*Winner of the 2004 Nautilus Award*

"This remarkable book has taught me a whole new way of thinking."
—HAROLD KUSHNER, author of *When Bad Things Happen to Good People*

"A beautiful piece of work destined to become a perennial classic."
—MARTHA BECK, author of *Expecting Adam* and *The Joy Diet*

"Greenspan writes intensely and compassionately. This is a committed, serious look at the emotions most of us would rather sweep under the rug."
—*Publishers Weekly*

"This is a beautifully written, deeply compassionate, and revolutionary approach to working with the most difficult human emotions. Miriam Greenspan teaches us how to trust our emotions and how to listen to hear the truth they reveal. This is a practical guide that illuminates how the wisdom of the heart can heal ourselves, each other, and our world."
—JANET SURREY, PH.D., founding scholar of the Jean Baker Miller Training Institute at the Stone Center, Wellesley College

"Miriam Greenspan will help you turn the lead in your life into gold of joy and peace. Of equal importance, she helps us see that such changes are not for ourselves alone, but for the whole world."
—HENRY GRAYSON, PH.D., author of *The New Physics of Love*

"This book is essential reading for all people. It beholds that which is tragic about the human condition but embraces it in a therapeutic and consoling way. Greenspan describes enormous grief and terror—her own and the world's—and explains what it means to surrender to fear, to face straight into it, to 'let it be' as the royal road to sanity, exuberance, and freedom. She is a trustworthy guide for us in these times."
—PHYLLIS CHESLER, author of *Women and Madness*

*(continued on page 317)*

# Healing
### through
## the Dark
# Emotions

## The Wisdom
## of Grief, Fear,
## and Despair

## Miriam Greenspan

*Shambhala*
Boulder
2004

Shambhala Publications, Inc.
4720 Walnut Street
Boulder, Colorado 80301
www.shambhala.com

15   14   13   12   11   10

Printed in the United States of America

⊗ This edition is printed on acid-free paper that meets the American National Standards Institute z39.48 Standard.
♻ This book is printed on 30% postconsumer recycled paper.
For more information please visit www.shambhala.com.
Distributed in the United States by Penguin Random House LLC
and in Canada by Random House of Canada Ltd

Library of Congress Catalogues the previous edition of this book as follows:
Greenspan, Miriam.
Healing through the dark emotions: the wisdom of grief, fear, and despair/ Miriam Greenspan.—1st. ed.
p.   cm.
Includes bibliographical references.
ISBN 978-1-57062-877-1 (hardcover)
ISBN 978-1-59030-101-2 (paperback)
1. Affective disorders—Popular works. 2. Grief—Popular works. 3. Fear—Popular works. 4. Despair—Popular works. I. Title.
RC537 .G726 2003
616.85'27—dc21
2002008069

*With love and gratitude, this book is dedicated to my family of spiritual teachers*

Aaron—for the blessing of your spirit

Anna—for the light in your eyes and the fire in your soul

Esther—for knowing "the secret of life is love people" and showing us how to live it

and especially Roger—for your courage and for a mind and heart as large as the world

# Contents

# *After 9/11*

## A Note to the Reader

ALMOST ALL OF THIS BOOK was written before September 11, 2001. I was putting the finishing touches on the last chapter when I heard the news and ran to see on television the crash that shook the world. Throughout this book, but especially in the last two chapters, I have made the case for the profound connection between our personal experiences of grief, despair, and fear, and the world we inhabit. After September 11, this connection has become all too transparent.

My subject is alchemical transformation—from the lead of grief, despair, and fear to the gold of gratitude, faith, and joy. These spiritual strengths, as well as the power of courage and compassion, come to us when we are open to the wisdom of the dark emotions and learn how to live openheartedly in a world damaged and broken by human actions and inaction, a world that needs healing as urgently as we ourselves do. If we ever needed the wisdom of the dark emotions, we need it now.

I hope that this book will be a source of guidance and comfort for those who seek a peaceful heart in dark times.

# Preface

THIS BOOK IS PART of a larger cultural conversation about the critical importance of emotion to individual and collective well-being. More and more, as a society, we have come to comprehend that the ability to feel, understand, and manage our emotions, especially those we call "negative," is a vital aspect of overall intelligence and essential to living a good life.

While millions of people who have worked on their feelings in psychotherapy may not find this idea new or surprising, it is an idea whose time has come in popular culture. It took off after the 1995 publication of *Emotional Intelligence* by Daniel Goleman. This landmark book put the subject of emotions at the forefront of our national awareness. Subordinating the "feeling brain" to the "thinking brain," Goleman argued, is essential to emotional intelligence. To succeed at this, we must cultivate certain basic emotional skills, including self-awareness, mood-management, empathy, and impulse control. Of these, the "master aptitude" is knowing how to control the flow of negative emotions.

Since then, dozens of books on emotional literacy and healing have flooded the marketplace. Many of these have been geared toward helping the reader master negative emotions and avoid their potential harm to body, mind, and spirit. Books about guilt, shame, anger, grief, depression, and anxiety continue to have a wide readership.

So why yet another book on emotions? The latest neuroscience research on emotions makes headline news these days and appears on TV specials. Psychotherapy, recovery programs, and emotional healing methods of all kinds have been de-stigmatized and popularized. Dozens of systems of emotional healing abound. "Emotional intelligence" has become a popular phrase. It would seem that we know all we need to know about how to manage our negative emotions and raise our emotional literacy.

A quick look at the world stage reveals another picture altogether. The images of grief, terror, and despair around the globe affect us all, whether we dwell on them or not. Random acts of terror; national, ethnic, religious, and regional wars in which long-standing antagonisms erupt in horrific bouts of rageful vengeance; and the mounting violence of everyday life assault our sense of safety and erode our confidence in the world at this dawning of the twenty-first century. The seething emotions at the core of these human-made infernos pollute our psychological, moral, and spiritual environment. Emotional intelligence and healing, in these contexts, seems remote indeed.

If negative emotions are so harmful, why can't we seem to tame their ferocious energies? If we know so much more about them now than ever before, why are we humans so embroiled in them? If, as the Dalai Lama tells us, the basic wish of all human beings is to be happy and the very purpose of human existence is happiness, then why do we humans seem so intent on creating misery for ourselves and each other? The fact is that while books about emotional intelligence may have hit the *New York Times* bestseller list, true emotional wisdom, for human beings as a whole, remains a distant dream. The world has a long journey ahead before anything resembling emotional healing takes place on a global scale.

This book will argue that our emotional illiteracy as a species has less to do with our inability to subdue negative emotions than it does with our inability to authentically and mindfully *feel* them. What looks like a problem with emotional control actually has its source in a widespread ignorance about how to tolerate painful emotional energies and use these energies for emotional, spiritual, and social transformation. And while emotional control certainly has its uses, it is transformation that our anguished world so urgently calls for. In particular, we need to honor three basic emotions that are an inevitable part of every life: grief, fear, and despair.

These are the "dark" emotions and their healing wisdom is the subject of this book.

Why grief, fear, and despair? Certainly there are other emotions we call "negative." Envy, guilt, shame, and anger, among others, account for a great deal of human suffering. But in my thirty years as a psychotherapist, I've come to believe that the inability to bear the core triad of grief, fear, and despair is the source of much of our individual and collective emotional ills. These are the emotions we most avoid and that we most need to attend to in our time. Suppressed grief often turns into depression, anxiety, or addiction. Benumbed fear can easily lead to irrational prejudice, toxic rage, and acts of violence. Overwhelming or unconscious despair often leads to severe psychic numbing or expresses itself through destructive acts to oneself and others. As we shall see, intolerable despair is also a core ingredient of the increasing incidence of chronic depression worldwide. The inability to tolerate grief, fear, and despair, as most any psychotherapist knows, is a major feature of the epidemic of addictions to alcohol, drugs, technology, entertainment, work, sex, etc., that afflict our civilization.

In short, aborted grief, fear, and despair are at the root of the character-istic psychological "disorders" of our time—depression, anxiety, addiction, irrational violence, and psychic numbing. Sadly, these destructive patterns play themselves out on the world stage as much as in the individual psyche.

Does this mean that the dark emotions are "negative"? In my view, there are no negative emotions, just unskillful ways of coping with emotions we can't bear. While generally devalued in our culture, the dark emotions have a wisdom that is essential to the work of healing and transformation on both individual and collective levels.

Initially, this book had a chapter on anger. In the end, I decided that anger needed its own book. As a response to violation and injustice, anger is a fiery moral passion that impels us to act in the protection of one's life or integrity. It is an honorable emotion—so long as we don't use it as a fuel for hatred and violence. Many of my references to anger in this book, however, explore anger as a by-product of aborted grief, fear, or despair. When the latter "softer" emotions are denied or suppressed, their energies are easily converted to, and masked by, the "harder" emotions of anger and rage. While anger has an important and largely overlooked place in the process of self-empowerment, it can also be a shield against one's vulnerability. Much of the anger we see in the world today is this latter kind, and it calls for a crash course in how to tolerate and befriend grief, fear, and despair.

I offer this book as a guide and companion on rough emotional terrain. It describes a healing process through grief, fear, and despair to gratitude, joy, and faith that I call the *alchemy of dark emotions*. I'll explore how to practice this alchemy—and what gets in its way. My intention is to foster the expe-rience of emotional alchemy as you read—as well as to reveal the profound relationship between your dark emotions and the state of the world. My passionate belief is that our emotional lives as individuals are always con-nected, for better or worse, to the emotional environments in which we live; and that what we call "healing" is incomplete without what in the Jewish tradition is called *tikkun olam*—the repair, healing, and transformation of the world.

This book was written over a thirteen-year period, crammed between the cracks of my life as psychotherapist and mother of two children, one dis-abled. I don't fancy myself a scholar of depth psychology, Hasidic Judaism, or Buddhist meditation practice, but each of these has strongly influenced my unique approach to emotional healing. So too has the personal experience of authentic heart-centered prayer to which my life has led me. Some thirty years as a psychotherapist; an equal number of years as a feminist committed to a vision of a more humane civilization; twenty years as a practitioner of mindfulness meditation in the Vipassana (Insight) tradition; and perhaps most importantly, my personal experience of childhood suffering and of motherhood under challenging conditions—these are the major influences for the emotional healing process you will find in these pages.

Sometime in 1997, the metaphor of "emotional alchemy," a transmutational process in which something ordinary, hard, and dull—a lump of lead—becomes something extraordinary, valuable, and beautiful—a nugget of gold—struck me as an apt description of the transmutation from grief to gratitude, fear to joy, and despair to faith that this book explores. I wrote about this alchemy in an essay called "Befriending the Dark Emotions" in the May/June 1998 issue of the journal *Common Boundary*. The book's working title at this time was *Emotional Alchemy*.

Then, in 2001, along came Tara Bennett-Goleman's book of the same name, and my book needed a swift title change! While initially dismayed, I soon realized that, from a less ego-driven perspective, this was all to the good. The idea of emotional alchemy is in the air. Many people are doing this kind of work, in differing but overlapping ways. Emotional alchemy is a process that is critically needed—so the more methods, the better. Bennett-Goleman uses mindfulness practice from the Buddhist tradition to attend to mental reactions to emotions (cognitive patterns such as "I don't belong" or "I'm not worthy"). I use an eclectic collection of different practices to attend to emotions as bodily energies—as distinct from our mental reactions to them. (You will find these practices in chapter 10.) Whereas Bennett-Goleman's book explores "how the mind can heal the heart," this one is about how the heart can heal itself.

My hope is that *Healing through the Dark Emotions* will contribute to changing some familiar ways of thinking about emotions in general and so-called negative emotions in particular. More than ever before, our age asks us to reevaluate the accepted notion that individual healing takes place in a social vacuum. Emotional alchemy, I will argue, is connected to what I call "emotional ecology." The inescapable relationship between individual heartbreak and the brokenheartedness of the world is a central feature of my view of what emotional intelligence and healing, from an enlarged social and global perspective, might look like in the years to come.

In addition, Western culture's hypervaluation of reason and denigration of the "passions" still holds great sway in this arena. It is my view that the constraint of emotion actually does as much harm as good. Emotions, including those we mark as negative, have a wisdom of their own, their own kind of "reason"—as critical to human continuity and planetary survival as the traditional Western notion of rationality. Emotional intelligence, from a more culturally feminine perspective, breaks with the masculine norm of the conquest of emotion and puts more trust in its inherent value.

One important aspect of such a perspective is the idea that no understanding of emotional healing is complete if it neglects the body. This book develops a user-friendly way of approaching our dark emotions as bodily-felt energies. These energies can be so overwhelming that we compulsively numb or distract ourselves away from them. They can also be so intellectualized that we are barely aware of them as physical energies at all. We could all use some help in knowing how to tolerate the energies of the dark emotions as they course through our body-selves and learning what they have to teach.

What would happen if we knew how to ride the rough waves of the dark emotions on the surfboard of mindful awareness? What would happen if we stopped calling painful emotions "negative" and had faith that the heart— even in the throes of intense pain—can be trusted? What my life and work have taught me, repeatedly, is that the heart heals itself when we know how to listen to it. Befriending and mindfully surrendering to our most dreaded emotions, we discover the heart's native intelligence. In learning what grief, fear, and despair have to teach us, we find a kind of magic that we hadn't known existed—a magic that the world desperately needs in order to come to its senses.

I hope that this book will help you discover this magic and that it will encourage you to find your most profound healing where you least expect to: in your heartfelt grief, fear, and despair for yourself and the world.

*Healing through the Dark Emotions*

# Introduction

> One does not become enlightened by imagining figures of light but by making the darkness conscious.
> — C. G. JUNG

"HEAL US, OH LORD, that we may be healed," prays Tevye the milkman in *Fiddler on the Roof*. "In other words," he adds, with his knack for humor in the face of misery, "God, send us the cure. The sickness we've got already."

Like Tevye, we all suffer and search for the remedy. We turn to gods and men, doctors and priests, gurus and talk-show hosts. Searching for relief, recovery, redemption, oblivion—anything that will put an end to our emotional pain. We pay psychotherapists to cure it, take Prozac to mute it, seek counsel from religions that exhort us to rise above it, read inspirational books to overcome it, join recovery programs and self-help groups to cope with it, spend millions of dollars to escape it, use alcohol, drugs, food, work, possessions, sex, entertainment, and all the techno-toys we can get to distract ourselves from it.

When it comes to the dark emotions, we are all experienced sufferers: grief, despair, and fear are our human birthright as much as joy, wonder, and love. There is no life without loss and therefore no life without grief. There is no life without vulnerability and therefore no life without fear. So long as we live in a world where terror, violence, environmental degradation, injustice, and scarcity exist, despair will find its unwelcome way into our hearts and souls.

These are our worst feelings, and they are part of every life. When I call them dark, I don't mean that they are bad, unwholesome, or pathological. I mean that as a culture we have kept these emotions in the dark—shameful, secret, and unseen. As a result, we tend, for the most part, to shun them. But the emotions that we reject and suppress can become dark in an altogether different sense: like a rich, fertile soil from which unexpected flowers can bloom.

In the throes of grief, fear, or despair, we generally believe that giving feelings like these too much space in our psyches is a sign of emotional weakness or breakdown. We turn away, not toward them. The enlightened

Buddha saw that such aversion to suffering only worsens it. Still, for those of us who are not yet enlightened, when things go wrong, we want out. When we are besieged by afflictive emotions, we try to find a way around them. The last thing we want to do is go through them—even if doing so would lead us to unimaginable gifts on the other side.

In my work as a psychotherapist, I once saw a client who was on the verge of divorce from his second wife. His wife was fed up with his almost total lack of emotion and responsiveness. She told him: "I have no husband, I have only a shell of a husband." She was ready to throw him out. This man's first wife had died of breast cancer while still a young woman. He had no children from his first marriage, and his second wife was infertile. He had never grieved the loss of his first wife or of his dream of progeny.

"All I have is this relationship, and I don't want to lose it. Please help me," he begged. "Tell me what I can do."

I told him that I thought I could help him if he was willing to befriend his grief. "What do you mean?" he asked, looking frantic at the suggestion.

"I mean letting yourself grieve your losses."

His response was swift and unambiguous: "I can't imagine anything I'd want to do less. Isn't there another way?"

I told him that if there was, I didn't know of it. His wife wanted a man who could feel, and he had stopped feeling after his first wife died. I asked him: "Why would you rather deaden yourself to your emotions than feel your way through them?"

"Because," he said with finality, "I'm sure that I couldn't survive it."

Dread of the dark emotions is not always this extreme or so openly acknowledged. But it is always a force to be reckoned with. The fear of falling into the darkness, of going down and not being able to come up, lurks right at the edge of our ability to feel at all. Like a child who locks the closet door in terror of the monster inside, the more we lock up our dark emotions, the more we fear that they'll jump out of the closet and devour us. Our culture reinforces this fear, which I call "emotion-phobia."

As a result, when we are deluged by dark emotions, we are rarely in shape for dealing with them. We find ourselves adrift in a sea of overwhelming feelings without the ability to swim—and no life raft in sight. Just when we think we need the biggest painkiller we can get, we find out that even Prozac won't simply remove our suffering.

Distracting ourselves from emotional pain may work well enough for most of our garden-variety displeasures, so long as life doesn't slam us on the head. But sooner or later, we all get slammed. Your wife dies of cancer.

Your husband at midlife runs off with a younger woman. You lose your job. Your child becomes ill. You are assaulted or raped. Memories surface of being sexually abused as a child. You are diagnosed with a serious disease. Your mother dies. Your father dies. Your cat dies.

Or perhaps it's none of these. Perhaps, like many people today, you are deeply aware of living in a world that is both dangerous and endangered—an environment that triggers the dark emotions on a daily basis. Perhaps not personal adversity but awareness of the enormity of pain in the world, and of danger to our planet itself, is the source of your grief, fear, or despair. Or perhaps you feel these emotions and don't know what to connect them to or how to cope with them.

Our culture exhibits a curious ambivalence toward such emotional pain. On the one hand, it teaches us to control our pain or medicate it; on the other hand, we are urged to feel, express, and release our emotions.

"Get ahold of yourself." "Get a grip." "Stay in charge." These metaphors of management and control illustrate what we believe to be the "positive" way to deal with "negative" emotions. We must manage feelings that would otherwise be destructive.

Our distrust of the dark emotions has been heightened by recent mind-body research that concludes that negative emotions are bad for you, contributing to life-threatening illnesses from asthma to cancer, cardiovascular disease to immune system disorders. By and large, this research neglects to distinguish between emotions that are experienced mindfully—that is, fully experienced in the body in a direct and open way, as they occur—and those that are not mindfully experienced or have become "stuck" in the body.

At the same time, the explosion of healing modalities in the psychotherapy, New Age, and recovery movements in the past several decades has heralded a new epoch of "getting in touch with your feelings." It is now hip to be in therapy, where it was once a stigma. It seems that everyone is in some kind of therapy, recovery program, or healing path. Or on Prozac, Zoloft, or Paxil. As a nation, we seem to believe that, with the right effort, we can completely eradicate emotional suffering. In either case, whether it's control or catharsis we seek, we regard negative emotions as a dangerous hindrance to the good life. The focus is on dispelling such feelings, not learning from them.

In this book we will explore another way: the healing wisdom of the dark emotions. We will discover that there's something good in so-called bad feelings—but that we can only get to the good by fully experiencing the "bad." Grief, despair, and fear are really neither positive nor negative but simply human emotions; it is our attitude toward them that's negative. The dark emotions can be our best, albeit most demanding, spiritual teachers, when we can get beyond the compulsion to control them. By learning how to attend to, befriend, and surrender to the energies of grief, despair, and fear, we create the conditions for something new to arise in ourselves and in the world. We discover an unexpected gateway to healing and transformation. We release ourselves from the strangled grip of pain into an amazing alchemy by which grief, despair, and fear are transmuted to gratitude, faith, and joy.

Part one, "Emotion-Phobia," looks at how emotional alchemy is obstructed by our culturewide fear of the dark emotions. It is listening to emotional pain that initiates us into the emotional alchemy process (chapter 1). To listen well, we must become comfortable with our vulnerability, a challenge for any of us (chapter 2). The primary obstacle to this is our culturally conditioned fear of emotion itself (chapter 3). When we compulsively and chronically disconnect from the dark emotions, disavowed dark emotional energy can become stuck in the body, producing toxic emotional states such as depression, anxiety, and psychic numbing, as well as addiction and psychosomatic ailments. It can also run amok in the form of explosive anger and violence.

Part two, "Emotional Alchemy," is the heart of the book. Chapter 4 introduces this process both conceptually and pragmatically. Chapters 5 through 7 focus on the alchemy of grief, despair, and fear, respectively. These chapters start out with a description of the texture or feel of each emotion in its social context and then move on to re-visioning its value and power. The alchemy process is explored both discursively and narratively. Looked at from a wider angle of vision, grief, despair, and fear are then connected to a larger, world context. Each of these chapters concludes with emotional exercises designed to initiate you into the alchemy of grief, despair, and fear.

Part three, "Emotional Ecology," enlarges the frame of reference, moving the focus from individual journeys of healing to the larger social and global contexts of the dark emotions in our time. In the dominant paradigm of psychiatry and psychology, emotions are seen as events that occur within a boundaried, separate ego ("It's all in your head"), fundamentally rooted in a nuclear family of the past. In contrast to this kind of psychology, I emphasize the emotional *ecology* of grief, despair, and fear, looking at how these emotions are situated in larger systems, extending beyond the nuclear family to our society and the world as a whole. My intention is to break through the characteristic splits of our civilization—between head and heart, mind and body, self and world—and to arrive at a model of healing that embraces the connection between the self and the world. This part of the book invites you to look into the pain of the world and see how your dark emotions are connected to larger global currents. It is meant to nourish you to build the necessary emotional fitness and compassion to which we are called by a world in crisis.

While the exercises at the end of chapters 5 through 7 are specific to grief, despair, and fear, the thirty-three emotional exercises of part four comprise a home course in emotional alchemy and are general enough to include any challenging emotional state—including anger, anxiety, depression, shame, envy, and self-pity. As a complete program, these exercises would be useful as well if you are in recovery from addiction, or if you are emotionally numb and want to recover your capacity to feel. The exercises here can be done at any point in your reading, in conjunction with the rest of the book, or independently of it. I hope this systematic presentation of the emotional alchemy process will be useful when you need it most.

## Telling Stories

Many years ago I taught English composition to college students. During that time I discovered the power of first-person narrative as a way of learning. Students who wrote about their lives were able to make connections that were central to understanding not only themselves but the world. Stories are the way that we learn about the world as children, and they continue to be a good way to learn as adults. We may forget any number of theories, ideas, facts, and figures, but no one forgets a good story.

As a privileged companion to hundreds of people bravely journeying through grief, despair, and fear, I have heard many stories. Some of these stories are told here—stories of depression, addiction, anxiety, abuse, divorce, phobias, incest, illness, and other common emotional struggles. All of these stories have been disguised to protect confidentiality. Somewhere in these stories, you may find yourself.

However, these stories are not written in a professional voice alone. I speak also as a fellow traveler. Most of what I know best about the healing wisdom of the dark emotions I learned the hard way—by suffering through my own misery mindfully. This is really the only way to learn it. We can read about those who have endured and triumphed. We can study ancient spiritual texts. We can use New Age inspirational books. We can consult psychotherapists. But in the end, Life is the ultimate guru, and pain the most effective wake-up call.

That call came for me twenty years ago when I gave birth to a beautiful boy who died two months later. Aaron's life and death are the ground in which this book is planted. It is his spirit that has guided me through the thirteen long years of writing and living that this book entailed. Aaron was my master mentor. And Esther, born fifteen years ago with multiple disabilities, is my gifted continuing-education teacher. A magical moment in the midst of a serious medical crisis with Esther was my most powerful personal experience of the alchemy of fear to joy chronicled in chapter 7. It was in this moment of terror for my daughter's life that this book was conceived. The truth is, I didn't come to the book, it came to me. I have tried to be a faithful scribe and write as clearly as possible what I've been led to.

In addition, my family background as a daughter of two resilient survivors of the Holocaust has been the crucible in which my early awareness of grief, fear, and despair took shape, an awareness that has accompanied me all my life and is the formative experience of my life's work. I came to consciousness in a post-Holocaust era and live now, as we all do, in an ecocidal world tormented by terror and violence, degraded by pollution, a world whose future is highly uncertain. My early awareness of dark emotions in the aftermath of genocide is another aspect of the personal genesis of what you read here.

Personal odysseys through the dark emotions as a path of sacred power are the backbone of everything this book has to offer. These narratives are threads that weave themselves throughout the book. I have intentionally made extensive use of my own story, for a number of reasons. For one thing, my own stories are the ones I know best. As Thoreau said in *Walden*: "I should not talk so much about myself if there was anybody else whom I knew as well." The detail of these stories is designed to give you a sense of the contours and colors of alchemical journeys through the dark emotions, and to reassure you that these healing alchemies are possible, even under very dire conditions.

Another thing. When I read a book of popular psychology or one about healing, I'm engaged with the author in a personal way and want to know: How did she come to believe this? What in her life made her understand this subject in this particular way? I know I'm not alone in my nosiness.

Most engaged readers of books on subjects like this one are voyeurs like me. The stories from my own life that you will read here will give you a sense of the ground from which this book sprouted.

Most importantly, a major contention of this book is that we must become friendlier with our dark emotions in order to use their energies for healing and transformation on both the individual and collective level. To do so, we have to stop thinking that feeling emotional pain means we're sick. In breaking through the taboo against the public disclosure of therapists' suffering, I want to depathologize the experience of grief, fear, and despair; to explore these emotions in a more universal, as well as more socially conscious context.

Emotional suffering, as I write about it here, is not a sign of mental disorder or illness. It's a universal fact of life—the Buddha's first noble truth; an inevitable result of living in a damaged and damaging social context; and a unique pathway of spiritual awakening, growth, and transformation.

Steeped in the medical model of psychiatry, we have lost the sense of grief, fear, and despair as universal experiences and as responses not just to personal but also to social and global conditions. A culture that insists on labeling suffering as pathology, that is ashamed of suffering as a sign of failure or inadequacy, a culture bent on the quick fix for emotional pain, inevitably ends up denying both the social and spiritual dimensions of our sorrows.

Denial is present in a different way in a great deal of the New Age literature on healing. Here an airy spiritual focus offers a healing path that often bypasses the reality of suffering on the ground—avoiding or denying the social roots of our pain and dissociating itself from the darkness in our world.

If healing is to mean more than a welcome relief from individual pain, or a fear-driven avoidance of collective pain, it must be connected to a process of inquiring deeply into the suffering that is part of everyone's life and spiritual journey, and that is an overwhelming fact of life on the planet today. If you're someone who cries when you read the newspapers or watch the news on TV, if you have become numb out of overwhelming grief and fear for our world, if you're someone who sees the connection between your own emotional state and living in an age of global threat, if you love the world and want to see it heal itself, I hope this book will be of some use to you. Now is a fruitful if not urgent time to learn the alchemy of the dark emotions.

For those who desperately need a way to feel more hopeful, resilient, and joyful, take heart! The emotions that appear to afflict us can be the vehicles of our liberation from suffering. Experiencing our grief, fear, and despair in a new light, we renew our capacities for gratitude, joy, and faith. We grow in courage and compassion. We approach the world with less fear and more wonder. We have more energy for changing the things that matter.

These gifts can only be found when we are unafraid to dance the dance of dark emotions in our lives.

Let's dance.

# PART ONE

## Emotion-Phobia

# 1 *Listening to Pain*

Help us to be the always hopeful
Gardeners of the spirit
Who know that without darkness
Nothing comes to birth
As without light
Nothing flowers
— MAY SARTON,
"The Invocation to Kali"

Blessed are the men and women
who are planted in your earth, in your garden,
who grow as your trees and flowers grow,
who transform their darkness to light.
— *The Odes of Solomon*

FOR SOME THIRTY YEARS as a psychotherapist, I've listened to painful stories. When people come for the "talking cure," they generally wear their heart's pain as a badge of shame. They believe that they are suffering because of some core defect resulting from bad parenting, and that therapy will rid them of this defect and take away their painful emotions—hopefully forever. Many have the idea that if they could stay the course of a complete cure in psychotherapy or read enough self-help books, they could achieve a life completely free of suffering.

The truth is more in line with the famous biblical observation: "Man is born to sorrow, as surely as the sparks fly upward" (Job 5:7). No one gets away without some share of it. We all grieve life's inevitable losses. We fear the inherent uncertainty and vulnerability of existence. And increasingly, as a population, we are familiar with the despair of troubled relationships, unexpected traumas, inner emptiness, and global degradation and terror. As much as joy, wonder, and love, these dark emotions are part of our human endowment, however much we may sometimes wish they weren't.

The Baal Shem Tov, a legendary eighteenth-century Jewish mystic, taught that to master our sorrows, we must know how to be fully immersed in emotion, yet not ruled by it. I call this process the alchemy of the dark emotions: knowing how to stay connected to the energy of painful emotions, to attend to and befriend it, to surrender to it, mindfully, without being overwhelmed. This is how we listen to the language of the heart.

Healing through the dark emotions is an unarmed journey into vulnerability—a journey through, not a departure from, pain. Often, we come to this process when we are desperate. Perhaps we've already tried a number of ways to "self-medicate" our painful feelings with drugs, food, entertainment, distractions, or other means, and none of these have worked. Or worse, our attempt to medicate or anesthetize our pain only complicates and extends it.

At such times, it becomes clear that there is no way out but through.

Healing through the dark emotions is the opposite of arming ourselves against a sea of troubles. It is a shamanic journey to the dark emotional underworld where the only way to master dark emotional energy is to experience it fully. Just as the tribal shaman ventures into the world of spirits in order to bring back knowledge of remedies for troubled souls, so does the emotional alchemist descend into the depths of his or her own pain to discover its wisdom for self-healing and transformation.

The good news is that the dark emotions can serve as guides on this journey—when we know how to listen to them. Though listening is not always easy, it's an art that can be learned. Like most things, it becomes easier and we get better at it with practice. It's like learning to swim as a child, when the water is inviting but also frightening. If we want to swim, we must listen to our bodies. We must learn all the different movements—the arm stroke, the leg kick, the head motion, the synchronized breathing—and how to coordinate them. But in the end, it comes down to taking the risk and plunging in. Then, feeling our bodies in the water, we notice something wonderful that helps us overcome our fear: We are buoyed up! The water holds us up and carries us.

So it is with the emotions that make us feel most vulnerable: grief, fear, and despair. These dark emotions are in-the-body energies mediated by beliefs we have gathered from the culture of family and society around us. Their purpose is not to make us miserable, drive us crazy, or shame, weaken, or defeat us, but to teach us about ourselves, others, and the world, to open our hearts to compassion, to help us heal and change our lives. They bring us information and supply us with energy—the raw material of spiritual empowerment and transformation. When we know how to listen to them, we can ride their energy, like a wave, with awareness as our protection. Emotional energy flows, and a hidden doorway in the heart opens.

Something shifts. A transmutation occurs: a movement through pain to spiritual power.

This is emotional alchemy: a process by which something ordinary is transmuted into something very precious.

From ancient times, the alchemists sought to discover a means by which base metals could be transmuted into gold. Though some believe that the early alchemists were actually able to accomplish this, mostly the term has come to be a metaphor for a process of spiritual transformation. In the alchemy of dark emotions, the feelings we resist most are the leaden ore with which we begin. Our ability to attend to, befriend, and mindfully surrender to them is the means by which this lead is alchemized to the gold of spiritual wisdom.

Finding the power of the sacred, not despite suffering, but in the midst of it: This is the alchemy of the dark emotions. Through this alchemy, grief moves us from sorrow for what we've lost to gratitude for what remains. Fear of life's fragility is transformed to the joy of living fully, with openness. And even despair becomes the ground of a resilient faith—not just an opiate for our pain, but a profound commitment to life as it is.

Your life exactly as it is contains just what is needed for your own journey of healing through the dark emotions. It starts with learning to listen to your heart.

## *The Power of Listening Is the Foundation of Healing*

My first child lived and died in a hospital for children. Aaron arrived, long and pink, an unnamed sorrow in his seemingly ancient eyes, his spirit encased in a flawlessly formed body that, like a flower, faded and died sixty-six days after his birth.

In the days of my vigil with Aaron, I didn't leave the hospital except to go home to sleep. For the two months of his life, my world was Division 33, the neonatal neurology floor, a world of infants with shunts in their heads; children with bombed out, vacant stares; others whose brain chemistry was being slowly eroded by persistent, uncontrollable seizures. A world of beeping heart monitors, brain scans, and endless medical tests, of parents with the darkened eyes of unrelenting grief. A world of daily vigil, prayer, and incessant fear: What was wrong with my baby? Would I ever take him home?

One of my first ventures outside of this world was a necessary trip to the dentist. Dr. Ross inspected my teeth and gums and did whatever he did. I was not paying attention to my teeth because I was elsewhere, with Aaron. "Are you okay? Are you ill?" the dentist asked me. His unexpected solicitousness was touching. I responded simply, "I'm not sick. I've given birth to a child who can't leave the hospital." The tears flowed from my eyes, unbidden.

Without a word, the dentist turned and walked out of the room. At first I thought he had gone to get some implement, something he needed to finish the dental work. Clearly he wasn't done, because I was left pinioned to my elevated chair with a dental tray in my lap. But Dr. Ross never came back. I waited for some time before extricating myself from the chair and jumping down to the floor. I remember walking out onto the street, where I could see only in black and white and shades of gray. My perception had altered. The colors had drained from my world.

Why was this moment so memorable? The dentist was not a friend of mine. I had no expectations that he should attend to anything but the state of my teeth. His lapse in professional manners was no big deal. Yet the absurdity of being left stranded in a dental chair because this decent man couldn't bear to be in the presence of my pain sent profound shock waves through me. It tapped into something larger—a common experience for people who are grieving—a sense of living a life that cannot be listened to. The isolation of feeling this way is stark enough to drain the colors from one's world.

Without a listener, the healing process is aborted. Human beings, like plants that bend toward the sunlight, bend toward others in an innate healing tropism. There are times when being truly listened to is more critical than being fed. Listening well to another's pain is a primary form of nurturance, capable of healing even the most devastating of human afflictions, including the wounds and scars of violence, even the horrors of war and large-scale social trauma. Children speak their pain automatically when there is a listener, but learn to hide it when there is no ear to hear.

I learned to listen to pain early in my life. My birthplace and first home was a Displaced Persons Camp for homeless refugees in southern Germany—the remnants of Hitler's war against the Jews. The Holocaust, not recorded in my personal memory but imprinted in my cells, was my legacy. My Polish Jewish parents had survived starvation, forced labor, imprisonment, the destruction of their families and their world. Their shattered yet persistent faith in life was the direct inspiration for my conception.

I didn't hear my parents' stories until I was thirteen years old. But as far back as I can remember, I felt their grief, fear, and despair. Attuned to the unspoken emotional energies that permeated my childhood, I grew up with a sense of their power and developed a strong faith that listening to suffering would bring its own gifts.

Not too surprisingly, listening became my life's work. I'm comfortable with suffering that is spoken rather than silenced. I'm energized by listening. From this work, I've seen again and again that the essence of healing emotional pain lies in listening to what hurts—in both knowing how to listen to oneself and being listened to by another.

This is one of life's little ironies: Though all emotional healing requires it, listening to pain is difficult—and the greater the pain, the more difficult it is to listen to. The dark emotions are uncomfortable; they are also contagious. Their energies flow through and between and among us without regard for the boundaries we erect to keep ourselves separate. If we are unable to tolerate some discomfort, it's hard to listen to dark feelings in ourselves or others. Our best, most compassionate intentions are thwarted, our connections marred by the shadow of intolerable emotions. We become inured to the incessant cacophony of the world's suffering, limited in our authenticity and responsiveness. And we suffer from not knowing the darker side of ourselves.

Because of the difficulty and the power of listening to pain, millions of people spend millions of dollars seeking out the help of professional listeners called psychotherapists. To be a professional listener is to enter a terrain without destination. Listening is more than hearing words or deciphering meaning from the cuneiform of body language. *Webster's* tells us that listening is "hearing with thoughtful attention." But in listening closely, there is also a kind of suspension of thought. One listens with the limbic system, the third ear of intuition, as much as with the cerebral cortex—emptying oneself to allow another's story to enter, opening to the energetic movement of emotion, empathically joining with someone else's experience. This is the secret of all successful therapy, regardless of the training or theoretical orientation of the therapist: by a kind of grace, good listening transforms suffering. In a culture that honors head more than heart, the skills of good listening are generally not taught to trainees in the art of psychotherapy. The would-be therapist learns to theorize and analyze, to diagnose and prognosticate, to interpret and interrogate. But not to listen.

When a person's suffering is well listened to in psychotherapy, an alchemical process is initiated. Something that starts out as a desperate but inarticulate anguish or a mysterious, painful sensation in the body begins to cohere as a story. Sometimes a new, unexpected story or story fragment emerges. A hazy memory of being sexually attacked by a gang of boys becomes personalized with the faces of the attackers, among whom is a brother and a cousin. A quick flashing image of a father holding a gun to his head as he ponders killing himself emerges in an instant. Is this story real? the storyteller will often ask. Did it really happen? New story fragments are jarring and must be incorporated gradually.

Other times it's not a new story that emerges but an old one felt for the first time, known in all its fullness, the emotions no longer sequestered away in a dark room where no one can hear them. A sense of renewed vitality emerges.

The rewards of listening, however, are not always expected or welcomed. Robert comes to therapy wanting to explore his marriage. He has been married for twelve years and has three young children. He is not happy with his wife. He would like her to be a better listener. Gradually, as Robert speaks more and more honestly of his suffering in this relationship, he begins to realize that it is not just Jane who has not been listening to him; he has not been listening to himself. As he starts to listen to himself more, he is appalled by what he hears. His fear that his wife doesn't love him reverses itself. He realizes that his bigger fear is that he doesn't love her . . . that he has in fact never loved her, that he married her as a young man unaware of himself, of whom or why he was marrying. The story of Robert's suffering shifts, from the story of an unsupportive wife to the story of a man who fears that he has never loved anyone and doubts that he is capable of love. This new story is worse than the story Robert came in with. It forces him to confront a terrifying choice: Should he stay in this marriage or leave it?

To answer this question, Robert has to go through an arduous and challenging journey, to heal through his dark emotions. Listening to suffering can result in a dangerous knowing. What will we find out, if we really listen? Will we be able to bear what we then know? What will knowing ask of us? This journey takes courage. The courage to heal.

Just as being well listened to helps people heal, listening to oneself is the secret of self-healing. The most profound healing often comes with the deepest suffering precisely because a great pain will not let up, forcing us to face into it, and the only alternative to paying attention is cutting ourselves off from life itself. In this way, pain can be a great teacher of listening.

In listening to ourselves, we learn who we are, what our bodies know, the emotional wisdom of our cells. And slowly, if we honor what we hear, we begin to heal and to live fully. When we listen closely to what hurts, we learn what life is asking of us. We become fluent in the language of the heart. We get the counsel we need.

## Learning Not to Listen

We sit in a circle. I have asked a group of six women who have come together for the purpose of emotional healing to speak of what they learned in their families about painful emotions. The room is aglow with lights from several candles, lending an air of ceremony to the simple act of telling their stories.

Meg begins. "Whenever I expressed a feeling, especially sadness, I was told: 'Don't be silly.' So when I felt anything, I ran off to be alone in the woods. This was my only comfort, except for drugs. No one was there to hear me. I had to deal with my pain alone. I cried myself to sleep at night. I cried silently so no one would hear."

"I got the same message," says Marie. "I learned to direct all bad feelings at myself, blaming myself and hating myself for my failures. I didn't cry. I pushed everything down, never let myself express anything."

Nancy continues the theme. "In my family the message was: 'We only have happy feelings here. Anyone who is upset is ungrateful.' If anyone wasn't happy, they were sent to their room to shape up. Worry and anxiety were the only feelings I allowed myself to have. I lived with a sense of foreboding: Don't get emotional or something terrible will happen. So I funneled everything into organizing, being busy, doing things, working hard to be good. I was the good girl."

"My parents just ignored anyone who felt anything," Dorothy offers. "We pretended no one had feelings of any kind and did what we were supposed to do. I never let anyone know I felt anything—not even myself. I numbed myself, tuned out, avoided conflict."

"My mother was the only one allowed to have feelings in our family," says Rosalie. "She was pretty out of control. When she was upset, she would open the doors to our rooms and yell, 'Stupid!' She'd scream and wail and carry on. We had to tiptoe around her. We weren't allowed to disturb her. It was like living in an emotional minefield, never knowing what would provoke her. We all grew up resolved not to be emotional like her. Instead of feeling, I stole things. It was only years later that I realized how much anger there was in my compulsive stealing."

Patricia speaks last: "I learned that the only way to handle feelings is to get hostile, drunk, or stoned. That's what my parents did. That's what my brothers did. And that's what I did. I was addicted to drugs for years before I began to realize that if I didn't deal with my feelings, I would be dead."

These stories tell of a culture in which the common denominator in our emotional education is suppression, intolerance, shaming, punishment, and neglect. It is a culture in which our role models are often emotionally out of control or illiterate, in which we learn to do all kinds of things to avoid the power of emotion—becoming overly busy, avoiding conflict, numbing out, acting out, doing drugs. The energy of the dark emotions in such a context is routinely converted to a host of toxic behaviors and mental states including anxiety, depression, addiction, abuse, psychic numbing, violence, and isolation.

Some of us, the lucky ones, had a full palette of emotional colors when we were young. We cried when we were sad. We laughed when we were glad. We yelled when we were mad. We said when we were scared. Nobody told us that we were bad, crazy, or sick. We were held, loved, comforted, disciplined with respect. But most of us didn't reap these early benefits. We were hushed when we were sad, shushed when we were mad, pushed away when we were scared. We were exhorted to control our feelings or hide them out of sight.

We learned to fear the raw power of emotion and its expression, an endemic, culture-wide fear that I call emotion-phobia.

It is in our families we first learn to distrust our feelings and to be shamed by them. Not listening to painful feelings is a family tradition shared by a variety of ethnically, racially, economically, and religiously diverse families. When shaming and ignoring emotion don't work, there's always the direct threat of punishment. Punishment for visible suffering is particularly visited on boys, but girls too learn to silence themselves. By and large, girls learn to suffer in silence, boys to deny that they are suffering at all.

Even if we were not humiliated, punished, neglected, or whipped into shape for ordinary human feelings, by the time we are adults, we are expected to restrict their free flow. We've mastered the internal regulation processes of emotion-phobia. We've been taught to believe that emotions are not appropriate in any context but an intimate personal relationship. In public, we compose ourselves, compulsively apologizing when we cry, as though displaying authentic sorrow is bad form, a sign of emotional weakness. One of my clients was told by her mother whenever she cried as a girl: "Don't cry, or you won't have any tears when you really need them." Another was accused of having a "nervous breakdown" whenever she displayed her sadness.

Often, in the process of constructing these adult ways of coping with emotion, we become strangers to ourselves. The fires of our passionate human nature subside or sputter out. The colors on our emotional palettes are no longer so vibrant or alive. For many, they have hardened and dried into a dull, gray residue.

Some children do escape this fate, but at a cost. It's common for children who maintain their ability to feel the emotions that others ignore or deny to be labeled "oversensitive"—and thus disparaged for their emotional authenticity and aliveness, their self-awareness and empathy. Kate, a particularly "sensitive" child, remembers running to her mother one day, crying: "I feel like I was sent to the wrong planet. I can feel everything, and everyone acts like you're not supposed to." Fortunately, Kate had a mother who respected her ability to "feel everything." Despite this, Kate was internalizing the emotion-phobic messages of the larger culture.

Ignoring, stopping, and shaming or punishing emotion are the three parenting styles that most often result in emotional illiteracy in children. Our culture as a whole propagates just this kind of illiteracy. In an emotion-phobic culture, most of us don't know how to listen very well to emotional pain for the simple reason that we have never been taught that doing so is a good thing, or how to do it. In school, about all we learn about "negative" emotions is that displaying them is bad conduct. We're taught little about what these emotions are or how they work. In religious institutions, we're often taught that fear, despair, or anger is a sign of sin or insufficient faith.

Similarly, in the populist spiritual renaissance of recent years, "bad" feelings are sometimes considered a hindrance, an obstacle to spiritual development. The spiritual journey is seen as an airy, light-bearing bypass of painful on-the-ground darkness. Though the culture of popular psychology appears to celebrate or even overindulge being in touch with feelings, the focus here is often on letting go of "bad" feelings, not on listening to and learning from them.

What's missing is any sense that emotions—whether we call them "positive" or "negative"—are there for a reason and have something to teach us.

The victory of psychopharmacology that has produced the Prozac revolution as our culture's cure for despair has contributed its share to the conquest of pain by any means necessary. In medicine and psychiatry, the prevailing message is: If it hurts, medicate it. As we shall see in later chapters, the pharmaceutical answer to depression has been both a boon and a bane. While offering many patients an effective remedy for a condition that is disabling when severe, the new antidepressants have also been part of an increasing tendency to equate the absence of painful emotion with sound mental health. As a result, it has become increasingly impossible to attribute despair to anything but a drop in serotonin levels—a biochemical blip that can be managed or obliterated through brain-altering chemicals.

Increasingly, we are conditioned to a low threshold of tolerance not only for "bad" feelings but for any kind of information that doesn't come in ten-second sound bites, or arrive on our computer screens in a nanosecond, or dazzle us with dizzying fast-cut images that move with a kaleidoscopic frenzy. The shadow side of the information revolution, the techno-toy craze, and pop culture visual values is this lowering of our capacity for sustained, mindful listening to ourselves and each other, to the earth itself.

In short, if listening to pain is a necessary skill of emotional alchemy, it's not one we cultivate in a fast-moving, "feel good," throwaway culture. From almost every standpoint, our culture teaches us not to listen.

## Emotions Live in the Body

Contrary to the popular idea that feelings are "all in your head," emotions live in the body. They explode us into ecstasy or devour us with pain. They make us fidget and squirm, surge with adrenaline, or go numb and lifeless. They affect the rate at which our hearts beat and the level and balance of various hormones, influencing the way that we breathe, think, work, digest our food, make love. As any therapist knows, the body carries a host of emotional wounds: of sexual abuse or emotional neglect, of unmourned losses and unspoken grief. We will not learn the wisdom of the dark emotions so long as we internalize a culture that abhors or ignores the body's intelligence.

Think about how your body feels when you're frightened or in despair, sad or jubilant. While it's obvious that emotions are visceral, in-the-body experiences, many of us don't really get this. When I ask new clients in psychotherapy, "What are you feeling right now?" they often don't know. They are likely to say, "I'm upset," which is inexact at best. Asked to locate their feelings in the body, many seem disoriented or puzzled by the question, as though I am speaking in a foreign tongue. Or they confuse feelings with thoughts: "I'm feeling that my husband is not really sensitive to my needs," or "I'm feeling that this is the last time I'll ever let my son drive the car," or

"I'm feeling that life sucks and then you die." Most of us are overly cerebral about feelings. We can spend twenty years in psychoanalysis and in the end know how to talk about emotions but not how to feel them.

When our emotions are very intense or painful, we often escape their in-the-body discomfort by having an "out of body" experience—taking our awareness away from our bodies and into obsession, anxiety, or any one of the numerous distractions available to us. We numb ourselves to feeling. In the extreme, this kind of separation of consciousness from body and emotion is what psychiatrists call dissociation—a defense commonly found in people who have been victims of trauma through abuse, incest, violence, or war. But in milder form, dissociation is routine; we all dissociate in small ways on a daily basis.

Ours is a dissociative culture—a culture that separates body from mind, body from spirit, feeling from thinking. This kind of dissociation is a special requirement of masculinity in patriarchy. From boyhood on, men are subjected to a relentless conditioning process that teaches them to armor their bodies against emotion. (How many movies have we seen in which a sorrowful event—a death, a murder, a divorce—is followed by a bar scene in which the hero manfully drinks his feelings away?) In effect, this amounts to a kind of routine emotional abuse required by the norms of masculinity, evident everywhere from our school halls to the military, in the ways that young boys as well as nations behave. The result is that for many men, the capacity for emotional sensitivity is drastically impaired, with devastating effects on men's abilities to be at home in their own emotional bodies and to connect in relationship. These effects include the proclivity to wage war as a solution to international problems.

Women, on the other hand, are trained to be sensitive to the needs of others but not necessarily to their own needs and to view their bodies as objects to allure the interest and passion of others. In a very different way, girls learn to abuse their bodies and bodily sensitivity, as we see in the growing epidemic of eating disorders in preadolescent and adolescent girls as well as among more mature women. Double-binded from the start, women are expected to carry, feel, and display the emotional vulnerability that is taboo for men; but, at the same time, we are devalued for doing so. As a result, though women are generally more in touch with their feelings in the body and able to name them, we also bear the shame of feeling, the internalization of a culture in which emotion is devalued.

In a postfeminist age, many believe that women are better at "doing" emotions than men are. As I see it, both men and women are impaired, in different ways, by our culture's disability in relation to emotion and emotional communication. Emotional vitality and authenticity, a mature sense of emotional wholeness and freedom—these human capacities are hard to come by in a culture that doesn't honor the body and the heart.

For both men and women alike, discovering the power and wisdom of the dark emotions takes an active intention, a willingness to risk emotional exposure, a courageous attention to our vulnerability, and the ability to listen to the body's emotional signals. Without these skills, the dark emotions tend to cook themselves into a toxic stew that adversely affects our bodies, minds, and spirits.

## Emotions Live in the World

As much as emotions are in-the-body experiences, they are mediated by socially conditioned beliefs. We don't just feel; we make sense of what we feel. We think as we feel and about what we feel. And our thoughts both trigger and subdue our emotions. Our dark emotions are subject to the transmission of cultural meanings. Individuals account for their suffering by ascribing meanings that are conditioned, supported, and reinforced by the culture as whole.

In our culture, we believe that there are experts in suffering, and we trust them to explain our pain. These experts—psychiatrists and psychologists—tell us what our suffering means. And generally, these meanings are intrapsychic and/or biochemical in nature. If we are in emotional pain, it must be something in our early childhood or a biochemical imbalance. Psychiatry has replaced religion as the accepted way of explaining human suffering. The psychiatric culture in which we are steeped has by and large ignored Freud's views about the inevitability of what he called "normal misery" and more and more cast all suffering in the pathology mold. The emotion we used to call despair, for instance, has been redubbed "clinical depression," a biochemical disorder that should be treated with medication.

Suffering has not, of course, always been construed in this way. For most of recorded history, the meaning that culture gave to human suffering was very different. The link was between suffering and sin, not between suffering and personal psychology. The Christian tradition teaches the redemptive value of suffering in emulation of the Savior (*imitatio Christi*, the imitation of Christ) in order to be purged of sin and find salvation. In the Jewish tradition, suffering is transformed not through individual salvation but through "repair of the world" (*tikkun olam*). Most religious traditions teach that those who suffer are deserving of acts of charity rather than in need of psychotherapeutic treatment.

The idea that suffering is primarily a psychiatric issue is arguably an advance over the idea that suffering is a visible sign of transgression against God. Still, it is an idea that can be both distorting and damaging. It leads to certain fundamental, all too common confusions.

The first is our confusion between the self and the world. Nothing could be more obvious than the fact that we do not bring all suffering on ourselves through neurosis, psychiatric disorders, or negative "thought forms." One must be deeply enmeshed in the world-denial of contemporary psychologistic thinking to fail to see how much suffering has to do with large-scale political and economic forces, with pervasive social violence and collective forms of victimization. (For evidence, consult your daily newspapers.)

When we psychologize human suffering, we narrow our focus to the individual—perhaps in order to be less overwhelmed by the sheer enormity of human suffering, which, in the modern era, has reached a crescendo of atrocity. In doing so, we lose the connection to anything larger than our family of origin. The sense or meaning we give to pain keeps us stuck in a kind of narcissistic individualism that paradoxically fuels neurosis and emotional suffering.

In the process, we lose the distinction between neurotic and authentic suffering—between that which is avoidable and that which is a necessary condition of being human; and between suffering we can control as individuals and suffering that requires large-scale social transformation. Suffering that is rooted in the body's pain and degeneration, as Freud knew, and in the ego's attachments, aversions, and delusions, as the Buddha pointed out, is inevitable. The story of anyone's individual suffering, however, is also a story of that individual's social context, however hidden that may be to them or to the culture as a whole. We must learn to listen not only to our bodies but to the wider social context if we want to find the larger roots of our pain.

## Laura's Story: Transmissions of Fear from the Old Country

The alchemy of the dark emotions most often takes place in life's valleys: dark nights of the soul when inordinate pain, like a swollen river, breaks through the dam we've erected around our hearts and floods us with energy that unexpectedly guides us to new life. But it is not always adversity that triggers dark emotions. Sometimes it is a happy event that brings us to the healing path, because our fear of pain and our fear of happiness are really two sides of the same coin.

Laura came to therapy because she was afraid to be happy. She had a good life. She was content in her marriage and had three beautiful daughters. She'd overcome years of a debilitating chronic illness and financial struggle. Why was it so hard to let herself enjoy the life she'd built, to claim the happiness she deserved?

This question was underlined when Laura's firstborn daughter, Susan, was about to be married. Laura was a meticulous planner, yet she could not bring herself to complete the wedding plans. Each day she procrastinated and her anxiety mounted. She found herself in a panic. And like many people I see in therapy, she had a bad case of the "should feels": a malady in which you condemn yourself for feeling one thing when you "should feel" another.

"What's wrong with me?" she asked. "I should feel happy and instead I feel scared."

In working with Laura, I started with two basic teachings. First: Emotions are information. Treat them with respect. Let them guide your process of healing. Second: Let's not just talk about feelings; let's allow them to speak for themselves, from the body.

In a state of deepened bodily relaxation and heightened awareness, Laura readily located her fear in the area of her chest. I then suggested that she let her body speak from this place. (Children tend to be more open than most adults to this kind of suggestion because they are not bound by adult conventions of rationality and are able to just play and imagine. Adults in therapy often have to relearn what they once knew.)

The voice of Laura's chest spoke these words: "I'm scared. Susan will be married soon, around the same time of year that Sadie, for whom she was named, was married many years ago." (Among Jews of Eastern European origin, it is customary to name a child after a deceased relative. Sometimes a baby name beginning with the same initial as the relative's name is chosen instead.)

As I listened and asked questions, a story emerged.

Sadie was Laura's beloved grandmother. When Sadie was a little girl, her own mother had died in giving birth to Sadie's brother. Thenceforth, Sadie was raised by her grandmother. She came to the United States alone as a green girl of fifteen, in search of a new and better world, free of the grinding poverty and persecution of Jews in Russia. Here she found a young man who loved her and asked her to marry him. Now, at last, she felt her fortune would change and she would be happy.

The grandmother who had raised Sadie was invited to the wedding. Overjoyed, she prepared to come to America from the old country. But she never arrived. On the day of her departure, she was robbed and murdered. Her attackers took the money she had saved for the journey and left her life-less body on the street.

Thus Sadie, on the day of her wedding, was left to mourn the death of her second "mother."

In telling this story, with its O'Henry twist of fate, Laura's chest heaved with sobs. She grieved Sadie's losses of her two mothers. When her body "spoke," it was as though Sadie herself were speaking through Laura's flesh, Sadie's mourning completed.

The emotional conviction that joy gets punished by loss was lodged in Laura's body. Fear and grief were a kind of emotional legacy, inherited from her grandmother's history of trauma and loss in two critical moments of happiness—the birth of her brother, and her wedding.

When I asked Laura to have an imaginary conversation with Sadie about Susan's upcoming wedding, this is what Sadie had to say: "I felt both happy and sad on my wedding day. Now it's your time to celebrate your daughter's wedding. And I say to you: Let yourself be happy! For it is truly a joyous oc-casion! I will be with you during the entire day. And I promise you that no one will die."

Two months later, Laura danced at her daughter's wedding, radiant with gratitude. She felt Sadie's presence with her, as promised. The fear that she'd carried in her body had alchemized, making room for joy. She was no longer afraid to be happy.

Laura was, as we all are, much larger than she imagined herself to be. It was in enlarging her pain rather than reducing it that she could heal through the dark emotions she carried.

## An Ecology of Emotion

"Every man beareth the whole stamp of the human condition," said the es-sayist Montaigne. Every story of suffering contains a world of pain. No mat-ter how apparently individual, this story is played out in a larger social, cultural, global, and cosmic context—an ecology of emotion. We are not al-ways aware of these larger contexts. We cannot measure them in a laboratory.

But they are there, affecting each of us in ways we can barely speak, ways that we call unconscious.

Neurotic pain, the suffering we inflict on ourselves, almost always has a basis in authentic suffering—the fateful hand that Life deals us. This authentic suffering is not always what we have experienced directly in our own lives. It may be in our family history, the past of our parents or of generations dead and gone. One might have to go back several generations to find this core of non-neurotic suffering—a death, a sexual violation, or the trauma of war, oppression, or violence. When we come to know it, our own stories change. They become larger and deeper and wider than we thought them to be.

Amazingly, this larger story is rooted in the body. The boundaried body that we think of as our individual "self" carries the embedded emotional traces of those who came before us. Emotions in the body encode information that we can come to know when we let the body speak its truth. Psychotherapists in the past two decades have come to see this quite vividly in the case of incest survivors, whose stories have emerged from the body once they have a listener who, like a midwife, is there to receive the stories. How the body carries such information is mysterious—a part of the larger Mystery that ego psychology as we know it can barely glimpse, much less fathom.

We live in the world and the world lives in us. The dark emotions that our bodies carry are transpersonal energies housed in our flesh and rooted in our responses to the world—to the inevitable pain of being alive and being humanly connected to others. We see our "private" feelings through the lens of our separateness. But when we widen the lens, it becomes clear that everything we feel is experienced within a larger system of emotional ecology. The separate self, as we know it, is what Albert Einstein called an "optical delusion of our consciousness." In the words of Martin Luther King, Jr., we are all interconnected in an "inescapable web of mutuality."

We use a microscope to minutely examine ourselves or a telescope to sweep the stars, but we have no instrument by which to glimpse it all together: mind, body, emotion, culture, history, society, cosmos. At least not a scientific instrument, as yet. What enables us to see the whole picture is the clear, wide-angle vision that belongs to spirit.

It is in the spirit that emotional alchemy takes place—a spirit not divorced from the body but that flows from what the body knows. When we can broaden the story of our suffering from a place of rootedness in the body, emotional alchemy happens quite naturally. We learn that suffering does not have to deaden; it can also enliven. It does not have to weaken; it can also strengthen. It does not have to diminish but can enlarge us. We go to "shrinks" to reduce our suffering, when what we need is to open to it and let it expand us.

The world is in vital need of the truth that the dark emotions teach. Our aversion to pain actually sabotages our search for happiness. When we polarize light and dark, our healing remains partial and obsessive, easily undone. We search in the light for what we would find in the dark. In the dark is the accumulated sorrow, fear, and despair that lives in our bodies. In the dark is the enormous, seemingly insurmountable suffering that haunts our world.

The word *shaman* means "to see in the dark." There is a shamanism of the dark emotions—a way of maintaining awareness in the midst of the chaos and turbulence of the darker regions of the psyche—that ultimately alters our perception of who and what we are. Painful emotions challenge us to know the sacred in the broken; to develop an enlarged sense of Self beyond the suffering ego, an awareness that comes from being mindful of life's difficulties, rather than disengaging from them; to arrive at a wider and deeper perspective not limited by our pain but expanded by it.

Whether we listen to them or not, the dark emotions will emerge. One way or another, they exert their call through the body—as an act of grace or an act of violence, a cancerous growth or a surge of creative energy. Dark emotions don't go away. They simply come to us in whatever form we can bear. When we master the art of staying fully awake in their presence, they move us through suffering. We discover that the darkness has its own light.

# 2 *Vulnerability*

## The Power of No Protection

> One heals suffering only by experiencing it
> to the full.
> — Marcel Proust

WHEN WE ARE BUSY and everything is humming along, we are often in a state of deep forgetfulness. We forget what the Buddha called the first noble truth: life hurts. For the most part, the everyday self that psychologists call "ego" has a hard time with this unpalatable fact. We prefer the illusion of thinking ourselves invulnerable to the suffering that is part of being human.

But then Life has a way of waking us up. Something happens and we find ourselves in the grip of a formidable force that lets us know: We are not in control here. Life is larger than our ego's agenda. Before, we were probably not asking *Why am I here?* or *What is the meaning of my life?* But now we are besieged with the ultimate questions: *Where is God? What is the meaning of this suffering?*

These are Job's questions in the biblical story. A righteous man devoted to God, Job enjoys prosperity and good fortune. Then, suddenly, he is devastated by unbearable loss. Job's fate appears to be the whim of God. Roaming the earth for someone to afflict, Satan challenges God to a bet: Given a strong enough dose of adversity, even a good man will eventually curse God. Not to be put off by a dare, God allows his faithful servant to be the target of Satan's havoc, betting on Job's continuing good faith.

In one fell swoop, all of Job's good fortune is gone. His sheep, camels, oxen, and donkeys are stolen. His shepherds are attacked and murdered. All his children die—seven sons and three daughters, left lifeless under their collapsed house, destroyed by the wind. In the blink of an eye, the richest man in the East becomes the most bereft of human beings.

Job is flattened, but he doesn't lose his faith: "Naked I came from my mother's womb and naked I will return there. The Lord gave, and the Lord has taken; may the name of the Lord be blessed."[1]

But Satan is not satisfied. He argues: it's only because Job himself has not been afflicted with physical pain that he remains faithful. God then gives Satan free rein to do anything he wishes to Job, so long as his life is spared. Covered with boils and festering sores from his scalp to his feet, Job sits down in the dust. Apart from his longing for death, there is only one thing that animates him: the passion to tell his story, to proclaim his innocence and the injustice of his suffering, to argue with God.

Job has three friends who come to mourn with him. The Comforters are present while Job's words gush from his lips like blood: "God has ringed me with terrors and his arrows have pierced my heart."[2] As though blind to the totality of Job's losses, the first Comforter tells him that his faith will protect him from harm. The second Comforter reasons that since God is just, Job must be guilty of some offense and his suffering justified. The third urges the innocent Job to repent of his sins.

"How hollow then is your comfort! Your answers are empty lies," Job rails.[3] What he asks of his friends is to be accompanied in his pain and outrage. This is just what they cannot do. Instead, they blame Job for his adversity and explain it away, offering cheap salves that add a sharp bite to Job's blistering wounds. Their conventional theologies are their armor, protecting them against the vicarious experience of Job's radical vulnerability.

The power of the Book of Job lies in the contrast between the authentic voice of Job's suffering and the hollow theological "consolations" of his Comforters, between the poetry of calamity and the inadequacy of explanation or consolation for suffering of this magnitude, for affliction so unmerited.

By the end of the Book of Job, we know as little about the reasons for his suffering as we did in the beginning. At the heart of Job's vulnerability is Mystery.

What I know about vulnerability I learned in a crash course that started when my first child was born. I was thirty-four years old. I was deliriously happy. Colors were more vivid, music more transporting, the air pulsed with a vibrant energy. My senses were amplified, as though I'd lived with only a fraction of their force until now. I was lucky. By any reckoning, this was a good pregnancy. I had none of the usual assortment of pregnancy ills, and seemingly endless reserves of energy. I ate brown rice and vegetables, healthy organic sources of protein. No chemicals or preservatives passed my lips. I didn't even chew gum, because it contained minute amounts of artificial coloring. I walked every day—two miles around Jamaica Pond—and swam several times a week. Dedicating myself to nurturing this child within me, I felt stronger and healthier than ever before. Everything was going as planned.

Then abruptly, it was all swept away. A tornado came through, ripping out my roots and whirling me in a hellish circle before throwing me back into my life in an utterly new place. The dark emotions were the whirlwind in which I moved, the energies I had to master in order to stay alive.

Suddenly, I was in hard labor a month before my due date, filled with an ominous dread. Every cell of my body knew that something was wrong. My husband, Roger, found me on my knees in the living room, praying aloud. This was totally out of character. I was a secular humanist and a social activist, not a spiritual seeker or true believer. I had never prayed before. My prayers were wrenched from a fathomless depth, an acknowledgment of my smallness in the face of what was coming. I prayed because I knew I was going to need help.

All my plans were overturned. Instead of a cozy home birth with a chosen midwife, I entered a large Boston training hospital with a birth assistant I didn't know, laboring in a room with sharp lights and gray walls, and a host of people milling about. With the exception of Roger at my side, I recognized no one. Labor assistant, obstetrician, hospital staff—all faces were covered in blue face masks, the contemporary purdah of institutional childbirth. And instead of a miraculous bonding experience with a brand-new human being, flesh of my flesh and blood of my blood, I released a baby from my body who was whisked away after barely a glance into his wide blue eyes. He was limp and unresponsive. He would have to be observed. Tests would have to be done.

Time stood still until I was able to see Aaron. I remember approaching him as he lay in his little plastic bed in the Neonatal Intensive Care Unit and being awe-struck. He was perfectly formed. Lacking the usual baby fat because he was a month early, his muscles were finely contoured and pronounced, like those of a Greek statue in miniature. With his heart-shaped mouth and downy scalp, his beauty offered some modicum of reassurance. And yet it was clear that something was terribly wrong. Searching his eyes for a clue, I saw only a great and nameless suffering, an ageless sadness. More than anything, I wanted to comfort him.

But little comfort was to be found for any of us.

Aaron became the hospital's baby, living in a tiny isolette, a plastic baby cage in the neonatal intensive care nursery, surrounded by medical equipment, poked and prodded with needles and electrodes, tested and retested to determine what was wrong with him. And we lived with him, pleading with the hospital staff to make room for this seemingly irrelevant dyad— mother and child. Not to mention triad—mother, father, and child. We campaigned for a room in which Aaron could be with us. Apparently, this was the first request of its kind on the neonatal ICU. They would look into it. When no such room was available, I camped out in a sleeping bag on the floor of the ICU with Aaron at my side—a rampant breach of ordinary hospital etiquette. I was a mother and not a mother, trying to find a way to love this baby who was of me but did not belong to me.

Within a week, we were moved to Children's Hospital's neurology floor, where my son's condition was given a terrifying but altogether vague name: brain injury. Aaron had been a very active baby in utero. During my eighth month, there was a period of two days when I felt no movement. This was probably when it happened. For reasons we would never know, he had lost oxygen inside me. The medical term was anoxia. In the womb, universal symbol of safety, Aaron had been unaccountably vulnerable to harm. Something happened that had cut off his life support and sealed his destiny.

We think we are walking a path toward a planned destination. Then there is a turning in the road, and we find ourselves in a place nothing like the expected ground. We had thought there would be a bright meadow with a tranquil lake, but we find instead a deep crater and a devastated landscape.

At such times one has a sense of the inherent mystery of existence. There is a primal terror at the sheer vulnerability of being alive. In Job's day, that terror was perhaps mitigated by an overarching awe of God's power. For me, the experience was rather more precisely expressed by Shakespeare: "Like flies to wanton boys are we to the gods. They kill us for their sport." I had no faith in which to find shelter. So I looked instead for signs and portents, a talisman to clasp to me in this hapless wilderness into which I'd been thrown.

More than a year before Aaron's conception, I had a vision while doing yoga. While lying in the "corpse" posture on the floor, I saw a set of blue eyes, blazing with a radiant light. The eyes were riveting—and terrifying. A voice declared: "These are the eyes of your son, your first child." The vision came to me again as I dozed off in the passenger seat on a ride from Cape

Cod to Boston. Again I saw the eyes and felt the fear. It was disconcerting. Writing in my journal didn't help me understand anything more about this experience, which I decided was a case of psychic indigestion. I completely forgot about it.

Until now. Looking into Aaron's eyes, I was haunted by these visions. Were these the eyes that I had seen before, and was this why the visions were so frightening? Was it possible, in defiance of all reason, that my visions were prophetic? And did this mean that Aaron was going to die?

These visions vied in my consciousness with a dream that came to me at the start of my eighth month. In the dream, I looked down at my pregnant belly and saw the big mound shrinking into a small ball the size of a grapefruit. My baby was coming out—prematurely slipping out of me! Long and pink and still encased in his amniotic sac, he emerged and fell onto the carpet, with dust and lint gathering around him. I was in a panic, fearing for his life. He could get infected. He could die. So I talked to him. I asked him what to do, and he said "Don't worry. I'm all right." He was perfectly calm and omniscient. He reassured me.

At the end of the dream, I was exhilarated, shouting for joy: "My baby! My baby! I have my baby!"

Through all the endless tests, the bloodwork and the EEGs and the CAT scans; through all the fruitless attempts to feed an infant that couldn't suck or swallow; through all the hours that I sat with a mechanized Egnell pump draining my breasts of the milk meant for my baby's warm mouth; through all the times that Aaron regurgitated his intake of milk and had to be suctioned; through all the sleepless nights and endless days of doctors, I held on to this dream. I wanted to believe that it held the truth of Aaron's future. I'd had a number of clairvoyant dreams in the past, and much of this dream seemed prophetic. The baby was a boy who came early. He looked like the same singularly long baby of my dream. The doctors worried that he had an infection, as I did in the dream. The end of the dream was joy in my new baby. With all my heart, I prayed that this would be the end of the story.

But as the weeks of Aaron's life progressed, the dream's promise seemed more and more remote. Aaron was fading instead of flowering. Each time I held him close to me, I was terrified that if I moved the wrong way I would tangle up his heart monitor and rip out his IV cord and that he would die on the spot. I was frightened of his fragility, of the slender thread that held him to this life.

Rocking him in the nursery chair, I closed my eyes and saw what seemed like a tunnel at the bottom of the sea. And looking up, I saw dark shapes like strange underwater plants waving back and forth in the deep. Above these wavering forms there was dim light, very far away.

Was this Aaron's point of view I was seeing? From that moment, I imagined a face looking at him from above the wavering oceanic forms, shining on him like the sun. I put my face into the picture and beamed down my maternal love, reassuring him that above and beyond the dark dark sea, there was the lit-up face of his mother. I spoke to him softly. I said: *Aaron, whatever else you may know, I want you to know that there is love in this life. Besides the bright lights and the noise and the cold instruments and the pain, there is my love and your father's love. We are the suns that shine down on you in your little world beneath the sea. We shine our love down on you.*

Once, as I whispered to Aaron, I saw his eyes begin to redden and tear up, then to bulge slightly. His mouth puckered up like a fish. He looked directly at me and turned blue around the mouth as milk ran out of his nostrils. The nurse arrived just before his heart monitor registered the awful siren of his heart drop. His face got bluer. Oxygen was administered. The doctor was called.

From these moments I knew, early on, that my dream was only a dream. The end of the story could be anything. Perhaps, against all odds, Aaron would recover. Or he might survive this ordeal with what the neurologist called "massive" brain damage. Or perhaps he would die. I knew that anything could happen and that nobody knew what would happen, that I was at the mercy of something much larger than my hopes and dreams or the doctors' instruments. Whatever was wrong with Aaron was not in my power to fix—or their power to control. I was utterly helpless to keep this child alive.

My womb had betrayed my first, my dearly beloved child. There was no safety anywhere. I was besieged with raw grief, terror, rage, helplessness. My illusions of safety were exposed. My visions and dreams were hollow comforts and empty lies. I wanted so badly to believe they would protect me. But it was clear to me that there was no protection from reality. What would be would be.

I did not take this gracefully. In the evening, after hospital visiting hours were over, I anguished to friends and a therapist who could do nothing but listen.

Slowly, I began to learn about surrender. More than anything I'd ever wanted in my life, I wanted Aaron to live. Yet it seemed to me that Aaron was telling me, daily and in no uncertain terms, that his future was not up to me. Each day it became more and more clear that he was on his own journey. Our love could accompany him and warm him, but not alter the destination. Gradually, I became less demanding, less insistent that Aaron live. I wanted only to be with him for as long as I could. All I had was this present moment in which to be Aaron's mother and to love him. All I had was this present moment.

When I could be with Aaron in this way, I felt all right, energetic, ready for whatever would happen. When I thought about the future and the cards stacked against him and the doctors doing their tests, I sank into despair.

In this way, my life with Aaron became a prolonged intensive training in how to tolerate helplessness. Aaron was my teacher, the Zen master who taught me how to be mindful in the midst of vulnerability.

On the sixty-sixth day of Aaron's life, I awoke to a dream: My son was encased in a box with clear plastic around the perimeter. Around the box, menacing dogs barked. Their barks grew louder as they got closer and closer to him. I woke up in a sweat and rushed to the hospital.

I arrived in time to see the nurse piercing Aaron's spine with a thick needle. She insisted, as all his attendants did, day after day of Aaron's life, that this procedure did not hurt him. The lumbar puncture was necessary, she explained, because Aaron was very ill. They suspected he had pneumonia. They were testing him for meningitis. They drew blood to see how his blood gases were doing. But there was no need for their tests to explain what was obvious. Aaron was dying.

That night, he was taken to the intensive care unit. Roger and I followed. The floor was uncannily silent. We passed a large windowed area. Looking out, I saw the night sky spread out, a black carpet dotted with white stars. It seemed to me that they shone with unusual brightness. Large snowflakes blew against the windowpanes, melting on impact.

And here was Aaron: ensconced in a tiny chair surrounded by the plastic oxygen tent of my dream. Seated upright in his tented chair, his agony was plain. His little chest heaved up and down as he gasped for air. And for the first time in his life, Aaron was crying—not with the lusty cry of the newborn, but with the pain of his slow asphyxiation, the struggle of his dying.

Then the puzzle pieces all fit. Finally, after all the days of uncertainty, of praying, hoping, loving, hurting, and trying to understand, it was all made clear. Aaron was born to die. He would die of an infection. Not an infection he was born with, but a bacterial pneumonia he contracted in the hospital. All that was left for me to do, as his mother, was to help him make the passage.

The hospital had its ways of death, just as it had its ways of care. Aaron was still hooked up, as he had been throughout, to an IV and a heart monitor. The IV now carried a morphine drip to ease his suffering. (Finally, in these last moments, the hospital staff acknowledged that Aaron was in pain.) Every fifteen minutes, his line would be checked and his blood pressure measured.

"Call me if anything happens," the neurologist in charge had said after examining him. I had trouble deciphering his coded language. What could he mean, "if anything happened"? Then I realized that he was alluding to Aaron's death but unable to speak the word. "You mean if Aaron dies?" I saw him shudder as he nodded. I felt sorry for him, sorry that my words had pierced his medical reserve. It was clear that death was not something one spoke of directly on the ICU. Death was the enemy here; it meant that everyone had failed.

"Human beings cannot bear too much reality," T. S. Eliot wrote. Proximity to birth and death, those most exquisitely vulnerable of all human moments, was not what the hospital was set up for. They were too real to be endured without procedures that put participants in these events at a distance from them. The procedures, the euphemisms, the technical measurements surrounding Aaron's dying (why record a dying infant's blood pressure?) kept the reality of it at a safe distance. They made it possible to go on with business as usual. Perhaps they kept nurses and doctors from crying on the job—which, however human, would be deemed unprofessional.

But for me, these illusory protections made Aaron's dying alone in a cordoned-off box a kind of crucifixion. I needed to have this final experience with him. Aaron's death, no less than his birth, was a passage that called me to be with him. We needed each other. I wanted him removed from the oxygen tent, which only prolonged his dying. I wanted him to be in my arms, where I could hold him and speak to him, sing to him and soothe him. I wanted him to be disconnected from the hardware that held him to this life. And I wanted us, Aaron, Roger, and I, to be left in peace so that we could do this dying together as a family.

These requests on the ICU at Children's Hospital were as odd as our insistence on extended time to hold Aaron in the neonatal nursery. But the staff was gracious. They would not unhook Aaron from the heart monitor or IV until after his death. But they did take him out of his oxygen box and hand him to us. We were allowed to hold him in our arms and to rock him. To look into his face and to whisper: *Bless you, Aaron. Thank you for coming to us. Bless you for your unfathomable eyes and your beautiful soul. Thank you for entrusting yourself to us. And now, little one, it's time for you to let go. It's time for you to stop trying so hard, struggling to live. It's time to let your breathing stop. To let your life be over, and to be at peace. We will always love you. We will always remember you.*

Aaron's cries subsided after a time. He lay in our arms more quietly, and his breathing became less labored, more shallow. Gradually, his color changed from a bright red to an ashen gray and finally a ghostly white. It took Aaron as long to die as it did for him to be born—six hours and twenty minutes. He was born at 4:48 the morning of October 25. He died at 4:48 the morning of December 29. He had come full circle, his death a birth in reverse.

At the moment of Aaron's death, I heard a baby's cry. Loud and insistent, it struck me, oddly, as a sign of hope: somewhere else, though Aaron was dead, another child was alive.

*I accept what is now and what is to come.* This was the mantra that had come to me in the early weeks of my pregnancy with Aaron, and that I repeated every day until he was born. And now, finally, I knew what it was I was meant to accept.

Ten years later, it is bedtime and I am reading aloud to Anna, the radiantly healthy daughter born a year after Aaron's death. Her mind is alert and inquisitive, her wide eyes open with the wonder of life. Along with learning about the life cycle of the butterfly, the Greek gods and goddesses, and her multiplication tables, Anna has been learning more and more about the everyday social world that she hears about and sees on television: about violence, sexual abuse, and rape, about the harm that humans inflict on one another. Anna's unanswered questions about these scary subjects tend to come up at night. When we are cuddling, she finds the courage to ask.

These are some of the questions she asks me: Could a robber break into our house? Could a crank caller get your address and stalk you? Do kids get kidnapped off the street? How do you know if a stranger is just a friendly, safe person or if he is going to do something bad to you? Why do people use guns? What percentage of people are bad? What is a serial killer? Are there any earthquakes in this part of the country? Why do people do bad things to each other? Why do people die young?

All children develop their sense of self and world in the face of concerns like these. When an innocent child looks directly into your eyes and asks you to explain evil, natural catastrophe, and human vulnerability, there is nothing more compelling than wanting to reassure her. We want to say: You are perfectly safe. There is no danger to you. You will not be kidnapped, killed, or hurt. You will not die by earthquake, flood, tornado, or fire. We will take care of you and protect you. Nothing bad will ever happen to you. The bad things only happen to other people. Far away. Not here. Not you. Ever.

These answers, we know even as we speak them, are lies. The white lies we tell for a good cause: to reassure a frightened child. They are the reassuring illusions that deny the truth of human vulnerability. And as any parent knows, we spin them for ourselves at least as much as for our children. Of course somewhere we know that we are teaching our children the illusion of invulnerability. Of course we know that there is never an absolute guarantee of safety for any child or any adult, that we cannot shield them or ourselves from unexpected harm. But we try to shield them from the fear of harm. Often, we end up teaching them how to be afraid of fear, and afraid of vulnerability, rather than how to know that fear and vulnerability are part of every life and how to cope with them.

Anna and I talk of robberies and house locks, kidnappers and pranksters. I give her pertinent information in language and to the degree that I think she can take in and that can serve her. I tell her that there are ways to protect herself, that she has the right to speak up, scream, or run in order to defend herself. We speak of good and evil, serial killers and guardian angels. I tell Anna: The body is vulnerable, but strong. Sometimes it gets hurt. But it also heals. And eventually we all die. But the spirit lives on. It cannot be killed. It is invulnerable. I know this because after your brother Aaron died, he let me know that he was okay. As I speak these words, I am in awe, remembering.

The day of Aaron's funeral was a clear day in December, the air cold and crisp. I looked into the mirror and announced to myself: Today is the day you bury your son. And to my surprise, the moment was as crisp and clear as the air. What I saw and what, in that instant, I was able to accept, was that Aaron's life had been lived to its completion, and that it was now over. It was only much later that I realized that this simple acceptance was a gift of grace—a word I'd never used before.

At the cemetery, we lowered his small casket into the cold ground and took turns shoveling earth over it, as is the custom in Jewish burials. We sang to Aaron the songs we'd made up for him while he was alive and that we recorded for him to hear when we weren't with him. Then, softly, as though spoken in my ear, I heard these words: *You are looking in the wrong place.*

My attention turned then, from the casket in the ground to the cloudless blue sky. And I saw there what I can only describe as a magnificent radiance—the light of Aaron's blue eyes, magnified and shining through the heavens. The communication was clearer than speech. It was Aaron, reassuring me. He was saying, *Don't worry about me. I am all right.* The words were the same as those of the omniscient baby of my pregnancy dream. I was flooded with peace and remembered the phrase "the peace that passes understanding." I was awash in the pure joy of Aaron's presence. These were the eyes of my child, my firstborn. This was the end of my dream—joy in my baby. In this most unlikely place, where my child's body was laid to rest, I discovered the invincibility of spirit.

In the telling, this sounds like a tall story. Yet, at the time, it was no more extraordinary than any nonverbal communication between a mother and her baby, an everyday occurrence that is no less miraculous for being commonplace. I was surprised that my husband could not see what I saw, could not feel what I felt. It was as visible as the sun, this spirit of Aaron that shone down on me. After its appearance, it remained with me, no longer visible, but an unmistakable presence, for the rest of the day of his burial.

The year was 1981—well before the current wave of spiritual populism in America. Before the spate of angel books and before *Conversations with God* made the *New York Times* best-seller list. Had someone asked me, before this moment, "Does the spirit outlive the body?" I would have answered: I don't have a clue. Having grown up with an intimate knowledge of human evil, I'd been, for as long as I could remember, a deeply committed agnostic; a down-to-earth Taurus, feet planted firmly on the ground; a sensible psychotherapist and a fervid social activist. My mind was set on changing this world, not on peeking into worlds beyond. I was well aware that my profession would view my communion with my dead child as delusional. But there was no way to turn back from here. I knew I wasn't crazy, though I knew others would probably think so. Poor girl, they would say, unmoored from her senses by extreme grief. And it was true, grief had everything to do with this sudden glimpse into an alternate reality that I could neither explain nor deny.

From being fully present to my experience of loss without any set of dogmatic beliefs, a fundamental transformation had taken place. The road took another turn, and the devastated landscape opened out into an expansive vista of limitless sky. Attending to a dying child without protection, I discovered a new land, one that was perhaps always there but that I had some-how never noticed: a magical land inhabited by spirits; a world in which life expands out of death, parallel with this constricted world we know, in which death is merciless; a world that offers up the blessing of an unex-pected and unforgettable consolation.

## Vulnerability and Humanity

There is no safety net against vulnerability so long as one has a body and an ego. Though there are those who are protected against some of the slings and arrows of outrageous fortune by wealth, power, and privilege, we are all vulnerable. And to be vulnerable is to travel the pathway of the dark emo-tions. Helplessness and fear, grief, anger, and despair: these are the raw emotions of Job's poetry, markers of our human vulnerability. Dark feelings unfelt in the past emerge as special vulnerabilities in the present. Being fully alive in the present does not mitigate our vulnerability; it only makes us more aware of it.

But vulnerability is not just about hurting. It is about openness. Not only to pain, adversity, loss, and death, but also to the things we most desire and cherish: to love, intimacy, creativity, sex, birth, wonder; to being truly touched by another human being, being truly seen for who we are; to the sheer adventure of being alive; to the sacred spirit that imbues the world.

Vulnerability is what we share as human beings: our openness to being affected by one another, for better and for worse, is at the core of our inter-connectedness. Because we are vulnerable, we feel pain—not only our own pain, but the pain of others. What we do to others we also do to ourselves. Vulnerability is at the heart of our human capacity for empathy; for suffer-ing but also for joy; for hurt but also for compassion; for loneliness but also for connection. It is the open heart, fragile but strong, easily wounded but capable of great mercy and love. When we are most vulnerable, we are most alive, most open to all the dimensions of existence. In our vulnerability is our power.

I counseled a woman who was raped by her father as a young child. After years of work on the trauma of incest, she had come to a place of some peace about her history. Now, being pregnant with her first child revived it all. These days young girls are counseled to speak up and tell someone if they are sexually abused. But Christine's abuse began before she could speak, before she could have any idea of what was happening to her. It started when she was utterly helpless to respond in any way that could protect her. Her vulnerability was total. The idea of being in a hospital, subject to procedures she might not want, the pain of labor, the openness of her vagina in the act of childbirth—all of these are normal concerns for pregnant women. But for Christine, these concerns tapped into the reservoir of traumatic fear she'd experienced as a small child. She was afraid that her trauma would be triggered in the birthing room and that she would not be able to give birth to her baby.

Christine was a remarkable woman with enormous emotional and spiritual resources. In the course of her therapeutic work she discovered that in the midst of her early helplessness, there had been help that she had not been able to see at the time. She had seen them since, the spirits who had helped her endure her early violation, soothed and protected her and kept her alive. They had taken her to a mossy place where they surrounded her and bathed her in their warm, nurturing energies. She called them "the lily ladies."

Now, at this time of challenge in her late pregnancy, I asked Christine if she could consult with the lily ladies, to see if they had any wisdom to impart to her. These were the words she heard: "Your vulnerability is the source of your strength. Do not associate it with harm but with your creative power."

The lessons of the lily ladies helped Christine birth her baby and go to a deeper level of her own healing.

## Vulnerability and Control

The lessons of the lily ladies are not what we learn about vulnerability in our culture. Seeing vulnerability as strength is more of a feminine perspective. In a culture in which masculine values are normative, vulnerability is the opposite of strength. Strength is about sporting a stiff upper lip, being armored and combat-ready. Vulnerability is seen as weakness, defenselessness, readiness for victimization. We learn to cope with vulnerability through control or denial, steeling ourselves against feeling, avoiding or numbing the sensation of emotion. Because we all know deeply that, like the losses of Job, a great deal of the world's suffering is arbitrary or inexplicable, we have ways to ward off the discomfort of this knowledge, ways to rationalize vulnerability, to make it palatable. Like Job's comforters, we try to make ourselves feel less vulnerable by cleaving to conditioned theologies and dogmas, sets of learned beliefs designed to make vulnerability tolerable by explaining it away. Since we feel safe only when we are "in control," and since control is not always in our individual hands, we tend to deny how little control we are given over life-and-death matters.

The attempt to control vulnerability is understandably human. It is, in fact, an inbred aspect of what we think of as normal psychology. It is how the ego grows and develops its innate grandiosity, the normal delusion of its own invincibility. Especially in the midst of life's more adverse moments, control may feel like the ego's only way to survive. It bestows a limited sense of protection against the primal terror of existence.

At the same time, this kind of control locks out a great deal of the wonder of being alive, the mystery of the cosmos. It diminishes our capacity for living and for listening to what life has to teach us. It effectively bars us from discovering what lies beyond ego and beyond the body. It aborts the alchemy of the dark emotions. If this century of devastating wars, holocaust, genocides, and environmental destruction has anything to teach us, it is this: that unless we acknowledge and honor our vulnerability, unless we become increasingly aware of how "intervulnerable" we are, how vulnerable the earth is to human interventions, we will continue to pose a threat not only to our own survival but to the fate of the earth.

## Vulnerability and Surrender

As the first part of the Book of Job is the poetry of human suffering, the last part is the poetry of cosmic Mystery. God speaks to Job from out of the whirlwind, singing the panoply of the cosmos. Where were you, the Unnameable thunders, when the cornerstone of the earth was laid down, "while the morning stars burst out singing / and the angels shouted for joy"? A rapt Job, once so full of sound and fury, is rendered speechless. "I have spoken of the unspeakable / and tried to grasp the infinite," he says. "Therefore I will be quiet, comforted that I am dust."[4]

In the end, Job is humbled. Having argued with God—refusing to bypass the enormity of his unjustified pain or to relinquish the voice of his authentic sorrow—he finds comfort, at last, in knowing that he is dust. He has learned not submission but surrender. We are told that in the end, all of Job's former riches are restored. He is miraculously reunited with his family. He dies a happy man.

Job's life flows with abundance again only after he is completely humbled, after he lets go of his need to know what cannot be known. Having faced his vulnerability without refuge and refused to bypass its truth, he surrenders to the Unknowable and is rewarded with renewed life. In the

end, the Job story is about spiritual transformation through conscious suffering and the acceptance of human vulnerability.

It is through surrender to the unwanted that we embrace our vulnerability.
Our helplessness teaches us humility. When we are humbled by pain, we
see our smallness in the vastness of the cosmos. The ego gives up its hold
on reality, its paltry attempts to control and to dictate its terms. It lets go of
its agenda. Its grandiosity thus diminished, there is an opening, and a larger
vision can emerge. Amazingly, this letting go, which is a kind of death, is
also one of the great joys of life—an effort that is the end of all effort. When
we unfurl the gnarled fist of control, letting the hand open up to receive and
to give, our smallness—once the source of our agony—becomes a source of
comfort.

The way of surrender is not a way our culture endorses. The opposite of
control, surrender is seen as passivity or cowardice: the white flag of the los-
ers raised up to the victors. Yet conscious surrender is often what life asks
of us in those times when we most want to control the outcome. Embracing vulnerability does not mean wallowing in passivity, abdicating responsibility, or relishing being a victim. It means being fully present to what is
happening and staking no claims on the outcome.

Surrender is essential to the alchemy of the dark emotions. Without it,
the grandiosity of the ego inflicts itself on our best spiritual intentions. We
confuse ourselves with the Unnameable. To become larger spiritually, it is
often necessary to get smaller. We must become fully human, to know the
contours of human suffering without flinching, lest we become demonic
with an overbloated sense of our own power. What vulnerability asks of us,
ultimately, is not control of our emotions but transformation of our consciousness through emotional openness.

The way of surrender is the way of the mystics, of the dark night of the
soul, of the descent of Isis into the underworld, of being wracked upon a
wheel of pain, and returning, transformed. In my case, having no beliefs
about God or spirituality probably helped me learn the art of surrender.
True agnosticism is not a position of doubt. It is a statement about life's inherent uncertainty, a position of openness that entails the ability to tolerate
the unpredictability and chaos of existence without resorting to a comforting belief. It neither defines nor defies anything. It says: I don't know. I
don't know, so I am open. I am open because I don't know. This "not knowing" expresses the limits of what can be understood with the rational mind.

Then alchemy becomes possible, something new can happen—a vision of spirit after death that is as real as the flesh, a felt experience of Mystery.

This is what I learned through Aaron: The safety we seek by hardening our hearts to vulnerability can be found when all our protections are destroyed. In my surrender to sorrow, a doorway opened in the fabric of existence. I was able to see clearly beyond the confines of ordinary consciousness. I saw that beyond the body, there is spirit. That beyond death, there is life. Flowers of faith bloomed from the soil of vulnerability.

How wonderful it would be if faith permanently erased human suffering. But in my experience, the spiritual journey is a spiral dance, not a trip with a final destination. However life-altering, my vision of Aaron's spirit did not kill my ego. A month after Aaron's death, though his spirit was with me, I was still living with the daily grief of losing him. I was struggling to integrate my experience of his life and death. I had this dream:

I am looking into the pages of a wondrous book, with colorful images and beautiful words. The dream voice says: *Look at these creations. Aren't they beautiful?*

I answer: *Yes. But what good is all this beauty when I am in such pain?*

The dream voice replies: *Love. Love is the meaning. Love is the practice. Love is what this book is all about.*

In this dream there is a dialogue between a smaller self and larger Self. The larger Self is the overvoice, pointing me to the cosmic beauty and wonder of the Book of Life. My grieving smaller self asks the typical egoic question: *Why me?* The ego can't see beyond its own pain, its vision dimmed by tears. But the enlarged sense of Self beyond ego has the final word—and the word is Love. When the ego is shattered, the heart of Love is found in this brokenness, where we least expect it.

"Even in the pit of hell, it's a mitzvah to be joyful." So said Rabbi Nachman of Breslov, a mystic in the Hasidic tradition. A mitzvah is an act that honors the Divine. Even in hell, it is possible to be joyful, because both heaven and hell are here on earth, created by our minds and actions. Transformation is always possible. We can transform pain to joy by keeping our hearts open.

Keeping an open heart in hell, we learn the art of vulnerability, the power of no protection. This is a spiritual power, not an egoic conquest. To learn its secret alchemy, we must be willing to accept suffering and vulnerability as a normal part of life. Because we are vulnerable, life hurts. We are not here to be free of pain. We are here to have our hearts broken by life. To learn to live with vulnerability and to turn pain into love.

"There is nothing so whole as a broken heart," said Rabbi Mendel of Kotzk, another Hasidic sage. The world breaks our hearts wide open; and it is the openness itself that makes us whole. The open heart is the doorway, inviting the angels in, revealing that the world—even in the pit of hell—is charged with the sacred.

# 3 How Dark Emotions Become Toxic

You can hold back from the suffering of the world
. . . but perhaps this very holding back is the one
suffering that you could have avoided.

— FRANZ KAFKA

The man who fears suffering is already suffering
from what he fears.

— MICHEL DE MONTAIGNE

LENNY BRUCE SAID: "We all live in a happy ending culture, a what should be culture, instead of a what is culture. We're all taught that fantasy. But if we were taught *this is what is,* I think we'd all be less screwed up."

When it comes to primary human emotions like love and anger, fear and joy, grief and gratitude, despair and hope—what is, is. We all want to sit at the happiness banquet and feast on the bread of contentment, the wine of joy. We'd rather skip the emotional food that doesn't go down so well. In life's many meals, not everything is equally palatable; but it all needs to be digested. We can't laugh heartily unless we know how to cry. We can't be fearless unless we know the taste of fear. We can't be happy if we're afraid to feel sad. Our faith is not faith until it's tested. To be at peace, we have to be at home with all of our emotions, to get comfortable with vulnerability.

Grief, fear, and despair are primary human emotions. Without them, we would be less than human, and less likely to survive. Grief arises because we are not alone, and what connects us to others and to the world also breaks our hearts. Grieving our losses allows us to heal and renew our spirits. Fear alerts us to protect our survival, extending beyond our instinct for self-preservation to our concern for others. Despair asks us to find meaning in the midst of apparent chaos or meaninglessness. Making meaning out of suffering is the basis of the human capacity to survive evil and transcend it.

The purposefulness of these dark emotions is evident when we can experience them mindfully, tolerate their intense energies, and let them be. Unfortunately, we don't learn how to do this in a culture that fears and devalues them. Emotion-phobia toxifies dark emotions, leaving our hearts confused and numb, depressed and anxious, isolated and lonely. In emotion-phobic culture, we internalize the idea that befriending what hurts will hurt us, whereas suppressing and avoiding it will make us feel better. We only end up feeling worse. The cultural baggage we carry weighs us down, a major impediment to the art of emotional alchemy.

But we weren't born with our bias against the dark emotions. We can change what we believe and how we react to grief, fear, and despair. We can transform the way we experience these emotions and begin to taste the freedom and power of letting our emotions be.

### Emotions 101

Fourteen first-graders sit before me, their eyes sparkling, their faces upturned in readiness. I am a volunteer parent, here to teach a class on understanding our emotions. This is not a subject generally offered in this private, progressive elementary school in Cambridge, Massachusetts—nor in most other schools, public or private, progressive or otherwise, anywhere on the planet. As a society, we haven't valued the understanding of human emotion enough to teach it to our young.

I wonder what these seven-year-olds have to say on a subject so close to us and yet so little understood.

When I ask, "Who can tell me what emotions are?" a slew of hands go up.

"Emotions are what you feel inside, like when you're happy or sad," says Laurie, her round face warming to the subject.

Jane, a skinny girl with an electric energy, jumps in with "You feel them in your body. Sometimes they make you want to cry or yell or jump around."

"Emotions tell you what you feel about things that are happening around you," adds Camilla. Her large dark eyes look like they probably take in a good deal of what's happening around her.

Next I do a naming exercise with the kids. Students are invited to come up to the blackboard and write down the name of any emotion that they know. Within minutes, the entire board is filled: happy, sad, angry, nervous, annoyed, frightened, hating, hopeless, loving, caring, bored, surprised, confused, depressed, disappointed, irritated, excited.

When I ask the students to think about what these emotions tell us, my question initiates a vibrant classroom discussion. Laurie tells the class that her mother's irritability in the morning means she hasn't had her first cup of coffee. Ritchie notes that when his father gets mad and loses his temper, it often means that Ritchie's done something really bad because his father is usually pretty calm. Joanne sadly conveys her impression that her father is frequently depressed when he comes home from work, and this probably means he doesn't like his job. "When my parents aren't talking at breakfast, it means they're mad at each other," offers Carol.

The kids talk about what makes them happy (a new bike), sad (when someone dies), and mad (when their parents blame them for something they didn't do). Mark notices the way certain emotions are like others, only more so: "Angry is like annoyed, only worse." Naomi has a comment about how some emotions camouflage others: "I cry when I'm mad," she observes, "and when I'm sad, I act mad."

When I ask the children if they have any feelings about the world as a whole, there is a pregnant pause. Lawrence with the sapphire blue eyes speaks first: "I'm sad that there's so much violence." Several children nod their heads, echoing Lawrence's sadness.

"I get mad when animals are mistreated," says Anna. "Like when people hunt and kill them for no reason."

"The Gulf War made me really scared," Danielle reports. "I don't really understand why it had to happen."

The last to speak is Will, a small boy with big eyes: "I think at the rate we're polluting the earth, by the time I grow up there won't be much left that's clean and good for me."

By comparison to the emotional intelligence of many adults, these kids are emotionally gifted. They have an intuitive grasp of what feelings are and what they're for. They know that emotions are energies in the body that convey information, seek expression, and motivate action. Their emotional vocabulary is nuanced and wide-ranging. And they know that emotions, while "inner," are responses to the larger world.

Not yet fully socialized in what psychologists call the conventions of emotional display, they tell it like it is. They are unabashedly direct and honest about their feelings. There is an excited spirit of information-sharing in their conversation, and not a hint of self-consciousness. Displays like this, in adults, might be called inappropriate. Yet these kids, untrained in adult notions of privacy, are respectful of their own emotions and those of their classmates.

All of this is quite different from what I would expect in a therapy group for grown-ups. Adults often take a long time to speak of feelings and, when they do, tend to monitor and edit what they say, to refer to their feelings only indirectly, or to use words that don't communicate much detail ("It's been a hard week"). It takes some time for adults to distinguish their sadness from depression, to know that their "upset" is about feeling scared or sad or hopeless. Adults feel shamed by "negative" emotions.

Not all kids are as emotionally literate as this largely middle-class, articulate group. But children live in their bodies more than most adults do and are therefore more attuned to emotional energy unmediated by preconceived judgments and beliefs. Their antennae are exquisitely sensitive to the emotional energy within and around them. Their emotional intelligence is part of their innate curiosity about themselves and the world. Until they learn that emotions are shameful, they have no shame about them. They are unafraid to show their true colors.

As they grow up, all this will change. Their ability to express their emotions openly without shame will be drastically reduced. Their emotional IQ will be lowered. Their sensitivity to the violence, war, and pollution in the world around them will be decreased. Their intuitive grasp of the connection between their emotions and what's happening in the world will be supplanted by adult ways of ignoring, rationalizing, and denying what they can't bear to feel. The more educated among them, trained in a post-Freudian worldview, will believe that the prime cause of emotional suffering lies in early childhood experience. Their understanding of the impact of the social environment on their emotional lives will shrink to a list of parental failings, particularly those of their mothers. Many of them will be at a great remove from the felt experience of emotion in their bodies, preferring to locate feelings in their heads. The natural pathway by which emotions seek expression will be constrained by adult prohibitions or obstructed by denial. The enthusiasm and impassioned inquiry in these young students will be replaced by a strong wariness and fear. Once so colorful and interesting, emotions will now appear dangerous, inferior to reason, best kept under tight control. The children's hearts will have forgotten the magic of emotion.

In short, by the time these kids are grown, emotion-phobia will have set in. Disembodied, intellectualized, evaded, and shamed, their dark emotions will lose their power for alchemy.

Grown-up ideas about the dark emotions reflect this internalized emotion-phobia. In groups and workshops I've led, I ask participants to complete an Emotion-Beliefs Inventory consisting of a series of sentence completions: (1) What my grief (fear, despair) says about me is . . . (2) If I got in touch with my grief (fear, despair), and let myself feel it fully, I would . . . (3) What I would most like to do with my grief (fear, despair) is . . .

Here are some typical responses:

- What my grief says about me is that I'm pitiful. If I felt it fully, I would never stop crying. What I'd most like to do with my grief is be done with it.
- What my fear says about me is that I'm weak, unable to cope, a coward. If I felt it fully, I would be unable to function, become immobile, be paralyzed, die. What I'd most like to do with my fear is kill it.
- What my despair says about me is that I'm desperate, weak, spiritually undeveloped, totally defeated. If I let myself feel it fully, I would be isolated, wouldn't want to live anymore, would die, would kill myself. What I'd most like to do with my despair is overcome it.

Most adults have the entrenched idea that emotions like sorrow, despair, and fear are crippling, destructive, and "negative." That last word says it all. If we thought there was anything honorable or valuable about the dark emotions, we wouldn't refer to them this way. These emotions not only *feel* bad; we think they *are* bad—signs of emotional weakness, moral decay, spiritual inferiority, and personal inadequacy.

## Negative Emotions or Negative Attitudes toward Emotions?

As I bit into a bagel one morning, this headline screamed out at me from the *Boston Globe*: "Emotions Make Us Sick." The article went on to report that research in the new science of psychoneuroimmunology has shown that anger and hostility harm the heart. Anxiety and fear undermine the intellect and immune system. Depression and sadness make us more vulnerable to illness. The body's immunological protections against bacteria, viruses, and cancer, our ability to heal from illness of all kinds, is impaired by "negative" feelings.[1]

The research is in synch with our own experiences of grief, fear, despair, and anger as emotions that isolate us, keep us down, make us sick, or turn us into raving maniacs. As our society becomes more and more emotion-conscious, one would think that we'd see a general decrease in emotion-phobia, but in fact, "negative" feelings have been gaining more and more of a bad rep lately. Mind-body research has confirmed the idea that negative feelings are bad news.

The truth is that emotions may be pleasant or unpleasant, but they are not good or bad. The Latin root of the word *emotion* is *movere*, meaning "to move." Emotions are energies that move us—to feel, to express our feelings, to act. Emotional energy is neither positive nor negative. It is just energy. Only our attitude toward these emotions and what we do with the energy can be called "positive" or "negative."

The belief that the dark emotions are paralyzing and destructive reflects our distrust and overall negative attitude about them. The distrust aborts their potential. Similarly, it's our inability to handle the energy of the dark emotions that makes this energy negative—especially when we "act out" our emotions before we have fully experienced them with awareness. But the energy itself can be put to good use.

The same energy that powers the dark emotions has been variously called *chi, prana, élan vital*, and life force. This energy is sacred. We are endowed with it at birth and it guides what is most human about us as much or more than what we narrowly define as "reason." Computers can reason; but they can't feel. Animals can feel; but their emotions are instinctual, not conscious. Only human beings have the capacity to feel mindfully and to act consciously, informed by our emotions.

While it is true that emotions can be overwhelming if we don't know how to tolerate them, the emotional energy itself enlivens us. Without a smoothly flowing emotional energy system, our ability to live with authenticity and joy, to have satisfying and meaningful relationships, to distinguish right from wrong, to learn from life, are profoundly diminished.

So what about the research that "proves" that "positive" emotions are good for us and "negative" emotions are bad?

The research gets it wrong for two reasons. It suffers from alexithymia—the scientific word for an impaired ability to name emotions. Diagnosed in an individual, alexithymia is thought to be caused by an organic brain disorder. But our culture itself seems deficient in this area. One of the striking aspects of the mind-body research on emotion is its less than literate use of emotion terms. Anger, hostility, rage, and aggression (the latter is not an emotion at all but a behavioral disposition) are lumped together as though they are synonymous. Worry, anxiety, fear, and distress are used interchangeably. So are depression, sadness, and pessimism. These emotion-terms are used imprecisely at best; and poorly defined terms make for questionable science.

Hostility, rage, and aggression may contribute to heart attacks, but without certain forms of anger we would be morally inert. Anxiety and worry may weaken the immune system, but fear is the organism's response to danger. Without it, we would be as vulnerable to harm as if we couldn't register physical pain. Sadness is not the same as depression and pessimism. In fact, a low tolerance for sadness is a major predisposing factor toward depression. Even despair, a discrete emotion, is not synonymous with depression, a chronic mind/body state. The research is trying to get at something, but it ends up only confusing matters further.

The second reason the research doesn't get it right is that it makes no distinction between emotions mindfully experienced and emotions that are "stuck." It's true that unbefriended dark emotions can and do turn nasty and harmful. Disavowed anger often becomes chronic hostility and rage. Denied fear feeds into phobias, psychosomatic pain, prejudice, and irrational anger. Buried grief can give rise to chronic anxiety and depression. And intolerable despair can lead to suicide or homicide. When we can't tolerate the energy of a primary dark emotion, it is unable to move and so isolates rather than connects us. But condemning the dark emotions as "negative" is like blaming Pandora for opening the box. What's in the box needs to be known.

When we don't know what's in the box, we run into trouble.

## Kay's Story: Discarded Grief Feeds Addiction

Kay grew up in the projects, raised by parents whose lives were etched by the despair of poverty and alcoholism. The eldest of eight children, Kay was responsible for taking care of the kids while her parents were working, and when they were drunk. When bill collectors came to the door, Kay sent them on their way. When her father was in a "state," remembering his World War II experiences, under the influence of booze and trauma, Kay stayed up with him in a nightlong vigil to keep him from becoming violent. Like many children of alcoholics, she was smart, brave, feisty, and hypercompetent. She knew how to parent her parents and keep the household going.

As she grew up, Kay's pillow was the only witness to her tears. For years, she cried herself to sleep. But soon enough, Kay put a stop to her crying. She was too old; and nothing in her culture told her that crying was anything but a weakness. She did a good job of suppressing every last vestige of it.

With no more release for her sorrow, Kay found other means to soothe herself. By the age of twelve, she was doing pills and cocaine. By fourteen, she was a heroin addict. She managed to live on this edge for many years, but at a ravaging cost to her body and soul. By her mid-twenties she had twice heard the last rites recited over her. Several of her friends had overdosed and died. She knew if she continued the life she was leading, she would be next.

By the time Kay came to see me, she was in recovery. Through a combination of grit, luck, and devotion to a twelve-step program, she had saved her life. She'd been clean and sober for seven years.

When I asked her what she wanted from therapy, Kay said, "I don't want to feel sad." Recovery had made Kay's life manageable, but it hadn't killed her sorrow. She was hoping that therapy would.

"Being sad means I'm weak and pitiful," she told me, echoing the values of her parents and the culture as a whole.

## Vanessa's Story: Unfelt Fear Reinforces Victim Psychology

Unlike Kay, Vanessa spoke with ease about her sorrows. She'd had a sad childhood with a harsh and distant mother and a physically abusive father. For years, she had suffered with chronic fatigue syndrome, a condition that left her listless, jobless, and in despair. Several times, she'd been a victim of violence, including a rape at knifepoint and a date rape two years later.

Remarkably, despite these experiences, or perhaps because of them, Vanessa was fearless. While fearlessness is an ideal of our culture, it was actually part of Vanessa's post-traumatic stress disorder. She seemed to have no access to inner warning signals. She had never named her experience of violent sexual assault as a rape. She lived with a man who abused her emotionally and physically, and who had an obsessive fascination with men who murdered women, clipping news stories about them that he kept in a scrapbook. When I asked Vanessa if she was afraid of this man, her response was: "He'd never hurt me."

Vanessa's internal alarm system didn't work. She had a problem with self-protection because she was unable to register or listen to her fear. She learned to listen to fear's signals eventually, but only after her boyfriend had beaten her into unconsciousness and left her for dead.

## Carolyn's Story: Disavowed Despair Leads to Emotional Numbing

Carolyn was a recognizable contemporary woman on life's fast track. Attractive and high-functioning, she worked in the banking industry. For years, she had put up with the discriminatory conditions of her workplace: the double standards and harassment that she believed came with the job. Because she was excellent at what she did, she found satisfaction in this work and enjoyed working in a field where few women were allowed to excel. The challenge of having to be twice as good as her male counterparts to earn their respect (and two-thirds of their salary) was one she took on with gusto.

But this challenge came with a price tag: a life of unrelenting stress. Carolyn found herself enjoying very little in this life that had taken so much of her to build. She had a lovely house and a handsome husband, dined at fine restaurants and had impeccable clothes. But a dull ache pressed against the gleaming success of her life—a numb emptiness that she found hard to define, much less discuss. She wanted therapy to make her life less stressful.

One day I said to Carolyn, "I see you riding in a car. It's a beautiful car, shiny and fast, and has all the latest conveniences. You're a great driver. And you're driving fast and hard. The only thing is: Where are you going?"

Carolyn was sensible and stoic about hardship. She was not a weeper, even when talking about sad things. For the first time in a year of therapy, I saw her eyes fill up with tears. "I don't know," she said, "and I'm afraid to slow down enough to find out." When I asked her what she was afraid of, she said, "Of finding out that I'm going nowhere. That there's nowhere to go."

We'd hit the bedrock of Carolyn's unnamed despair, hidden beneath the nonstop work, the rush-around world of high finance, the elegant social scene she inhabited—a sense of emptiness at the core. This was probably the most significant moment of Carolyn's therapy. But it was one she didn't wish to return to. She recovered her composure and quickly moved away from this nowhere-to-go place inside her.

"I'm probably premenstrual," she concluded, trivializing and banishing her despair.

Kay wanted therapy to rid her of her grief. Vanessa didn't recognize her fear until she was attacked. Carolyn kept her despair hidden even from herself. All three, in different ways, tried to banish their dark emotions.

But banishing emotional energy didn't make it vanish. The energy just resurfaced in different forms. Kay's discarded sorrow fueled her addictions. Vanessa's denied fear reinforced her victim psychology. Carolyn's disavowed despair made her emotionally numb.

Though she didn't much want to, Kay found a way to befriend her sorrow in therapy. This helped her in her recovery process and reduced her stress and anxiety. Vanessa learned to listen to her fear after she was attacked and found a way to keep herself safe. Carolyn, with some coaxing, faced into her despair and used her greater awareness of it to make some needed changes in her life: less time at work and more with her husband and friends.

## Susie's Story: Aborted Grief Devolves into Depression

In ways too numerous to chronicle, our difficulty or inability to face our dark emotions takes its toll on our emotional, physical, moral, and spiritual lives.

The aborted alchemy of grief is a well-known precursor of depression. Those who have lost a parent or child, in particular, and do not grieve these losses because they are encouraged to "get on with their lives" too soon, often end up with serious depressions later on.

Susie was the daughter of alcoholics. Abandoned by her mother at the age of four, she was raised by her grandmother, who told Susie, "We will never talk about your mother again."

While her grandmother didn't drink, she was emotionally and physically abusive. She beat Susie with a strap and admonished her, "Don't cry or I'll give you something to cry about" (yes, people really do say these things to their children). Susie made a decision at the age of five that she remembers vividly: "I told myself that no matter what she did, I wouldn't shed a tear. She could kill me if she wanted to."

Susie would spend hours watching the clouds while lying on her back, and these moments of communion with nature helped her soothe herself. She kept her promise to herself and never shed a tear. When her grandmother collapsed and died, Susie didn't cry. When her brother died, she didn't cry. She never mourned her mother's abandonment. She kept her promise not to cry for the rest of her life.

Thirty years later she came to therapy and described her life in these terms: "There's a glass between me and the world. I want to break through the glass and feel my life, not tell it in the third person."

Psychologists would call the way that Susie described her life "depersonalization." She was at a remove from the flow of her emotions and her life force, as though she were a character in a story rather than a real, living human being. When Susie was four years old, her decision not to cry was a badge of her honor, dignity, and integrity. She would not give her abuser the satisfaction of seeing her vulnerable. But this choice had come with a price—the lifelong depression of unmourned losses. Susie would need to learn in therapy how to undo her childhood decision and let her tears flow again in order to free herself from the grip of depression.

### William's Story: Suppressed Fear Turns into Toxic Anger

William was a fearless kid. Reckless, many would say. As a young child, he had made a decision similar to Susie's: he wouldn't cry when reprimanded or hit by his alcoholic father. And he would never, ever show fear. He too had a favorite spot out in the open fields of his hometown where he could go to calm himself and manage his feelings. As a teenager, he became an angry rebel without a cause and a fearless daredevil. His motto was "Stay in control," but his out-of-control antics nearly got him killed in a motorcycle crash.

William had a lot to fear in his family: his father was a violent alcoholic. His mother was highly critical and cold. William's response to the grief and fear of his childhood was fairly typical for normally socialized boys: stay in control of your emotions. William remembers consciously deciding to do this. Not crying was a sign of his control. So was not feeling fear. He never saw a connection or contradiction between his "in control" emotions and his out-of-control, reckless, impulsive behavior.

Whereas girls and women tend to turn their toxified grief into the kind of depression described by Susie, boys and men are more likely to turn it into anger—which often masks a more male style of depression. This is especially true when undigested grief is mixed with unacknowledged fear. William's anger was enormous. He remembers running after one of his brothers with a knife, crashing his car and his motorcycle, slamming doors, throwing things, breaking windows. His anger was the clue that his life was out of control, despite the fact that his sorrow and fear were under control.

Years later, he made the connection in therapy: having resolved, as a young boy, to suppress his grief and fear, he funneled their energies into his more "masculine" style of angry acting out.

As an adult, William had given up his impulsive, angry ways and become a serious, highly responsible person. He worked as a counselor for adolescents and was very good at what he did. But in his intimate relationships with women, he was haunted by the question: "Am I capable of connecting to anyone? Am I capable of love?"

Toxified fear and grief in men often result in masked depressions characterized by angry, impulsive behavior and in impairments in relational abilities.

### Tom and Barbara's Story: Silenced Despair Fuels Toxic Anger

Tom and Barbara had been married for six years when they came to see me. They were smart and compassionate in every respect except one: when it came to their own relationship, they were combatants in a long and ugly war. More than any other couple I'd ever seen, they were engaged in the deadly game of "Marital Mortal Combat." Tom's idea of communication was to have an all-out verbal brawl with Barbara with no holds barred. With a raised voice and an in-your-face stance, he would accuse her of intentionally messing up his life, call her names, blame her for all of his misery, threaten her with divorce. Barbara would stiffen up and argue with him, point by point, to prove that nothing he said had any validity.

My attempts to intervene in this duel were invariably met with resistance. "If I'm angry, I have a right to express it," Tom told me. He saw no difference between aggression and assertion, hostile belligerence and anger. Barbara welcomed my attempted interventions at first. She wanted to make some ground rules so that both she and Tom could feel "safe" to talk about their feelings. But every ground rule we set up was almost immediately broken by both of them.

Tom felt entitled to his rage and bristled at the suggestion that it contributed to the sense of threat in the relationship. Barbara felt entitled to bring Tom down with a more apparently reasoned but vitriolic style of criticism. She wanted to muffle him but not herself. The currency of their relationship was unbridled, toxic anger.

Understandably, both Tom and Barbara harbored a great deal of despair about their ability to live together harmoniously. But neither of them could say: "I'm in despair about this endless war we call our marriage." They blamed the other instead. And it was easy to see why: any vulnerability they displayed was seen as weakness. Rather than speaking their hurt and despair, they girded themselves for battle.

This kind of chronic, unyielding anger is one way in which sorrow, fear, and despair become toxic when they cannot be spoken and heard. The despair of a marriage in which neither partner knows how to make peace is one of the most intense forms of suffering in relationship. Toxic anger both grows out of and fuels this despair in an increasingly vicious cycle.

Inevitably, this kind of anger will kill a relationship. In the case of Tom and Barbara, their decision to divorce was one of the few things they agreed on in their seven lonely years of marriage.

## Toxified Emotional Energy

Most of us experience a constant flow of emotions on a daily basis. Even smaller dark emotions can become a problem when we don't know how to handle them and they accumulate as unhealthy stress. But when the dark emotions are more of a tidal wave than a small ebb and flow, emotional energy can become highly toxic. Like all energy, emotional energy doesn't just disappear. It changes form. The essence of emotional alchemy is the mindful flow of emotional energy—a process in which we are consciously attentive to what is happening. When we can master this process, the dark emotions organically transform to spiritual strengths such as gratitude, joy, faith, courage, and compassion. But when we unmindfully suppress emotional energy it often converts to mental states and destructive behaviors that are subsequently diagnosed as "mental disorders."

In my work with hundreds of people suffering from anxiety and depression, I have seen again and again how these mental states are rooted in aborted grief; and I have witnessed as well how toxic anger often has its source in benumbed fear or despair. Unbefriended emotional energy can fuel a host of mind/body symptoms and conditions such as asthma, gastrointestinal disorders, high blood pressure, migraines, and back pain—to name just a few of the most common ones I see in my practice and that have been documented in the mind/body research. (This doesn't mean that these disorders are *caused* by dark emotions. My view is that stuck, toxified emotional energy is an important aspect of what keeps the physical ailments in place and prevents healing.)

When unminded emotional energy becomes overwhelming, it is tempting to "self medicate" it through a variety of addictions. Not just legal and illegal substances, but also work, power, status, entertainment, sex, relationships—anything can be used addictively. The use of alcohol and other substances both disinhibits emotional energy and numbs it, resulting in a great deal of unhealthy emotional drama and further toxifying of the dark emotions.

In addition, unconsciously suppressing the dark emotions takes its toll in psychic numbing. A silent plague of our era, psychic numbing was first described by the distinguished psychiatrist Robert Jay Lifton in his study of survivors of concentration camps and Hiroshima. The inability to feel anything at all, the compartmentalization of feeling and knowing, the death-in-life quality he saw in survivors—these have become fairly common contemporary mental states, in less extreme form. Psychic numbing is a way of coping with trauma—and in an age of ecocide, when the earth itself is not safe, we are all to some degree traumatized. Psychic numbing is also what happens when we banish the dark emotions for an extended period of time. When we numb certain feelings over and over again, the habit of numbing generalizes, and eventually the capacity for feeling itself is crippled. We end up feeling deadened to life itself.

In these various forms, unbefriended dark emotions can become dangerous. Emotional toxicity keeps us stuck in the same place or moves us into downward spirals that take us further and further away from emotional alchemy. We get trapped in vicious emotional cycles: unmindful dark emotions turn toxic, and the resulting emotional toxicity keeps us from trusting our dark emotions and learning from them.

Toxified emotional energy is at the root of four of the most common emotional afflictions of our age: anxiety, depression, addiction, and psychic numbing.

Approximately 12 percent of adults or 28 million people in the United States suffer from a diagnosable anxiety disorder. At some point in their lives, one in four adults—65 million people—will seek professional help for anxiety.[2] About 20 million Americans are clinically depressed. Twenty percent of the population are active alcoholics. Millions more are addicted to illegal substances. Whether we are anxiety sufferers, chronic depressives, active alcoholics, violent adolescents, benumbed workaholics, or just plain undiagnosed folks—we all suffer from unbefriended dark emotions. Without grieving our losses, listening to our fear and despair, we become lifeless and loveless, anxious and depressed, angry and destructive.

## Five Common Ways to Cope with Dark Emotions

It's not the dark emotions that hurt us but our negative attitudes, unskillful ways of coping, and emotion-phobic reactions to them. When we don't know how to listen to our pain, we rely on the stock ways of coping with the dark emotions that we learn in the culture at large. Probably none of us has ever had a single class in grade school, high school, or college called "How to Cope with Emotional Pain." Nevertheless, through family conditioning and religious teachings, and in the culture as a whole, we are schooled to endure, deny, bypass, avenge, and escape painful emotions. These five common ways of coping have their strengths and weaknesses, but for the most part they aren't conducive to healing and transformation.

## ENDURE

Endurance is the ability to withstand suffering without collapsing. In enduring, we survive—and humans have shown that we can survive even the most unimaginable and unspeakable suffering. At times, endurance is a simple matter of putting one foot in front of the other and moving on. Some people are helped to do this by faith. As an antidote to the pain of life, religion offers the balm of God's plan and a glorious day in the hereafter. It's easier to endure the sorrows of death and loss, or of desperate social circumstances if we believe that God has a plan we don't understand and that we will meet our loved ones in the world to come. The assurance of God's hand in our individual destinies, and the promise of tomorrow's perfection, as Karl Marx observed, is one of the most effective opiates for suffering.

Those who are not blessed with this kind of faith must base their endurance on a secular view of the world in which endurance and stoicism are synonymous. Not everyone subscribes to the White Anglo-Saxon Protestant masculine ideal of stoicism, but we are all affected by it, because it's the norm of the dominant culture. In this belief system, adults are people who can rule their emotions and endure suffering without emotional display. Negative emotions are a wilderness within that must be conquered to preserve "civilized" order. A lack of control over emotions is a sign of moral turpitude or spiritual weakness. Emotional control is a special requisite for men, who are taught early and often violently that any emotion but anger is effeminate. But women too—if they are "classy"—must learn to endure their emotions in silence.

I remember having a discussion with my best friend in college about the widespread American reverence for Jacqueline Kennedy, which was somehow captured and forever fixed in the moment that she appeared at the funeral of her slain husband, eternally dignified as she walked that lonely path to the cemetery without shedding a tear. My friend thought this showed her profound strength and courage. My less popular opinion was that she was cold and numb. Why is crying at your husband's funeral considered a sign of weakness? Why is suppressing your grief considered a sign of strength?

Jackie Kennedy personified the ideal of stoic endurance. She handled herself in her widowly duties without "breaking down"—that is, showing emotion. This emotion-inhibited stoicism was seen as the mark of her dignity. In our culture, endurance implies an ability to detach from emotion and to carry on as though we are not really torn up inside. In this idea for coping with suffering, emotion itself is the overt sign that we are not coping well.

## DENY

Denial is unconscious detachment from emotion and the truth that emotion holds. We think of it as aberrant, but it's actually an extension of the normal mode of coping with emotion that our society values. In Western society, we learn to detach what psychologists call "affect" from cognition—to separate feeling from thinking. This normal dissociation actually contributes to more extreme forms of denial. Extreme denial is one of the most destructive forces in the world, a kind of "hear no evil, see no evil, speak no evil" consciousness that paradoxically allows evil to flourish.

Victims as well as perpetrators of evil use denial—but for different purposes. Many perpetrators deny that their violent actions ever took place, or that they were harmful. The victim's denial, on the other hand, is a way of coping with emotional pain that is too overwhelming to experience directly. Denial is a survival mechanism that must be gradually replaced by the authentic experience of the dark emotions before healing can happen.

## TRANSCEND OR BYPASS

Transcendence is about "rising above" our feelings. Sometimes we can do this by setting our sights on something "higher." But in most cases, to transcend suffering authentically, we must be willing to live it fully. To rise above, we must go through—without any guarantees of what we'll find on the other side.

Problems arise when we mistake what some have called a "spiritual bypass" of suffering with genuine transcendence. The latter, in my experience, is not something you can plan, predict, or control. It's the gift of grace. Spiritual bypass, on the other hand, is usually based on false beliefs that mask denial. The cult members who took their own lives in the belief that they would leave the planet on a spaceship and live happily ever after in another, higher plane of existence were not transcending their suffering—they were attempting to spiritually bypass it in their denied act of mass suicide. The strand of New Age metaphysics that denies the evils of earthly existence and declares that only love and light are "real" is a more popular form of false transcendence.

## AVENGE

In vengeance, we neither bury nor rise above our suffering; we get mad and we get even. In the fall of 1997, after the raped and murdered body of ten-year-old Jeffrey Curley was found in a plastic container in a Maine river, the Cambridge neighborhood in which he had lived and all of the Boston area seemed to be overwhelmed with helpless anger. The normal denial of our children's vulnerability, which allows parents to set their children loose on the streets without any supervision, was demolished. Within hours of hearing of his son's death, Robert Curley began talking to the media about reinstating the death penalty in Massachusetts. And after the boy's body was found, the emotional reaction nearly accomplished what years of political bickering in the State House could not: but for a single changed vote, the state Congress would have passed a law ratifying the death penalty. Of course the death penalty would not bring back Jeffrey Curley or save other children from murderous sexual predators. But in visions of vengeance, we find some small relief for feelings that are intolerable.

Angry vengeance is socially conditioned as a masculine way to cope with grief. The opposite of spiritual detachment, which teaches us not to act on our emotions, vengeance is about finding an action as violent as the act that has left us steeped in unbearable grief or despair. The hypermasculine mode of dealing with helplessness and vulnerability is to kill someone as a release for your own intolerable pain. The intractable areas of unending violence in the world—between Israelis and Palestinians in the Middle East, between Bosnians, Serbs, and Croats in the former Yugoslavia, between Hutus and Tutsis in Rwanda—are places of chronic vengeance where whole populations are continually traumatized and re-traumatized by the violent death of loved ones. These cycles are both fueled by and contribute to intergenerationally transmitted unredeemed grief.

Seeking relief from suffering in angry acts of vengeance only ends up enclosing us in our wounds. If "enemies" could grieve together for all the wasted blood, they might find a way to peace. But communal sharing of grief that crosses the lines dividing race from race, tribe from tribe, ethnic group from ethnic group, nation from nation, is not one of our common ways of coping with suffering.

## ESCAPE

Escape would probably win the contest for most popular way of coping with suffering in the West. And nobody does it better than we do. Americans have mastered the art of distraction and escape to the highest point of any nation, and we are teaching what we know to the rest of the world—exporting more and more entertainment, celebrity worship, and addictive consumerism. Buying, owning, using gadgets, consuming experiences—these are the hallmarks of a culture of escape; so is the inability to tolerate silence.

The most extreme forms of escape with the most devastating consequences are addictions. Ours is a "user" culture. Americans are the most addicted people in the world—and our primary addiction is to feeling good. Whatever else addiction is, it is always a way to numb or soothe the dark emotions we cannot tolerate. Even milder, less destructive forms of escape like renting a stack of videos when you're sad can abort the alchemy of dark emotions.

According to Daniel Goleman, distraction is a bona fide skill of emotional intelligence that helps us cope with "negative" emotions. I would add: only temporarily. Distract yourself from a deep sorrow and it will come back to haunt you. While distraction can stave off feeling overwhelmed by intense emotional energy, it can also suppress a necessary flow of emotion. In a culture of distraction, we resort to this "skill" too often, and lack other skills that are more useful to emotional and spiritual growth. Distracting ourselves from our emotional pain, like taking painkillers to blunt physical pain, doesn't help us get to the root of what ails us.

In my view, distraction is actually one of the less skillful ways of coping with the dark emotions—a method we resort to when we have a low tolerance for discomfort or when we don't know any other ways to cope. Indulging in a distracting "getaway" is sometimes just what the doctor ordered. But ultimately coping with grief, fear, or despair is not the same thing as using these emotions as vehicles for healing and transformation.

These five common ways of coping with suffering have their uses. They can be a crucial part of surviving and affirming life. We can outlive what we endure. We can use "positive denial" to mute our latent fears in the interest of accomplishing a given task or goal. In this way, denial can be an important part of courage. Genuine moments of transcendence are possible to those who follow a spiritual path and can work skillfully with painful emotions. Distracting yourself from emotional pain is a good skill to use—so long as you're aware of what you're doing. Even revenge can find benign forms. The mother who founded Mothers Against Drunk Drivers "avenged" her child's death in a way that brought some good into the world and helped other people heal from similar tragedies.

In balance, these ways of coping with emotional suffering don't have to be a problem. But they become a problem when they are contaminated by emotion-phobia. Our fear of the dark emotions and difficulty tolerating them are primary obstacles to endurance without denial, transcendence without spiritual bypass, escape without addiction. Emotion-phobia gets in the way of our best intentions to truly transform suffering.

## Emotion-Phobia and the Head/Heart Split

For many centuries, we have lived in the shadow of the great divide between reason and emotion—the head/heart split in which the Western world, since Plato, has been schooled. We believe that our rationality is what makes us human and thereby distinctly different from the apes. Emotions, as part of our instinctual animal nature, are seen as dangerous and inferior to reason. We believe that submitting to their unencumbered, uncontrolled, free flow would destroy our capacity to think and function rationally, would make us dangerous, or win us a permanent place in the loony bin.

Although the distinction between mind and body originated with the Greeks, it was Descartes, the seventeenth-century French thinker, who made this philosophy the systematic basis for the sciences. Only reason, he argued, is a reliable guide to truth and certainty ("I think, therefore I am")—not the senses or the emotions. Ever since Descartes, the head/heart split has been the basis of how our society defines rationality. We think that the inferior heart is trustworthy only when dominated by the superior head. This split of head and heart is what we hold as the gold standard of maturity, even if we never totally live up to it.

In fact, the head/heart split is a source of profound disconnection. Affect is detached and dissociated from cognition. We learn not to feel through what we think, not to think through what we feel. In separating reason from emotion, we've been conditioned to place our trust in the former, culturally masculine attribute, and not the latter, culturally feminine one. We associate reason with strength, merit, safety, and men; emotion with weakness, wildness, danger, and women. Emotion-phobia—the fundamental fear of the raw power of emotional energy—is bolstered by this set of normative, gender-polarized beliefs about the supremacy of reason over emotion.

The head/heart split and emotion-phobia are so endemic to our way of thinking and feeling that we barely notice their presence. Dr. Laura, probably the best-known pop therapist in the world, daily broadcasts her version of it to her devoted fans. Emotions are dangerous and lead us to behave immorally, stupidly, and self-destructively. Having affairs and abortions, being mean and selfish, abandoning our children, everything bad Dr. Laura can think of comes from allowing our emotions to rule our behavior. During the December 2000 election battle between Bush and Gore (before the Supreme Court's decision on the winner), a *Boston Globe* columnist, sick with frustration about it all, wrote that Gore would be hunting down the ballots until every last legal avenue was exhausted. "On an emotional level it's understandable," she opined. "But at some point, logic, order, and finality must take precedence over emotion."[3]

The appeal to reason is designed to hush the opposition. Never mind that the journalist herself might be motivated by emotions she doesn't admit to. The point is that anyone who appeals to reason is automatically presumed to be taking the higher ground. All those emotional people who want every last vote to count should go home and calm down.

The head/heart split is not just a matter of what we think about what we feel. It's also about how we actually experience our feelings. Few of us have ever experienced a free flow of emotion unimpeded by "rational" control yet monitored by full awareness. Few of us know how to feel our emotions fully in the body and to completion. Most who have done so are women who don't particularly value this ability and in fact tend to trivialize their skills in this area. The power of emotions as a profound way of knowing and healing is barely recognized in a society that worships science and more masculine forms of knowing.

This is why the Juror's Creed—the code of honor that every juror must swear to—advises prospective jurors to "be led by intelligence, not emotions" in order to arrive at a fair, unbiased judgment. Intelligence is thought to automatically render an impartial judgment, while emotion is associated with prejudice.

The idea that reason and emotion can be neatly split is debatable. In most cases, reason that shows no trace of emotion is simply reason that has been dissociated from visible or conscious emotion. This dissociation, when extreme, is actually a symptom of pathology or trauma. Compartmentalizing our feelings and beliefs is hardly an ideal way to live. It's just as likely to produce bias and irrational behavior as emotion unbalanced by a reasoned appraisal of the facts.

The Juror's Creed assumes that only facts, not emotions, are valuable and informative. But some of this century's greatest crimes were committed by people who thought they were operating from a basis of fact and rationality; the resulting atrocities were done, for the most part, without emotion. The "final solution to the Jewish problem" was thought to be a rational program of national recovery and was supported by much of the German intelligentsia and scientific establishment. It resulted in the manufacture of death as a smoothly running industry. Heinrich Himmler, the head of the Gestapo, congratulated his fellow Nazis for being able to rise above their emotions in order to dutifully dispatch Jews to their death by shooting them into mass graves or gassing and cremating them.

The separation of reason and emotion, at its extreme, is the hallmark of the psychopath. But a society that worships reason is concerned only with the excesses of emotion, not those of so-called rationality. In such a society, the very idea of "excesses" of rationality seems absurd. But reason unmediated by the heart can be a serious problem.

## Mark's Story: Reason without Emotion

Mark came to therapy to sort out his relationship with Molly. He'd been with her for ten years. They'd been separated three times and each time he took up with another woman.

The striking thing about Mark was how rational he was. He had an advanced degree in engineering and was smart as a whip. He spoke slowly and deliberately, without a trace of emotion, even when speaking of painful matters. Mark was the ultimate rationalist, but he couldn't make a decision of the heart. He loved Molly, but he couldn't imagine being happy with her. Did loving her mean he had to stay with her? Then how come he wasn't sure he wanted to? Was he bad for not wanting to? Or was he just trying to be happy? And if he was just trying to be happy, why couldn't he be happy with someone he loved? On the other hand, why not love one of the three women he'd had an affair with? Perhaps they could make him happy. Was this happiness, or just lust?

Mark was riddled with splits. His head and heart didn't communicate. His body, emotions, reason, and morality all seemed to be in different places. He knew how to make a mental list of Molly's attributes and those of the other women he'd been with, but he didn't know how he enduringly felt about any of them, or what his feelings meant. Without his heart's guidance, his capacity for love and intimacy were seriously limited. Because Mark was smart, he realized that finding happiness and peace had something to do with listening to and understanding his emotions. "I have no experience of this," he said. "It's as though I'm a stranger on a strange planet."

Mark was a living, if extreme, embodiment of the reason/emotion dualism. This wrenching split of head and heart is a cornerstone of patriarchal culture, which teaches detachment from emotion as the highest goal of emotional intelligence. The result, in the body politic as in an individual like Mark, is a fragmentation that breeds a great deal of unnecessary suffering.

## Masculine Models of Emotional Control: Contain and Manage

When we don't trust the energy of "negative" emotions, the best we think we can do is to contain and manage it. Containment, as a strategy of emotional coping, bears the stamp of the masculine norm that guides our thinking and behavior in the murky, feminized realm of emotion. Starting with Aristotle, who posited that reason's control over emotion is what distinguishes men from women and children, we have all lived in the shadow of this patriarchal belief system.

As an overall emotional management strategy, control is useful in a limited way. At best, it helps us to reign in impulsive, destructive behavior. But control is not always a rational choice. It can be and often is a socially sanctioned compulsion. Destructive behavior can be a result of too much control as well as too little control. We compulsively control the dark emotions when we lack the ability to tolerate them. This kind of suppression is not necessarily a conscious choice, especially since conscious awareness is not something promoted in our culture, while avoidance, distraction, and escape are. Too much of this kind of control breeds its opposite: emotional explosion.

When we can't tolerate an emotion consciously, its energy submerges and often ends up as fuel for impulsive or compulsive behaviors that are destructive to self and others. Therapists call this "acting out," and it is a common mode of relief from intolerable feelings. I call it the emotional boomerang effect.

I remember a bit of acting out I did just before I got married. I was in my late twenties. The man I was marrying was wonderful. Everything was just right. The only problem was that I didn't want to admit to myself that I was terrified. Why should I be scared of marriage? It was an irrational feeling, unworthy of my respect, so I thought nothing of it. My fear was so much under control that it was out of control.

Two days before the wedding, I ran into an acquaintance on the street. She had an unusual haircut—pretty much like the crew cut my younger brother sported when he was eight years old. When I excitedly exclaimed, "I love your hair!" my friend said she'd cut it herself and would be glad to give me a similar style. So on the spot, I accompanied her to her house and had all my hair shorn—and I mean shorn, like a sheep—with a big, thick razor with multiple blades. To get the full picture, you have to understand that I had never once more than trimmed my hair since early adolescence. Long, straight, thick brown hair flowing down to midback and parted in the middle was a distinctive feature of my identity. Another part of my identity was being reasonably cautious and thinking things through. I was not an impulsive person.

When I got off the plane for the wedding in New York, my mother took one look at me and said, "You look like a concentration camp survivor." Everybody was perplexed, most of all me, at this sudden change in my behavior and appearance. What was I thinking? Fortunately, my husband-to-be found my new hairdo very sexy. It wasn't until after the wedding that I really dealt with my fear of getting married.

Acting out is not always so harmless. My most controlled clients are often the ones most likely to act out, and in the process do some serious damage to their relationships and themselves. The married man at midlife who enjoys what looks like a decent marriage and a highly ordered life and then launches a torrid affair with a younger woman that wrecks his marriage and his life may sound like a cliché, but this is a common form of acting out that destroys marriages and produces a great deal of suffering for children who get caught in the cross-fire.

The emotional boomerang effect is evident on the cultural level as well. One example is our national obsession with emotional intensity in the media—the emotional mudslinging we adore in everyone from the outrageous Jerry Springer to the more apparently rational but equally provocative pundits of cable television who "analyze" everything by barking at each other nonstop until someone outshouts the others. From talk-show extravaganzas to the latest disease-of-the-week movie, to the violent thrillers and horror films our culture specializes in, with their cathartic release of rage and terror, we are a nation of emotional spectators. Our obsession with watching emotional intensity and experiencing it vicariously is actually a kind of addiction to emotional pornography.[4] People who chronically suppress their emotions need to have their emotions artificially stimulated.

The flip side of our fear and devaluation of emotion is this endless fascination with it. Freud called it "the return of the repressed": what you suppress returns in the form of the symptoms and behavior of neurosis.

Without the free flow of emotional energy, we're all deader than we want to be, and like any addict, we want a fix that makes us feel better—something that allows us to feel more alive and cellularly connected to emotional energy. The latest diva who's just come out of rehab or actress who has gone into a depressive tailspin spikes our emotional neuropeptides and gets them going. In getting lost in the emotional lives of distant others we have multiple opportunities for vicarious emotional experience and release. But they only erode our capacity for authentic emotional connection.

Because we both fear and long to live passionately, unconscious suppression of our emotions doesn't keep us from unhealthy emotional drama; it can even contribute to it. Conscious control may be an important element of emotional intelligence, but it doesn't answer our longings for emotional authenticity and aliveness. To be alive emotionally, we have to be at home with the dark emotions and find a way to let them be. We must find an alternative to the "contain and manage" approach to our pain, something more like "connect and flow."

## A Story of Emotional Flow

My third child was born with a neuromotor disability that has no name. She walks with leg braces and a body brace. Her hand use is severely limited. Her muscle tone is neurologically weak throughout her body, her coordination so poor and her muscle-sense so limited that she broke eleven bones in the first eight years of her life.

Esther has spent too many moments of her young life in pain. Her life is more limited than most. Yet she's one of the happiest people I know. While her neurological system bogs her down, her emotional genius keeps her buoyant. Most of what I know about emotional alchemy comes from what she teaches me on a daily basis.

Esther was the first child with disabilities to attend the Barn Day Camp in Plymouth, Vermont. She was thrilled to swim, run (in her way), feed the goats, and sing her heart out after lunch. She experienced the delight of camping out under the stars and pushed herself to hike as far as the other kids, though it left her spent. From age six to eleven, she passed her summers at this camp. The next step would have been the residential camp for older children, but the physical rigor was out of her reach. So at age eleven, having completed her last overnight, Esther sat for the last time at morning circle, surrounded by campers, counselors, staff, and parents. Morning circle started with ten minutes of silence, after which the "talking stick" was passed around—a Native American tradition for holding council meetings—and everyone who wanted to had a chance to speak.

When it was Esther's turn, she had this to say: "Thank you, Helen [the director] and my counselors and friends and everyone here. Thank you for having me here at the camp. It's meant a lot to me and my family that I could be here even though I have special needs. I'll always remember my counselors and how great they were. And morning circle and the overnights (I won't talk about the skinny dipping!) I'll always remember looking out of the tent at the beautiful trees. I'll miss you all and I will never forget you. You'll always be in my heart."

As Esther spoke, her emotion was palpable, even if you weren't sitting close enough to notice the tears in her eyes. She was grieving and grateful at the same time and it all came through in the ineffable way that emotional energy is communicated to others. Around the circle, counselors, campers, and parents, men and women, boys and girls were dabbing at their eyes. A few were sobbing quietly.

A few minutes later we were all smiling and singing "'Tis a Gift to Be Simple." Esther's grin and her sparkling blue eyes were infused with an exuberant, cheerful energy. She sang, laughed, and hugged everyone goodbye, then went home happy.

This is emotional flow. When the dark emotions are tolerated, mindfully expressed and allowed to flow to completion, they change their valence. Esther's sorrow about losing camp and her gratitude for camp were two sides of the same coin.

Emotional flow is a source of connection to self and others. Esther's sorrow and gratitude were felt by everyone in the circle in his or her own way—a transpersonal energy linking the sorrow and gratitude in everyone's hearts. This empathic connection had a deepening effect on the circle, bringing a sense of intimacy to this group of friends and strangers. Everyone left with their hearts just a little more open.

It's in allowing the dark emotions to flow and expand our consciousness, rather than to fragment it, that the gifts in grief, despair, and fear can be discovered. The flow of the dark emotions moves us toward the spiritual strengths we most cherish: gratitude, joy, faith, courage, compassion. We all have the capacity for emotional alchemy. But we must first overcome the internalized messages of an emotion-phobic culture. We must learn to think about feelings in a new way and undo the head/heart split. We must learn to attend to, befriend, and mindfully surrender to the dark emotions.

Perhaps Esther's emotional genius has flowered because she is somehow more protected against the emotion-phobic messages and consciousness splits of our culture. She has never outgrown her childlike ability to stay in touch with emotional energy and to let it show without shame. She hasn't tamed her emotions like a lion tamer who takes the wildness out of the lion. She doesn't rule her feelings like a despotic father figure. She lets it flow and lets it go. She knows the secret of emotional alchemy.

Even if we've lost the secret, we can get it back.

# PART TWO

# Emotional Alchemy

# 4 *The Alchemy of Dark Emotions*

## Three Skills and Seven Steps

> Your heart will give you greater counsel than all the world's scholars.
>
> —*The Talmud*

THE PUBLICATION OF DANIEL GOLEMAN's *Emotional Intelligence* in 1995 marked a turning point in popular culture. Finally, emotions were deemed critical to human intelligence. Ironically, the book presents a model of emotional intelligence that is founded on the subordination of emotions to reason.

We have two brains, says Goleman, one that thinks and one that feels. The rational brain is reflective, logical, analytic. The emotional brain is impulsive, illogical, intuitive. While useful in emergencies, when we must act quickly, the emotional brain is outright dangerous unless dominated by the rational brain. Goleman calls the latter the "Manager." The unmanaged emotional brain, in his view, is responsible for much of the world's violence, mayhem, and destruction: "Intelligence can come to nothing when the emotions hold sway."[1]

An odd notion indeed in a book that ostensibly honors emotions! The age-old reason/emotion split is alive and well in this paradigm. Despite its considerable contribution to valuing and understanding emotions, Goleman's work is limited by a masculine bias against the emotional brain itself. In this system, the ability to impede the flow of emotions is dubbed the "Master Aptitude." Dominance and subordination are major metaphors. Emotional control is the goal.

Contrast this to the work of Candace Pert, a pioneering neuroscientist and author of *Molecules of Emotion: Why You Feel the Way You Feel*. In Pert's model (backed up by her research), emotional intelligence is suffused throughout the body. The neuropeptides and receptors that carry emotional information exist not only in the brain but in the endocrine, gastrointestinal, and immune systems as well. Emotional intelligence hinges not on one part of the brain dominating another, but on a smoothly flowing system of emotional "infoenergy" throughout the body/mind. Emotions don't need to be ruled; they need to be tolerated and expressed. They have an intelligence unto themselves, not when they are dominated, but when they are free-flowing.[2]

Goleman's focus on the need to control potentially destructive impulses neglects the value of free-flowing emotional energy when it's mindfully tolerated. The free flow of the dark emotions can't happen in a contain-and-manage model. The alchemy of the dark emotions is not a management kind of process. What Goleman wants control to accomplish is better accomplished through emotional tolerance and mindfulness. These skills prevent the dark emotions from becoming destructive. When we can tolerate emotional energy mindfully, we can control our impulses without suppressing our emotions. Strictly speaking, it's not our emotions that we control, but our actions. The emotional intelligence of the dark emotions moves us not to management but to transformation.

In his book *Flow: the Psychology of Optimal Experience*, Mihaly Csikszentmihalyi writes about a state of peak consciousness that comes from absolute concentration on an activity. His name for this state of focused concentration is flow.[3] When we're in flow with an activity, says Csikszentmihalyi, we can tap into extraordinary capacities and superlative performances. To do this, we have to control our emotions. Once again, the control of emotion is a culturally masculine ideal with all sorts of good uses.

But what would happen if we got into flow with emotion itself?

## Emotional Flow: Riding the Surfboard of Awareness on the Wave of Emotion

Emotional alchemy is the conscious flow of emotional information and energy. As we shall see in the following three chapters, each dark emotion has its own particular quality of energy and its own kind of flow. Emotional flow is not about letting it all hang out and acting in whatever way we are impelled, but about tolerating the energy of grief, fear, and despair in the body and allowing the wisdom of these emotions to unfold.

The flow of emotional alchemy is not a passive, powerless process—like lying down in emotional waves and drowning. Nor is it a hyperactive, controlling process—like erecting a dam to prevent the water from coming through. Emotional flow is a state in which one is connected to the energy of emotion yet able to witness it mindfully. We ride the wave of emotion on the surfboard of awareness.

When we do this skillfully, emotional energy in a state of flow naturally moves toward healing, harmony, and transformation. You don't have to force the alchemy of the dark emotions. It happens when the conditions are right.

When we can mindfully attend to, tolerate, and surrender to the energy of the dark emotions as it flows, we open the heart's doorway to the magic of emotional alchemy. These are the three basic skills: Attending, Befriending, and Surrendering (ABS). The ABS process won't transform a flabby midriff and give you that sleek washboard look, but it may well see you through many a dark night. Without mastering these three skills, you won't get the information carried by grief, despair, and fear, and you won't be able to transform their energies to gratitude, faith, and joy. This doesn't mean you're a bad person. With luck, you'll survive and be happy anyway, and not become an alcoholic or drug addict, or spend twelve hours a day in Internet chat rooms. Maybe you don't need the ABS process, because you're content with the way you feel. If so, you don't need to develop these skills. But if you're having trouble with sorrow, despair, fear, or any other difficult emotional state, then these three basic skills will never fail you.

## ATTENDING: LEARNING TO LISTEN

To attend to the dark emotions is to sense them in the body, focus your awareness on them, and name them accurately.

Ever see a mother in a supermarket with four kids in tow, pulling on her sleeve, crying "Mommy, Mommy, Mommy!" over and over again as she absently checks out the asparagus? She's thinking about what to cook for dinner, and they want to know if they can have that box of Cracker Jacks and some gum. You know what happens next. Little Max runs up and down the aisles. Bobbie and Joey pick a fight. Baby Jane breaks into a wail. Mom's absent attention is instantly refocused.

The dark emotions are attention-grabbers, goading us into awareness. They're like young children: If you attend to them, they reward you. If you don't, prepare for trouble. They have their ways of letting you know they need your attention.

The root of the word *adversity* is the Latin *vertere*, meaning "to turn" and also "to pay heed or attention." In the midst of adversity, the dark emotions ask us to turn our attention to what's going on emotionally. They demand not just attention but *quality* attention—emotional mindfulness. When we can focus our awareness on emotional energy in this way, we can turn our lives around, using adversity as an opportunity. But the more we ignore the darker emotions, the louder they get. This is annoying, but it's also a gift. Because the human organism wants to heal, dark emotional energy won't give up until it's gotten our attention.

Attending to emotional energy is a bodily-grounded awareness. It means knowing how to feel your feelings, as opposed to knowing how to describe them without feeling them. It also includes emotional literacy, the ability to find accurate words for emotional states.

Suppose you are not much of a feeling person. If your body is numb to emotions, attending to the numbness is the first step toward emotional alchemy. Just pay conscious attention to the numbness, and see what happens.

I once did some bodywork therapy with a gifted therapist. The therapy method was simply to be aware of emotions, thoughts, and sensations in the body and stay focused on them as they appeared. In a state of relaxation, I became aware of what looked like a white box of static energy surrounding my body. My body seemed to be lying in the box, numb and inert. Attending to this numbness was difficult. It was hard to stay focused because numbness is actually uncomfortable and boring. Encouraged by the therapist, I just kept paying attention to the numbness for quite some time.

After a while it began to look like a kind of cocoon. My tendency was to try to break out of this cocoon in a dramatic and explosive way, but I didn't. I just paid attention. Gradually, the cocoon began to break up of its own accord, but very, very slowly, requiring great patience on my part not to just flail out. When I finally came through it, I felt an electric surge of energy streaming throughout my body—an intense, all-body orgasmic-like release of the grief that the cocoon had been holding inside, masked by the numbness.

Don't assume that being numb to your dark emotions means you can't do this work. Just attend to whatever state you're in. Amazing transformations can occur from the simple act of paying attention. (See chapter 10, exercises 7–9, for help with bodily awareness of emotion.)

BEFRIENDING: YOU HAVE TO FEEL IT IF YOU WANT TO HEAL IT
Befriending emotional energy is a further extension of attending to it. It entails extending our emotional attention span. Befriending emotional energy is what psychologists call "affect tolerance." When you build your tolerance

for the dark emotions, they don't become overwhelming or lead you to act out. In befriending the dark emotions, you let them be. You don't try to suppress, dispel, avoid, deny, analyze, or distract yourself from them. Nor do you melodramatically indulge or mindlessly vent them.

In the realm of physical exercise, most of us believe "no pain no gain," but when it comes to emotional exercise, we want the quickie route to emotional fitness. The fact is, as with the body, so with the emotions: no pain, no gain. You can't be emotionally flabby and expect to come to a place of emotional transformation and spiritual power. To befriend the dark emotions, your intention must be to get close to what you want to run away from. You need to take your time and give yourself permission to let yourself feel whatever you're feeling without shame, doubt, analysis, or condemnation.

Think of a time when you felt inundated with sadness, fear, or despair. When emotions like these are intense, they flood the body and mind, often causing us to pull away or contract from them. Most of us don't know what to do when we are "flooded" in this way. This is when we're likely to look for diversion or distance, use avoidance, or escape into addictions. But flooding itself can be mindfully observed if we turn our attention to our bodies.

When you are flooded with sorrow, what happens to your body? Do you feel tears welling up in your chest? In your eyes? What is your reaction to this welling up of grief? Do you then begin to feel agitated and speedy? Or depleted and tired? What stories does your mind begin to spin? For example, do you think, "Here I am, feeling sad again. What's wrong with me?"

Similarly, when you are scared, how does your body feel? Do you even let yourself actually *experience* the feeling or do you immediately call a friend, turn on the television, or go out for a drink? What is your mental reaction to your fear? Do you think, "I'm such a wimp"?

When you begin to feel despondent or despairing, how does your body feel? Again, have you ever trained your attention to the bodily experience, or do you simply go immediately into mental overdrive, trying to analyze or explain away your feelings? Do you think, "Oh, no. I'd better get out of this mood or I'll never be able to function." Or, "Uh oh. Better get my medication increased."

We each have unique bodily experiences of and mental reactions to the dark emotions. Befriending emotional energy is about focusing our attention on these sensations and reactions nonjudgmentally, allowing the body to feel what it feels, and the mind to think what it thinks, while maintaining a witness consciousness—a mindful awareness of the stream of sensations and thoughts as they pass through our bodyminds.

## SURRENDERING: TO LET IT GO, YOU HAVE TO LET IT FLOW

Surrendering is an extension of befriending emotional energy. It's about allowing emotional energy to flow to its end point. Surrender is not about becoming passive and saying, "What the hell—I don't give a damn what happens anymore, so I'll just drink this quart of scotch and slobber in my sorrow." It doesn't mean letting go of your senses or your awareness. It means being fully present to emotional energy and letting it pass through the body until it's gone.

A basic axiom of surrender is: To let it go, you have to let it flow. You can't fully let go of a dark emotion until you've fully experienced its truth. That usually means a whole lot of befriending has to happen before you can let go of the emotion. Like befriending emotional energy, surrendering to it is a "let's get into it" process, not a "let me out of here" process. You don't surrender by moving away from what hurts. You surrender by moving into what hurts, with awareness as your protection. This is not "detachment" in the conventional sense; it's connected detachment: staying connected to emotional energy mindfully. The detachment comes from being mindful, not from disconnecting.

Surrendering to grief, fear, or despair may sound ill-advised at first. You may ask, "If I surrender, won't I become overwhelmed and dysfunctional?" Actually, the opposite is true. Surrender is a form of deep acceptance. It's saying yes to emotions we'd prefer to say no to. Paradoxically, it's saying yes that allows the emotional energy to flow and helps you to let go of it.

Think of the difference between holding on tight with a closed fist and letting go by opening your hand. Then think of this in relation to your heart. What would it be like to just surrender and let go into the feelings you've been trying so hard to control and contain?

One of my clients learned early in life that sadness was not an acceptable emotion. She got a strong message from her family: "We're all happy here—and we better keep it that way, or else." Later in her life, she gave herself a hard time for being sad, even when the occasion called for it. I asked her: What would happen if you just sat with your sadness for a while and didn't try to change it?

The next session, she told me she'd sat with her sadness all week and discovered that sadness is actually not as painful an emotion as she thought it was. What was more painful was trying to stop her sadness and getting anxious, depressed, and self-hating instead. She'd surrendered to her sadness and found, to her surprise, that it was actually a kind of "sensual" emotion, much easier to bear than the spikey self-lacerations she experienced when she didn't let herself feel sad. From that day forward, she referred to herself, in the Native American style, as "Sitting with Sadness." Surrendering to this long-forbidden emotion, she found not only her sadness, but also her sense of humor. This is emotional alchemy.

## Seven Steps of Emotional Alchemy

While the alchemy of the dark emotions is a nonlinear and creatively chaotic process, its three basic skills can be taught and learned. We learn these skills by practicing them. The emotional exercises at the end of the next three chapters (and in part four's "home course") are designed to help you practice the skills through a series of seven interrelated steps: (1) intention, (2) affirmation, (3) bodily sensation, (4) contextualization, (5) the way of non-action, (6) the way of action, and (7) the way of surrender.

I will briefly introduce these steps here. If you prefer immersing yourself in the narrative experience of the alchemy of dark emotions, you might want to move straight ahead to the next chapter and come back to these steps later. If you prefer a more left brain approach, read on!

### STEP 1. INTENTION: FOCUSING YOUR SPIRITUAL WILL

The aphorism "Be careful what you ask for, because you might get it" underlines the power of intention. Intention, as I define it, is a kind of spiritual will. By will, I don't mean a put-your-hand-in-the-flame willful effort. Spiritual will is the means by which the mind, heart, and spirit are engaged and focused. This kind of intention is a powerful attribute of consciousness, though we may not always be aware of it.

For example, people often come to therapy with the expectation: "The therapist will fix me by taking away my bad feelings." Their intention often reflects a profound, unconscious longing to be rescued from their own emotions. There is nothing wrong with this longing. In fact, paying attention to it will draw out all the dark emotions one would rather not face. The expectation of being fixed is like wanting to be airlifted out of a war zone. Of course you want the helicopter to come and take you away. But the fact is, this is a down-to-earth journey, and you have to actually walk through the terrain to get where you're going—to arrive at a place of emotional peace and freedom. If you want to be rescued, you are likely to wait passively for someone to do it for you or to you instead of engaging your own resources for emotional transformation.

To want to be fixed is to feel broken. This is where the emotional action is. The feeling of brokenness must be experienced before it can be healed or transformed. So the therapy-goer's initial intention needs to be modified from "I want someone to take my emotions away" to "I want to get to know these emotions better and find out what they're trying to tell me."

We all feel broken in some way. In framing your intention for the alchemy of the dark emotions, you try to accept this. You let yourself off the hook and don't blame yourself for your wounds. And you consult with your spirit. Your ordinary ego wants relief, wants out, wants escape. But your spirit has a wider view of things, can be patient, wants to realize itself— even in the midst of pain.

### STEP 2. AFFIRMATION: DEVELOPING AN EMOTION-POSITIVE ATTITUDE

The second step in the alchemy of the dark emotions is affirming their wisdom. It entails changing what you think about what you feel. We're all conditioned in an emotion-phobic culture and have internalized many ideas about the "negativity" of painful feelings. There's a difference between what you'd like to believe and what you do believe on a body level. Subconscious beliefs are deeply entrenched and have a tenacious way of holding on—the same way that unconscious emotions do. Even the most lapsed Catholic, for instance, can harbor the idea that God will punish her for bad thoughts. This belief triggers guilt and fear. In the same way, negative thoughts about the dark emotions produce more suffering.

Psychologists call changing what you think about what you feel "cognitive restructuring" or "reframing." For instance, thinking "I'm weak" when you feel sad or scared can be reframed as "I'm strong and courageous enough to let myself feel sad or scared." In re-visioning and reframing the power of grief, fear, and despair we come to think about them not as obstacles or enemies but as guides to spiritual transformation. This kind of affirmation is an essential foundation for trusting emotional energy and using it wisely.

### STEP 3. BODILY SENSATION: SENSING, SOOTHING, AND NAMING EMOTIONS

I can't say this enough: Feelings are in your body. Talking about feelings is not the same as experiencing them. Emotional intelligence is a bodily intelligence, so if you want to do emotional alchemy, you have to know how to listen to your body. This is the skill of emotional sensitivity.

Even if you're tone deaf to your body's emotion signals, don't worry. Your body has a way of calling your attention to emotions. In the absence of a skilled ability to listen to the emotional language of the body, "symptoms" arise, calling us to pay attention. As a mild stomachache over time can become an ulcer, an unrecognized grief can become a full-blown anxiety disorder or clinical depression. Denied fear makes itself known in a lowered immune system and psychosomatic disorders. Disavowed despair lives in our bodies, enticing us to act out in ways dangerous to ourselves and others.

The manufacture of these kinds of signs and symptoms may seem disheartening, but it shouldn't be. It is an aspect of the bodymind's innate tropism toward healing. If you can't locate feelings in your body, you can at least be aware of your symptoms and investigate them mindfully, to see what emotions they are carrying and/or disguising. If you attend to your ulcer, your asthma, or your aching back in this way, you will discover hidden dark emotions.

Listening to the body's emotion language is often harder for men, who are encouraged to develop strong "body armor" to defend against the fluidity and vulnerability of emotional energy—which, in our culture, is associated with femininity. Women are generally more in touch with their feelings; but this doesn't mean that women are necessarily better at emotional alchemy. Women are socialized to locate feelings in the body and to name and express them more accurately than men. But we are also socialized to condemn ourselves for our feelings, and therefore we often abort emotional energy and don't reap the benefits of our emotional sensitivity.

Both men and women can use an increased understanding of the body-emotion connection, and a greater fluency in reading the body's feeling signals. This skill can open a door to profound shifts in the ability to connect to oneself and others.

In addition to sensing emotion in the body, it's important to know how to soothe emotional energy when it becomes very intense. Thich Nhat Hanh, a Vietnamese Buddhist monk and spiritual leader, speaks of how we must "lullaby" our anger and despair. Soothing these emotions is essential, he says, because it prevents us from acting hastily or carelessly.

Most of us never got enough soothing as children. When we were emotionally troubled, we were more likely ignored, shamed, or punished than soothed. As adults, we still suffer from a lack of soothing. Given the state of the world and its everyday assaults and stressors (including the speed at which we in the West are now living and the overwhelming inundation of information we have to contend with, as well as the everyday violence of the culture), we could all stand to be rocked like babies every day! But even if you've got someone to do this for you, it's important to be able to soothe yourself.

Finally, emotions in the body need to be named accurately. If you want to transform how you feel, you have to know what you feel. Sensitivity, the ability to sense emotion in the body, goes along with literacy, the ability to identify that emotion with clarity, subtlety, and precision.

This is a skill we don't learn in school. Lots of very intelligent people, with Ph.D.'s, M.D.'s, or "Esq." after their names, people who can make all sorts of subtle intellectual distinctions, don't have a clue as to which words mean what when it comes to emotions. Here's an example from my therapy practice.

Melissa is talking to her husband, Daniel, in couples therapy: "I've been reaching out, and you don't seem to notice. I'm sad and angry that it's all one-way. I don't like feeling that I'm the only one who cares if we make it or not."

In the face of what feels like an emotional onslaught, Daniel slumps down even further into his chair. Staring down at the small stone he has lifted from the altar in my office, he absently shifts it from one hand to another. He is silent.

I wait to see if Melissa will pursue her question. When she doesn't, I decide to go after Daniel's response myself. I want to give Daniel a try at naming his feelings while modeling some persistence for Melissa.

Turning my attention to Daniel, I ask: "Do you have any response to what Melissa just said?"

Daniel's brow furrows slightly: "Of course. It makes me upset."

"What do you mean by 'upset'?"

"Upset . . . you know . . . I just feel bad about it."

"Bad is like upset. It's a general term but doesn't tell me much. Bad how?"

"How bad? Very bad . . . really bad."

At this point, Daniel is a bit agitated. I sense that he feels criticized by my persistence. I explain that my questions are not in pursuit of the right answer but come from wanting to understand what "feeling bad" means to him, since it could mean so many different things.

His interest sparked, Daniel asks: "For instance?"

"For instance, feeling bad could mean: I feel sad. Or: I feel guilty. Or: I resent you and wish you would leave me alone. Or: I'm mad at you. Or: I'm anxious about our relationship. Or: I feel hopeless. Or: I feel bad about my-self. Or: I feel depressed. Or: I want to make things better."

The stone comes to a full stop in Daniel's right palm. "Oh," he says, "I see what you're saying. Feeling bad to me means all of the above."

Daniel is a psychotherapist. But his lack of emotional literacy should come as no surprise. Therapists don't learn to name emotions in their schooling or internships. When it comes to emotional literacy, we all could use some help.

### STEP 4. CONTEXTUALIZATION: TELLING A WIDER STORY

Every life contains emotional pain. There's the pain; and there's the story we tell ourselves about it. We all have a story about our suffering. Most of these are narcissistic stories—narratives in which the self is the exclusive focus. The individualist culture of psychology has actually contributed to this narcissism. We have come to view the "inner child" as a reality that has little connection to anything outside of itself except the nuclear family.

To practice emotional alchemy, you have to be acquainted with the story you are currently telling about your emotional suffering and recontextualize it in a broader social, cultural, global, or cosmic context. There is a pro-found connection between emotional alchemy and emotional ecology. Without knowing that connection, we're doomed to the ego's endless whin-ing. Making the connection between our own personal pain and the pain of the world is an essential part of emotional alchemy because it gets us out of the isolation that the dark emotions tend to impose, especially in an emotion-phobic culture.

For example, the story of your emotional suffering may be: "I am sad and angry because my mother was cold and unnurturing." This is one of our cul-ture's most typical stories. (Historically, psychiatry adopted the story of ma-ternal insufficiency as an explanation for all sorts of emotional suffering.) Along with these kinds of stories about a defective parent is another story, which I call the "core defect" story. How come your mother was cold and unnurturing? At the root, there is often a story about your own defective-ness: My mother was cold because I was unlovable. Your core defect story explains your suffering by reference to a core sense of shame about who you are. (In emotion-phobic culture, feeling shame about one's pain is normal.) When you are in pain, you tend to resort to your core defect story as an ex-planation for it. Your boyfriend just left and you feel abandoned, sad, and angry. The reason he left, you tell yourself, is that you're not pretty enough, thin enough, sexy enough. In fact, the truth may be that he left because he's not ready for a relationship with the level of intimacy that you want. This latter idea doesn't occur to you, because core defect stories tend to be absolute—offering a self-denigrating explanation for complex human behavior and events. Many of us constellate an entire identity around an unconscious core defect story These stories contribute to our suffering and keep us from befriending it.

To experience the alchemy of the dark emotions, it is necessary to widen the story of your pain and see the larger picture. The nuclear family story is itself only a piece of this larger picture. Contextualization is about locating our own personal story in its widest possible contexts, which can be pictured as a series of concentric circles that include your family, community, nation, and world.

The larger stories may be: My mother was cold because her mother was abusive. Her mother was abusive because she was abused by her husband and took it out on the kids. Her husband was abusive because he was traumatized while serving in a war. Abuse and violence of all kinds are intergenerationally transmitted in families. What happens to the capacity to love in these larger contexts of abuse and violence?

These larger stories may seem remote, but they live in our bodies.

If this step seems odd and cumbersome to us, it's because world-negation is the *modus operandi* of conventional psychology and psychiatry. But the fact is, there is a world out there that continues to influence our emotional lives on a daily basis—and this is as it should be! The aim of emotional alchemy is not to shut out the world and cultivate your own garden. If indeed there ever was much use for this way of conducting one's emotional and spiritual life, in the context of today's emotional ecology it can easily become a more sophisticated evasion of our responsibility to love and care for one another. Moreover, in an age of global threat, this narcissistic hiding of the self from the world becomes more and more impossible.

In the step I call contextualizing, your own ego's pain is seen and experienced in connection to the pain of the world. When you can see your emotional suffering as part of a much larger story, you build wisdom and compassion for yourself and others, for the world as a whole. Compassion is both a necessary ingredient and a lasting gift in the alchemy of the dark emotions.

STEP 5. THE WAY OF NON-ACTION: BEFRIENDING WHAT HURTS

The way of non-action develops the skill of affect tolerance. When you can tolerate the feeling of grief, fear, or despair in the body without acting prematurely to suppress it, you are practicing the way of non-action. Being able to focus and sustain awareness in the midst of turbulent or painful states of emotion is perhaps the most critical skill of emotional intelligence.

Any mindfulness practice builds this capacity. T'ai chi, yoga, and other forms of physical practice that build mindfulness are particularly useful. What I teach my clients is *vipassana* (insight meditation), a simple Buddhist practice popularized by Jack Kornfield, Joseph Goldstein, Jon Kabat-Zinn, and other American students of Theravada Buddhism.[4]

The way of non-action may seem to contradict the basic nature of emotions like fear and anger, which motivate us to act. But in order to act mindfully, it is necessary to "not-act" mindfully. Mindfully befriending emotional energy is the best protection against the potential dangers of acting carelessly and catalyzing events that we will later regret. The way of non-action can be discovered and cultivated through the practice of meditation and envisioning our emotions in the body. (See the emotional exercises for these practices at the end of chapters 5, 6, and 7, as well as in chapter 10.)

STEP 6. THE WAY OF ACTION: SOCIAL ACTION
AND SPIRITUAL SERVICE

The quickest way to change what you feel is to change what you do. This is the basis of behaviorism and behaviorist therapy. It is also what you intuitively know when you decide to distract yourself from your sadness by going for a walk or watching television or calling a friend. When we distract ourselves from our emotions, we act despite what we feel. But in the way of action, we find an action that uses the energy of emotion with the intention of transformation.

The dark emotions ask us to act in some way. Fear asks us to act for the sake of survival or protection of life. Grief and despair are emotions that ask us to be still; yet the stillness itself actually requires a number of actions. To mourn the dead, we must act in ways that allow the flow of grief rather than abort it. To sit with despair, we must find practices that allow us to tolerate our emotional state and surrender to it consciously. The dark emotions call us to find the right action, to act with awareness, and to observe the transformations that ensue, however subtle.

The way of action is strong medicine in times of trouble. Social action and spiritual service both have to do with serving others not for personal gain but because there is joy in being of use. Both are ways to practice this step. When we move our grief, fear, and despair into conscious acts on behalf of ourselves and others, these emotions become transformative. But the way of action can also be practiced through personal acts of kindness to self and others, however small. This is something we can practice even when we are at a loss for what do to. As one of my clients said when she found herself feeling helpless about her brother's drug addiction: "When you can't do anything, you can always love."

STEP 7. TRANSFORMATION: THE WAY OF SURRENDER (FLOW)
The art of conscious emotional flow is the art of surrender. Emotional flow is not something you find by sitting down and thinking about your feelings a lot or analyzing how you got to be the way you are—which is why years and years of talk therapy often create little emotional change. Emotional flow has its source not in the talking, analyzing part of the brain but in the intuitive, creative part.

Emotional energy in a state of flow moves automatically in the direction of healing, renewal, harmony, and transformation. This step can be cultivated through creativity, prayer, energy work, and play. (See the emotional exercises at the end of chapters 5, 6, and 7, and in chapter 10.)

Ultimately, the way of surrender brings us to the emotional skill of making new meaning out of our suffering. This quintessentially human ability to create new meaning out of emotional pain allows us to heal from the past and transform the present.

## Seven Foundations of Emotional Alchemy

Since we all suffer, we might as well learn how to make exquisite lemonade from life's lemons—to find ways to transform turbulence to tranquillity, pain to wisdom. The foundations for this journey are summarized here. (Again, if you're eager to get into the heart of emotional alchemy, skip ahead to the next chapter; if you prefer the analytic mode, read on.)

1. *The energy of the dark emotions is not "negative" energy; it's just energy.*
Emotions are mind/body energies that summon our attention and prepare us for action. Energy comes from the Latin *energia*, meaning "activity." Energy is defined as vitality of expression, power forcefully exerted, and the ca-

pacity for doing work. Like all energy, emotional energy can be used to lend power to an activity, to get something done. It can be conserved; it can be transformed. But it doesn't disappear. This energy is available to be used in some form—for good or ill.

Energy is information. The energy of the dark emotions brings us information about the self and the world; about the past, present, or future; about the inner and outer worlds and the connections between them. The information we get alerts us to be attentive to something important and guides us to transformational change.

2. *Emotional alchemy starts with intention.* "Intention implies little more than what one has in mind to do or bring about," says my dictionary. The surprising phrase is "little more." The fact is, in the realm of emotion, as in life as a whole, what we have in mind to do or bring about is a very powerful force! No kind of emotional alchemy can come about without our conscious intention for it. Intention sets the whole process going. Without it, not much happens with your dark emotions except pain.

To become adept at emotional alchemy, you must have the clear intention to use emotional energy for the purpose of healing and transformation. Once you have this intention, you're more than half the way there!

3. *Emotional energy is directional.* When you mindfully attend, befriend, and surrender to dark emotional energy, it moves in the direction of greater harmony, healing, and transformation.

Emotional energy sets us in motion. It takes us from one place to another—if we don't get in the way of its flow. Alchemy happens. You can't make it happen, but you can let it happen. This is something like the "effort without effort" that is the essence of mindfulness meditation practice. Or, if you prefer (and many do), it's like having an orgasm. Trying to force it is not the way. Orgasm happens when you're at home with the intensity of sexual energy and surrender to its flow. Ditto for emotional alchemy.

4. *Conversely, emotional alchemy is aborted by the fear of emotional energy.* When you are not mindful or skillful in the ways of emotional energy, the energy can easily convert to toxic emotions (such as shame, envy, and self-pity) and toxic mental states (such as anxiety, depression, and psychic numbing)—or into mind/body symptoms that alert you to the fact that your dark emotions require attention. It can also move you to harmful behaviors

like addiction and acting out. Therefore, it's always necessary to work with emotion-phobic beliefs and unlearn our habitual ways of thinking about and reacting to grief, despair, and fear.

5. *The dark emotions are purposeful.* Just as physical pain alerts you to pay attention to the body, emotional pain has a purpose for the soul. The purpose of painful emotions is not always obvious, but it can be discovered with the proper intention and patience. Looking for the purpose in dark emotions is an important part of attending to them and learning what they have to teach.

Put another way, finding the purpose in grief, despair, and fear is about making new meaning out of pain. This doesn't mean putting a gloss on it. It means digging into the deepest recesses of your heart and soul, searching for what your pain is trying to teach you. Even in the worst forms of adversity, making meaning is possible—and a necessary part of the healing process.

6. *Emotions live in the body.* Emotional alchemy is a process of going down into your body from your usual perch in your head. You have to feel it to heal it. To be an emotional alchemist, you have to know how to distinguish your emotion as sensation in the body, from the beliefs that trigger it, and from your reactions to it. Awareness is not just a mental process; it's a full-body process. Attending to, befriending, and surrendering to emotional energy can only happen when you're on friendly terms with your body.

7. *Emotions live in the world.* Emotional alchemy is not only a process of going deeper; it's also a process of getting wider—telling a wider story, recontextualizing your private, personal pain. The wider we get, the more our dark emotions connect us to the world and the more we grow in wisdom and compassion. As the Dalai Lama has repeatedly said, compassion is the most potent human power for healing and transformation, on both a personal and global level. It is the emotional elixir at the end of the alchemy process, the most precious gold of all.

The three basic skills and seven steps of the alchemy of the dark emotions are condensed distillations of a process that is ultimately mysterious. This process cannot easily be reduced to a set of skills, ideas, or biochemical events. The systemization of any emotional process gives it an aura of scientific credibility. But emotional alchemy is an art, not a science.

In the next three chapters, I seek to communicate some of the mystery and magic of the alchemy of the dark emotions. My intention is to re-vision the power of grief, despair, and fear while offering some solid companionship and practical wisdom to sustain you on your own journey of healing through the dark emotions.

# 5  *From Grief to Gratitude*

For grief has darkened my eyes;
my body is like a shadow.
My days fade like an echo;
the strings of my heart have snapped.
— *The Book of Job*

There is nothing so whole as a broken heart.
— MENACHEM MENDEL OF KOTZK

## The Landscape of Grief

### SHATTERING

IT IS SAID THAT WHEN SOMEONE WE LOVE DIES, a part of us dies too. In my experience it is not a part but the whole—the self we've known is all at once shattered.

This is how it was when Aaron gasped his last breath on the ICU. Holding his body in death, I was both a mother and not a mother. Expiring in my arms, he was set free, released from the prison of plastic tubes and electronic monitors that attached him to his life. For the first time since the moment of his birth, I could hold him without the tubes and wires. Dead, he was nakedly mine and altogether gone all in the same instant. Time stood still and the world fell silent. I was drawn into a vortex, and the self I knew was irreversibly shattered.

What happened next: an energy larger than my body could contain broke through in a rush of strange, unfathomable syllables. In retrospect, searching for a way to describe this experience, I thought of the phrase "speaking in tongues." I know very little about speaking in tongues except that in certain moments of altered consciousness, some people seem to manifest this "gift"—if that's what it is. Mostly, I've heard of this happening to Pentecostalists. It's the last thing I would expect to happen to me.

What came through me, as I stood and wrapped my arms around my dead baby, was a form of speech emanating from a source deeper than personality. Though utterly indecipherable, these strange sounds were a kind of prayer. I was standing behind a curtain on the ICU, surrounded by the sanitized hospital air. Having asked for several moments to be alone with Aaron just after he expired, this incomprehensible prayer was the last thing I uttered before they took his body away.

Was I speaking in a long forgotten but suddenly remembered shamanic tongue to ritualize the moment of parting and make it bearable? One thing is certain: this was not a way I would have behaved if not for the power of grief.

Everyone has his or her own way of grieving. Not everyone speaks in tongues at the moment of grief's greatest impact. But anyone who's ever lost a parent, child, lover, spouse, or close friend, knows that grief is one of the most powerful emotional forces there is—powerful enough to shatter the self we've carefully constructed.

Leaving Children's Hospital after Aaron was taken away, this shattering was briefly lulled by the merciful numbing of shock. Aaron's body had been taken out of my arms. The doctors and nurses, looking shamed, had expressed their condolences. We retrieved the few things that Aaron had with him in his hospital crib: a stuffed koala bear, the gift of a friend; a lavender hippo from the hospital gift shop; a red parrot that we'd held before his eyes because we were told that newborns see red more easily than other colors; a tiny purple velvet pillow sewn by another friend, replete with wishes for health and healing; and the white cotton cap that kept Aaron warm in his hospital home. These things we took with us.

The storm of grief hit once we arrived home. Our arms were empty. The house was empty. And most of all, Aaron's room—the room he never saw—was empty. Traditionally, Jews don't give baby showers or prepare a baby's room before the birth. Perhaps a history of persecution has made us wary of counting our chickens before they hatch. Without a cradle or crib, without baby clothes neatly tucked away in drawers or a mobile hanging from the ceiling, we'd nevertheless prepared this room for Aaron. The room that had been Roger's office was emptied for the new arrival.

Walking into what was to be Aaron's room, I felt myself pulled away from shore by a rip tide, toward death. All the life force in my body ached to go, to be with Aaron, wherever he was. A primitive howl emerged from my mouth. I understood, in this moment, how someone can die of a broken heart.

And then, suddenly, a voice that certainly is not that of my everyday self said "No! It's Aaron who is dead, not you. You're alive!"

Abruptly, I was called back to life. I felt myself spinning, as though through a tunnel, and then landing back in the room. Whose voice this was, calling me to be here, urging me to choose life, despite my everyday self's desire to follow Aaron into the next world, I do not know. But the voice was undeniable, and I listened.

In the weeks and months that followed, I came to know these two selves: the one that urged me to give up the ghost, and the other that, despite everything, was alive in a new way. The simultaneous shattering of ego and expansion of consciousness is a common experience for people who are grieving. Before we are personally affected, we know, of course, that death is an inherent part of life. People each day die of cancer or heart disease, of AIDS or accidents. People are raped and murdered. People are sick or have children who are sick and who die. We "know" this. But we cannot emotionally absorb the fact that we could easily be one of them. Only when we ourselves are diagnosed with a serious disease or lose a loved one do we know, in a different way, that loss is not just something that happens to other people. The normal ego maintains its illusion of control and invulnerability until disaster strikes and it all begins to unravel.

This ego dissolution is the first phase of the extraordinary healing process we call grief.

As I write, Boston grieves the deaths of seven people at Edgewater Technology, Inc., their lives cut short by a coworker who hunted them down with an assault rifle and machine gun. No sooner had the deed been done than ministers and television reporters were exhorting the bereaved to "let the healing begin." At a church service three days later, the congregation was advised to release their pain and hold on to the positive memories. In the face of grief after violent loss, this is the all-too-common counsel: stay positive, forgive, move on.

In grief's alchemy, however, the first phase is not about moving on but about being broken, a searing experience that cannot be pacified by all the compassionate counsel in the world. Healing through grief doesn't start when we give up feeling bad; it begins with the agony of loss. The merciful numbing of shock must wear off and the reality of death take hold. Grief must sink in. In the alchemy of grief, going down always precedes coming up. Understandable but misguided attempts to speed up the process tend to derail it. Generally, a grief deferred is a grief prolonged. There are no short-cuts in the alchemy of the dark emotions.

Grief is a universal response to death and loss, built into our neurological systems. Animals grieve too. My cat Mojo, a friendly beast, hid in a corner for two weeks after the death of his mother, Little. His appetite, ordinarily ravenous for a good portion of the day, receded to a paltry shadow of its former level. He looked around for Little in every corner of the house, then took himself into seclusion.

While animals grieve, they don't reflect on their emotional state (as far as I know). The grief process does not alter their sense of self or the meaning they attribute to loss. They do not change or grow from a spiritual stand-point. Because loss is an inevitable part of life, grief for human beings is an important and largely neglected aspect of psychospiritual development, as well as a profound healing process. Whatever the nature and extent of the loss, we grieve because we are not alone, because we are interconnected; and what connects us to one another also breaks our hearts.

Grief exists on a spectrum, from the "milder" sorrows of a best friend moving to another state, to the more absolute losses: the death of a marital partner, parent, or child. I use the words *grief* and *sorrow* interchangeably. *Sorrow* is the milder word, used to describe the emotions one feels in the wake of neglect, betrayal, abandonment, and abuse. But *grief*, the stronger word, is equally applicable to all of these kinds of loss in relationship. The grief following separation and divorce (given that one out of every two American marriages ends in divorce) is one of the most common forms of this dark emotion.

Grief is a psychospiritual process. As the conventional ego begins to give way, the spirit can do griefwork. Griefwork is not a return to the pre-loss status quo. People do not get "back to normal" after a child dies, or after any profound loss. Grief is an opportunity not for "resolution," as in the popular parlance, but for transformation: a wholly new awareness of reality, self, beloved, and world.

Death unseats the dominance of the conventional self that psychologists call the ego. The ego falls apart, awash in feelings of sorrow, anguish, de-spair. These painful states alternate with periods of emptiness, numbness, lifelessness, paralysis. Everything seems an effort. A stack of dishes in the sink can be utterly defeating. At the same time, there is a perceived dis-crepancy between the ego's pain and the seeming indifference of the uni-verse. The ego screams its "NO!" into the void.

Many in mourning ask: How is it that the world can go on turning, just as it did before, that people go about their business in precisely the same way, that the mail comes and the sun shines, and everyone looks pretty much the same, when in fact life, as it has been lived, has been destroyed?

This question is asked from the strikingly narcissistic point of view of the conventional self, based on its "normal" distortion of reality: the illusion of being the center of the universe. The world turns as it did before precisely because the conventional ego is not at the center of it! Loss, particularly sudden or unexpected death, shatters the ego's normal grandiosity, its center-stage illusion of control.

This subversion of the normal ego creates an opening for a transformed sense of self to emerge. In the alchemy of grief, the shattered ego's surrender to the inescapable reality of death ushers in a wider perspective—a larger self that can accept death, not as punishment, but as part of the circle of life. While the ego suffers, in T. S. Eliot's words, "like a patient etherized upon a table," this larger self grows, and with it, an awe before the mysteries that lie at the heart of existence, an ability to live fully in the present moment, and a gratitude for all things that are born and die.

### EXPANSION

> Excess of sorrow laughs. Excess of joy weeps.
> Joys impregnate. Sorrows bring forth.
> —WILLIAM BLAKE, *Proverbs of Hell*

We don't choose grief, it chooses us. But we do have a choice in how we deal with it. We have the choice to let it be, not to rush it, to honor it in the way that we are called to. "Choosing" grief, in this sense, provides the grounding for the alchemy of grief to unfold. It is an inner intention that says: I will let this grief mold me to its purpose, rather than try to rein it in, stay in charge of it. And this inner intention, this choice, is what begins the process that I call "expansion"—the development of an enlarged sense of self through the grieving process.

Expansion is not absolute. The larger self doesn't take over—or we'd all have become enlightened long ago! The common phrase "A part of me died" in the aftermath of loss is also true: some piece of oneself gets buried with every death of a loved one. Some people feel diminished by this burial for the rest of their lives. But if we open to grief, nothing is ever wholly lost. The burial is not the end. In the seed of grief, there is the promise of a blossoming.

The flowering can happen only if we get past some of the deeply internalized cultural beliefs about the grieving process: "Get this over with and get on with life. Don't let your feelings get the better of you. Don't fall apart or go under. Just lift your head up and move on. Be stoic. Be strong." If you follow these cultural commandments, you're not likely to discover the alchemy of grief. One person who refused to follow them was my client Doris. When her mother died, she found herself crying a lot, and she decided to let the crying happen. This was different for her. She was used to stifling sadness and being "strong." But for the first time, she felt that inhibiting her grief would not be the "strong" thing to do, and she chose to let it be. One day she would be "fine" and functioning; the next day she would barely be able to force herself out of bed. One day she felt numb; the next day she was howling.

In the midst of one such moment of active grieving, as Doris sat in her dining room feeling the rush of grief's energy, her roommate appeared at the door. "It's not healthy to cry like this," she said to Doris. "You should get up and do something."

Doris felt as though she'd been slapped in the face. But she was able to say to her roommate: "This is what I need to do right now, and I don't want you to judge or stop me."

What people in grief need most is to be compassionately accompanied, to feel that those who care about them are willing and able to tolerate the pain that they are in, to be there with them, to be present. A touch, a simple expression of caring, and the ability to sit with the grief goes a long way. Because emotions are contagious, however, grief is hard not only for the mourner but also for those who care about her. This is why many people who are grieving at some point come up against the judgments, inhibitions, and unsolicited advice of well-meaning others. And the advice is generally in the same vein as that of Doris's roommate: Don't grieve too much. Don't show your grief too visibly. Get busy, move on, don't look too sad.

The message is: Get your old self back in shape. And it is a message that is reinforced by psychologists in the bereavement field who mark the stages of grief by the capacity to return to "normal." The "get back to normal" message impedes the flow of grief. If we are in a hurry to dispel grief in order to get back to baseline, we are in danger of wasting the profound opportunity in grief for transformations of consciousness that make baseline appear quite limited.

Grief, like despair, is an emotion that asks us to depart from the "normal"—to be still, like a pool of frozen water in the winter. From out of this apparent stillness, an imperceptible movement occurs, from sorrow for what has been lost to gratitude for what remains. The trick is to let go and descend into grief's cold waters.

Descending, the heart breaks open and the ego loses its moorings. "Normal" seems far away indeed. The conventional ego is lost. The ego as we know it is part role, part compendium of beliefs and memories, part deeply ingrained habit patterns from the past, part narrative that we've internalized

from our family and social culture. Boundaried, isolated, and beset by endless cravings, competitive strivings for recognition, and compulsive aversions to pain, the normal ego—so prized in Western psychologies—is, from
a spiritual standpoint, an unhealthy state of consciousness. The alchemical
opportunity in grief is precisely the profound wrestling with the everyday
ego that is so much a part of the process.

Once shattered, the ego struggles to reconstitute itself, having been so
unceremoniously unseated by the loss it could not control. It tries to
reestablish the solidity, predictability, and familiarity it once knew by returning to routine. This return has its place and its comforts. Folding the
laundry, we remember that although one child may be dead, the others still
need their clothes to be washed and cleaned. Or we remember that we ourselves have a body that must be tended to. Or we feel the soft fabric and are
reassured that life goes on.

But going too quickly into daily routine also has its dangers. Once we are
"back"—going to work, doing the laundry, watching television—we tend to
abort the process of grief. We don't have time for its intensity. Grief is an
inconvenient, unwelcome intrusion, interrupting the organized day, which
keeps us anchored to our accustomed sense of self. We are rarely counseled
to understand that it is precisely the surrender of the normal self that makes
grief transformative.

Among observant Jews, the practice of "sitting *shivah*" keeps the
mourner from returning to routine too soon. In the seven days following the
burial (*shivah* means "seven" in Hebrew), the mourners stay at home and
receive visitors for most of the day. People come to comfort and console; to
bring food and drink; and perhaps most of all, to give the mourners an opportunity to remember the dead and to give voice to their grief. Ancient
mourning customs are followed, including the draping of mirrors with a
black cloth so as not to interrupt grieving with attention to grooming and
appearances. The ritual is about encouraging an openness to the grief
process. Mourning is gradually stepped down—the seven days followed by
a thirty-day period of less severe mourning, and then an eleven-month period when the mourner's prayer is said twice a day; after that, the dead are
remembered ritually once a year.

There is a psychological and spiritual wisdom to this practice. If we can
hang in, and maintain our openness to grief, we find that the ego reestab-
lishes itself with an expanded vista: less isolated and bound up in its narcissistic shell, more open, compassionate, and free of compulsive maneuvers to
avoid pain, more connected to spirit.

In a sense, grief is a birth process from ego to spirit. The broken ego struggles to maintain itself in the face of the expanded awareness of its own smallness and limitation. When the heart breaks open, the ego starts its journey out of isolation—ironically, just when it is most bereft.

The alternating or simultaneous experience of a smaller and larger sense of self in grief is not an abstract idea; it is a deeply felt experience. It is common for mourners to feel utterly inconsolable and yet to feel buoyed up by the indestructible love of the person who has passed away. The ego is gripped by its loss, but the larger self is actually expanded by it. While the physical connection is broken, the spiritual connection with the beloved attains a greater force precisely because it extends beyond the physical.

For me, this alternation between a smaller and larger self, which started immediately after Aaron's birth, continued after his death. Certainly my ego found Aaron's death intolerable. Yet something larger than my ordinary self had an astoundingly matter-of-fact attitude and accepted his death with a mysterious equanimity.

I remember how these two very different selves behaved at Aaron's funeral. That morning, I'd looked into the mirror and said to myself: "This is the day you bury your son." The larger self must have been in charge at this moment, because there was an altogether unexpected kind of acceptance. *Yes*, it seemed to say, *that's the way it is.*

It was a beautiful sunny day in December, the air clear and cold. The funeral director, when we arrived, pinned a torn black ribbon to my coat, explaining that in ancient times, Jews rent their garments as a display of grief when burying a loved one, but that nowadays, clothes costing what they do, we don't really want to rip them apart. I understood his little joke as an attempt to normalize mourning. Everything had a crisp clarity to it that I had never experienced before.

Then, walking to the gravesite, gazing at the shocking smallness of the unadorned wooden coffin, I was jolted out of the expanded consciousness of the morning's equanimity by the voice of my conventional ego: *Wait a minute! This is not the way a mother of a dead baby is supposed to behave!* it screamed. *You should be crying! You should be looking distraught!* And instantaneously, I began to cry, obeying the ego's command. But even as I did, the larger self gazed at this display of the ego's distress with compassion.

Messages from the larger self accompanied and comforted me for the next several months. Often, they came to me in dreams, sometimes in remarkably succinct form, like Post-it Notes from the larger self on the page of my consciousness. In one dream I was told: *You never lose two things: your memories and your goodness.* In another: When in trouble, remember these three things: *Don't feel sorry for yourself. You are not alone. Give to others.*

Nineteen years later, I still keep these messages on my refrigerator, to remind my ego when it gets too uppity.

But even as the self expands, the ego keeps on ticking. The ego is a natural-born victim. *Why me?* is its central question. (You won't find too many grieving people asking, "Why not me? Since there is so much suffering in the world, why should I be spared?")

Through countless walks around Boston's Jamaica Pond, I asked *Why? Why? Why?* This was my mantra, repeated to the rhythm of my lonely steps. I thought endlessly of why it shouldn't have happened: I had a radiant pregnancy. I was very healthy. There were no signs of any problems. The birth was normal. The doctors don't understand why either. And on and on.

Sometimes this thought cycle was interrupted by disturbing explanations such as: This happened to Aaron because in the first trimester I cowrote, produced, and performed a multimedia project on Jewish Resistance during the Holocaust. The images and energy of evil drained his life force. Or I thought of some of the "explanations" offered by those around me. The doctors called it "hypoxia"—loss of oxygen in utero. But this was only a description, not an explanation. "He was an old soul and had to return," said a friend. (To where?) "It's best this way," said my auto mechanic. (Best for whom?) One of Aaron's doctors at Children's Hospital, a native of Jamaica with a lovely lilt to her voice, had this to say when I informed her of Aaron's death: "He must have done something very bad in his last life." An astonishing diagnosis, coming from a Western physician! But then people say all sorts of crazy things to others who are grieving—mostly, I think, to soothe themselves.

Eventually, I grew tired of asking why. One day the question stopped, exhausted by its own futility. And a wiser response came to me: *The answer to the question Why? is: You'll never know.* The preoccupations of an agonized ego that wanted to know everything so as to regain some semblance of control then gave way to a more productive line of questioning. I began to ask questions I could answer. Not *Why?* but *What shall I do with my sorrow?*

A friend suggested I try insight meditation. She introduced me to a teacher who taught me how to focus on my breath as I inhaled and exhaled, and to observe the contents of my mind in its gyrations. This opened a new door: the door of mindfulness. It encouraged me to inquire into my grief with curiosity. My vision began to expand beyond the narrow tunnel of my grief. I started to look at people walking down the street in a new way. I saw people with sorrow in their eyes, heavy with care and despondency. Every-one grieves something, I thought, whether a fresh loss or something long buried. Everyone grieves because everything passes, everyone dies.

Realizing this, not just abstractly but viscerally, I began to let go of the *Why me?* question at last. *Why me?* was the ego's question. And the ex-panded self's answer was: *The Mysteries of loss and death are not yours to un-derstand through the rational, analytic mind.*

Through daily meditation, I inquired into grief in another way, with the enlarged perspective of the inner witness. Ultimately, through this process of meditative grief, I came to believe that Aaron and I (in our larger-self forms) chose his fate together, prior to his birth. This was a shocking idea that my rational mind and everyday ego found altogether absurd and totally rejected. Yet it insisted on making itself known in some unfathomable way. A gradual dawning took place in my walks around Jamaica Pond—a sense of Aaron's death as an event that could be only partially understood from this side of the veil between the worlds—a sense of life's inherent Mystery.

Not everyone, of course, would attribute this meaning to my situation. But each of us must make some meaning of loss or be devastated by it. The need to find meaning in loss and death is as urgent as the thirst for drink or the hunger for food. Without meaning, despair sets in and stays, a perma-nent, uninvited guest.

Is the loss we've suffered inherently meaningful, or do we impose a meaning on it in order to bear it? One way or another, we construct a mean-ing story, and it is through this story that we find acceptance. In making meaning of loss, we discover the third aspect of grief's alchemy: surrender.

## SURRENDER

> One may lie down weeping at nightfall,
> but at dawn there are shouts of joy.
> —*Psalm 30:6*

The rabbis of the Talmud said that when Adam and Eve were expelled from the Garden, God saw the loneliness of their exile and, out of compassion, gave them the gift of tears. With this gift came the promise of healing their grief.

Tears are grief's natural lubricant. For Adam and Eve, tears were the balm for their expulsion from Edenic grace. They are also, the Talmud tells us, a way back to the Source: Even when the gates of heaven are shut to prayer, they are open to tears.

In my experience, tears, fully and unselfconsciously shed, are a powerful kind of prayer. And, like all prayers, they are the medium of surrender to what some call God's will and others call simply "what is."

In the months after Aaron's death, my tears flowed freely—in private and public, of their own accord. I made no attempt to hide them as I ordinarily would. I thought nothing of people seeing me crying. I walked around Jamaica Pond and cried. I wrote Aaron's story and cried. I went shopping and cried. I wrote poetry and cried. I went to meditation group, talked about Aaron's death, and cried. The tears were like waters washing the grief away. My arms literally ached—a common experience for mothers who suffer what experts clinically call "a neonatal death." But I was not depressed or anxious. The tears kept my grief from turning into these chronic states of negativity, which commonly afflict mourners who ignore grief's compelling call to make space for its powerful energy.

Tears are the medium of the ego's surrender to death. Surrender, like every part of the alchemy of grief, happens unevenly: sometimes in a blinding flash, sometimes incrementally. It happens and then is undone and happens again. Then, one day, usually when it is wholly unexpected, there is a new awareness of peace.

I remember a moment in the kitchen. I had just brewed some hot water for tea, and I poured it into a blue ceramic teacup. The hot steam rising from the teacup, the white flowers on the rounded blue ceramic, the minted aroma of the tea—there was a numinous quality to this moment, a clarity, a sense of wonder and fullness. Life was good. There was magic in the everyday. I heard these words: *The world is charged with the sacred.*

When not sad after Aaron's death, I was happy. Happier than I had ever been. This happiness had everything to do with living in the present and appreciating my life in a heightened way. With not taking anything for granted, knowing that the future is an illusion and that every moment is precious. Going shopping with Roger after Aaron's death, I remember laughing in the aisles while looking for a can of soup and reading food labels. The laughter was the sheer exuberance of being alive—and feeling alive in a new way. The present moment had a fullness to it. When I was in the depths of sorrow, there was only sorrow. When I was laughing, there was only laughter.

I spent many days in the cemetery after Aaron's death, sitting at the gravesite, talking to him. This is a common practice for mourners, even those who have no belief in God, the afterlife, the immortality of the soul, spiritual redemption, or reincarnation. No matter how much my ego thrashed about in the weeks and months after Aaron's death, I could find some peace here.

The small stone is inscribed: "Aaron Michael Gottlieb. Whose spirit blessed our lives." Going to the cemetery reminded me, and still does, of the blessing of his life and death, his legacy. Here I remember what is important and nourish my larger self.

In an oft-told Buddhist story, a woman loses her son and is inconsolable. She approaches the Buddha and begs him to bring her son back. He instructs her to go around the village from house to house, seeking a single mustard seed from any home where no one has died. If she can find such a mustard seed, he will restore her son to life. So the woman knocks on each door and finds that there is no household that has not experienced loss. She returns without the mustard seed but with an enlarged awareness of the universality of loss that leads her to a path of compassion and peace.

Sitting cross-legged on the grass, facing Aaron's small gravestone, communing with his spirit, I find my own gift of peace. All around me, the dead reassure me of the democracy of death. Everyone dies. We are all bound for the same place. I exhale, a long, slow breath. There is nothing to hold on to. The trees sway in the breeze, the birds chirp in the grass. Everything is alive. I am alive. I am here. And I am talking to Aaron, who, I am certain, hears me.

Surrendering to death changes the way that we see, and the way that we feel about being alive. Where there was only loss and deprivation, we begin now to perceive wholeness and interconnectedness, the cosmic panorama of life and death and rebirth that the ordinary ego is too myopic and desperate, too greedy or clutching, to notice. With this altered sight, the preoccupation with what we've lost imperceptibly alchemizes into gratitude for what we've been given: for the gift of the beloved. For the gift of life itself.

Gratitude comes from seeing through the eyes of grief. We can stop clinging to life and just live it gratefully.

## A Universal Journey

Many have made the journey of grief, which, despite cultural variations, is a universal experience. It is reassuring to read about the ways that others have traversed this rough terrain.

*A Grief Observed* is a beautiful book detailing the inner journey of C. S. Lewis in the aftermath of his wife's death from cancer. It was amazing for me to read this book after Aaron's death and to see the parallels between

Lewis's journey and my own, despite the obvious differences in time, culture, and the nature of the loss.

For Lewis, the first phase of grief, the shattering, is reflected in the collapse of his religious faith like a house of cards.[1] He examines this collapse and begins to distinguish between authentic faith and wishful thinking. "If I really cared, as I thought I did, about the sorrows of the world, I should not have been so overwhelmed when my own sorrow came."[2] Here Lewis's ego is upbraided for its narrow narcissism. As aware of the pain of the world as he was, his awareness was limited. Grief opens him up to the sorrows of the world in a new way.

Lewis observes the *Why me?* phase of the ego's shattering with a remarkable lack of sentimentality. His bitter anguish is short-lived and moves seamlessly into the expansive phase, which is described with this same candor and clarity. Lewis comes to feel the presence of his wife, Joy, not as a dramatic mystical union with the dead but as a matter-of-fact meeting, like getting a telephone call or a wire from her. He simply has a sense of her presence, "a chuckle in the darkness."[3] This matter-of-factness is remarkably similar to how I experienced Aaron's presence the day I buried his body and beheld his radiant spirit, gazing down at me from the heavens, reassuring me that he was all right.

In the end, the alchemy of grief brings Lewis to an expansive gratitude for Joy's presence in his life, as well as a transformed spirituality, informed not just by theological belief but by direct experience. He ends his journal in a state of surrender, at peace with his loss.

## The Value of Grief

I am well aware that meetings beyond the body are not everyone's story in the aftermath of profound loss. (Though it might be a much wider experience than we know. Somewhere, I read that approximately 20 percent of respondents to a national survey believed that they had communicated in some manner with the dead; and more than 80 percent accepted that such communication was possible.) No two grief journeys are exactly alike. Each journey has its own way of unfolding, its own gifts.

These gifts are not possible if the alchemy of grief is aborted. In a culture in which death is desacralized and treated as the enemy at the gates, to be warded off at any cost, grief itself is suspect as a "tainted" emotion, and the grieving process is seen in a pathological light.

According to the fourth edition of the *Diagnostic and Statistical Manual of Psychiatric Disorders* (the bible of the mental health profession, known as DSM-IV for short) bereavement is a condition in which sadness, insomnia, poor appetite, and weight loss are expected "normal" grief reactions. Other "symptoms," such as moving slowly and with less animation ("psychomotor retardation'), functioning at a lower level ("marked functional impairment"), even visions or voices of the dead ("hallucinatory experiences") are considered "normal" in a state of bereavement. But not for long—for two months, to be precise. Should these "symptoms" persist beyond the two-month cut-off point, the diagnosis of "major depressive disorder" is warranted.[4] So, if two months after your mother dies, you're not up to par and fully functioning, if you still have "symptoms" of sadness, sleeplessness, or suppressed appetite, or if you're still hearing or seeing her spirit, head straight for the shrink's office and stock up on antidepressants (perhaps with a little antipsychotic medication thrown in for good measure).

This is not the alchemical approach to grief. If bereavement is normal, why call the common experiences of grief "symptoms"? Symptoms of what? Of loss? Is loss a pathology?

This way of thinking about grief wants to knock out the "symptoms" quickly, so that you won't have to undergo the often prolonged process of transformation through grief. Not everyone wants to go through such a process, certainly. But institutional psychiatry's bias against loss, death, grief, and darkness in general is part of what has conditioned us to see grief as a "deviation" from life rather than as a normal part of it. The pathology model makes the universal emotion of grief into a psychiatric problem.

The gift that grief offers us is the capacity to see deeply into the way things are. Life is limited. We are here for a short time. Grief asks us to know this, not only in a disembodied, cerebral way, but in the marrow of our bones—to look into the reality of death and loss without our usual egoic blinders on. The alchemical gift of gratitude comes from looking into the face of death, not from turning away.

It would be a mistake, however, to think of the alchemy of grief as a linear process: A plus B equals C. Loss plus grief equals gratitude. This is not the way it works. One doesn't "do" grief and then get to the other side, where one is "done" with it. Grief takes different forms—from the most acute phases to the painfulness of "anniversary" days, which, even years after the death, come upon us suddenly, and with great force. Every mid-October for several years, often unawares, I would feel a kind of spiritual chill, along with the colder weather, as Aaron's birthday approached. On

October 25, the chill would crystallize into a day of pure grief. Then it would fade.

After seven years, I noticed a change. The blessings of Aaron's birth and death had somehow "set in," and I began to anticipate Aaron's birthday with a kind of joy. Roger and I decided to celebrate the day with our two daughters. We'd buy a small cake with "Happy Birthday, Aaron" written on it (no age) and a flower ornament. We'd toast our glasses of grape juice champagne and drink to Aaron's happiness and peace—and to our own. We'd go around the table and say what we were grateful for that day. Usually it was the simple things: each other, the beautiful color of the leaves in fall, our friends. The transformation of grief to gratitude was thus ritualized. But it took considerably longer than two months to get to this. The "resolution" of grief and the transformation through it are not the same process.

My advice to all readers who have grieved, are grieving, or will one day grieve a major loss: Throw out the psychiatric manual! Do it in your own way, in your own time. You can't run at someone else's pace. The alchemy of grief is not a timed, linear process. Grief comes and goes, ebbs and flows like the tide—but without the predictability. One doesn't get to the other side at some particular moment, so much as notice that the landscape is changing. Where it was winter, it is now spring. Spring is slow to come. There is a long, slow thaw. The buds come in imperceptibly. And then one day: glory! It's all blooming—the full, spectacular array of leaves and flowers, the panoply of nature's beauty. One can see and smell and feel life pulsing everywhere.

## The Grief of Lost Relationships

The grief journey is not always a response to physical death. The loss of a primary relationship through separation or divorce is a common experience that can become an alchemical journey. In my experience, people grieving about a lost relationship are eager to share their grief stories and need to know that even devastating relationship losses can be healed and can usher in unexpected gifts. Here are two such stories.

### DIANE'S STORY: GRIEF AND SELF-BIRTH

Diane came to therapy because her marriage was in trouble. She and her husband Dick were in couples therapy. Dick wanted sex to be as it had been in the honeymoon phase of their relationship and despaired of its ever being that good again. Diane felt she had bent herself to accommodate

Dick's demands for exciting and frequent sex, but that this had only alienated her from him and from herself.

In the first session with me, Diane said she felt as if she was "opening a Pandora's box" full of the pieces of herself that she had put away to please and placate Dick.

In the next seven months, the communication and emotional intimacy between Diane and Dick improved. Diane felt ready for a new, more mutually satisfying sexual exchange with her husband; but Dick was even more convinced that their glory days were over and it was time to move on. In the middle of therapy, Dick decided to leave Diane and moved out of the house. Diane was devastated. How could Dick not want to work this out? How could this thirteen-year relationship come to an end just when she'd begun to think it was most possible to fix it? She was overcome with wave upon wave of grief.

Part of my job as a therapist is simply to accompany the client in her dark emotions. In the storm of grief, everyone needs someone who can be present without fear of being overwhelmed. Ultimately, therapy is a relationship in which the connection between client and therapist is the medium of transformation. Through this connection, and the therapist's ability to model a fearless approach to difficult emotions, the mourner is empowered to go through a healing process at a greater depth than is possible in isolation.

In this journey, everyone has a particular creative gift that helps him or her through. Diane's gift was her vision: her ability to "see" her emotional process. Her images had the vividness, power, and clarity of dreams, but she could see them while awake. She didn't need me to practice any particular technique to help her get to these images, though it was always helpful for her to close her eyes and breathe consciously. Diane's first image of herself after Dick's abrupt departure was of moving through the narrow part of a funnel packed with shit. The passage was dense and suffocating. She could see very little, but dimly, she could sense that, at the other end, there was a light and a wide opening.

This was Diane's image of rebirth. Many people grieving or recovering from trauma have these kinds of images. Always, I encourage them to let the image be and allow it to guide them, rather than to mentally manipulate it to something more pleasant. These images, from my experience, move organically in the healing process of emotional alchemy.

In the next few months, Diane's image of the funnel continued. She sometimes awoke at night choking and in a panic. With encouragement, she was able to breathe through it, to let her body follow its process rather than distract herself from it. As she did so, her anger began to surface. She found herself railing at Dick, though he was no longer there: "You never fought for our marriage!" She saw herself stomping her feet and roaring. Allowing these angry feelings and images required great courage for Diane, who was a gentle soul and had been taught to suppress her anger.

A short while later she noticed that the funnel was now aerated and she could breathe more easily. Gradually, the stuff in the funnel became less dense, more movable. She saw herself just two inches from the top of the canal, ready to emerge.

Diane's grief journey was not, however, a steady progression. Even as her funnel image moved toward imminent birth, she saw herself at the bottom of a sinkhole, twenty to thirty feet down. *Where am I? How did I get here? How do I get out?* she asked herself, stunned and shocked at the bottom of the pit.

Then one day, an image of a rope ladder appeared. This took her by surprise. She wondered where the rope ladder came from and how it got there. Exploring this in therapy, she realized that this was the ladder of support that was provided by loving friends and family during the most intense period of Diane's mourning for her lost marriage. Diane had always been a very independent woman. Now she was learning: *I don't have to do this alone.* This sense of interconnectedness and the permission to need help were unexpected gifts that Diane received in the course of her journey through grief.

Shortly after the rope ladder image, and seven months after she first started therapy, the funnel was transformed. Diane emerged from the narrow tube, surrounded by color and light. This was the proverbial light at the end of the tunnel. She came through, her arms shaky but raised high to the heavens, having given birth to herself. She felt more vital and more alive than ever before. As a bonus, the migraine headaches that had plagued her since childhood were gone.

Diane's grief was a journey as treacherous and risky as any unprotected trek into the raw wilderness, a process that took great courage and that enabled her to master her sorrow, fear, and anger. This process, for many women, is often a journey of return to those parts of themselves that have been lost in a culture antagonistic to women's development or in a relationship in which they have given their power over to another. The alchemy of grief is consummated by a grateful rediscovery of the surrendered or lost self.

So it was for Diane. "My heart is broken," she said. "My emotions have been challenging. But my life is better. I'm grateful for finding myself."

## SARAH'S STORY: UNFINISHED GRIEF

If we are lucky, we mourn our losses. Mourning is a privilege we don't always have. Under conditions of war or other social dislocations, mourning is often impossible. Children who lose a parent are often discouraged from grieving by well-meaning adults who do not allow them to attend the funeral, or clergy who admonish them to be of good cheer because God has taken their parent for a good reason and they will be reunited in heaven. Many people live their entire lives never having fully mourned the death of a parent or a child, never confronting the losses of their early years.

The dark emotions offer us a passage, a way to heal and liberate ourselves from the past. Unfinished grief lives in our cells. Thus it is never too late to do griefwork. Healing is always an option. The body, when we listen closely to its story, is the place in which the alchemy of the dark emotions is rooted. Transformation is never out of reach, because the body holds what needs to be healed and offers it to us when we open to its wisdom—a miracle!

I am privileged to witness this miracle every day in my work as a therapist. One of the most miraculous of these was Sarah's story. A striking, gentle, and compassionate woman of forty-six, Sarah came to see me at the end of a five-year relationship with Barbara, the only serious relationship of her adult life. In one of our early sessions, she said, "I realize that my grief about losing Barbara is grief about everything in my life."

This is true for everyone. Grief in the present taps into the deep reservoir of grief from the past. In Sarah's case, this grief was extensive. Her infancy was marked by neglect, her childhood by abandonment, and her adolescence by abuse. Sarah's mother married because she "had to" (being pregnant with Sarah's older brother) and took care of her two children minimally until Sarah was six years old. Then, one day, her mother disappeared, never to return. Sarah was raised by an aunt and uncle until she was thirteen. During these seven years, she was initiated into sex by her uncle, who had no trouble making her comply because Sarah was a "good girl." At thirteen, she relocated and lived once again with her biological father, who had remarried. The sexual abuse to which she'd become accustomed took another form with her father and continued for the next two years.

Sarah had spent several years in therapy working on the trauma of this sexual abuse, but her grief for her absent mother was untouched. Her story of her mother was skeletal: "She had me, she didn't want to be a mother, and she left. She chose herself over her children—running away with a man and leaving us behind."

Sarah kept a few paltry tokens, the only reminders that she'd had a mother at all, in a "mother box"—a pair of gloves, an earring, a scarf. Everything else was lost. Her only memory of her mother was of being four years old and running toward her with a bouquet of daffodils, freshly picked, which she offered as a gift. She remembered running and then suddenly stopping in her tracks, ashamed, feeling as though she'd intruded upon someone who didn't want her to be there. Her bright yellow daffodils were not received. This unreceived gift of herself and the big hole it left in her soul was painful; yet having this memory was better than the feeling of having no mother at all.

Mother loss was the unhealed wound of Sarah's life. Breaking up with Barbara opened up this gaping wound. It had been stitched over and made bearable; now the stitching came undone, preparing Sarah for a more complete healing.

When I worked with Sarah, I always started with a few minutes of meditation and deep breathing, followed by focusing on the sensations in her body. Fortunately, almost a decade of sexual abuse had not impaired Sarah's bodily awareness, as it often does for others. She was acutely conscious of her body's signals. Like Diane's images, Sarah's bodily awareness was the particular gift we could tap into, the medium of her healing. After the meditation and breathing, Sarah would immediately find a place in her body that was the focus for her "dropping into feelings."

In one of our earlier sessions, she felt a tense ball in the center of her diaphragm. Focusing on this sensation, she found her entire body tingling. The words *Why didn't you take care of me?* emerged, from a place deeper than thought. As she said the words, she experienced an acute pain in her left arm, which she associated with "the smallest part of me." Here, in Sarah's body, was the neglected and abandoned infant. Sarah was flooded with images of herself as a child locked in a closet and then, going further back, as a baby who cried for someone who wasn't there.

In the next session, Sarah arrived carrying a picture of herself as a winsome, chubby baby. Looking at the photograph, she felt a kind of disgust. "I don't like this baby," she told me. When I asked her why, she said, "This baby is grouchy."

For the next few months, Sarah found herself both wanting to be rid of the baby and wanting to hold it. She gave the picture of the baby to me and asked me to hold it until she was ready to take it back. This unlovable "grouchy baby" became the focus of Sarah's lifelong grief. The baby was the unattended inner child, a source of self-contempt and shame.

Each time we worked with her bodily sensations, Sarah experienced the familiar pain in her left arm. The pain brought her information she could not have pieced together with her rational mind. Gradually, by staying with the arm pain and the imagery of the grouchy baby that it conjured up, Sarah began to shape a fuller story of her mother's abandonment: "My mother wanted to take care of me, but she didn't feel she could."

Sarah was beginning to piece together a meaningful narrative where there had been only emptiness. With this emergent narrative, she began to experience some compassion for the baby: "Being uncared for could make any baby grouchy!"

The turning point came when Sarah asked me to support her painful left arm. As I held her arm and she scanned her body, Sarah felt all the grief of her infancy and childhood coalesce into a howl. Then there was "a flicker of a shadow," a fleeting image that Sarah could barely catch. Focusing in on it, she saw a face peering down at her. The face wore glasses and had a flat expression. "Mommy!" Sarah cried, "Why did you leave?"

This was the core of Sarah's grief—and with it came the first and only image of her mother's face. Having that image, and a story to go with it, was the completion of Sarah's work. She had had a mother. Her mother's abandonment was not simply an uncaring act; it had some measure of love for the baby she didn't feel she could care for. This mother now had a face. Having a fuller story and seeing this maternal face, Sarah could finally let go of the ancient grief she'd been harboring in her body for forty years.

In one of our last sessions, Sarah brought me a bouquet of yellow daffodils. I received them with great joy and returned her picture of the grouchy baby, which Sarah was now ready to take back and to hold.

It was a privilege to know Sarah, a wise and beautiful soul, and to be present to her amazing grief journey. The waters of grief had become redemptive for her.

These were Sarah's words about the grief's alchemy: "Our relationship has been like a bridge over the painful waters of my lifelong sorrows. A bridge that allowed me to stand, look down and see the waters clearly, and then to drink them in until they changed to a life-giving source."

## Unredemptive Grief in the World

The spiritual fulfillment of redemptive grief is the capacity to feel a vibrant gratitude for life. This can happen when there is a complete shattering, expansion, and surrender. It is because we do not encourage such a process in our culture that the gift of grief is too often aborted.

It has been said that we live in a culture that denies death. The conventional wisdoms related to grief are, at best, contradictory: Grieve but don't show it too much, especially in public. Too little grief is cold but too much is unacceptable. Get your grieving over as quickly as possible and move on. Yet a peaceful acceptance of death looks suspiciously like a lack of love for the departed.

Training as a psychotherapist, I learned that the grieving person has six months to feel sad after a major loss, after which the grief response is no longer "normal" and merits the diagnosis of clinical depression. The current diagnostic manual has reduced that time frame to only two months. Dictums such as these only discourage emotional alchemy. The prevailing psychiatric view of grief is based on the assumption that the ego as we know it is the one and only ground of consciousness. With no awareness or acknowledgment of the spiritual dimensions of loss and death, the psychiatric view sees "resolution" as a process of the conventional ego's readaptation to life after loss, not as a transformative opening to a profoundly new sense of self.

Religious blandishments as well can be used to discourage the alchemy of grief. While emotion-phobia is not necessarily integral to religious perspectives on death, any religious dogma can be used to bypass the full and conscious experience of grief's power. Exhortations to forgo grief because death is "God's will" are often heard when we most need to be encouraged to go through grief's difficult passage.

In these ways, the terror of death and loss in a materialist, positivist culture, on the one hand, and the glib consolations of clerics, on the other, can be impediments to the alchemy of grief.

Our world is haunted by large-scale unredemptive grief (I prefer the term "unredemptive grief" to "unresolved grief"). Attempts to defend against grief's power through conscious acts of suppression as well as unconscious avoidance and denial guarantee that the toxified energy of grief will emerge in displaced, unrecognizable, sometimes violent or destructive forms. We see and hear and read about these manifestations of unredemptive grief every day in our world.

For example, Palestinians and Israelis, two chronically grieving peoples fighting over their piece of turf in the Middle East, are destroying the possibilities of peaceful coexistence through their inability, on the leadership level as well as on the ground, to allow a redemptive process of grief that would enlarge their respective points of view and lift them out of the national victim egos in which they are both tragically stuck.

Unredemptive grief poses numerous dangers for the individual and society. It is passed on from generation to generation, guaranteeing that the various individual, interpersonal, and social ills that spring from such grief will be ongoing. The problem of unredemptive grief becomes more urgent in our time than ever before. Our largely denied and unacknowledged sorrow about the silent destruction of the earth produces more and more symptoms. These include documented higher incidences of depression, anxiety, loneliness, boredom, violence, drug abuse, and malaise in the generation growing into adulthood in our era.

At no time in history has it been more crucial for us, as individuals, as nations, and as a species, to honor grief and learn its alchemy.

## Emotional Exercises for the Alchemy of Grief

For the exercises in this and the next two chapters, as well as the comprehensive set of emotional exercises in part four, you'll need an "emotional alchemy journal" in which to record what you experience and learn.

### STEP 1. INTENTION: TO GRIEVE IS TO HEAL

If you're grieving the death of a loved one, you need to bring a clear intention to this process. Don't let anyone—family, friends, doctors, psychiatrists—tell you how or when to grieve. Let this be a time that you trust your heart to guide you.

What is your best or highest intention with regard to the grief in your life? Spend some time reflecting on this. How can you grieve this loss and honor it, while still nurturing yourself?

Frame your intentions carefully and write them down in your emotional alchemy journal as clearly as you can. Waking each morning, take a deep breath and remind yourself of your intention. Do the same before you go to bed.

## STEP 2. AFFIRMATION: THE VALUE OF GRIEF

Affirming the value of grief may seem counterproductive or counterintuitive in a culture that values "moving on" from loss as quickly as possible. Many people judge others for the manner in which they are grieving. If you've had a negative, judgmental attitude toward others who are grieving, this is a clue as to your own condemnation of this emotion, your internalized emotion-phobia.

On one side of your emotional alchemy journal, write down every "negative" thought you have about grief and sorrow, about grieving too much or too little, or about how you express your grief. Example: Crying in front of others is shameful. Or: Thinking you don't want to live after someone dies proves you're weak.

Then, on the other side of the page, write a set of affirmations in your own words, about the value of grieving. Example: Mourning is a universal expression of interconnection and loss. It's wise to feel sorrow and express it. My grief is a measure of my love.

Repeat these affirmations as needed, as a reminder to give yourself permission to grieve. (See chapter 10, exercises 2–4, for additional suggestions about affirmations for grief.)

## STEP 3. BODILY SENSATION

Grief can be a very depleting emotion—physically and mentally. Soothing is much needed right now. Start with the soothing breath. (See chapter 10, exercise 6). This form of conscious breathing will bring you sustenance when you are faltering or feeling anguished, empty, or fatigued.

Also, see chapter 10, exercises 7–9, for additional suggestions about the mindful experience of grief in the body.

## STEP 4. CONTEXTUALIZATION: WIDENING YOUR STORY OF GRIEF

In the alchemy of the dark emotions, finding the larger context of your pain is an essential step. But it may be very hard for you to see the "larger picture" at this time. You may be hurting too much. Perhaps all you feel is longing and anguish. Perhaps you're just numb. Perhaps the meaning of this death or loss is absolutely incomprehensible to you at this time. Perhaps it just feels senseless and tragic.

Don't force finding a larger context for your grief. Telling yourself that "it was his time to go" is only reassuring if you can really believe this to the marrow of your bones. And no one can tell you this but yourself. Don't let other people's contextualizations get in the way of your own grief process.

Example: If friends try to reassure you by saying things like, "Everyone has an appointed time for death. It's all for the best," or "It was her karma," or any other universalizing reassurances, make sure that it's okay with you to hear these things. If you find them comforting, then fine. If you find them off-putting, or feel that these kinds of remarks only make you feel worse, don't hesitate to let people know that these kinds of statements are not helpful to you at this time. (Most people who care about you will appreciate your candor.)

Give yourself time, and trust that you will find some way to make meaning of this loss. (If you find this impossible to even contemplate, you might want to make it one of your intentions.) Mentally place yourself in a wider circle of those who grieve and contemplate grief as a universal emotion. At the same time, find a way to get support from others who have endured or are in the process of grieving similar losses. Such support has been shown to be literally life-saving.

See chapter 10, exercises 13–17, for more suggestions about contextualizing grief.

## STEP 5. THE WAY OF NON-ACTION: MINDFUL GRIEVING

The way of non-action is allowing sorrow to be sorrow. "Medicate, distract, and avoid" is not a recipe for alchemy. But be kind to yourself if you need to do any of these things. Distraction is an important balance to grief's cruel shattering. Find simple, soothing ways to distract yourself: Call friends. Watch an innocuous, nonviolent or humorous movie. Take a walk in the sun with someone you trust.

Medication usually interferes with grief's alchemy. But if you feel acutely suicidal or unable to get out of bed for many months, medication may be an ally for a period of time. If you do seek medication, make sure you find a trustworthy psychopharmacologist or family physician who has some expertise in antidepressant medication. Primary care providers may prescribe too soon and in unnecessarily high doses because they are not well informed about the judicious use of antidepressants. Whoever prescribes should be willing to talk to you at length about how you feel about taking medication, how you respond to medication once you start, and about potential and actual side effects. They should also be willing and able to talk to you about your grief. If they can't do this, find someone who will.

As an alternative to medication, try meditation!

Practice mindfulness meditation and emotion meditation. (See chapter 10, exercises 18 and 19.) Try to make a sacred space and time for these practices each day or as frequently as you can, for a specified amount of time. Three minutes a day is better than no minutes.

Also: Try the heartflow meditation (chapter 10, exercise 29). Circulating your breath through the heart furthers the process of allowing your grief to go through its various aspects of shattering, expanding, and surrendering. Let your heart-breath be a steady, daily practice if you can. It will move the process along safely.

STEP 6. THE WAY OF ACTION: DON'T LET YOUR GRIEF STOP YOU
Grief, like despair, invites stillness. One would think that "action" is either irrelevant or impossible. But certain kinds of actions can help, if they are done authentically and when you are ready.

One kind of action is to not let tears or visible signs of grief stop you from going where you want to go, doing what you need to do, or talking to whomever you need to talk to. Give yourself the permission to break through your conventional patterns of relationship and take some risks to connect.

I remember a tough decision I had to make after Aaron died. Around the time of his death, the parent prenatal group that I had been attending while pregnant was holding its postpartum get-together. This would be a gathering of proud new moms and dads with their new two- and three-month-old babies. I got the invitation and cried. Of course, there was no reason for me to go: I had no baby to show. I would have to call the new mom who was hosting the gathering to R.S.V.P. But every time I picked up the phone to make the call, I found myself frozen in my grief. The thought of not going was agonizing. So was the thought of going. It didn't make sense to go; and yet, after thinking about it, I felt that attending with a picture of Aaron would be better than not going at all. It would be a way of saying: yes, I had this baby, and he was beautiful, and he will always be my baby. Not going would erase the fact that he ever lived. Then I thought in horror, how can I do this to this group of new parents? In their moment of joy, to bring the smell of death into such a happy occasion?

In the end, I chose to go ahead, because I knew that staying home would push me into a profound sense of isolation. I called and explained my predicament and was welcomed to the reunion. I showed my pictures of Aaron and spoke his name, described his personality and his spirit. I enjoyed, with a poignant ache, the newborn beauties that had just arrived on the planet. I left early, came home, and breathed a sigh of relief. I had not let my grief stop me, and this felt like a small triumph.

Grieving alone is dangerous. So is allowing the shame or fear of grief and/or death stop you. Grief has a tremendous power. When we submerge it in avoidance, we can't use it for spiritual growth. Allow grief's power to propel you. You may find that you want to do things you've never done before, like taking a watercolor or writing class. Don't let any conventions or prohibitions about grief stop you. Now is the time to take good care of yourself and indulge your authentic needs and wishes. They will guide you well.

STEP 7. THE WAY OF SURRENDER: LET GRIEF FLOW

The simplest exercise for the way of surrender to grief is through prayer. You don't have to be religious or believe in God to pray. You just need the intention to commune with something larger than your ego. The only requirement is the need to receive help.

By prayer, I don't mean reciting words by rote. Prayer is an utterance straight from the heart into the universe. Even if you are not a theist, you can pray so long as you can let yourself open your heart and invite the spirits in. The spirits don't have to be literal entities that you believe in; this can be a metaphor for opening yourself to the universe, to what is, to being alive. To experience emotional alchemy, you have to get out of ego psychology and into something more expansive. Prayer helps you do this. When you pray, you get out of your own way and let something larger guide you.

See chapter 10, exercise 31, for the three basic prayers: *Help me. Thank you. I surrender.*

Start with asking for help. Every grieving person needs help. No one can do this alone. The purpose of grief is to teach you this wisdom: that we are all interconnected, and in our interconnectedness is our hope and our solace. You may want help from friends, family, spouses. Sometimes these people may be there for you. And invariably they will disappoint you as well, because the need for help and solace at this time is inordinate. There is no one person who can fill this need. This is one reason prayer is so important. Pray to God, Goddess, Higher Power, the One, the Source, Yahweh, the Divine, the Sacred. If none of these words feels right, pray to the Mystery. Pray for help.

And then open your heart to receive the help you've asked for. Open your ears to hear the response.

*Thank you* seems like an impossible prayer when your heart is shattered and broken. And yet, now is a good time to remember what you are thankful for. Think of how grateful you are for those who are still alive and who help hold you up at this time. Think of your life: Are you grateful for it? Or are you in too much pain to feel gratitude? Only pray *thank you* for what you're authentically thankful for. Even if it's only a small, minute thing. Example: I'm thankful for this bed in which I can sleep.

*I surrender* is another prayer hard to speak at this time. "In Thy Will be my peace" is not a prayer that comes easily. Try saying: *I accept what is now and what is to come* and see what happens in your heart. Then just accept the response, whatever it is. Be mindful of your constrictions, your expansions. Give yourself permission for all of it.

Try also whatever creative outlets for grief you may be drawn to: writing, singing, chanting, drawing, dancing. Creativity is the great healer. (See chapter 10, exercises 25 to 28.)

Finally, remember: Even when the gates of heaven are shut to prayer, they are open to tears.

# 6   *From Despair to Faith*

> He hath set me in dark places as those who are
> dead forever. He hath made a fence around me and
> against me, that I may not go out; He hath made
> my captivity heavy. Yea, and when I have cried and
> entreated, He hath shut out my prayer . . . He hath
> thwarted my steps . . . and broken me into pieces.
> —SAINT JOHN OF THE CROSS,
> *The Dark Night of the Soul*

> There is no sun without shadow, and it is essential
> to know the night.
> —ALBERT CAMUS, "The Myth of Sisyphus"

## The Landscape of Despair

For almost three decades, I've listened to people in despair. Despair is the most common dark emotion that people bring to psychotherapy, in the form now known as "clinical depression." This is how they describe their emotional state: *I've descended into a dark abyss. There's an empty hole inside me. I'm trapped in this dark place. I don't feel I'm really alive. I'm wandering through a desert. Nothing makes sense.* The imagery of descent, stasis, emptiness, captivity, sterility, and darkness vividly communicates the interior landscape of despair as a place of inner paralysis, abject loneliness, spiritual barrenness, and existential meaninglessness.

The word *despair* comes from the Latin root *sperare*, meaning "hope." To despair is to lose all hope; to feel empty and desolate, adrift in a lonely sea, to exist without a sense of purpose or faith, to be disconnected from the flow of life, exiled from a universe of meaning. Despair is a dark weight that will not lift, a deadness at the core. In its stark bleakness, despair is hard to miss; it dominates mind and body, heart and soul. And yet, like the other dark emotions, it can be submerged from awareness for long periods of time and become the emotional substratum of a life or even a culture. Milder despair can be lifted to some extent by a pleasurable or exciting activity or person; relieved, temporarily, by alcohol and other substances that in the long run only intensify it. But in its more extreme manifestations, despair is not easily distracted. People in despair find it difficult, if not impossible, to soothe themselves. The wretched self-loathing of despair, one of its hallmarks, is inconsolable. *I'm a failure, I'm a bad person, I'm nothing.* These self-hating thoughts both breed despair and fuel it.

Despair is a profound dispiritedness, a fatiguing emotion that saps the life force. The smallest action may seem to require a gargantuan effort. When despair is in full sway, there is an overwhelming sense of futility. In the Greek myth, Sisyphus, with great effort, rolls a large rock up a mountain. At the top, the rock, of its own inertia, rolls back down again. Doomed to roll the rock up the mountain over and over again to no avail—this is what life often feels like to those in extreme despair.

"There is but one truly serious philosophical problem," said Camus in the famous first sentence of his essay "The Myth of Sisyphus," "and that is suicide." When life is without meaning and all effort feels futile, suicide is an ever-present possibility, beckoning as a way out of the no-exit pain and emptiness. "To be or not to be?" is the question that many people in despair ask themselves at the lowest point of their descent. In the midst of despair, death has its allure, but it is a cold exit from an unredemptive universe.

Wracked with self-loathing and hopelessness, the spirit in despair has gone down to the underworld where existence is a state of death-in-life.

When my daughter Anna was a little girl, she loved all kinds of animals. Our home was a menagerie. We had two caged rats, Blackie and Bozo, eyed with much interest by our two cats, Zuckie and Mojo. Our amphibian was a frog named Froggie, and our reptile population included Max the turtle and a garter snake named Sam.

The most fascinating of these creatures for both me and Anna was the snake. Sam was a bright green with darker markings. We never did find a way to detect snake gender and decided, by fiat, to make Sam a girl and give her a masculine-sounding name that could also pass as a nickname for Samantha. Sam (whose gender identity was no doubt terribly confused) slid around her cage gracefully, looping in and out of the holes in the wooden structure in her fish-tank home. She slept a lot but always seemed interested in being taken out to have a look around. Every few days, Sam ate three to five small guppies for dinner. We'd watch in amazed, horrified fascination as she swallowed each fish whole and the bulge slid down her throat. (Do snakes have throats?) Sam was active and energetic. She loved to be touched and enjoyed circling herself around Anna's neck like an emerald necklace as Anna did her chores.

Then, one day, Sam became more subdued than usual. She wasn't swooshing around in her snake house. She seemed sluggish, and her appetite was suppressed. She ate poorly and then not at all, the fish lying belly up in Sam's water dish. We worried and watched over her.

After more than a week of this depressed behavior, Sam seemed on her last snake-legs. Her bright green skin, so alive and vibrant, had turned brown and dull. She lay on the floor of the cage, motionless. "She's dead," I thought. Feeling a pang of sorrow that deepened as I thought about announcing the news to Anna, I rushed off to work.

Several hours later, I returned—and Sam was gone! There on the cage bottom was a perfectly formed snakeskin, its zigzag design intact but hollow. The snakeskin lay there, a translucent sculpture—but where was Sam? Taking the top off the cage, I picked up the wooden snake house with its circular holes in which Sam did her morning exercises, and gasped as Sam jutted out of a hole, leaping and slithering around the cage at breakneck speed—more vital and full of energy than when we first took her home from the pet shop. Sam's little red tongue darted in and out of her jaws. Her eyes sparkled. Her skin was a brighter hue of green. Having shed her skin, she was more lively, beautiful, and alert than ever. She was a born-again snake.

Despair's alchemy is this kind of transformation. There is a descent to a state of death in life. We look and feel dead, but something is happening under the skin—if we let it. The mask of the old self is dying—a harbinger of resurrection.

When we're in the throes of despair, a metamorphic process is at work. The call to spiritual death and rebirth in despair can be easily mistaken for a call to suicide. This is when we're likely to reach for a pill—to ease the pain or to do ourselves in. Imagine if the snake thought it was dying when it sloughed off its skin. Imagine if the caterpillar was relieved of its cocoon before it had completed its metamorphic process. The transformation would be aborted.

The dark, enclosed place of the cocoon is necessary for metamorphosis to complete itself.

## Is Despair a Normal Emotion?

> I have taken the pit as my home
> and made my bed in the dark.
> I have called the grave my father;
> and the worm my mother, my sister.
> And where now is my hope?
> — *The Book of Job*

From the Book of Job to the work of T. S. Eliot and Samuel Beckett, from the melancholy of the Old Testament Psalms to the dark nihilism of punk rock music, despair has been a perennial theme in art, literature, poetry, music, and philosophy. Sophocles. Aeschylus. Dante. Shakespeare. Dostoyevsky. Kafka. Van Gogh. Camus. Elie Wiesel. What would their work be without the element of despair? Many of the world's greatest artists and thinkers have pondered this essentially human experience. Even Jesus Christ had his moment of despair while nailed to the cross: "My God, why hast Thou forsaken me?"

While despair is a more complex emotion than either grief or fear, it is altogether human. The youngest person I ever worked with was nine years old, the oldest in her mid-seventies. Both were familiar with despair.

The nine-year-old, a charming girl named Rose, came from a "good" family. She was smart as a whip and had a dry, precocious sense of humor. She loved her family—mom, dad, and younger sister. They lived in a well-to-do suburb of Boston amid backyard gardens and flowering trees. There was no history of mental illness in the family. But Rose was chronically irritable, listless, dejected, and angry. Her gracious, soft-spoken mother couldn't understand why. Her gentle father, whose worst shortcoming was an occasional propensity to panic, was equally bewildered. What's wrong with her? they wanted to know. She was not a victim of incest, child abuse, or neglect. She wanted for nothing. Yet she suffered from a pronounced depression that, according to research, has been increasingly affecting each successive generation since the turn of the twentieth century.[1]

In a workshop on befriending the dark emotions, I met seventy-four-year-old Anne Marie, a white-haired, long-term survivor of incest. As a child, she was locked in a small room and left there whenever she wasn't "a good girl," usually after her father molested her. She remembered sitting in a corner in the room, no bigger than a large closet, gazing at a picture of two young children holding hands while crossing a bridge. In the picture, an angel hovering above them seemed to be watching over the children. She prayed that such an angel would guide her out.

Sitting across from me some sixty years later, Anne Marie told me that somehow her prayers had been answered. She had managed to marry and have two children and to raise them in a loving home. Doing battle with the demon of despair for many years, she had liberated herself from the locked room in her mind. She had conquered despair, on her own, without the help of a psychotherapist or medication. Her greatest accomplishment, as she saw it, was not transmitting the despair of abuse to her children.

Young and old, men and women, rich and poor: Despair afflicts all manner of people. It is a democratic emotion, cutting across lines of race, age, gender, sexual orientation, ethnic and religious affiliation.

Prior to the advent of modern psychology, despair was an expected part of the human condition. It is only in the last several decades, with the ascendancy of psychiatry and the ability to produce psychopharmacological agents that effectively mitigate despair's impact, that we have come to think of it as abnormal. Feeling despair for a prolonged period doesn't mesh with our culture's vision of the good life. In the secular view, God may no longer be in His heaven, but modern science and technology promise to help us feel that all is right with the world. Despair, with its particular combination of desperation, dread, hopelessness, emptiness, helplessness, and sorrow—insisting that we look into the dark side of life—is not in keeping with this cultural ethos.

What's to be done about despair? The question itself comes from a very modern sensibility. In ages past, the answer was simple: Bear it! There was nothing to be done except to seek solace in God. Misery of this kind was a spiritual challenge tended to by the clergy. But with the rise of psychiatry, our culture's story of despair has been rewritten. The word *despair* itself begins to have an archaic ring. We speak instead of "clinical depression"—a mental disorder that can and should be "treated." In the age of Prozac, the feel-good allure of the serotonin boosters, like the "soma" of Huxley's *Brave New World*, appears to make despair obsolete.

This is not my view. Despite its bad reputation and the sense of shame associated with it, despair is a legitimate and eminently human emotion. More than grief and fear, it has a moral and social dimension that calls us to pay attention to and make meaning out of human suffering. *Enter this dark night of the soul*, insists the voice of despair. *Look at the world's pain without your usual protections. Descend to this place of near-annihilation. If you can bear your way through this night with patience, you will be moved to a muscular faith that has looked into the heart of darkness and emerged to affirm life.*

## Despair in the Age of Melancholy

### DESPAIR AND DEPRESSION: WHAT'S THE DIFFERENCE?

"The mass of men lead lives of quiet desperation," said Thoreau. Only in the last fifty years have we come to think of the quiet desperation of despair as a mental illness. William Styron, in his account of his own depression, *Darkness Visible: A Memoir of Madness*, says: "Since antiquity . . . chroniclers of the human spirit have been wrestling with a vocabulary that might give proper expression to the desolation of melancholia."[2]

That vocabulary, in our time, has become entirely medical. What the ancient Romans called "melancholia" has been renamed "depressive disorder." There's a spectrum of these "disorders," including "major depressive disorder," "major depressive episode," "depressive personality disorder," and "dysthymic disorder." Taken together, these conditions are so widespread that depression has been called "the common cold of mental illness."

Currently, it is estimated that 20 million people in the United States suffer from some kind of depression. This number records only those who are diagnosed by a physician or psychiatrist; it does not include the millions who self-medicate their depressions with alcohol and drug dependence, and others who have not been psychiatrically evaluated.

Another estimate: 100 million people worldwide are depressed. One wonders how such a number was arrived at. Have a team of psychiatrists gone to the site of every civil war, military dictatorship, ethnic-cleansing locale, refugee camp, war zone, inner-city ghetto, every home where girls and boys are secretly sexually molested, and asked: Do you have a lowered mood? trouble sleeping? problems with sexual desire? increased or decreased appetite? Do you ever think of killing yourself? These are the kinds of questions doctors and therapists ask to determine if someone is depressed. I imagine that most people in the world with very real causes for their despair are not too likely to appear for psychiatric evaluation. These statistics probably underestimate the pervasive reality of despair in the world.

Two large government-sponsored studies begun in the 1970s document a serious rise in depression in the United States over the past century.[3] Another study, a massive survey of parents and teachers, shows a worldwide trend in the younger generation: Each successive generation is more lonely and depressed than the one before.[4] The rise in depression is not limited to this country but is a global phenomenon. Gerald Klerman, a prominent psychiatrist, has referred to our era as "The Age of Melancholy."

If so, melancholy is not a mood we tolerate. Joanna Macy—Buddhist teacher, deep ecologist, and social activist—speaks of the "social taboos against despair."[5] Just as fear is equated with cowardice, despair is often seen as a profound failure of character, will, spirit, and faith. I believe this is one reason we currently prefer to see despair as a medical condition. In a culture that condemns despair, it's hard to look at this emotion in a way that honors its dignity, power, and wisdom. Viewing it as an illness beyond our control, we don't have to feel to blame for it. This lessens despair's stigma and gives us some hope.

Are despair and depression simply different words for the same condition?

According to the *Diagnostic and Statistical Manual of Mental Disorders*, 4th edition, depression is a "mood disorder." The manual doesn't actually define "mood disorder," assuming that this entity is a primary medical fact, a condition as empirical as a case of measles or a broken leg. The unquestioned assumption is that the normal mood is a "good" (pleasant) mood. Sunny, optimistic, upbeat cheeriness is the measure of how a normal person feels or should feel (one can't help wondering how many psychiatrists live up to this norm) about life, most of the time. It is not normal to feel sad, dejected, or hopeless, say the experts, for more than two weeks at a time. These timelines are nothing if not arbitrary, but appearing in a diagnostic and statistical manual, they attain the ring of hard science. In this framework, the dark emotions are, by definition, pathological mental processes.

As we've seen, according to psychiatric experts, grief devolves from an "adjustment reaction" into the more serious territory of clinical depression if it lasts more than two months. Apparently, this was Job's problem. According to a paperback book on depression now being sold at the local drugstore, Job's symptoms were "loss of interest, social withdrawal, self-deprecation, and insomnia."[6] (One can't help wondering how it was determined that Job suffered these symptoms for more than two months.) The modern take on the monumental suffering of Job is that he had "a disease that can be traced back to antiquity."

Sanity, it has been said, is the consensus of the majority. In our culture, the consensus is that the mask of comedy is normal; the tragic is sick. Even "dutiful self-denial" (as opposed to a more carefree and self-indulgent lifestyle) is viewed as a symptom of a mood disorder called dysthymia—a low-grade, chronic depression. Just a generation ago, dutiful self-denial was considered a mark of good character. It's still what many parents in many cultures (and even some today in our own culture) expect of themselves as an important aspect of good parenting. Priests and nuns learn dutiful self-denial as part of their training in the proper worship of God. But in the God-is-dead secular humanism of contemporary psychiatric jargon, this character trait is a symptom of a mood disorder.

Ideas like these perfectly exemplify the bias against the dark emotions in our culture. This bias is even more interesting in the context of research studies showing that depressives tend to both remember and predict events more accurately than nondepressives.[7] The more gloomy predictions of the depressed are more on target than those of their more cheerful counterparts. The optimists, it seems, tend to "edit" reality, leaving out the painful bits, while the depressives are more realistic. The distortion of optimism is based on the fact that people who wish to remain cheerful often avoid or deny the darker side of life.

This emotional cutoff is the rock upon which the norm of ideal mental health is built.

From the standpoint of almost every culture and time except this era in the United States, the psychiatric approach to despair would be seen as naive or nutty. The idea that only cheeriness is normal has a distinctly Brave New World feel. It's no wonder that despair, the darkest of the dark emotions, is virtually taboo in our society. Feeling this bad in a feel-good culture is transgressive; it goes against the grain in a culture of denial.

With its medical cast, declaring depression a disease does for those in despair what declaring alcoholism a disease did for alcoholics: It removes the taboo against talking about it and the stigma of "having" it. While I'm all for destigmatizing any form of human suffering, I'm concerned that the medicalization of despair has, at the same time, created a reified "condition" about which people have become altogether disempowered. If you're depressed, go see your doctor, and he or she will give you a pill. Paradoxically, this way of thinking has lowered our affect tolerance for despair. And this lowered tolerance, in my view, actually predisposes us to depression.

Depression, as I see it, is unalchemized despair. It's what happens when despair becomes chronically stuck in the body. Depression is certainly not a medical condition in the way that heart disease is. Rather, what we call depression is a culturally acceptable concept for chronic, toxified despair. This is not to deny that the thing we call depression takes a very real toll on too many lives. There is no doubt that the pervasive and rising incidence of depression in our country, and perhaps in the world, is a serious mental-health crisis. The problem is that the way that we think about depression makes the alchemy of despair next to impossible and, in its way, contributes to the escalation of this condition in our time.

When I see someone who calls herself depressed, I ask a series of questions such as: What do you mean by depressed? What are the various emotions in this "depression"? Is depression the same as feeling sad? What does it have to do with anger? Is there any relationship between your depression and things in your life that make you feel disempowered or without a voice?

In the context of today's take on depression, these kinds of questions no longer seem to matter; they are superseded by questions such as: How long have you been feeling this way? Does depressive illness run in your family? Have you ever been on antidepressant medication?

In my experience, both personally and professionally, despair is a complex emotion that contains core elements of grief, anger, and helplessness. It is fundamentally related to social conditions and to how we make meaning of our suffering and pain. It has a distinctly moral and social dimension that cannot and should not be ignored, whether or not an antidepressant is administered.

Despair invites us to a journey into the fertile dark. This is no trip to Tuscany where we walk the vernal hillsides watching the sun's light on the landscape. It's a journey to the dark inner core of our banished selves and our failures to create a humane world.

Despair asks us to make meaning out of apparent meaninglessness; to grieve our unmourned losses; to examine the unexamined life; to legitimate our anger at the world; to struggle out of the cocoon and be reborn. It is a harsh and demanding taskmaster. It insists that we stop with business as usual, pause from the daily routines of our lives, reflect on the meaning of our existence. The voice of despair says: *Go deeper*. It's a voice that can barely be heard above the din of the world, which impels us: *Go faster, go further, go go go.*

What's needed is a way to rewrite our culture's story about depression, to make it a story that allows not only for treatment with brain-altering chemicals, but also for a redemptive process of spiritual renewal and transformation.

## DESPAIR AND SEROTONIN

What about the research indicating that depression is the result of insufficient levels of serotonin in the brain? On the level of brain chemistry, depression has been linked to neurotransmitter deficiencies in serotonin, norepinephrine, and possibly dopamine. But even this is debatable. It's a working hypothesis that has by no means been proven—though it is widely believed, even by physicians, to be a medical "fact."[8] Even if this is true, it's a far cry from the idea that these deficiencies exist to the idea that they are causative. And yet, television commercials are now telling us that a serotonin deficiency causes depression and that depression is a physical illness comparable to diabetes.

Again and again psychiatry seems to make this fundamental error: The fact that there is a biochemical substrate to an emotion or mental state does not mean that this biochemical correlative causes the condition. Nor does it mean that the condition or emotion is pathological. Every mood, according to this logic, could be seen to have a biochemical cause. Yet we don't say that love is caused by endorphins running amok. Nor do we label love a mental illness.

What makes depression intractable has a lot to do with how much we fear and devalue despair and how difficult it is to tolerate this emotion. When all our efforts to keep despair at bay fail, we tend to panic. We want it to go away immediately. Sometimes a quick fix is just what's needed to avert disaster. In the emergency of a serious suicidal depression, one might not have the option to risk taking a longer route through despair. But generally, the desire for a quick fix only complicates the duration and experience of any emotion. When we hate ourselves for the "weakness" of despair, for the experience of helplessness that is so much a part of it, and when we panic in response to it, these reactions sink us into the condition we call depression.

WHY LISTEN TO DESPAIR WHEN YOU CAN LISTEN TO PROZAC?
For some thirty years, I've worked with hundreds of depressed people. Most of the people in my practice are depressed, and most of these are women. Abject misery, loneliness, self-loathing, a sense of futility, submerged anger and grief, longing for death are the bread and butter of my line of work. For almost twenty years, I sent no one for a medication consultation.

In 1993, six years after Prozac came out on the market, my not doing so began to seem like a kind of odd, stubborn refusal on my part. The culture had shifted. My stance was that while antidepressants could be helpful, first and foremost, I believed in accompanying people in their despair, giving them support for their journeys through these treacherous realms, and doing a fair amount of education on the value of creative expression, physical exercise, and spiritual practice for healing through despair. With the cultural shift, this stance now seemed intransigent and unduly laborious.

Since then, I have referred ten people, all women, for a psychopharmacological consultation with a psychiatrist who specializes in prescribing medication. Four clients refused to go and felt their dignity was insulted by the suggestion. They got better without the drugs. Two took an antidepressant medication, felt better, and never looked back. One felt better but was uneasy about it. Three couldn't endure the side effects.

What I've noticed is that, before Prozac, people didn't expect to feel better so fast. Now they do. Prozac has lowered our affect tolerance for despair (no doubt to the delight of the pharmaceutical behemoths). Before Prozac, people in my practice felt better within four to six months by journeying through despair and healing their souls. Now there is less patience for this kind of time frame.

In the dystopia of the Brave New World—a society built on oppressive genetic hierarchies, a rigidified class society, and police-state enforcement of absolute conformism—soma was the little pill that made all of these misery-inducing conditions bearable: "Ten cubic centimeters of soma cures ten gloomy sentiments." Since the release of Prozac in 1987, more than 40 million people have taken it. The selective serotonin reuptake inhibitors, or SSRIs (as these kinds of antidepressants are called), are the soma of our day. It's hard to think about them clearly because they make people who feel lousy feel good. How can this be bad?

After much questioning, Peter Kramer, in the best-seller *Listening to Prozac*, concludes that Prozac has forever altered our way of thinking not only about depression but about what it means to be human. Whatever its drawbacks—and they are, by his own admission, quite considerable— Prozac is here to stay, and it's useful. Kramer is especially enthusiastic about its use for "dysthymics." Those who see the world through a glass darkly are, he says, at a distinct disadvantage in our cultural landscape, where we prefer "hyperthymia" (the more energetic, efficient, upbeat, business-as-usual temperament). While acknowledging the American cultural bias, Kramer nevertheless concludes that no one should be denied the benefit of fitting in with cultural norms.

I disagree. The judicious use of antidepressants where it's a matter of life and death is one thing. No one wants to feel bad all the time, and it is by no means a moral failing to use the new antidepressants if one chooses to do so. But helping people "fit" into the culture and preserving the cultural status quo is hardly the endgame of psychotherapy, or at least it shouldn't be.

It contributes little to our nation's mental health and only guarantees continued mental health problems. Our hyperthymic culture has a dark underbelly that, in many respects, is the ground of the current epidemic of despair we call depression. Depression, paradoxically, takes root in a soil that is antagonistic to despair. The ways in which conventional psychology has become a force for conformist individualism have been roundly criticized by many, and justly so.

Moreover, beyond helping them "fit in," what can we offer to those who carry despair for the culture? Women, the elderly, the disenfranchised, and artists, among the most vulnerable to despair, might have something to contribute to the culture from out of their despair, rather than in spite of it. What gifts lie in these darker realms? And what about confronting the denied darkness of our culture and society?

This is where listening to Prozac just doesn't cut it.

"Psychiatrists have no option but to blame people for their own suffering," said Germaine Greer. "Admitting that unhappiness might be justified would undermine the entire rationale of medicating the mind."[9] I'm not opposed to the wise use of antidepressants, but doing so in a medical model, in the absence of any validation for the emotion itself, can make despair's journey seem like an absurd exercise in anguish to no end. Discovering the value of despair demands a great deal of internal work and patience. Listening to despair is difficult. (Even Job's wife couldn't listen to him, advising him to "curse God and die!") None of us have an easy time with this emotion.

And yet, listening to despair can have a fertile richness that cannot be found in a capsule.

## The Value of Despair

> Despair . . . is the only cure for illusion. Without
> despair we cannot transfer our allegiance to reality—
> it's a kind of mourning period for our fantasies. Some
> people do not survive this despair, but no major
> change within a person can occur without it.
> —PHILIP SLATER, Earthwalk

### DESPAIR AND THE SEARCH FOR MEANING

One winter, in the grips of an acute despair about my youngest daughter's chronic ill health, I took two days off. Esther had been ill, off and on, for a good part of the last year. We'd consulted the primary care physician, the asthma specialist, the pulmonist. We'd administered antibiotics, homeo-pathic remedies, herbal medicine. None of this had helped. Esther missed sixty-five days of school that year. She had the pale, sickly complexion of a chronic invalid, and no one knew why. The uncertainty of the illness made it all the more difficult to bear. My husband, seeing my downward spiral, in-sisted I take some time away.

I went up to Cape Ann and took a long walk around Halibut Point, just at the border of Gloucester and Rockport. The trees were bare. The earth was cold. The breeze was harsh. Approaching a deep quarry, I was taken by the limitless depth of its frozenness. The water, lapis lazuli in the heyday of summer, was now a leaden gray. Nothing moved. The wintry world, the dead stillness of the frozen water, perfectly reflected my mental state.

Despair moves us into the still point, the deep, frozen pool at the center of everything in our lives and in the world that makes us question the mean-ing of existence. It calls us to ask questions like: *Why do the innocent suffer? Why is there so much unnecessary cruelty and pain in the world? Does God exist? What am I here for?*

In its density, despair brings us to the experience of existential empti-ness. This emptiness is experienced not just by those who have been trau-matized by history or personal experience, but by those whose lives are full. We love our children, our partners. We are engaged in our work. We have good friends. And yet, very few people with a conscious interior life can deny that at some point, there is an experience of emptiness, and the ques-tion arises: *What's the point?* Given a certain lighting on the stage of life, we lose sight of our purpose. "Tomorrow and tomorrow and tomorrow creeps in this petty pace from day to day to the last syllable of recorded time." We strut and fret our hour upon the stage and then are heard no more.

Despair is a more cognitive emotion than grief or fear, involved with our beliefs about the nature of things. When I walked around Halibut Point, I was the one struggling with existential meaning, not Esther. She was sick and in pain, but she was not in despair. She was sad and disappointed about missing school so much. But the futility of our efforts, as parents, to pre-serve the health of our sick child led us to ask despairing questions about the meaning of our lives.

Watching the innocent suffer will bring these kinds of questions to the fore. But so will a lot of other things: reading the morning news, losing a loved one to cancer or murder, thinking about the state of the world . . . or nothing at all. In a moment, everything that was full and ample and re-warding becomes stale and empty, lifeless as a withered flower.

After I took my walk around Halibut Point, I went down to the ocean. Unlike the water in the quarry, the ocean water was not frozen. Here the waves crashed on the rocky shore. I found a spot and sat down, feeling the spray of water as I closed my eyes, throwing my questions out to sea: *What do you have in mind?* I asked, of I know not what deities. *Isn't it enough that she is disabled and in chronic daily pain? Must she also have these mysterious respiratory illnesses? What possible point is there to all of this? And if there isn't any point, then why must she endure this pointless pain?*

I heard no answer to my questions. Opening my eyes, I saw a row of sea-gulls stretched out against the leaden sky. Not flying but just suspended in my line of vision, they appeared to be staring straight at me. I had the odd idea that they had heard my cries. The thought came to me, suddenly: *The universe holds Esther. You don't need to do it all yourself.*

And with this thought, my heart, which had been as cold as a stone for many weeks, began to crack open. Inside the stone, the waters of my sorrow began to flow. And then I felt, as I have intermittently over the eighteen years since his death, Aaron's presence. As always, it reassured me. The mother-self in me melted into something larger. Where there had been emptiness and pain, there was once again some sense of meaning: I was here to love my daughter and to learn what she was here to teach me, not to single-handedly rescue her. Esther's spirit needed no rescuing; rather it was my spirit that needed care.

The grayness of the day took on some color as meaning flowed back into my life. The walk in the wintry landscape of Cape Ann, my questions (which were really prayers for Esther), the seagulls, Aaron's spirit, the crashing waves—all reminded me that I was part of a larger web of life, and so too was Esther. I no longer felt alone.

This is a condensed story. It took me more than two days to make peace with Esther's illness. Making meaning out of the chronic pain of the inno-cent is an ongoing process, not one that is finished and done for all time. All the parents I know who have a child with complex disabilities go through this process time and again as our children mature. What our lives teach us is that despair is an emotion that comes and goes, asking painful questions, calling us to go deeper to find a meaning we can live with—a meaning that frees us from unnecessary care and allows us to love unconditionally the children that have been given to us.

Arising as a response to something in ourselves or in the world that we cannot bear to accept, despair asks us to look at the Medusa's head and not be turned to stone, to face into a dark truth from which we'd prefer to avert our gaze, and to create meaning from pain. It invites us to change our lives and ourselves, to transform the way that we look at the world. And it moves us to let our grief flow. Though we may want to push out of our discomfort zone immediately, despair asks us to slow down, take our time, be still. Sometimes, it compels us to stop everything in order to painstakingly remap our world.

The metamorphosis of meaning is an important part of the call of despair and its fulfillment. Sometimes, despair hits with a sudden jolt. This is how it was for William Styron, as he recounts it in *Darkness Visible*. Chosen to receive the Prix Mondial Cino del Duca, one of the most respected literary honors in France, he flew to Paris to accept this award "that should have sparklingly restored my ego."[10] But instead of a sparkling ego-bath, he found himself drowning. He didn't give a damn about the award. That which had once provided pleasure and meaning was now found to be empty. Styron's benumbed despair began to eat away at his soul, and he moved into his headlong, rapid descent.

For Styron, this was the beginning of an "illness" that afflicted him in the way that a storm overtakes a landscape. Though he later on notes that his depression started when he was in crisis about his writing, he doesn't connect this "illness" to a necessary reexamination of meaning in relation to his career and his literary fame. What Styron wants, when his depression hits hard, is for life to be just as it was before.

This is precisely what despair will not allow. *Transform yourself or be damned*, the voice of despair seems to say. This call to transformation is the despair's message.

Styron's despair took a precipitous turn for the worse after he lost his taste for alcohol and could no longer turn to his habitual source of inspiration. Despair's descent often begins in the wake of a critical loss of some kind: of a marriage, a job, a child, a house—anything one counted on to provide a sense of meaning, order, identity. People who are used to thinking of themselves as cheerful by nature often experience despair as a sudden drop of a leaden curtain of pain. Others, more accustomed to melancholy, may not even notice that despair rules their lives until a doctor points it out and writes a prescription.

Whatever way it arrives, despair comes with an urgent call to grieve our losses and to examine the meaning of our lives. The agony of meaninglessness is at the heart of despair. Recovering faith in a meaningful universe is central to its alchemy. Meaningful pain—the pain of childbirth or of wartime battle or of sacrifices made for a good cause—may be difficult but doesn't necessarily lead to despair; whereas pain without apparent purpose, meaning, or coherence almost always does. Meaninglessness is a breeding ground for despair. Young people without hope of achieving anything meaningful in their lives are extremely vulnerable to despair and its ravages: suicide, homicide, addiction, violence. Veterans of the Vietnam War were more likely to suffer from despair and post-traumatic stress syndrome than World War II vets precisely because the cultural meaning ascribed to vanquishing the Nazis was a clear and compelling "good guys versus bad guys" scenario, while the meaning of the war against Vietnam was contested: Were we there to protect democracy, or to ruthlessly destroy a colonialized people?

Science is discovering that animals can think and feel in much more complex ways than we, in our human hubris, had ever thought possible. Gorillas taught to use sign language exhibit the capacity to formulate complex thoughts and to communicate them. They can remember the past and think of the future. They can play. They can feel and communicate sorrow, fear, and anger, as well as compassion, empathy, delight, and love—in some cases more eloquently than many human beings! What they cannot do, as far as we know, is assign any meaning to their existence. Only humans have the capacity—and the need—to do this. We are also the only animals who consistently put ourselves and others in the unenviable position of having to find meaning in self-created situations that defy all sense and give rise to despair.

Meaning-making is a defining characteristic of what it is to be human. As we need food in order to survive and grow, so too we humans seem to need a sense of meaning in order to thrive and to avert despair. According to the psychiatrist Viktor Frankl, a survivor of Auschwitz and Dachau, the search for meaning is the primary motivational force in human beings. Existing without purpose or meaning, for humans, is like existing without air. You can only go for so long before you choke. A life without meaning chokes the soul. Spiritual suffocation is the bedrock of the emotion we call despair—and a major reason for its pervasiveness in a spiritually and morally vacuous culture.

The age in which a traditional web of meaning encircled and anchored the tribe has long since passed. In our era, individualism has become its own locus of meaning, unfettered and, alas, also unattached to anything beyond its own insatiable, manufactured needs for acquisition, consumption, status, power, and pleasure. This state of affairs engenders the anomie of meaninglessness that is the cultural backdrop for despair in our time.

At some point, many of us have had the experience of looking deeply into ourselves and finding the darker side of our social personae—a self riddled with shortcomings and failures, a self that feels empty, and that we believe to be unredeemable. This journey to the interior often meets the congealed despair hidden within. Increasingly, in our postindustrial, secular, information-glutted, urbanized, and consumer-driven culture, divorced from a traditional net of meaning or any larger sense of spiritual connectedness, the atomized self of the twenty-first century is vulnerable to this kind of despair.

To a large extent, we don't actually feel this despair. But we see it acted out in the escalating violence among the young, or in our destruction of the environmental underpinnings of our collective survival. The wake-up call of despair beckons us not only to personal but to social transformation. It asks us to rewrite the meaning of our individual and cultural stories in ways that are more conducive to living faithfully on this earth.

## The Alchemy of Despair to Faith

> He who learns must suffer.
> Even in our sleep, pain which cannot forget, falls drop by
> drop upon the heart and in our own despair, against our will,
> comes wisdom through the awful grace of God.
> —AESCHYLUS, *Agamemnon*

Despair's journey is both a search for renewed meaning and a call to grieve our losses. Though it may seem sudden and precipitous, despair has its roots. Sometimes, these have been growing and branching over long periods of time. When the roots are suddenly exposed, despair is diagnosed as "acute" depression. When slowly and insidiously revealed, it is labeled "endogenous" depression—despair with no immediately apparent referent or source. But even if the source is not acutely apparent, there is always a source. Usually there are several.

Long-standing grief over unnamed or unmourned losses is one of the most common sources of despair. These losses include the more dramatic forms of violence and abuse, but they also encompass the silent losses of emotional neglect. The pain of losing (or never having had the consistent presence of) a loving, nurturing, empathic parent often appears, years later, in what gets diagnosed as depression. These kinds of losses, unlike the death of a spouse, are generally not mourned; often they are barely recognized. Despair is the emotion that brings them to our attention, sometimes decades later.

At the end of *Darkness Visible*, a brief paragraph refers to the death of Styron's mother:

> I'm persuaded that a . . . significant factor was the death of my mother when I was thirteen . . . early sorrow—the death or disappearance of a parent, especially mother, before or during puberty—appears repeatedly in the literature on depression as a trauma sometimes likely to create nearly irreparable emotional havoc. The danger is especially apparent if the young person is affected by what has been termed "incomplete mourning"—has, in effect, been unable to achieve the catharsis of grief, and so carried within himself through later years an insufferable burden of which rage and guilt, and not only dammed-up sorrow, are a part.[11]

One wonders what would have happened had Styron been fortunate enough to receive help in grieving the loss of his mother with someone who could go into that darkness with him and make it visible. Instead, what he had was a doctor, many decades later, who prescribed an overdose of Halcion—a sedative that has a known side effect of suicidal obsession and depression.

Buried in the frozen landscape of despair, there is usually a seed of grief. To experience the alchemy of despair, you must find and release that seed.

In Mary's journey through despair, grief in the present is the trigger. In Belle's story, despair is a journey of uncovering grief from the past.

MARY'S STORY: DESPAIR'S HARD LESSONS
Six months before Mary came to therapy, her world had been familiar, cozy, and predictable. She lived with her husband, Joseph, and their daughter, Amy, who was fifteen and a sophomore in high school. Their elder child, Mark, was in college and doing well. Mary worked as a counselor in a local high school, where she was appreciated as a savvy and skilled professional. Devoted to her work, she felt lucky to have a job in which she could have a positive influence on adolescent girls. She loved her job and her family. The

latter, she told me, was not without its problems, but these had been "within normal limits."

Then, suddenly, her life came undone. Rummaging through her husband's pockets for a pen, she found a note from a family acquaintance that implied a rendezvous with her husband. When she confronted Joseph with this evidence of an affair, he denied everything at first, then broke down and told her that he was not happy in their marriage and was considering a separation. Mary was aghast. How could their marriage be so troubled without her even knowing it?

But that wasn't all. As their marriage came apart at the seams, so did her daughter. Within a month of this initial confrontation with Joseph, Amy began behaving strangely. She overslept and was late for school. She began to disregard her curfew. Mary suspected her daughter of drinking or using drugs, but Amy denied it. Mary was beside herself.

"Raising Mark was so easy," she told me. "He practically raised himself. He was always disciplined; we never had to hound him to do anything. He was responsible from an early age, motivated, smart, handsome, athletic, and social. Everything just *worked.*"

But now, nothing was working. Her daughter seemed to have changed overnight into a different girl.

"Amy was always morbidly shy. She kept to herself too much. I tried different ways to encourage her to get out more. Perhaps I pushed her too hard to be more outgoing. Now I'm terrified every time she leaves the house."

One day, Mary walked into Amy's room and found her staring into space. She looked at Amy's wrists and went into shock. There were lines. Mary knew these kinds of lines from her work with girls. Amy had been cutting herself. As a counselor, Mary knew that the self-mutilation colloquially called "cutting" was on the rise among teenage girls. Once a fairly rare behavior of sexual abuse survivors, cutting was now more common. Seemingly "normal" girls who had intact, nonabusive families, who got good grades and weren't bulimic or anorexic or seriously depressed, girls who were popular and good-looking, all kinds of girls one would not expect to be mutilating themselves were doing so.

Wearing her guidance counselor hat at school, Mary was sure-footed and confident, a strong, straight-talking role model. The girls trusted her. She knew how to take them under her wing, to support and encourage them, and to educate them about the culture's toxic influence on a girl's sense of self, to help them find themselves. But now that it was her own daughter who needed help, she felt ashamed, useless, and defeated. She and her husband agreed to put all questions of a separation on hold in the interests of presenting a united front for Amy. Nothing worked. Amy was alternatively defiant, distant, and depressed.

One night, Amy didn't come home. Mary paced the floor, contemplating at what point she would call the police when, peering out of her living room window at 5:00 A.M., she saw her daughter staggering out of a red car. A young man Mary had never seen before helped her out and sped away. Running to the door, Mary and John had to practically lift their daughter up the stairs. Amy was drunk and disheveled. She refused to tell her mother where she'd been or whom she'd been with.

Amy went to bed and Mary went to pieces. Everything she'd ever had faith in—her marriage, her daughter, her skills as a mother and as someone "good with girls"—could no longer be counted on. They all seemed to be slipping away. This loss of certainty unmoored her.

This is how Mary described her emotional state: "I'm out on an ice floe in the middle of the Arctic Ocean, and I don't know how to get back to shore."

Mary's intense despair forced her to take a close look at herself, to re-feel and rethink her life. She saw now that she'd been in denial for several years about the state of her marriage—refusing to feel the deep estrangement, preferring to just go through the motions and keep up a facade. She had to ask herself why she'd been hiding from her pain and the pain of her husband. Doing so was excruciating for Mary, who prided herself on facing things squarely.

Worse than this, for Mary, was facing herself as a mother. Her professional identity as a helper of girls had been so strong that Mary found it hard to admit that she'd never felt confident as the mother of a daughter. Mothering her son came easily. Somehow, she'd always felt separate from him and yet connected in a comfortable way. There was an ease between them. But with Amy it was different. From the start, she was more critical of her daughter, who seemed too shy, too withdrawn, too hidden. Amy didn't know how to connect to a daughter like this. She'd always fantasized that having a daughter would be a totally fulfilling experience. She began to see that the ways that she'd driven herself to be "superwoman" had made her less than empathic with her daughter's less assertive approach to life; and that she had, for years, been driving Amy to be different than she was. Facing these "flaws" in how she mothered Amy was one of the hardest things Mary did in therapy.

Despair, for Mary, was like a mirror held up to her weaknesses and flaws.

Painfully, and patiently, she came to acknowledge and accept that neglecting her relationship with her husband had contributed to the deterioration of her marriage. And that her judgmentalness, lack of confidence in Amy, and condemnation of Amy's shyness had made for a less than optimal bond with her daughter.

In the midst of this crisis, the sense of meaning that had anchored Mary to her life had come undone. Mary came face-to-face with an emptiness inside her that she'd studiously tried to avoid: a place of spiritual stasis. As a young child, she'd been a good girl with a strict Catholic upbringing. She had gone to Catholic grade school and was considered one of the school's best and brightest. But in adolescence, she had rejected the Church after reading about the Inquisition. By young adulthood, she'd become a "lapsed" Catholic with a bitter distrust of anything that smacked of religion. She'd put all of her faith, instead, in living a secular life.

Now that life seemed meaningless. All of her roles—as counselor, wife, and mother—seemed to be tainted with the "sin" of her inadequacy. It felt as though her identity itself was built on a house of cards that had now collapsed.

One cornerstone of Mary's transformational work in therapy was learning to accept responsibility for the less than perfect parts of herself with some compassion rather than the harsh self-condemnation of thinking of herself as a "sinner." While she no longer overtly subscribed to Catholic doctrine, this unconscious theology was a core part of Mary's despair. A part of her that she thought she'd left behind years ago felt as though she had committed unpardonable sins against her husband, her daughter, and a God she no longer had faith in. Getting through her despair was connected to descending into the dark night of her confusion and disconnection from faith.

This work was unexpected for Mary. She hadn't been inside a church for thirty years. She saw religious believers as people lost in illusion and prayer as a false consciousness resorted to by the desperate and high-minded. She thought she'd made her peace with the loss of her Church as a community. Now it was all coming up for her in surprising ways. She found herself privately praying for her daughter and then wondering if she was losing her mind. The fact that she would pray was another indication of her weakness and desperation, both of which threatened her former sense of self as supercompetent and self-sufficient.

Mary went through a long period of reviewing her religious history and realizing that her abrupt departure from the Church was not just an intellectual decision: it was a profoundly traumatic moment, spiritually speaking.

No one in the Church had understood her questions and her anger about Church history. She had no one who would listen to her pain and confusion. She left "in the sin of pride," she told me, laughing. And for thirty years, she'd forgotten she ever had faith in God, ever prayed with sincerity to be aligned with God's will, ever seen the world in a spiritual light.

This loss of faith was the last thing she thought she would need to talk about in therapy. And yet, it was essential to her journey through despair that she come to a new place in relation to God and spirit. Painstakingly, Mary came to feel that she needed some kind of spiritual solace and that this was okay. Praying did not make her a weak person, even if she wasn't sure whom or what she was praying to. She began to allow herself some spiritual practices she'd long ago shed. She prayed each day for her daughter and for her marriage. And she decided that she needed some kind of community outside of her work and family networks. She began to attend a local Unitarian church and to find some comfort there.

"I don't know about God," she told me, "but the idea of a community of seekers and some kind of truth beyond the social roles we play makes sense to me."

Facing her demons, Mary found new strengths, and new wisdom. In the crisis of her despair was the opportunity to become more self-aware, to renew her sense of herself and her relationships with those she loved. Her heart expanded as she learned more and more about unconditional love for her daughter and her husband. She felt that she had become a better, more accepting mother, and that this was connected to being more tolerant of her own limitations. Amy stopped cutting herself and began to emerge from out of her own dark night with the help of a therapist. Mary and Joseph decided to give their relationship a chance and were working on it in family therapy. Mary continued to attend the Unitarian church and formed some important relationships there that began to heal the religious rupture of leaving the Catholic Church as an adolescent.

This is not to say that all was secure and certain for Mary. In my last session with her, she was still unclear about whether or not to do a trial separation from Joseph; and she was still worried about Amy, though much less so. But a vital shift had taken place, an unexpected gift had arrived: The trauma of religious disconnection had been healed, and she had begun to find a deep well that nourished her spirit.

In Mary's words: "I'm not sure how it will all turn out for Amy or for me and Joseph. But I'm no longer out there on the ice floe. I've found a place of solid ground, a place to stand in community."

BELLE'S STORY: DESPAIR'S METAMORPHOSIS

> I said to my soul, be still, and let the dark come upon you
> which shall be the darkness of God.
> ·  ·  ·  ·  ·  ·  ·  ·  ·  ·  ·  ·  ·  ·  ·  ·  ·  ·  ·
> I said to my soul, be still, and wait without hope
> For hope would be hope for the wrong thing; wait without love
> For love would be love of the wrong thing; there is yet faith
> But the faith and love and the hope are all in the waiting.
> Wait without thought, for you are not ready for thought:
> So the darkness shall be the light, and the stillness the dancing.
> — T. S. ELIOT, "East Coker," *Four Quartets*

Belle came to see me in a state of acute despair about her marriage with the urgent question: Should I stay in this relationship or leave? She had been living a good life with her husband and two daughters. Located in a quiet neighborhood in the suburbs, her house was immaculate and beautifully decorated, her well-tended gardens extensive. She'd been married for fifteen years, apparently happily. She and her gentle husband, Doug, were devoted to raising their girls, aged ten and twelve, who were both healthy, bright, and adorable.

"Everyone thinks we have the perfect marriage, the perfect family, the perfect life," she told me the first time I saw her in therapy.

"And what do you think?"

"I think there's no room for me in this life. I think I haven't been there all along, and I want out."

In her words, Belle had "come uncorked" after attending a workshop on opening the heart where she had, for the first time in her life, considered the questions: What is my heart's desire? What is my life's purpose? To her surprise, a lock in her heart snapped open, releasing the long-imprisoned griefs of a childhood in which no one concerned themselves with questions like these.

At the same time, something came alive in Belle that had been dormant for a long, long time: her passion for life and connection. Coming home from the workshop, she wanted to share this opening with her husband, to connect to him in a deeper way. His response, she told me, was to push her away. "I felt like a football kicked into a dark space, spinning."

The meaning of her life, so clear and transparent for the past fifteen years of her marriage, was suddenly dislodged: "I slammed into a wall and woke up." She found herself questioning the very basis of her life with her husband and children. Why had she married Doug in the first place? Had she ever really loved him? Or had she coupled out of a quiet desperation to achieve the normalcy, stability, and solidity she couldn't muster for herself?

It is not unusual for people in therapy to come to a turn in the road where everything known and secure suddenly seems alien, and where the lure of the new both beckons and terrifies. People at the age of forty, Belle's age when she started therapy with me, are particularly prone to these kinds of inner upheavals, which are known colloquially as midlife crises. I always advise people in such crises to slow down their process, to take time to listen to themselves before jumping to any premature conclusions born of an inability to tolerate their feelings. Belle's crisis was more profound and sudden than many; it had the quality of a spiritual emergency. Abruptly, after a seemingly contented life, she felt "my forty years have been wasted."

Belle and Doug had married in their twenties because it seemed the right thing to do at the time. Doug was a kind man who wasn't sure about marriage but was sure he wanted children. Belle was in a panic about what to do with herself. "I needed a job or a man," she said. "I didn't have the job. I didn't know what I wanted."

Doug seemed like a sensible choice, though he was not the man Belle loved. Her heart belonged to Paul, a man who wanted to marry Belle but who, with a wife and two children, was a choice Belle's mother would condemn. Belle had been a "good girl" all her life, raised to be dutiful and make no waves. Doug gave her a way to break from her family without shattering her mother's expectations. She gave Doug the possibility of bearing children.

They eloped, and Belle never looked back. Not even when their sexual life ended for several years did she question her choice. Now that her heart had opened a crack, she saw something terrible that was altogether obscured by the "created fantasy" of her life: that her marriage was hollow. She and Doug had "played house," but all along, she'd been "missing."

Now Belle felt she as though she was coming out of a long sleep, "like a chick struggling to get out of its shell." Half out, she was like someone who'd been slowly starved. Her hunger for authenticity, passion, and self-expression was enormous. Long-ignored wishes could not be neglected anymore. She could no longer fit herself into the role of the suburban mom, which she found "too small." Her dreams were to find meaningful work outside the home, to have an impact of some kind on the world. Along with these dreams came a desperate clawing to get out of her marriage, which she felt would suffocate her if she stayed. She urgently needed "to define myself from the inside."

This is precisely what Belle had not been allowed to do in her family while growing up. Belle's mother had lost her first husband to cancer and married, grief-stricken, a second man who also had seemed like a sure bet: a man who had wanted to be an artist but was raised to be a corporate lawyer and so dutifully went with the career his family chose for him.

Belle was a lively child, full of an ebullient, creative energy. The grief of her mother's deceased husband and her father's lost artistic ambitions were well out of sight by the time she was born, the last of their three children. But then tragedy struck: Beth's father drove his car into a ravine and came home paraplegic.

The house then became a place of grim, bleak endurance and Belle a child with the sad, steely face of hidden grief that afflicts children who survive serious trauma. Belle's mother put away her brightly colored dresses and shoes and dutifully took care of her husband. A stark stoicism branded everyone in the family from this day forward. As the youngest, Belle had a special role: "My mother took me to be her comforter. I was the one who wouldn't be a bother."

From this time on, Belle's childhood self, as she remembered it, was mute and grimly dutiful, locked up in a prison of silenced grief, anger, and guilt. The energy, vibrancy, and mischievousness that shone in her face from a photograph taken before her father's accident were missing. Her emotions, her dreams, the aches and pains of growing up, were not seen or attended to.

Early on in therapy, Belle drew a picture of her heart, weighed down by a large rock. The rock reminded Belle of the Easter theme of resurrection. Christ, after his crucifixion, was entombed. A rock had to be rolled away before he was resurrected. This was going to be a long, stormy journey in search of a resurrected self.

The rock sitting on Belle's heart since her childhood was the dead weight of the submerged despair that came from locking away her grief and anger about her family's tragic losses, and from having to erase herself for the sake of her devastated mother. Inside this silent rock were the howling emotions that had never been addressed, a self that had never been seen or encouraged to be. Now, decades later, the rock was unearthed by the inner revolution going on inside her. "I was raised to be beyond reproach and to make no noise," she confided, "and now I feel like I need to make big trouble."

By "big trouble," Belle meant putting herself at the center of her life, which in her book was tantamount to a cardinal sin. She craved self-expression and emotional connection—neither of which she felt were possible in this companionable but hollow marriage. Her husband, naturally, responded with panic and anger. Who was this woman? This was not the same girl he married. Belle was unrecognizable, even to herself.

In the first part of her journey, Belle wanted to take the large black rock that sat on her heart and forcibly remove it. But it wouldn't leave so fast. I suggested that we take some time with it. "The rock may not want to be lifted just yet." I said. "Perhaps it needs to be seen and known first." Looking closely, Belle noticed that this rock, though dark and scary, was also beautiful and interesting. As depicted in another drawing, it had a patina of green moss. Something was growing here in this seemingly infertile terrain.

The alchemy of despair called to Belle, asking her to cry the tears she'd never cried, speak the anger she'd never spoken, and find the self that had been stopped when her father came home without the use of his arms and legs.

After six months of work in therapy, Belle's drawing showed a heart seated on a cushion, surrounded by vibrant lines of bright energy. The colors were rose, blue, and yellow. The rock had lifted.

Yet despite this, and despite her improved relationship with her husband, Belle found that she was not inclined to stay married, except out of duty to her children. The prospect of derailing their lives and breaking up their beautiful home struck her with terror, dread, and guilt. But a force inside her that wouldn't give up insisted: *Listen to yourself!*

Belle dreamed of giving birth to herself. In one dream, she was pregnant, toward the end of her term, and yet hadn't felt any movement for several days. She felt the oncoming labor, wondering: Is this baby viable? The dream question asked: Would Belle's new self be born alive, or would it be stillborn? The answer, Belle decided, hinged on whether she could tolerate her despair: "I need to let the darkness and despair out, not enclose it in a cyst, like I have been doing all my life."

Walking this path, Belle came to a decision: She would move out into an apartment of her own. The separation would help her know what she wanted. This was the period of her deepest "inner child" work—the healing of the small, sad girl within her. In a state of deep relaxation, Belle saw a dark cave of stalactites—black, pointy mineral deposits. "This is a cold place of uncried tears," she told me. I asked Belle to invite in the little girl who never cried. Seeing this child, so sad and alone, Belle cradled and comforted her.

Some weeks later, Belle did something she'd never done before: announcing in church that she had separated from her husband, she cried in public. In defiance of the childhood message about grief, which said to enclose your sorrow in a locked box and never look in, Belle was now unashamed to let her grief be seen. And to her amazement, she discovered that people were responsive and caring, offering their support and concern. Her tears did their transformative work, surfacing the congealed grief within her despair and releasing it. In this moment, Belle came to see that people cared, and she began to have faith that she could get through whatever she needed to go through.

In a card she sent me during this period, she wrote: "In spite of and because of this crisis, when I enjoy something these days, whether the foaming storm-charged surf at the beach or my daughter Susanna's beautiful smile, I really enjoy it. More than I ever could enjoy it before."

Belle was becoming a more engaged, more real, more fun mother. She was able to set limits firmly but kindly, to talk to her girls about their feelings and help them get through their grief and anger about the separation, to soothe them. Her journey through despair was deepening her abilities to be there for her children in a way that she hadn't experienced herself as a child. She also found a job using her skills as an artist.

Belle worked very hard to find a way back into her marriage. She confronted her own ambivalence about being in any intimate relationship. She improved the quality of her relationship and communication with Doug. And yet none of this ignited the relationship or made her want to stay in the marriage. This phase of her journey involved facing into the "bad mother" archetype that afflicts women in our culture who consider leaving a marriage for any reason other than an abusive or alcoholic husband.

In the end, Belle and Doug mutually agreed on ending their marriage. In a drawing, Belle showed me a sunset followed by a sunburst. The sunset was the demise of her marriage. The sunburst was the self she was becoming. This self, she said, was all about "learning to love myself and to be open to loving authentically."

Her mother had once confided in Belle, "When I married your father, I didn't love him. But we had a home and raised kids together and became comfortable." Belle now felt free of the need to replay her mother's life. Despite the enormous sorrow this freedom caused her, it was also the harbinger of a new kind of faith: "I have faith in my path and trust that wherever it leads me is good."

More and more, Belle was able to enjoy the simple things—her work, her children, the ocean, the trees—and to experience these as sacred. Whereas she had once interpreted her pain as a symptom of her failure to "do my life right," she was now making a new kind of meaning of it: "Being in pain and struggling doesn't mean you're doing something wrong or that there isn't joy in it or alongside it."

Belle's divorce papers said that her marriage was ending due to "irretrievable breakdown." But Belle's "breakdown" was not "irretrievable." Through this journey of despair, she had found the courage to weep and redeem her losses, to redefine her pain and her life. The snakeskin had sloughed off, and a new self, green and fresh despite its long ordeal, was born. She sent me a card in the shape of a butterfly, with beautiful orange and green wings. Inside, she'd written: "Metamorphosis is not for the faint-hearted!"

In one of our last sessions, Belle said: "I feel like the real me. I'm more myself than I've ever been. Nothing much bothers me anymore. I know now that I can rely on being honest and having faith in the universe and in the goodness of human beings. I've come through."

At the very start of Belle's work in therapy, she did a drawing of her emotional landscape: Stark black mountains jutted up and down the left side of the page, looking formidable if not impossible to scale. These were followed by a series of circles labeled *disappointment, anger, loss,* and *grief.* After the circles, a small dark heart appeared, cut, as with a serrated knife, down the middle. It read: "Broken Heart."

Then came a large empty rectangle labeled "Empty Space." And just after this, a series of lines—yellow, pink, orange, red, blue, indigo, purple—a small but clearly drawn rainbow. The word "Destiny" was at the far right side of the page, followed by a question mark.

Here, at the outset, Belle had drawn an accurate map of the emotional terrain of the long journey through despair that she would complete some two years later. The jagged black mountains would be scaled before she could reconstruct her entire world of meaning—a task that would be arduous and would require much courage. The circles of her disappointment, grief, and anger as a child and as a wife would be traversed. The empty space was the place in which a new sense of meaning and a redefined self would take shape. The rainbow was an image of hope and faith renewed at the end of this long day's journey into night.

This drawing, so true to Belle's interior, has been replicated in various forms by hundreds of depressed women and men I've seen in therapy over the years. Despair is a hard climb. There is usually a confrontation with the silenced, stuck emotions within. An unbearable desolation, when tolerated, proves to be fertile ground for metamorphosis: a profound rebirth of the self and a renewed faith in life.

A word about the despair of women. In the United States, depressed women make up the bulk of people in despair. Women are three times as frequently diagnosed with major depression as men. They suffer moderate depression at ten times the rate of men. Women in unhappy marriages are five times more likely to be depressed than their husbands. People living below the poverty line are especially prone to depression; and 75 percent of these people are women and children. Similarly, victims of sexual abuse are at high risk for depression and most victims of sexual abuse are women. The same is true for victims of rape and domestic violence. In addition, 50 percent of caregivers—those who care for the elderly, the young, and the frail or disabled—are depressed. Almost all of these caregivers are women.[12]

In short, women's experiences of oppression and victimization, and their caregiving roles in patriarchy, are more predictive of depression than any other factor. Being female in a male-dominated society puts women at risk for despair. This is exacerbated by the fact that women's anger at our social condition is still largely socialized to remain underground. Women's journeys through despair frequently involve a process of getting acquainted with, validating, and finding a constructive way to give voice to this anger.[13]

Many think that women's anger is passé, now that we live in what the media calls a "postfeminist" age. Would that this were the case. While there has been some substantial change in sex roles for a larger percentage of the population, patriarchy is still alive, if not so well. Its institutions are still firmly rooted in the culture. Until the social structure of male dominance is drastically and systematically altered, the despair of women continues to draw our attention to the fact that oppression is depressing. The alchemy of anger, closely related to the alchemy of despair in women's lives, merits a book of its own. The pervasive despair of women continues to be an ongoing social effect of the abuses of patriarchy. We see this in Jody's story.

## JODY'S STORY: DESPAIR AND HAPPINESS

> In the depth of winter, I found that there was in me
> an invincible summer.
>
> —ALBERT CAMUS, "Summer"

Despair, for many female children, starts in early childhood sexual abuse and becomes a longtime companion. Jody started thinking about suicide when she was eleven years old. For the next three years, these thoughts were an almost daily part of her life. By fourteen, she was planning her death in a number of ways: jumping out a window, slashing her wrists, downing pills from the bathroom cabinet.

Instead, miraculously, Jody decided to seek help. Certainly, she hadn't learned to ask for help at home, and received none from the people closest to her. From the time she was a toddler, she'd been sexually abused by her father. At first, he exposed himself and fondled her. But as she grew older, the abuse became more severe and assaultive. At the age of seven, Jody was violently raped and drugged so that she would not speak about it. Even if she had been able to speak, she would not have told her mother because she had long ago learned that her mother didn't listen.

"Despair" was not a word Jody used as a teenage girl, but "unbearableness" was. She needed help when she was fourteen years old because she felt that her life was unbearable. Telling her mother she wanted to talk to someone, she was sent to a therapist. At first, Jody didn't talk to the therapist about the sexual abuse. She talked about her illness. One year after the rape, Jody began falling down and limping as well as experiencing crushing, chronic pain throughout her body. No one could diagnose what was wrong with her. Her illness was treated as "psychosomatic," which, in the days before the advent of mind/body medicine, meant that Jody was thought to have a mental disorder. This only added to her suffering.

"I was lonely, guilty, self-hating, devastated," Jody told me. "Beyond lonely—there should be another word for it—an existential absolute terrifying aloneness beyond words."

Talking about this despair with her therapist was the beginning of Jody's journey through it. When she dreamed of monsters, her therapist instructed her to imagine a screen of light that the monsters would not be able to come through. This was the first time that Jody felt some hope. Having some control over her dream life meant there might be some way to feel less helpless. Perhaps she would not have to kill herself.

Fortunately, Jody seemed to have an innate sense of guidance in finding what would help her heal. In high school, she took up art and lithography, making prints that, in retrospect, were a way to release some of the traumatic harm she'd suffered. Through this creative outlet, she got on speaking terms with her unconscious.

Jody also had a teacher who loved and encouraged her. Time and again, I have seen how being truly loved and appreciated by just one person, even in the wake of catastrophic trauma or neglect, can make all the difference in someone's ability to get through despair and to heal brokenness of body, heart, and spirit.

Moving out of her house at age seventeen, Jody joined a twelve-step group where she could talk about her life openly and in community. In step meetings, people held the pain with her. This was in sharp contrast to the rest of her life, where few people could listen.

"I kept wanting to talk about the incest and my despair," Jody told me. "But I felt frequently that a tremendous energy met me, thwarting me, wanting me to move on. People could not go there with me. 'It's a beautiful day' they would say; 'let's have fun.' But what I needed most was to be listened to."

Something else happened in her twelve-step program that helped Jody. She began to experience a spiritual connection to something beyond herself. Though she was not at all sure that she believed in God, she learned the meaning and value of prayer.

"I had conversations—although I wasn't sure with who or what. I said, 'Please listen to me.' I rarely prayed for anything tangible. I prayed for emotional shifts—to open my heart, to be free from fear, to know what's true for me, to get through this day without killing myself."

For years, Jody prayed "all day every day." Prayer comforted her and gave her the feeling that she was not alone. She could feel a sense of connectedness that was an antidote to the unbearable isolation she'd known ever since she could remember.

During this same period, Jody was instructed in mindfulness meditation and began to practice daily. Because of her disability, which was still unnamed, sitting daily on a cushion was physically painful. But, as Jody put it, "my life was excruciating anyway, so I could put up with things that others found more difficult." Gradually, Jody extended her meditation time to include longer daily sittings. For years, she meditated for several hours each day. With aching, cramping, and a sore, bruised feeling throughout her body, Jody focused her mindful attention on her breathing and on her bodily sensations, as well as on her mind's reactions to them.

"This was an extreme remedy for an extreme situation," Jody told me in her characteristically matter-of-fact way. "It was a long time before I would say it was working."

When I asked Jody to tell me her thoughts about taking Prozac instead of going through so much pain and despair, this was her response: "Looking back, there were advantages to not having taken it. I learned something about inner resources and the value of human support in a way that I couldn't have if I had just taken a pill. I have pretty easy access to joy now, and I think this is related to how deeply I could go into my pain. My joy and my pain can't be separated. Also, I have a deep faith in my own capacity to heal, psychologically and spiritually. That's something I've learned from my experience, and it can't be shaken."

I asked Jody how she made sense of her suffering, and whether making meaning had been a struggle for her.

"Shit happens," said Jody. "That's the way I look at it. I don't see myself as that unique. Some people have it easier than me and, if you think globally, a lot of people have it harder. I'm just part of humanity."

This global, wide-angle vision was part of Jody's hard-earned wisdom through the alchemy of despair. She spent years coping with adversity before coming to this place of equanimity. She struggled with meaning in the way that all innocent sufferers do. She had to transform the meaning-story of her pain, which, for many years had been: "I'm in pain because I'm bad."

In Jody's family, the story of incest was that it never happened. When Jody, at nineteen, confronted her mother with it, her mother became furious and accused Jody of making it up. During the same period, her family and several doctors also told her that her physical pain and disability were something she could control if she really wanted to. This furthered the "I'm bad" meaning-story. For a long time, Jody was obsessed with finding out what her illness was and whether she was in fact "making it up." While meditating, she would try "mental experiments" to see how much control she could have over her pain. She became very adept at affirmations and visualizations. But nothing made the pain and disability disappear.

The glib New Age message that everybody can heal themselves only furthered this sense that Jody was somehow spiritually inferior to others: "I felt my physical illness was a sign of moral or spiritual weakness." The more Jody tried to fix her illness, the more demoralizing her meaning-story of pain became. Finally, she stopped trying to fix it and surrendered to her illness as an ongoing part of her life.

Years later, it is thought by some experts in pain management that chronic pain can be a consequence of severe early childhood sexual abuse (though the pathways by which people develop autoimmune, neurological, and connective tissue diseases in the aftermath of trauma is not yet fully mapped by medicine). Jody was eventually diagnosed with a collagen-vascular disorder and now has a medical story that accounts for her illness. Although little is known about this type of condition, Jody has stopped thinking of herself as spiritually inferior. She has accepted that some pain and despair will not be strangers to her: "There has to be this willingness that if I get into a despairing place, so be it. I've been there before and I know I'll get through it."

In many respects, Jody's journey through despair resembles a Zen story in which the seeker sits outside the Master's door and is told to wait before the Master will speak to him. The seeker waits and waits. And waits some more. Years pass before the Master welcomes the student in. By this time, the seeker, having learned patience and mindfulness, is enlightened. This is not to say that Jody would declare herself "enlightened." On the contrary, she is altogether humble when speaking of what helped her through her despair. She knows that she has limits that will not disappear. She takes care not to push herself into these areas or she can easily be overwhelmed. She knows that she still needs a great deal of support from friends who can listen when she says despairing things. Her healing, she knows, "took love, time, and a deep opening from other people." She is grateful for what she has received from others and knows how much she still needs their support. She is a human being, aware of her vulnerabilities and needs for care.

But Jody's way of mindfully approaching her despair and trauma became for her a source of emotional wisdom and spiritual power. Meditation taught her how to tolerate her painful emotional and physical states. "What my emotions really wanted," says Jody, "was to be attended to. Because of the depth to which I could pay attention to them in meditation, they didn't feel they had to keep knocking at my door. I came to see how the fear and resistance to emotions makes the pain all so much bigger. When my fear and resistance lessened, there was much more space to be taken up with other parts of life. That's when joy started to come in."

More than therapy, Jody told me, meditation allowed her to be with her emotions in a fuller, more accepting way, grounded in her body rather than lost in her thoughts. She had learned from meditation how to separate her thoughts about and reactions to her pain from the pain itself. This was the key to liberating herself from its devastation. She had a teacher who had once said: When a flower opens, it opens equally to sun and rain. Jody had allowed her heart to open in the same way: "Pain is what's there, and it opens into spaciousness and joy. An open heart requires the willingness to be in pain."

Jody found a meaning-story that honored her pain and her struggles, and herself. Her words are eloquent descriptions of the emotional alchemy process. Meditation did not cure Jody's illness. She still suffers pain and limitation. She's lived with a disease for almost twenty years that she will have for the rest of her life. Yet she holds herself with a dignity and grace-fulness that is rare. Draping herself on a couch because she is more comfortable reclining than sitting, she exudes a relaxed bodily awareness that is striking by comparison to the many more stressed-out people I see in therapy who have no chronic illness or pain. She holds herself like a flower, open to both the sun and the rain.

None of us can be altogether "cured" of the pain of life or of feeling despair or other dark emotions from time to time. But, like Jody, we can find a way to live fully and wisely. Jody's wisdom came through the process of treating her life as "guru" and approaching her pain with an open heart. Through the alchemy of despair, she learned the secret of contentment: "Happiness doesn't come from outside but from within."

## Despair in the World

Things fall apart; the center cannot hold;
Mere anarchy is loosed upon the world,
The blood-dimmed tide is loosed, and everywhere
The ceremony of innocence is drowned;
The best lack all conviction, while the worst
Are full of passionate intensity.
                    —W. B. YEATS, "The Second Coming"

Where does one go from a world of insanity?
Somewhere on the other side of despair.
                    —T. S. ELIOT, Family Reunion

Victims of violence like Jody are on the front lines of people facing into despair's dark night of the soul and summoning the courage to grieve and re-make their lives.

Increasingly, however, we are all traumatized by a culture of violence that is eroding our capacity to trust in the world. Children killing children in high school cafeterias. Random drive-by shootings. Workplace gunfire. Terrorist violence. An ecological crisis of unprecedented proportions. The wasting of the earth in the name of progress. These are some of the triggers for grief, fear, and despair in our world. All of us are deeply affected by the gratuitous suffering in the world—whether or not we are aware of it. The apparent senselessness of so much pain and death gives rise to a silenced culture of despair, masked by frenetic compulsions and escalating addictions, including unrecognized and pervasive workaholism, addiction to a frenzied pace of life, and the over-use of antidepressants.

A simple glance at the morning news demonstrates that our world, beautiful and sparkling though it may be when we're in a good mood, is contaminated with the grime of cruelty, horror, avarice, and indifference. Hidden in the back pages we find the by now familiar stories of the pollution and desecration of the planet. It is human to feel despair when there are seemingly insoluble problems beyond the scope of our individual power to overcome, especially when these problems are crucial to the fate of the earth and to future generations. These kinds of problems, if we live openheartedly in the world, challenge our faith in the meaning of our lives.

Confronting history can have the same effect. Looked at without blinders, the modern age, despite its promise of progress and enlightenment, has witnessed more barbarism than any other time in recorded history. The rivers of blood flowing into the sea of our common humanity have permanently stained the ocean; and yet they seem to have no end. Where there is senseless suffering and unredemptive death, where there is violence, oppression, injustice, atrocity, betrayal, and indifference—despair and doubt will be the darker guests in our consciousness.

There is a singularly relational dimension to despair that comes from a loss of innocence in a world that disappoints our longings for justice, meaning, community, and spiritual coherence. Despair grows not only out of our personal wounds, losses, and disappointments, but also out of our needs for community and a shared sense of meaning—spiritual necessities for which we harbor a profound and aching, though largely unconscious, nostalgia. We despair because, in ways that our forebears could not have imagined, we humans suffer the profound loneliness that accompanies our estrangement from the natural world and its nonhuman inhabitants.

Despair finds fertile ground in an indigestible truth. Often, it will not let up until we face these darker truths about ourselves and our world. Unpalatable as they may be, these realities haunt us, intruding into our consciousness when we least expect them. Watching our children at play, we may feel an unnameable pang of fear and despair for the world we are bequeathing them. Like any of the dark emotions, despair can live for long periods of time at the subliminal level, where it must be continually banished from awareness by the readily available distractions of our culture. Despair tells us what we'd rather not know. It asks us to look into our darkened souls and the broken heart of the world and make a journey of descent.

These journeys are hard, and we need one another's company. We need to know that despair is a legitimate emotion and that we are not emotionally or spiritually inferior for feeling it. It is not feeling despair but denying its impact that holds us hostage in a world imperiled by our own actions.

## BEN'S STORY: GROWN-UPS HAVE MESSED UP THE WORLD

> There are a number of signs that we in America may be on the threshold of a period as a nation when we shall no longer be able to camouflage or repress our despair.
>
> —ROLLO MAY, *Freedom and Destiny*

We live on an endangered earth. Though we may prefer to put this fact on the back burner of our consciousness, we all know it in our cells. The large-scale systemic actions and inaction that imperil our world can be described as a form of violence called by some ecocide. In this context, says Joanna Macy, despair is inevitable and, no matter how individual, always has a transpersonal and global dimension. It is not a pathological condition or a deranged nihilism. "Rather, as it is being experienced by increasing numbers of people across a broad spectrum of society, despair is the loss of the assumption that the species will inevitably pull through."[14]

Joanna Macy has been doing what she calls "despair work" for more than two decades. The work is designed to help people trust their despair and find individual and social empowerment through facing into it. Psychotherapy, argues Macy, has by and large ignored the social and global dimensions of despair and thus compounded the problem by isolating those who bear despair for the world.

From my knowledge of my own profession, I would have to agree with her. Despair for the fate of the earth and grief for the loss of those outside the egocentric circle of "my parent," "my child," "my spouse," are emotions that would be viewed within a psychiatric framework as displacements of more personal dramas. "I, me, mine" is the basic approach of ego psychology. So if you walk into a psychiatric evaluation and say that you feel grief and despair for the world, don't be surprised if you're diagnosed with a mental disorder!

The relationship between the state of the earth and our emotions is not a subject generally addressed by most psychologists. The impact of ecocide on our children's development remains virtually unexplored by conventional experts in the field. Given the fact that every elementary school child is now taught the realities of environmental pollution, this omission can only be explained by our horror of the subject, which has rendered it largely taboo. And yet, there is no doubt whatsoever that living on an endangered planet affects every man, woman, and child. The most vulnerable, of course, are the children.

Ben is one such child. Raised with love and devotion by two parents who gave him everything a child could need, Ben was a typical boy. He loved baseball and Nintendo. He was smart and cute, a good kid.

Then he hit puberty. Seemingly overnight, he became angry, defiant, and out of control. Hurling plates and other household items, he cursed his parents. The face of an angel, possessed by the force of rage and despair: this was Ben.

Of course, Ben was taken for professional help, to a family therapist and then an individual therapist, and then another individual therapist. He was diagnosed with a learning disability, then with attention deficit disorder. Then another diagnosis: oppositional defiance disorder. This would require some serious therapeutic intervention, and take some time.

But after one year of therapy, Ben hadn't improved much. One night, he threw a vase and just missed his mother's head. She called the police, who took Ben to the police station and gave him a warning. This sobered him up a bit. He was put on an antidepressant medication, which also helped a little. But Ben continued to be troubled and troubling.

What was bothering Ben? Where did his rage and despair come from? And why was it so overpowering?

Certainly, there are no easy answers to this question. Ben's problems were complex; and his parents' dilemmas are faced by millions of parents every day. Learning disabilities are on the rise—not just because they are being diagnosed more frequently but because more and more children are put at risk by environmental toxins. Attention deficit may be a primary diagnosis for a "disorder" of our entire culture, but knowing this doesn't make it any easier for the Bens of the world or their families. Oppositional defiance disorder is one of the up and coming diagnoses of the twenty-first century. Other psychiatric diagnoses for children are also on the rise, including childhood depression, bipolar disorder, dysthymia, post-traumatic stress disorder, conduct disorder, narcissistic personality disorder, and borderline personality disorder.

Notwithstanding the psychiatric jargon that puts these "disorders" into a pseudo-scientific framework, what most of them have in common is the experience of despair, anxiety, or rage for no apparent reason. More and more children, at younger and younger ages, are vulnerable to these emotions— the privileged no less than the impoverished or oppressed. Taken one by one, despairing, defiant children may all seem "disordered" or sick, but my contention is this: What's wrong with them is, on some level, a response to what's wrong in the world.

In a fit of rage one day, Ben spat these words out at his parents: "You grown-ups have messed up the world. Children should rule."

Ben was indicting not only his own personal parents, but the entire adult world. He had an explanation for his "oppositional defiance": He didn't think adults worthy of their power. And he had a solution: Children should have more power, adults less.

At face value, Ben's description of adult culpability is clear and unarguable. We adults have, in fact, been messing up the world. Ben's awareness of adult responsibility for bequeathing a messed-up world to the next generation may not be the only answer to the question of what's bothering Ben; but it is the aspect of the answer that tends to be most overlooked and denied by the very adult world he's indicting.

While we are all affected by living in an ecocidal context, the young and the sensitive are the most vulnerable to being psychically overwhelmed by it. Rose, another young girl I saw in therapy who also suffered from despair without apparent reason, was, according to her mother, "very sensitive." Being sensitive to a world in crisis triggers overwhelming emotions, including despair without apparent reason. Our most sensitive children are often the designated carriers of this despair. One by one by one, we diagnose the children-carriers while avoiding the larger picture.

Most often, such children are put on medication. This is understandable. It is painful to see our children in such distress and so out of control. We want to see them feel better. We want to see them happy. Our children are experiencing and reacting from a profoundly submerged level of the larger cultural despair. Feeling the unfelt despair of the adult world is too much for any child.

The plague of silenced despair in a culture in which a blind optimism is synonymous with "normalcy" and despair is pathological by definition, is currently treated by drugs developed by the pharmaceutical giants—soma for defiant children who rage at the adult world, for children with obsessive compulsive disorders reflecting their overwhelming and paralyzing fears. It's what we're giving to anorexic and bulimic girls who can't stomach the world they're growing into. It's what the doctor prescribes primarily for women, who far outnumber men in the despair department—women who've been violated and oppressed; who are overwhelmed by caretaking responsibilities for children, husbands, and elders; and who are trying to do too many jobs at once to put piecemeal patches on open sores that our society barely recognizes and for which it has found no social medicine.

"Maybe the real issue is that our culture doesn't give people a sense of community, support, and connection," said Peter Kramer in *Listening to Prozac*. "These drugs treat what ails us."[15]

Perhaps. These drugs may lighten the burden, but they will not cure the problem of despair in our time. This emotion continues to be measured and assessed according to criteria developed by those who work within a masculine model of health and illness that pathologizes the wisdom, power, and transformative potential of the dark emotions in general. Antidepressants help millions of people—men, women, and children—get up each morning, fit in, and function. This is fine, as far as it goes. But the Prozacking of America is a short-term bandage for one of the most serious emotional catastrophes we face as a species—a crisis that will not right itself unless we can learn the value and hear the call of despair in our time.

Facing into Ben's prescient cry about the messed-up world we have left for him, looking squarely at his despair and the despair of his generation, is, perhaps more than anything I can think of, an invitation to a collective dark night of the soul for our species.

Most of us adults don't have the heart for this journey. Or the time. We are too busy trying to be of use in guiding our children to adjust to and succeed in the world as it is. We would have to make space in lives that have little or no give for an emotion we can barely tolerate. If we are unable to face into our despair, this is understandable.

Yet how can our children have faith in an adult world that cannot name their despair in relation to the world? What kind of faith in life are we teaching them, that so closely resembles denial? All of us adults are implicated in this dilemma, which will have profound consequences for the generations that follow us. The pain of our children's despair invites us to remap our culture's values; to reexamine and transform the value of profit and consumption over sustainability and wholeness; to hear the dark cries of the earth itself for respite from our unconscious ways of destroying life.

The Bens of the world deserve adults who can take on this challenge. This is not something his parents, or any of us, can do alone. We are in this together, and together we must find the way out. What the alchemy of despair tells us is that the way out is the way through.

## A Final Word on Doubt and Faith

> If you seek a spark, you will find it in the ashes.
> —ELIE WIESEL

In the Jewish tradition, doubt and despair are not sacrilegious. They are not signs of weak faith or spiritual sin. On the contrary, struggling with God, arguing with God, fighting with God, even accusing God of crimes against humanity—these are all very much a part of the Jewish, particularly the Hasidic, soul.

The willingness and courage to be aware of and experience the dark side of life, and the consequent despair we feel when we do so, is what distinguishes authentic faith from wishful thinking and denial. Despair is faith's darker handmaiden. There is no faith without doubt and despair, just as there is no good without evil, no day without night. To be authentic, faith must be all-inclusive—encompassing Auschwitz as much as it encompasses paradise.

Despair, mindfully held, brings us face-to-face with the darkness within ourselves and in the world. Looking into the darkness of unredemptive suffering and death in the world, we let the dark night of the soul take us to wherever it may lead. When we return from this journey, life can be lived fully without turning away from anything, and this, not a blind unquestioning belief, is what faith is all about. Faith is choosing life despite it all, in the teeth of it all. As in the Hebrew toast: "L'chayim!" which means "To life!" To say yes to life we sometimes have to fully enter "no" and make the conscious choice of saying yes. The deepest faith is that which confers value on life even after having looked into the worst.

If psychiatry gives us only two weeks to do this before being declared clinically ill, don't let this worry you. The rewards of the alchemy of despair cannot be measured by psychiatric assessment.

Keep in mind the story of Buddha. As a young prince, he was utterly removed and protected by class privilege from the realities of aging, illness, suffering, and death. Venturing forth from the palace, his first glimpse of these existential realities led to a great sadness, a kind of despair. It was the Buddha's despair that led him to pursue enlightenment. What if this despair about universal suffering had been seen as a pathological disorder of mood? Had the young royal prince consulted a psychiatrist, there would be no Buddhist path to enlightenment.

From the great Hasidic rabbi Nachman of Breslov come these words of comfort: "Regardless of what happens to you, in the end you will find that all your descents will be turned into great ascents . . . because the purpose of the descent is the ascent."[16]

Don't be afraid of your despair. Be gentle with yourself. Take your time with this journey. Let despair guide you to the self you need to birth, the meaning you need to make, the world you need to serve. Let it reward you with a resilient faith in life.

## Emotional Exercises for the Alchemy of Despair

> Consequently I rejoice, having to construct something
> Upon which to rejoice
> —T. S. ELIOT, *Ash Wednesday*

### STEP 1. INTENTION: TOLERATING DESPAIR WITHOUT PANIC OR NUMBING

When we descend into the abyss, we panic. It is cold and dark here, a free fall in empty space with no markers to guide us, nothing to hold on to as we descend. We feel utterly alone—a feeling of disconnection and isolation from the human family, alienation from the world and from the universe of spirit. This is how the soul feels when choked in despair.

Because despair is so difficult, it requires soothing, patience, and care. It is easy to panic or numb ourselves. These reactions complicate despair until it settles into the body as chronic depression.

To find soothing, patience, and courage in ourselves, we must start with a strong intention. Medications like Prozac provide a blanket of reassurance when this intention is lacking; they soothe you when you can't soothe yourself. There's nothing wrong with taking medication if you feel you need to. But there are other ways that work without the side effects, if we can be patient. Patience is the ability to hang in there with feelings that appear to be going nowhere.

Tell yourself: *What I'm feeling is despair. It's an emotion, not an incurable condition or a final destination. I can tolerate this emotional energy and hang in there with it. If I pay attention and let it be, it will move me to a new place.* Make this your intention.

### STEP 2. AFFIRMATION: THE VALUE OF DESPAIR

Affirming despair's value goes against the grain of the culture. This is why it's very important to alter your beliefs about the negativity of despair and to be open to what it leads you to question and what it has to teach you.

Tell yourself that there is something important to be learned from this emotion and that facing into it will liberate you from the need to compulsively avoid or deny the dark areas within yourself and the world. Tell yourself: *Despair teaches the darker truths that will set me free.*

It's always helpful to have company on a rough trip. Read the Hasidic masters on despair—the Baal Shem Tov, Rabbi Nachman, Elie Wiesel. Read the Buddhists on cultivating courage, wisdom, and compassion, such as Pema Chödrön's *The Wisdom of No Escape* and Chögyam Trungpa's *Shambhala: The Sacred Path of the Warrior*. Read Saint John of the Cross. Read the Goddess literature that values the dark: Sylvia Perera, *Descent of the Goddess*; Vicki Noble, *Shakti Woman*; Patricia Reis, *Through the Goddess: A Woman's Way of Healing*. These works and others affirm the value of mindfully approaching despair and other dark emotions.

Write some affirmations about the wisdom that comes from mindfully facing into despair and repeat these when you need to.

See exercises 2–4 in chapter 10 for further suggestions on affirming the value of despair.

### STEP 3. BODILY SENSATION: TENDING TO THE BODY

The body in despair is a body that needs tending. It is tired and/or agitated; run-down, burnt out, numbed. It has lost its capacity to take in what's good about life—the sights, the smells, the touch that brings joy. So it is always wise to start with the body—with the intention to care for your body and to bring it comfort and pleasure, as well as to cultivate emotional sensitivity in the body.

*Conscious Breathing.* Start with your breath. If nothing else seems possible, you can always breathe! Breathe in deeply, allowing your belly to expand, then exhale slowly through the mouth. This simple releasing breath allows the body to calm itself and brings nutrient-laden oxygen to all the cells. Breathe in and out deeply for several minutes, and then just let yourself be silent. Depression, says William Styron, is a "fire in the brain." Simple, deep breathing dampens the fire and allows the brain to settle itself.

As you breathe, become aware of where despair lives in your body. Acknowledge its presence without trying to change or eradicate it. See what happens with it as you continue to breathe through it. (See also exercises 6 and 7 in chapter 10.)

*Aromatherapy.* Scented candles or scented aromatherapy oils are a simple way to inhale soothing relief. Lavender and other scents work well to balance energy and help you relax. Breathing in, take in the aroma and let your body absorb it. Breathing out, release your panic and agitation, letting the candle or scented oil receive it. Let the aroma move into the cells of your body.

*Massage, Bodywork, Energy Work.* This is a good time for simple, nonsexual, soothing touch. In addition to the many different kinds of massage available these days (Swedish, shiatsu, mixed bag), there are also many different kinds of energy work. All kinds of freelance bodyworkers are out there, few of them regulated in any way. A word of caution: Make sure you talk to the energy worker to get a sense of what exactly he or she does and how. This work can be very powerful, and it may actually make you feel worse if the person's philosophy is that you have to "release" everything you're feeling now. When you're in despair, cathartic forms of release can stir the pot when it needs to be soothed. Make sure you're with someone you trust who is sensitive to the impact of bodywork on you.

In my experience, a simple form of energy work that is trustworthy, reliable, and used by all kinds of people, including nurses in hospitals, is Reiki. Most Reiki practitioners have nothing to prove and do their work simply and humbly. I have never heard of anyone having ill effects from it. Healing the body and the spirit through Reiki is something you can learn to do for yourself.

*Music.* One of the greatest balms for despair is music. Even when all is desperate and without hope, music can bring life back to the weary soul. While contemporary books on emotional intelligence advise you to distract your-self from your bad mood, I would say the opposite: Start by using music not as an escape but as a way to get more present with the pain of despair.

Listen to Rachmaninoff, Tchaikovsky, Brahms. Or perhaps your cup of tea is Bessie Smith, Billie Holiday, B. B. King. Whether it's classical music or the blues, listen to music that evokes mood. Let yourself cry the sorrow that is the hidden seed in despair. Be a friend to yourself in this place; and let the music hold you.

After this, listen to more upbeat, rhythmic, or calming music. Observe how your mood is amenable to change.

### STEP 4. CONTEXTUALIZATION: TELLING A WIDER STORY

Look for the context of your despair in the larger world around you: in rela-tion to your family, your community, your society, the earth. Seeing despair in the wider context protects you against the virulent self-blame and self-loathing that often accompany this emotion, and prevents it from becoming corrosive.

Be aware of the difference between contextualization and blaming. In contextualizing an emotion we see it in a wider social framework of under-standing. It is natural for the poor to feel despair about their economic state in a country that privileges the rich, or for any oppressed group to harbor some despair in the social context of inequity or subjugation. Despair in this context is an expectable emotion; but turning it into blame and hate has never been a good antidote for it. Contextualizing despair means putting it in a wider social context and coming to understand it more clearly. This teaches us that suffering is larger than our individual egos and builds com-passion for ourselves and others. See chapter 10, exercises 13–17, for further suggestions on contextualizing despair.

### STEP 5. THE WAY OF NON-ACTION: MAKING A MINDFUL DESCENT

See the demon of despair and greet it: Hello, darkness, my old friend! Be with it, but don't indulge it. Read about it, speak about it, dream about it. Write down your dreams. Don't fight it. Fighting it only wastes your energy.

*Meditation.* Practice a form of mindfulness: mindful sitting, mindful breathing, mindful walking.

Meditate on your despair. Be aware of how and where it lives in your body. Pay attention to it without judgment. Be kind to yourself; tend to your despair as you would to a fragile flower that needs to be lovingly and gently cared for. Notice any self-denigrating stories you are telling yourself ("I'm so weak to feel like this," etc.). Try accepting how you feel without condemning yourself.

See chapter 10, exercises 18 and 19, for further suggestions on how to meditate on despair.

*One Beautiful Thing; One Beautiful Place.* Even in his jail cell, condemned to death, Merseult, the antihero of Camus's novel *The Stranger*, found that he could see a small patch of sky through the bars of his cell, and this made him happy. Natural beauty is a healing balm for despair, allowing you to feel despair without freaking out, and increasing your capacity to tolerate and balance the light and dark of existence.

Despair brings attention to the starvation of the spirit in the modern world. In despair, there is a great hunger for beauty and spiritual nurturance. Find one beautiful place or one beautiful thing each day and contemplate it. This doesn't mean you have to go to Hawaii. There's beauty all around us, if can see it. Any tree will do. Open your eyes and look closely at the trunk, the leaves, the branches when the leaves are not yet in bud. Do the same with a flower, plant, or rock. If you are blessed with a place of beauty within walking distance, walk there each day and sit or stand for a spell.

As a therapist, I have heard countless stories of abuse and torture—mental, physical, and sexual. Often, when I ask what helped the person get through this pain, the answer is: There was a spot in the woods I used to run to. Or: I lived near a stream and would go there when I couldn't take it anymore. Or simply: Nature. Nature was my only real friend, my ally, the one thing that would never let me down.

Let the beauty of nature bring you solace so that you can be with your despair more peacefully.

*Talking with Despair.* In a place where you will not be disturbed, in a state of meditation or relaxation, or just in your ordinary waking consciousness, ask questions of your despair: *What do you want of me? What are you asking of me?*

Some common answers to these questions: Change your daily habits. Eat better. Exercise more. Breathe deeply. Take better care of yourself. Speak your anger to your husband (or wife). Grieve your losses. Change your idea of who you are. Affirm your own worth. Make peace with something difficult (my mother didn't love me; my father abused me; my child doesn't respect me; I'm lonely; I don't know who I am). Find and attend to your spirit.

STEP 6. THE WAY OF ACTION: ACTING WITH AWARENESS
Acting mindfully encourages the alchemy of the dark emotions. Compulsively acting out of the emotion doesn't. Listen to your despair and find out what it's asking you to do. Then go out and do it!

Here are some actions that promote the emotional alchemy of despair.

*Exercising the Demon.* Research continues to show that exercise is as effective a treatment for depression as antidepressant medication. Twenty minutes of aerobic exercise three times a week: Do it and see how despair moves through you, like the weather. If you are too "down" to do anything very athletic, just walking is fine.

*Walking with Despair.* Slow or fast, walk with despair. Walk with your ruminations, anxiety, and deadness. Look up and see the sky. See the trees, the birds, the people you pass. Don't chase away your thoughts and feelings, but don't indulge them either. Let them be a part of the walk. Being present to what's going on inside you and what's going on outside of you at the same time, you develop a more balanced and active approach to despair.

*Creating from Despair.* Use whatever creative resources you have: writing, drawing, singing, dancing, sculpting. Write, draw, sing, dance, or sculpt your despair. Write how it feels, what it looks like, what it reminds you of. Draw it in colors. Sing your despair song. Make it up ("Life sucks and then you die; everything is just a big fat lie."). Put on the right music and dance your despair in slow, lugubrious movements (see Gabrielle Roth, *Maps to Ecstasy*, on how to dance with your emotions).

Then, when you're done, be done. Consciously put the creative activities away and move into the next moment, fully present.

See chapter 10, exercises 25–28, for more on creative actions for despair.

*Friendship Circles.* Do you have one friend or a circle of friends who will listen to you and not try to fix you? If so, you're one of the lucky ones. Be direct and ask: "I need someone to hear my despair for ten minutes without trying to make it all better. Would you do that for me?" Make sure that this is someone you trust and who understands that you do not expect anything but listening and compassion for a limited amount of time. True listening and compassion are lubricants for the alchemy of despair.

*Political Action and Spiritual Service*. There is an alchemy that can only come from action. Do one thing for the earth, whether it's working for Greenpeace or recycling with your children. Community service and political action are ways to enlarge your despair story to include the pain of the world. Find a way to put your dreams of world peace into action through some activity, however small. While acting for the sake of the world may seem overwhelming, it often has the opposite effect: It gets us out of the constricting straitjacket of our writhing egos and onto a larger field of consciousness. The enlargement does us good.

STEP 7. THE WAY OF SURRENDER: TRANSFORMATION
Surrender is about letting the emotional energy flow and letting it go. We can't make it happen, but we can do things that gently encourage it. Here are two.

*Chanting*. Repetition is both soothing and helpful to the art of surrender. Chant a cherished word, phrase, prayer, or mantra from your faith tradition or any word or syllable that you find soothing. Examples: Chanting "Shalom," the Hebrew word for peace. Or "Om," the primordial sound chanted by Buddhists and Hindus.

Do this daily, or as much as you need to—for a moment or an hour. Find a quiet place where no one will bother you, and chant with your despair, not to dispel it but to let it be. See where the sound takes you.

*Prayer*. For long periods when my daughter Esther was chronically sick, I would awake each morning with the Twenty-third Psalm on my lips: "The Lord is my shepherd, I shall not want. She makes me lie down in green pastures. She restores my soul." This prayer has always helped me to find the strength to carry on.

Scientific studies conducted on hospitalized patients who have been prayed for and those who have not show that the first group recovers more quickly—even though they don't know that anyone is praying for them!

Prayer opens the heart and moves emotional energy along. You don't need to pray to God—just pray. Pray as a way to connect to something beyond the small ego-self. Pray the three basic prayers: Thank you. Help me. I surrender.

If you do not like to use God-language, you can still pray for help and pray with gratitude. Prayers of thanks in the midst of despair are very effective ways to move its energy. Say thank you for all the things you may take for granted: your vision, your hearing, your body, your food, your children, and so on.

The same is true of prayers for help. Again, you need not ask God for help. Just ask for help! Perhaps help will come from an unexpected quarter. Watch out for it, so you notice when it comes!

The last prayer: I surrender. So be it. Let it be. Practice clenching your fist and then opening it, allowing your hand and fingers to fully relax. Now do the same with your despair and other dark emotions. Open up and breathe through it all.

Remember the words of Albert Camus: "In the depth of winter, I found that there was in me an invincible summer."

# 7  *From Fear to Joy*

> Courage is mastery of fear—not absence of fear.
> — MARK TWAIN, *Pudd'nhead Wilson*

> Where there is fear, there is power.
> — STARHAWK, *Dreaming the Dark*

## *The Landscape of Fear in the Age of Anxiety*

> I am troubled by shapeless fears. My God, these
> anxieties! Who can live in the modern world without
> catching his share of them?
> — VINCENT VAN GOGH

FEARLESS JACK IS A FOLKTALE HERO with an odd affliction: He can't feel fear. Because he is fearless, he is also joyless. He can't be happy until he is capable of trembling with fear.

So Jack sets off on a journey to find fear. He travels to a land where the king has promised his daughter's hand in marriage to anyone who will spend three nights in the enchanted castle full of horrible creatures. No problem for Jack. The first night, his sleep is interrupted by three huge, ferocious cats. He drives them away and returns to a sound slumber. The second night, he is confronted by a man with his torso cut in half. The two of them play a game of skittles with the bones of two skeletons. Jack wins the game and chases the halved man out of the castle. On the third night, he matches wits with a giant who threatens to kill him, pinning the giant to an anvil with his own ax. Jack sleeps like a log and emerges the next morning, having cleansed the castle of its monsters.

Success in his mission earns Jack the hand of the beautiful princess. But he is still unhappy, because he has not yet learned to feel fear. So the princess consults with the local wise woman, who knows just what to do. She instructs the princess to rise before dawn and draw some water from the fountain in a golden jug. When Jack is asleep, she is to throw the water at him, catching him off guard so that he'll awaken in a fright.

This is how the story ends: The princess does as she is told. Jack wakes up, trembling with fear. From that day on, he is completely happy!

Fearless Jack is not a popular folk story. It's virtually unknown. I found it in a children's book of folktales years ago, and I've never met anyone who ever heard of it. It's not a tale that has stuck with us because Fearless Jack is not exactly your typical male hero. His journey in search of fear, in our culture, would be regarded as singularly unmasculine. Why would a man want to find and feel fear? How can fearlessness be an obstacle to joy? The story seems to have it backward. In a fear-negating culture, we think of fear as the obstacle and fearlessness as the solution. Having no fear is the quintessential mark of courage.

But the courage in this story is not about fearlessly killing monsters; it's about breaking through emotional numbness and recovering the capacity to feel. Killing monsters is no problem for Jack, because he is numb. And being numb is a problem for anyone who wants to live with joy.

Fearless Jack's problem is our problem. The problem with fear is not that we feel it but that we don't feel it. Fear-avoidance and psychic numbing are common ways of handling fear in a culture that continually triggers this dark emotion and yet shames us for it. When we are numb to fear, we are oddly unhappy.

Again, this idea seems to have it backward. Isn't this the age of anxiety? Don't we all walk around fearful? And doesn't our fear get in the way of love, freedom, and happiness?

According to recent estimates, approximately 50 million people in this country suffer from phobias at some point in their life. Some of these phobias are episodic, but others continue and get worse throughout the life of the sufferer. This doesn't include the millions more who would be diagnosed with one or more "anxiety disorders": obsessive-compulsive disorder, post-traumatic stress disorder, acute stress disorder, generalized anxiety disorder, anxiety disorder due to a general medical condition, substance-induced anxiety disorder, and anxiety disorder not otherwise specified.[1]

Indeed this is the Age of Anxiety. This mental state is far more widespread than depression in the general population. The "shapeless anxieties" van Gogh alluded to more than a century ago have become epidemic. But anxiety is not synonymous with fear. Fear is a discrete and powerful emotion with a particular referent, while anxiety is a generalized state of unease. We fear something; we're anxious about everything.

There is also a difference between fear and phobia. We may fear sending our kids to school after a rash of school shootings, but we send them anyway. The difference between this kind of fear and a specific phobia is that if we are phobic about sending our kids to school, we don't send them. If we are phobic about planes, we don't fly. If we are phobic about enclosed spaces, we avoid elevators, and so on. Phobias are specific, extreme, and incapacitating. Put a snake in front of someone who has a snake phobia and he will break out in a sweat, have difficulty breathing, tremble, become lightheaded or nauseous. His heart will race as though he were in the jaws of imminent death, and he will have an overwhelming need to flee. These are the same somatic responses he would have if he were confronted with an immediate threat to his life. Most specific phobias of this kind are irrational because the trigger is not in fact a threat to one's survival. (We are all familiar with the more common phobias—such as fear of flying, heights, or enclosed spaces. But specific phobias can be very arcane—fear of colors, for instance, or fear of chickens.)

While it would be comforting to think that all phobias and fears are irrational, obviously this is not the case. The threats to survival in our era are numerous. Global warming, environmental pollution, nuclear and biochemical disasters, and terrorism are not individual but global threats. But this doesn't mean they don't affect us as individuals! In relation to these threats, it has become almost impossible to experience fear in the old individualized way that we once did when being chased by a wild boar. Our fears are rational, largely transpersonal, and overwhelming. They are also largely denied. In this unprecedented world context, fear is continually triggered and benumbed. Isolated in our own skins, without a community in which our fears can be shared, validated, and addressed, the authentic experience of fear in our time has become almost impossible.

We can't heal what we don't feel. The alchemy of fear is out of reach until we can learn, like Jack, how to feel our fear. When we don't know the contours of our fear, when we can't experience it authentically or speak about it openly, we are more likely to be afflicted with anxieties and phobias, panic, obsessive-compulsion, psychosomatic ills, and all kinds of controlling, destructive, and violent behaviors. Those of us who don't know how to feel our way through the real fears that haunt us; or who are not threatened by the immediate, in-your-face fears that plague millions of people on earth—fears of starvation, war, homelessness, disease, pervasive violence—have replaced the alarm of authentic fear with the host of "anxiety disorders" that have become epidemic in our time.

Equating these anxieties with fear, we think of fear is an irrational emotion. We forget that fear has its reasons.

Once I led a workshop in Boston on befriending fear. A thin woman with a look of permanent, frozen emergency on her face met me at the door. "What I want to know is this," she said. "Are we going to dwell on fear, or are we going to get rid of it?"

I began to explain that the idea was to befriend our fear and then see what happened with it. This was all she needed to hear. She turned and walked away before I'd finished my sentence.

The avoidance of fear is the way of our culture. In this context, befriending fear sounds suspiciously like "dwelling" on it—and what good could that possibly do?

Yet it's avoiding fear that turns it into a phobia. Fear of flying is not a phobia until it keeps us from getting on a plane. Avoiding fear on a large scale has contributed to the phobias, generalized anxiety, panic, and obsessive-compulsion that have been on the rise in our society for the past several decades. Like pain, fear is a wake-up call that says: Pay attention! It's not fear but the fear of fear that makes it a problem. When we are afraid of feeling fear, when we are unconscious of its hold on us, when we avoid it—then we can't use it or move through it. We become frozen in the fear of fear. And we're more likely to end up one of the millions of phobics and panic sufferers.

The word *fear*, like *anger*, is global and undiscriminating. It would help matters if we had more words with more nuanced distinctions. Fretting about making a good impression on a first date is not the same as fearing for your teenage son when you find out he's addicted to cocaine, or fearing for the earth in an age of environmental trauma. Some kinds of fear we can soothe by breathing deeply and talking ourselves through them: Put on your red dress and go out on that date! Some fears alert us to a necessary action: Find a way to communicate with your son and get him into a drug rehab program. Some fears, as we shall see, are prophetic signals from the realm of the "irrational" that give us needed information. Many fears today are overwhelming: What's to be done about the hole in the ozone layer, the toxins in the water, earth, and air?

Whatever the nature of the fear, getting friendly with the beast is always more helpful than becoming frozen and avoiding it. Even our neurotic and "irrational" fears have something to teach us about our limitations, our vulnerabilities, our need for healing. As for the "rational" fears—we ignore them at our own peril. When we are numb to fear, we lose our connection to basic emotional instinct. We forget that primary emotions like fear are part of our humanity and are there for a reason.

There is no existence without fear, so we'd best learn how to work with it. We all need a good dose of healthy fear to navigate our way through the shoals of life. Like Jack, we must wake up and recover the naturalness of healthy, instinctive fear.

The alchemy of fear is about moving through our frozenness to the authentic emotion. When we are capable of fully feeling fear, we are open to the secret of joy.

## What Fear Is For

> Fear is sharp-sighted, and can see things underground.
>
> — MIGUEL DE CERVANTES

In the movie *Fearless*, the protagonist, like Jack, is a fearless man. Max Klein starts out with an airplane phobia. On a routine business flight, the aircraft fails and Max faces into his worst nightmare: dying in a plane crash. But something unexpected happens. "I'm going to die," he thinks in the moments before impact, "and it's okay. I can let it go." As the plane goes down, Max's spirit is soaring. He has moved through his fear to an ecstasy beyond it.

Back on the ground, Max does not welcome his former life. He takes no interest in his wife and son. He finds himself standing on rooftop ledges and walking into traffic. As long as he can reaffirm the sense of invulnerability he felt on the plane, he remains fearless. And it seems to be working. Whereas before the crash he had a severe, life-threatening allergy to strawberries, he now can enjoy the fresh red fruit with no ill effects. He is in a transcendent realm, a ghost walking.

But Max's spirit, like the plane, is bound to crash back down to earth. Biting into a ripe strawberry toward the end of the film, his body goes into allergic shock. The look of fear returns to his haunted eyes and, along with it, a sense of being back among the living. "I'm alive! I'm alive!" he cries, as his wife cradles him in her arms.

Max's recovered fear heralds his rebirth into life on the ground, where fear comes with the territory.

Fear is as human as laughter and tears. Though few of us would care to admit it, we are all afraid. It gets down to this: the human condition is scary. Pain, loss, and death are guaranteed the moment we are born. So too is some degree of helplessness in the face of apparently random events over which we have no control. We fear uncertainty, helplessness, isolation. We want to live without pain or death. And these impossible wishes make us all the more afraid. These basic existential fears inhabit us, whether we are aware of them or not. Almost any phobia or fear you can name, at its core, gets down to these six: fear of pain, loss, death, vulnerability, isolation, and chaos.

To a large degree, we live with these six basic fears without paying too much attention to them. Few of us walk around saying, "I'm scared of pain, loss, death, vulnerability, isolation, and chaos. What about you?" (not much of an opener for a cocktail party conversation). But there are times when fear comes knocking on your door and walks right in, uninvited: You are diagnosed with breast cancer. You lose your job in a downsized economy. Your fourteen-year-old daughter has anorexia. A loved one is dying. When we are in the grip of unavoidable fear is when we have most to learn from it.

Fear arises in any situation where there is a threat of loss or harm to body, mind, and spirit. It is a basic emotion, built into the biological organism. Part of our deepest instinct for survival, fear is our emotional alarm system. Like the other dark emotions, it has an inherent intelligence. Without it, we would be unable to protect ourselves. Fear for those we love is often more intense than fear for ourselves—as any parent knows. Fear is part of the human glue that binds us to one another, in both helpful and harmful ways.

What fear tells us is that something requires immediate and close attention. Its purpose is to move us to action to protect life. An alarm signal goes off that says: Stop where you are—there's danger ahead. Get ready to fight or flee. The "fight or flight" response has, of course, changed over the centuries. We no longer throw our spears at wild buffalo or shimmy up a tree when our prey becomes predator. Still, there are other, less immediate, more complex, and yet frightfully dangerous elements to be attentive to in the interests of protecting life on earth. At perhaps no time in the history of the earth is fear a more appropriate emotion.

### FEAR AS A WAY OF KNOWING

Take a left here, says a still, small voice. Our rational mind may say, No! I need to take a right. Listening to the "irrational" voice, we narrowly avert a terrible car accident. Most of us have had some experience like this, a bolt of fear or queasy internal alarm that irrationally alerts us to a catastrophe waiting to happen or something urgent that requires our attention.

In a culture that dishonors the wisdom of emotion in general, and fear in particular, we're not likely to experience fear as a legitimate or rational emotion. We're even less likely to trust fear as an "irrational" way of knowing.

Yet consider the story of Adam Trombly. On a fine sunny day in the spring of 1974, Mr. Trombly, director of an environmental organization called Project Earth, was walking through a cow pasture in Rocky Flats, Colorado. Suddenly, he had a queasy feeling in his stomach. A feeling of fear and dread suffused his body, though it was a perfectly benign Sunday afternoon with cows grazing on the green grass. "There's something very wrong here," Trombly thought, "and I'm going to try to find out what it is."

He had some soil samples taken from the ground and had them tested. It turned out that the soil was saturated with an invisible toxic substance. The level of plutonium oxide in the earth at this particular site was many thousands of times the acceptable level. There had been a major fire at Rocky Flats Nuclear Installation, and plutonium oxide had been released into the atmosphere. Though this was the worst nuclear accident in the history of the United States up to that point, it was unreported in the press. Trombly's fear "discovered" the problem—and the cover-up.

For most scientists, the idea that Adam Trombly took his fear as seriously as he would any bit of evidence, and acted accordingly, would appear to be ridiculous. Yet through trusting his emotional response, he was able to receive information from the earth itself. This is a way of feeling and knowing that our culture does not recognize, much less endorse and support. On the contrary, by any contemporary psychiatric assessment, Trombly's way of listening to fear would be called an "idea of reference." Ideas of reference—the sense that inanimate objects are talking to us, bringing messages to direct our actions—are considered to be symptoms of a psychotic thought disorder. From this standpoint, listening to fear of this kind as a potential source of information is delusional.

Conventional social science does not recognize intuition: the nonrational information that comes to us from the emotional part of the brain. Listening to fear and learning to discern the important information that it may be conveying is an important part of developing the "sixth sense."

Many years ago, for a number of months, I experienced a pronounced sense of dread and fear whenever I walked up the back stairs of my home. The feelings would intensify as I approached the second-floor landing. Having no idea why fear seemed to descend on me as I ascended the stairs, I began to worry that I was developing a new, heretofore unheard of phobia: fear of hallways. But it was only this specific hallway that triggered my fear—not your classic phobia. One day I spontaneously decided to "follow" my fear up the stairs like a Geiger counter—to go where it led me. It led me to a pipe in the hallway, buried underneath a pile of old newspapers. As I removed the pile, I noticed that the pipe's white wrapping was flaking off onto the floor. This was years before "asbestos" became a household word; the home inspector had never warned me that this pipe, as well as many of the pipes in the basement of my home, were wrapped in asbestos insulation. Though I had no conscious knowledge of this toxic substance, my fear alarm went off with a loud blast as soon as I saw the white flakes in a little pile near the pipe. Believe it or not, the word "asbestos" actually came to me. I immediately called a company to come and check on it. Indeed, after a simple test, I was informed that asbestos was flaking off the pipe—and is most dangerous in its airborne form. I had it professionally removed. Inexplicably, my fear led me to discover this toxic substance in my home.

Don't be afraid to explore your fear—you never know where it could take you!

## THE VALUE OF IRRATIONAL FEARS

Right about now, you may be thinking: "But what about my fear of flying? of speaking in public? of intimacy? These feelings don't give me information. They're not prophetic. They're defeating, frustrating, and inhibiting."

It's true that many of our fears are groundless or neurotic. It wouldn't be particularly helpful to treat all our fears as though they were giving us accurate information. But this doesn't mean that our irrational fears are totally without value. The value of irrational fear is that it humbles us. It tells us we are human and less than perfect. It lets us know that we are in need of healing.

For example, your fear of abandonment may be irrational in the context of a solid marriage to a loving, devoted spouse. But it's still a signal. It tells you that you need to attend to some pain from the past. It alerts you to the fact that your heart needs to be healed if you are to grow in your capacity to give and receive love.

Your fear of abandonment may also carry some information about your partner's limitations. Perhaps your spouse cuts off emotionally when he's overwhelmed by feelings of his own. Your experience of his emotional cutoff as abandonment can teach him how his emotional withdrawal affects you, and lead him to inquire into his own fear of emotions. There is valuable information here for him too: Befriending his emotions would enlarge his capacity to connect to you.

Fear may be uncomfortable but it need not be a problem. The artist Georgia O'Keeffe said, "I've been afraid every day of my life, and I've never let it stop me from doing anything."

Remember: It's not fear but avoiding fear that leads to phobias. Because we are scared to feel fear, we avoid whatever triggers it. It's the avoidance that locks the phobia in place. Phobias are one result of fear when its energy is toxified by avoidance. For example, when you don't move off the sofa because you're afraid of going out and getting hit by a car, it's not fear that stops you; it's avoidance that stops you. Georgia O'Keeffe was not afraid of her fear, so it didn't hinder her in art or in life. She felt fear, but she wasn't phobic. If you are afraid of abandonment, this is not a problem unless you avoid relationships. You may be fearful of speaking in public, so you don't do it. You're afraid of flying, so you take the bus. It's not the fear that stops you. It's fear of *feeling* the fear that stops you. If you can feel it, you can heal it.

Psychologists call the capacity to feel an emotion "affect tolerance." When you are intolerant of fear, you avoid it. When you are tolerant of it, you can feel it and not let the feeling stop you. You can speak in public even if you're afraid you'll become tongue-tied. You can get on the plane and breathe through your fear. Fear is not the problem. Avoidance is the problem! If you can let yourself tolerate feeling fear, the feeling gradually decreases. Current programs of treatment for phobias are all based on increasing affect tolerance for fear through gradually increasing exposure to the phobic trigger. Steven Phillipson, clinical director of the Center for Cognitive-Behavioral Psychotherapy in New York City, puts it this way: When your fear tells you to avoid something "what you really need to do is face down the fear."[2]

The raw emotion of fear itself is actually not paralyzing but energizing. Fear moves us to act—and if we avoid instead, the fear only grows. The trick is knowing how to tolerate the potentially destabilizing energy of this powerful emotion, to face into it, and to find the right action.

Here's a story about how one woman learned to do this.

## JENNY'S STORY: FEAR OF DEEP WATER

Jenny came to therapy with a specific agenda: She was afraid of deep water and wanted to learn to swim. We assess phobias by the extent to which they impair a person's ability to function. In Jenny's case, by her own estimation, her fear was a deep-seated terror that interfered with her social life. An athletic young woman in her early thirties, she'd played lacrosse in high school, enjoyed working out at the gym, and took pride in her physical fitness. For most of the year, her phobia had no impact on her everyday life. But with each approaching summer season, Jenny became more and more anxious. She dreaded the fun-in-the-sun beach activities her athletic friends were into, because they underlined her phobia and made her feel she didn't belong. As a result, she found herself avoiding certain friends. One of her circle had recently purchased a small cottage on the Cape and invited a number of friends, including Jenny, to join him for a week during the summer. This was the direct trigger for her psychotherapy appointment.

"It would be great fun," Jenny told me, "except for the fact that I'm the only one who can't swim, which makes me feel odd person out." Jenny's self-image was that of an extremely independent person. She was used to feeling in charge of her life and hated feeling out of control, dominated by a fear she couldn't conquer. She had tried taking a swim class some years ago but dropped out when it was time to submerge her head in the water. This "failure" had deepened her phobia and made it even more intractable: "I can't imagine how I would ever want to get into deep water, but I can't stand being such a wimp."

Unlike many people who suffer from highly specific phobias, such as fear of air travel or enclosed spaces, Jenny had a specific traumatic memory regarding the origins of her fear of deep water. She remembered, at the age of six, being dunked by an older brother who thought it was time for her to learn to swim and thought the "sink or swim" approach would work. He forced her into the water and held her down while she flailed around, gulping lake water. Her parents were not present when this happened and had little sympathy for her when she came home "hysterical." After this incident, Jenny avoided pools, lakes, and the ocean. Now, as an adult, she was barely able to stand at the water's edge without panic.

With anyone who is phobic, I try to get a "fear history" of the family. Jenny was fourth of seven children in a large, close-knit clan. According to Jenny, hers was "an exceptionally fearless family." The children were encouraged, if not required, to be self-sufficient from an early age. "Independence was probably the most important value in our family," Jenny told me. Independence meant self-sufficiency and fearlessness. Anyone who expressed any doubts, worry, or vulnerability was ridiculed or held in contempt. After the lake episode, Jenny's fear of the water marked her as physically and morally inferior. Her brothers teased her mercilessly. Her parents reprimanded not her brothers but her: "This is not how a Connelly behaves."

When I asked whether her parents ever expressed or exhibited any fears of their own, Jenny replied: "My father was a corporate VP who regaled the family with stories of how he 'destroyed the opposition' at work. He was proud of his service in the army during World War II. He used to say, 'Life is a war, and if you can't be tough, be prepared to die.'"

Her mother's version of similar values was stated somewhat differently: "Fear is something people feel when they haven't the inner strength to meet challenges."

Jenny's father ran the family like boot camp. The three older brothers were good little soldiers until they hit adolescence, at which point two of them got into trouble for delinquent behavior. The four sisters were clearly inferior to the boys, simply by virtue of their gender. But of the girls, Jenny was the only one considered to be hopelessly wimpy, "the odd person out." Jenny spent her adolescence trying to overcome her bad rep in the family by playing lacrosse and striving to be a good athlete.

Fear was a taboo emotion in the Connelly household—shamed and denied, unfelt and acted out. Jenny bought the family myth of independence and fearlessness. But as therapy progressed, she began to realize that the independence preached in her family covered a dark cauldron of not-so-well-kept family secrets. Her mother, in fact, was a hidden alcoholic whose drinking was overlooked by the family until she had a kind of breakdown that was vaguely described as an "illness." Every child in the family bore some evident wounds and scars: Two boys got into trouble with the law as teenagers. The third was a self-hating, closeted homosexual. One of Jenny's sisters had a secret abortion. Another had no intimate relationships. The third seemed to have one destructive relationship after another. As for Jenny, she was concerned about her alcohol use and wondered whether she might be on her way to becoming an alcoholic herself.

Becoming more aware of these hidden frailties and secret dark emotions in her family had no immediate impact on Jenny's water phobia. But it laid the necessary groundwork for beginning to reevaluate her own fears and vulnerabilities and to come out from under the shame of being the identified "fear carrier" in the family.

When I first suggested that there was nothing wrong with fear, Jenny reacted as though I were mentally incompetent. But gradually, she began to get a glimpse of the possibility that she might have a phobia and still be a worthwhile human being. She began to see her fear of deep water as a metaphor for her family's fears of any deep emotional undercurrents and her own fear of the sadness, anger, and despair that she suffered in silence for many years.

As we did this work in therapy, summer fast approached. I suggested Jenny walk into the pool of her health club, on her own, and just get acquainted with the water. To her surprise, she was able, for the first time, to wade into the water up to her waist! She got out quickly, before the panic set in.

The next phase of Jenny's therapy was what psychologists call a "desensitization" program. Through a series of gradual exercises, Jenny visualized herself walking into the water until she was able to let herself go and just float. To do these visualizations, Jenny had to become more and more accustomed to feeling fear and not reacting to it with panic. Though not always the case, this therapy was immediately successful, largely because of Jenny's intention to make it work. Within several weeks, Jenny was able to immerse herself in the pool and swim, but only with her head above the shallow water.

Jenny was inspired by her ability to go this far and thought about ending therapy here. But having discovered a wellspring of "deep water" inside herself, she decided to continue. She wanted to learn to navigate the waters of her submerged rage at her parents, her grief about her parents' lack of nurturance, and her fear of being an "inferior" person. Jenny also decided she wasn't satisfied with her incomplete ability to swim: "I'll know I've really conquered this thing when I can swim across Long Pond on my own, with my head in the water."

This goal would have to wait for the following summer, at which time, with her friends cheering her on, Jenny swam across Long Pond on her own, as though she'd never known fear.

"The fact is," she confided after her victory, "I know I swam across, but the entire way, there wasn't a moment I wasn't scared."

Jenny worried that this meant she hadn't completely overcome her phobia and was surprised to hear me say, "This is what courage is all about, Jenny—feeling fear and not letting it stop you. All you need to do now is let yourself swim with the fear, and you'll find that the fear will change, as you will."

Two years after Jenny ended therapy, I received a card from her that read: "I've been swimming all year at the gym, and somewhere, in the middle of it, I realized that letting go in the water is a great joy! I feel free, for the first time in my life, not only to swim, but to enjoy myself and appreciate who I am!" She signed the card, "No longer a wimp, Jenny."

Shortly thereafter, in a "tune-up" therapy session, Jenny told me that being able to swim, and to feel fear without panicking, had spurred her to confront her father: "You were a bully to all of us, and none of us are happy with ourselves as we are because we were never good enough for you."

To Jenny's great surprise, her father broke down and cried, asking for her forgiveness! "I never meant for you to not like yourself," he told her. "I only thought I was preparing you for the world." Jenny was amazed that her father could be this vulnerable and found that, having worked through her anger at him in therapy, it was possible to authentically forgive him, rather than simply placate him.

In listening to her fear, Jenny found the actions she needed to do to honor fear's power. She learned to swim. She swam across Long Pond. And, perhaps most frightening of all, she confronted her father. The last time I saw her, she said, "I look at the deep water now, and instead of seeing my own failure, I see how beautiful it is. I'm no longer afraid to go deeper into myself."

The joy that Jenny found in her journey of healing through fear was not only in being free to swim in the beautiful ponds on Cape Cod, but in facing into her dark emotions, and learning to respect her fear and herself.

## *Fear in a Fear-Negating Culture*

> We are all afraid: without fear we become manic,
> hubristic, self-destructive.
>
> —ADRIENNE RICH

"The only thing we have to fear is fear itself." These words of President Franklin D. Roosevelt, spoken to a Depression-era audience, sounded reassuring at the time. But on closer inspection, this statement exemplifies the fear of fear in our culture. Actually, life presents us with many fearful things. And it would be good if we learned how to experience our fears mindfully rather than to deny them.

The basic lessons of a fear-negating culture are: Fear is a "negative" emotion that gets in the way of everything good. Feeling and exhibiting fear bring shame. Only wimps and cowards are afraid.

I learned these lessons early in my life. When I was a child, I lived with fear daily. In the refugee camp where I was born, I was a person without a country, one of the millions of homeless persons created by war in this century. For three years, we waited for visas offering safe passage to a nation where we would be allowed to live. Chronic fear takes up residence in circumstances like these, along with that most resilient of emotions, hope.

I left Germany on an outworn battleship when I was four years old. Traveling on rough seas for two weeks was my first lesson in the acute fear of the unknown. Men and women were separated and closely watched by the Americans who escorted us to the land of the free. I missed my father, who, along with the other men, was held in some unseen location in the bowels of the ship. I was frightened he wouldn't find his way back to us. The wide water, with its rolling waves that made me green with seasickness, was another source of fear. I remember asking, with dread, "Mama, will we always live on the water?" To this day, a breezy vacation cruise is my idea of pure, unadulterated hell.

Settling in the South Bronx, I met with the fear-inspiring stench of poverty: the dirty streets, the tattered poor, the palpable air of want and deprivation. I remember being chased home from school by a young male gang member with a knife, being relieved and thrilled that I could outrun him. The persecution was over for my family, but the Bronx clearly had its own threats to survival. I learned early that the world can be a dangerous place.

I responded to fear by becoming feisty and streetwise, ready to outfight or outrun anyone who tried to mess with me. Against the shame of being a refugee and member of the working-class poor, I adopted a culturally masculine attitude toward fear, cloaking it behind an aura of bravado. While the culture of America in the early 1950s went about schooling girls in how to attract and marry a male protector, I went about learning to be "tough." I wasn't about to hide or cower. "Scare the other guy before he scares you" was my *modus operandi*. No one, but no one, was going to get the better of me (as my six-year-old friend Norma found out when she tried to steal a precious piece of Bazooka bubble gum and felt my teeth sinking into her flesh; she dropped the loot and never tried that again).

My early machismo was a sign that I was even more scared in the South Bronx than I'd been in the refugee camp. The streets were dangerous. Showing fear in any way was a badge of shame, like the yellow star of David that marked Europe's Jews for extinction. It was a badge I refused to wear. This feistiness had its price. Internalizing the devaluation of fear in the culture, I've had some trouble ever since speaking my fear plainly rather than turning it into anger. I've had to be particularly careful to remind myself that fear is okay, and that speaking fear is often an important aspect of its alchemy.

## SHAMING FEAR

Some thirty-five years after my macho youth in the Bronx, I found my eight-year-old daughter, Anna, learning the same lesson about the humiliating nature of fear.

I remember the time her second-grade teacher was reading Roald Dahl's *Witches* to the children at literature hour. The book starts with a convention in which the ugly crones, dressed and disguised as ordinary women—and therefore indistinguishable from anyone's mother, aunt, or grandmother—are plotting to exterminate the children of England by turning them into rats. Several children in the classroom found this book frightening. One came in the next day with a note from her mother saying: This book is not appropriate for eight-year-olds.

As a result, the teacher split the class into two groups: the fearless ones would continue reading *Witches*. The scaredy-cats would read *The Rats of NIMH* (this teacher had a thing about rats).

Driving the car pool to school one morning, I listened to a group of seven- and eight-year-olds talking. Josh, a dark-haired boy with glasses, initiated the conversation. "I don't think the book is scary," he said, throwing out the gauntlet. Sarah, a tall third-grader with a bow in her hair and no discernible expression on her face, immediately agreed with him. Anna, ever the rationalist, declared forthrightly that there was no reason to be scared because it was only a story and everyone knows that there aren't any real witches trying to kill children.

That left Annie, the youngest and smallest, with a bright crop of red hair resembling the Broadway cutie, to add her two cents. Annie had nothing to say. In such an important conversation, her silence was conspicuous.

"What about you, Annie? Were you scared?" asked Josh.

The kids looked at her in anticipation. Annie's eyes looked skittish for a second. Then, lowering them, she spoke a barely audible "no" into her lap.

I drove along, a fly on the wall, struck by the force of this early peer pressure. Annie had succumbed, denying her fear to belong to the group. By the tender age of seven and eight these children had imbibed the same basic message that I mastered as a child: Fear is not cool. It's for babies, sissies, and wimps. Never admit you're afraid.

Of the dark emotions, fear is the most shamed and condemned. It lacks the legitimacy and dignity of grief or despair. Grief is understandable after a serious loss, a sign of our caring. With about 20 million diagnosed clinical depressives, despair, like alcoholism, has been morally redeemed by being seen as an illness. But no matter what way you look at it, fear is essentially humiliating.

Because we are human and not just mammalian, fear is not a simple survival response. It's shaped by the beliefs, values, norms, and myths of our civilization. We learn fear in our families and from the culture as a whole. We learn what to be afraid of, how to cope with our fears, how to act and not to act.

Ours is a fear-negating culture. Fear is a tainted trait, associated with weakness, cowardice, and irrationality, the province of the female and the infantile. We view fear as an obstacle to love, reason, creativity, courage, and power. We see no use for it. We learn to put fear away, with our childish games and toys, up in the attic or in the back of the closet, where no one notices it's there.

By the time we are adults, the devaluation and shaming of fear have taken root. In my work with clients, I sometimes ask them to do what I call a Fear Beliefs Inventory. These are free-associative sentence completions in which clients reveal their unconscious convictions about the dark emotions. Without thinking about it, finish the following sentences: I think of fear as . . . . What my fear says about me is . . . . What I'd like to do with my fear is . . . . If I got in touch with my fear and let myself feel it fully, I would . . . .

Some typical sentence completions:

- I think of fear as a weakness, shameful, isolating, a barrier, a monster that hangs over me.
- What my fear says about me is I'm a victim. I'm powerless. I'm weak, neurotic, unworthy, lack faith, am inadequate, a baby, dumb, unbalanced, cowardly.
- What I would most like to do with my fear is get rid of it. Ship it out express mail. Control it. Kill it.
- If I got in touch with my fear and let myself feel it fully, I would not be able to function, become immobile, be frozen for life, wither away to nothing, I wouldn't be able to breathe and I would choke. I'd become catatonic. I'd get stuck in it and be unable to move. I'd be scared to death, paralyzed. Never get out of bed. Never do anything. Hide, run away, die.

Asked to draw their fear, clients depict images of a sticky brown substance like mud or a black abyss that swallows one up, or a hovering monster that devours one's life. These drawings express our fear of fear, and the shame associated with it. To know the alchemy of fear, we must be willing to get comfortable with the muck and face into the abyss.

## THE WARRIOR AND THE VICTIM

Facing into the abyss is not likely in a culture that views fear as an emotional disorder or a moral defect. The devaluation of fear, like the devaluation of emotion itself, is a key characteristic of the culture of patriarchy—the social division of gender in which elite males dominate the political, cultural, and social landscape.

The core of the problem of fear in patriarchy is that fear is fundamentally associated with femininity and, like many other feminized characteristics (dependency, vulnerability, emotionality), devalued. From boyhood on, males are relentlessly conditioned—by peers, families, religious and educational systems, the media, and culture as a whole—to deny their vulnerability and to armor themselves against fear. While women, traditionally the "weaker sex," are socialized to carry the fear that male culture abhors or denies. Fear is the emotional gauge at the gender boundary, the emotion that distinguishes the men from the girls.

Men are the fear-conquerors, women the fear-carriers. Fear-conquerors are symbolically linked to heroism and power. Fear-carriers are symbolically linked to victimization and powerlessness. The masculine archetype of the Warrior and the feminine archetype of the Victim are the gendered embodiments of fear in patriarchal culture.

The Warrior sees fear as an enemy to be conquered on a battlefield, wrestling mat, boardroom, football field, emergency room. The quintessential Warrior activity is, of course, warmaking. The Warrior masters fear through acts of aggression against an "Other" seen as enemy. From the Pentagon to the Mafia, from the streets of the Middle East to the hallways of our high schools, unacceptable fear is conquered through various forms of organized aggression and violence. This is the ultra-masculine way. The pop culture hero is an armored male machine with no fear of injury or death, willing to risk anything to subdue or kill the enemy. His courage is not so much acting despite fear as acting without fear. Fearless men are rewarded with the gender prize of masculinity: top-dog status in the gender hierarchy.

Women, on the other hand, are taught to embody vulnerability and fear more overtly, and this is a crucial aspect of what devalues the female sex (which is why men who show fear are called "pussies"). Fear for women is not an enemy to be conquered but a warning track that says: Go no further. It is the demarcation line that points to the bounds of possibility and permissible female behavior. If you're a woman and you don't use fear to limit yourself, there is an implicit threat of violence. Because fear is culturally "feminine," men who show it are emasculated, dishonored, humiliated. Women, on the other hand, are often considered threatening when they adopt a more macho style of fearlessness.

The culture of patriarchy punishes fearful men and fearless women. It sets men up to be archetypal Warriors and women to be obedient Victims. These archetypes embody fear in ways that lead to ever more dangerous escalations of violence and vengeance from the Warrior and compliance of the Victim in her own subjugation. Neither the Warrior nor the Victim can see the value in fear. Fear is not mined for its gifts; it's banished, numbed, and acted out.

## BANISHING FEAR

Banishing emotion is based on the premise that if we don't feel it, name it, or speak it, it will go away.

Two dearly beloved professors at Dartmouth College, Half and Susanne Zantop, were murdered in the winter of 2001. No one knew why or who did it. The police and investigators weren't talking, so the murders were shrouded in secrecy. The president of the college, trying to cope with this blow and with the grief and fear it triggered on campus, decided to keep the dorms and buildings unlocked—as they usually are in this quiet town of Hanover in New Hampshire. His explanation, according to the *Boston Globe*: "Our hearts here are not filled with phantoms. I don't want people to become alarmed."[3]

Poof! Fear is banished. But why wouldn't some degree of alarm be a natural response to the discovery of two vibrant members of the community dead in a pool of their own blood? I'm willing to bet that the parents of these students would have preferred that the doors to the dormitories be locked until the murderers were apprehended. But locking the doors would mean there is something to fear. And the message that the reassuring president wanted to give was: There's nothing to fear (but fear itself). For some, this may have been reassuring; but for those who were in touch with their fear, the denial probably only made things worse.

Banishing phantoms is one of our culture's favorite ways of dealing with the dark emotions. But banishing an emotion doesn't make it vanish! Banishing fear is a temporary haven for a lingering unconscious energy. Like grief, fear needs a community in which it can be spoken and heard, not a sign that says: "No phantoms allowed."

Sometimes banishing fear is a good idea. Like all emotions, fear is often a passing, momentary energy. Right before a performance, a dancer may be afraid that her sprained right ankle will give out and she will fall on her face. She may choose to listen to her fear and skip the performance. Or she may choose to banish the fear and go ahead with the performance. She's experienced enough to know what kind of pain to attend to and what to ignore. But banishing our fear of larger concerns like AIDS or environmental pollution only contributes to making what we fear more likely to happen.

Banished fear is one of the main ingredients in the mindless eco-madness of our time. According to President George W. Bush, there's no need to regulate carbon dioxide emissions from power plants because carbon dioxide is not really a pollutant! The fifteen hundred members of the Academy of Sciences have long ago declared that greenhouse gases like carbon dioxide are known causes of global warming, which in turn is creating more and more flooding, droughts, and catastrophic weather events all over the globe. But the Bush administration simply denies that global warming is "real." This is banishing fear. It creates a kind of reverse alchemy process, resulting in actions that create an ever more fearful world.

Like the monster in the closet when you're a kid, the fear of fear enlarges our demons. You don't want to get up and look in the closet, because then you'll actually see the monster. So you bury your head under the covers, getting more and more scared. And the monster, which started out as a wee bit of a thing, gets larger and larger, until you're sure it's as large as the house.

When we avoid what scares us, the result is phobia, paralysis, or acting out. We are scared of environmental destruction, so we avoid reading anything on the subject in the newspaper, minimize what we know, and act as if there's nothing to be done, or as if nothing should be done. Avoiding fear, we become more and more disempowered. We don't get to the authentic emotion. We don't learn which fears to respect and which to shrug off. We don't heal fear from the past or learn from fear in the present.

## NUMBING FEAR

The most extreme form of banishment is psychic numbing. This drastic "defense" against the dark emotions in general is on the rise in our society.

Increasingly, fear is triggered and then numbed in the face of random, meaningless violence and overwhelming threats of global proportions. We may feel fear for a moment and then do our best to make it go away, because there is nothing to be done about it on an individual level. An environment that triggers fear daily and at the same time shames us for feeling it, that inspires fear and encourages us to deny it, is crazy-making. This kind of double bind is, to use the popular current lingo, "dysfunctional." This is the environment in which we live. The result is an ever-increasing psychic numbing to fear, and a steady rise in anxiety disorders and phobias.

Disempowered psychic numbing to fear is one of the most striking aspects of pop culture. When I was a teenager in the early sixties, Alfred Hitchcock's *Psycho* made an almost indelible imprint on my consciousness. I couldn't take a shower without locking the bathroom door for several weeks. I later found out that other girls my age had developed a similar shower-phobia after viewing the famous shower slashing scene. Later on, in the 1973 film *The Exorcist*, vivid images of a young girl possessed by the devil, replete with hideous revolving head, satanic-sounding voice, and projectile green vomit, had an even more powerful impact. The fear in the audience was audible.

By today's standards, these movies are tame fare. Teenagers and preteens laugh when asked if scary films are scary. We have become so desensitized to fear that gory cannibalism fests like the movie *Hannibal* are seen as an innocuous evening's entertainment. Among other things, we see the tragic consequences in teenagers and preteens who act out the murderous scenes they vacantly watch on the screen or the lyrics they hear in rock tunes. A thirteen-year-old boy knifes and kills an eleven-year-old outside a Springfield, Massachusetts, movie theater, just after viewing the slasher film *Valentine*. Violent rock lyrics are imitated by boys with guns. Nothing is real. It's all spectacle. The erosion of our ability to feel fear and to express it has devastating consequences on the emotional and moral intelligence of the young.

Our children are raised on a steady diet of fearful media images. They are growing up in a world in which all manner of violent acts are reported nightly on the evening news and can appear and disappear at the flick of a switch. The real images and the "entertainment" images blend together in a surreal infotainment pastiche, giving an aura of unreality to the hard-to-absorb reality of casual violence in our time.

Fear, in this context, loses its purpose as a warning signal and becomes a thrill we seek before moving on to the next channel. Our alienation from fear is a marker of how removed we are from emotional instinct—which explains why television shows like *Survivor* and *Fear Factor* become instant mass manias. Like Canadian geese who've been overfed on white bread, we have lost the wildness of emotional instinct, barely experiencing our primal fear for survival itself. We need the media to hook us up with the emotions we've lost.

Because fear (like sex) is both hyperstimulated and benumbed, we develop an escalating need for a pornography of fear. Movies and videos have to be more and more gory or scary to break through the numbing and give us a temporary feeling of fear. The pornography of fear stimulates the visceral, adrenaline-pumping emotion we've lost in the virtual reality desensitization of our overstimulated and benumbed civilization. Watching *Scream* or *Alien*, we temporarily break through the numbing. We feel fear moving through our bodies and let it go when the movie is over. We're having an ersatz alchemy experience. But we end up more alienated from the reality, purpose, and intelligence of fear in our lives, less able to cope with real fears about real things.

ACTING OUT

When fear is shamed, banished, and numbed, we are no longer free to act with it, and we are more apt to act out. Acting out is about skipping a step in awareness, moving from repressed, shamed emotion to an act that expresses unconscious feelings in behaviors that we don't consciously connect to the emotion. When we are shamed for feeling something, acting out is likely, and usually harmful to self or others. In keeping with our culture's devaluation of the female, women tend to act out in self-destructive ways, while men, trained to be aggressive, more often act out in ways that are destructive to others.

For example: Jimmy is not an athlete or a scholar. He has no spectacular talents. He doesn't play football or have a popular girlfriend. His schoolmates bully and harass him mercilessly. Those who don't do so actively mutely stand by as the bullies go about their business. He is scared to go to school and be humiliated. But after a while, he numbs out to his fear and turns it into a silent, bitter rage. Jimmy's particular penchant for psychic numbing has been fed by gorging himself on media violence for years. One day he's had enough and begins to plan his revenge. Piling up an arsenal of weapons, he decides on a hit list. He knows which students in particular he wants to kill: the ones who appear to be fearless—the school football hero, the three most popular kids in the school. Or perhaps just anyone at all.

This scenario has become chillingly real in our era. The experts keep searching for the causes of the epidemic of violence among young males. They look to family violence or neglect, the silent plague of male depression, drug abuse, and desensitization to violence in the media. And certainly all of these are factors. But overlooked is the Warrior culture of fear-negation, which makes violent acting out inevitable in the young male population. Violence is often a direct consequence of denied fear, fear acted out because the person has lost the ability to feel it authentically and mindfully, and to express it without shame. People act out because they are afraid to feel, afraid to speak, afraid of their fear.

Female forms of acting out are typically more self-destructive: suicidal gestures, eating disorders, self-mutilation, and unprotected sexual promiscuity (all of which are on the rise among teenage women). Benumbed fear in women, even when it is not acted out, bears grave dangers. Many years ago, I had a client, Andrea, who refused to let fear be a warning track for her. She lifted weights, walked in scary neighborhoods, worked in a male-dominated architecture firm, and could move furniture with the big boys. One night, her car broke down after midnight in a dangerous neighborhood. She thought nothing of getting out and thumbing a ride. She was picked up by a man who blindfolded her, drove her to a house, and called three of his pals. The four men gang-raped Andrea at knifepoint for the next five hours and then dumped her on the street.

The most traumatic part of the rape for Andrea was the loss of her fearlessness. "I don't want to live in a world where I can't be free," she cried. "I don't want to be afraid all the time. I don't want to let fear determine where I go and what I do."

Andrea had ignored the normal fear that women carry in patriarchy; and she had paid dearly. Her cry to live free in a world without fear is the expression of a universal yearning. But living without listening to fear, throwing caution to the winds, is not a solution to this yearning. Without fear, we feel safe when we aren't safe, compromising our ability to protect ourselves. Or we unconsciously channel fear's energy at inappropriate targets, acting out in ways that only make the world more fearful.

The more fear-inspiring our world becomes, the more afraid we are of this emotion. The more there is to fear, the more we avoid it. In a post-Holocaust, post-atomic, hyper-violent, environmentally traumatized era, a world in which "the dreadful," as the philosopher Heidegger says, "has already happened," fear is ever present, overwhelming, and largely unconscious. We become inured to fear, strangers to our own hearts.

In the process, we lose the intelligence of fear and the information we need to know about ourselves and our world. We forget what fear is for, what it can teach us about survival and about the human capacity to live happily and in harmony with each other and the earth.

"When the wayfarer whistles in the dark, he may be disavowing his timidity," said Sigmund Freud in *The Problem of Anxiety*, "but he does not see any the more clearly for doing so."

When our children are afraid of the violence around them and we say, "There's nothing to be afraid of. It's okay," we are teaching them to whistle in the dark. We might put our arms around them and say, "It's okay to be scared when scary things happen. Being aware of fear makes you stronger than pretending you don't feel it. Let's see if we can find something to do that would make you feel safer."

In this way, we could acknowledge the naturalness of fear and reward our children for their mindfulness and honesty. We could soothe them without teaching them to whistle in the dark. We could educate them to cope with fear by feeling, speaking, and finding an action for it. We could teach our children how to honor and befriend their fear.

## The Alchemy of Fear

> In order to experience fearlessness,
> it is necessary to experience fear.
> —CHÖGYAM TRUNGPA,
> *Shambhala:*
> *The Sacred Path of the Warrior*

### EVELYN'S ORGASM

Evelyn came to therapy wanting to talk about food and sex. She said she was afraid of both. Eating was a dangerous enemy, threatening to undermine her control. She avoided eating and then stuffed herself compulsively. She studiously avoided sex with her husband, Bill. She'd experienced little desire or arousal and had been unable to have an orgasm for six years. She wanted to feel less afraid. She wanted to have a more vital relationship with Bill. She wanted to come.

Evelyn was stuck in "frozen" fear. Avoiding food and sex was her way of coping with the fear these activities triggered. The last thing she wanted to hear from me was that the problem was not her fear but her fear of fear.

"What bunk!" she responded when I put this to her. "I've been afraid my whole life. What good does it do to feel fear?"

When I asked Evelyn to tell me where in her body she experienced her fear, she said, "I don't know what you mean. Fear lives in every part of my body, in every cell of my body."

Though she described herself as ruled by fear, Evelyn could not actually locate it bodily. Her years of avoidance had removed her from the direct experience of this emotion. Remember Fearless Jack? He was able to experience fear in the vulnerable hypnagogic state between sleeping and waking. Some form of mindfulness meditation or relaxation process that alters consciousness from the "normal" waking state is often helpful in recovering this direct experience. For this reason, I taught Evelyn to meditate. When she had learned the basis of mindfulness meditation practice, I suggested she focus her awareness on the fear in her body.

Evelyn wasn't pleased. She wanted her fear to be banished, not located. Nevertheless, she practiced meditation for several months as we talked about her fear, its roots in a history of a sexualized connection to her father, her father's near-suicide, her mother's alcoholism. There was no dearth of reasons for Evelyn's fears. Fear of intimacy and of isolation, of not being loved and of being loved, of being out of control, were all focalized around food and sex. Sex was both tantalizing and terrifying (given her father's lack of boundaries in this area). In her adolescence, Evelyn had been promiscuous, using sex as a compulsive way of escaping from feelings. During this time, she'd had a number of abusive boyfriends and begun to associate sex with humiliation. In early adulthood, she had avoided sex for several years. Only in the first few months with her husband had sex been a source of pleasure, fun, communication, and intimacy. But after being formally married, sex again became scary. She was back to avoidance, only occasionally letting it happen to please Bill and thereby stave off her fear of being abandoned by him.

In addition to her sex and eating phobias, Evelyn suffered from obsessive-compulsive behaviors and generalized anxiety (which is what she meant by the fear in every cell of her body). So Evelyn and I worked on befriending her fears.

One day Evelyn came to therapy all excited. She had meditated on her fear at home for forty-five minutes. An odd experience had occurred. She had felt paroxysms of fear in her chest, which she described as a kind of "peristalsis." She had tried to hang in there with these sensations. And to her amazement, being present with fear had transformed itself to a state of surrender. She was able to feel the fear and witness it without jumping up to numb it through eating. Something shifted. After the meditation, she was able to have some fun with Bill and to feel aroused in his presence.

Then she noticed something else. When she was afraid, she converted her fear to anger, which she then directed at her husband. Her fear about being vulnerable and being abandoned by Bill were at the root of her frequent fights with him. "My anger is just a mask for my fear," she said, amazed that she could feel this and not just think it.

As her week progressed, Evelyn realized that her way of being angry was creating problems in her marriage. She began to pray (though she was not a religious or churchgoing person) to be released from it. And lo and behold! She was released! She was able to talk to Bill about her fear and anger in a more vulnerable way, rather than to act out by having a fight or eating compulsively. She let Bill know that her anger was her way of coping with the fear that he would leave her. This brought them closer. They laughed and played. They made love. And for the first time in six years, Evelyn had an orgasm.

"Okay. I'm sold," she told me in the next session. "Maybe your idea about befriending fear wasn't so bad after all!" We spent this session talking about Evelyn's learned style of emotions. She lived in a family where emotions were taboo and scary. Her role models were a cold, critical, alcoholic mother who often had "fits" of out-of-control anger, and a suicidal father who sexualized his relationship with his daughter. Evelyn reacted by trying to control her emotions. But she had a volatile temper of her own, and was very passionate by nature. When she felt scared or mad or sad, she would try to do something to suppress how she felt. Her modus operandi was: Don't just feel something, do something. Stuffing food down her throat, reading compulsively, and having compulsive sex were three ways of handling her emotions when she felt out of control. Thus, she vacillated between avoidance and compulsion.

By meditating on her fear and just letting it be, Evelyn had tried some other actions. Instead of compulsively having sex, eating, or fighting, and instead of compulsively avoiding sex and eating, Evelyn spoke her fear directly to Bill. The unexpected fun part was how this process of listening to fear in her body and giving herself permission to express it had led to more intimacy with Bill, to sex that was desired rather than used to escape from emotion, and to orgasm.

Evelyn's experiment with befriending fear was not a total success story. She was not entirely satisfied with the idea of having to be mindful of fear for the rest of her days. She still wanted her fear to disappear altogether. But fear was now a tolerable emotion, an opening to communion, surrender, climax. She had found the connection between fear and joy.

## THE MAGIC OF SPEAKING FEAR

When Evelyn decided to speak her fear to Bill rather than to convert it to anger, something shifted in their relationship and a door to joy opened. This is one of the simplest yet most powerful ways to discover the alchemy of fear: the act of speaking it directly.

The shaming of fear makes speaking it a virtual taboo unless you're a young child, preferably female. There's no simpler way of breaking through this taboo than just doing it. Giving voice to fear goes a long way when it's most needed. It's a crucial key to the transformation of fear to joy that I've witnessed time and time again in my work as a therapist.

As an example, the embattled couple comes to mind. They've been fighting the same fight forever.

"Why can't you listen to me?" she cries. "Why can't you respond to my feelings?"

"Why can't you accept me as I am?" he counters. "Why can't you see all the things I do to please you?"

They are at an impasse. He wants more sex. She wants more intimacy. She wants him to be more emotional. He wants her to stop demanding that he change.

One of the first things I do with couples like this is to teach the skill of speaking fear. This takes some work. Even asking, "What are your fears?" can seem like an accusation if I don't preface it with a little preamble about how even the most solid relationships have their share of fears. With some reassurance, it's safer for these fears to emerge.

She might then say: "When you don't respond to me emotionally, I feel disconnected. I feel isolated and adrift, as though I'm floating in deep space with no one there, nothing to anchor me. This is scary for me."

He might say: "When you criticize me, I feel humiliated, unappreciated, and alone. I feel scared."

Many couples would prefer to do the Marital Mortal Combat game for years than to speak their fear to each other in words like these, which can feel altogether too vulnerable. The good news is that, when couples learn to speak their fear, something invariably shifts and a kind of magic happens. Hearts that have been hardened for years begin to soften. The distance that couples use to protect themselves when they are afraid, but are afraid to say they are afraid, begins to melt. The mutual yearning at the core of Marital Mortal Combat shows its face: the need for connection, without which we are all doomed to feeling alone and afraid.

When this happens, healing words usually follow.

She might say: "I need you to listen and respond to me in an emotional way because I need to feel connected to you before I can open up sexually."

He might say: "I want to have sex with you not just because it's pleasurable, but because it's the place I feel most connected to you."

Speaking and listening to fear ushers in new words, and a new sense of connection. Even a relationship that has suffered years of disrepair and neglect begins to renew itself. There is joy and connection again, where there was only pain and distance. This is the alchemy of fear.

## THE MOVEMENT FROM FEAR TO JOY

What I know about the alchemy of fear has not just come from the work I do. Mostly, it has come through facing my own demons.

Here's how fear's alchemy found me.

My daughter Esther had just learned to walk when she vaulted herself out of her crib. For more than two years, she'd been a fitful sleeper, especially after a particularly difficult motor milestone. Learning to walk was a mammoth accomplishment, requiring careful, continuous patience on her part and ours, because Esther did not learn to move without hours and hours of coaching and assistance. For weeks after her walking triumph, Esther didn't sleep for more than two or three hours at a stretch. Getting her down to sleep was harder than ever. Bleary-eyed with sleep deprivation, we'd consulted a sleep expert who advised us to let her know that we'd be in the next room and then leave her in her crib until she cried herself to sleep.

Roger and I retreated to our bedroom, holding our hands over our ears. Esther did not cry herself to sleep. She cried herself into a majestic leap over the bars of her crib, vaulted by tears of rage. The fact that she was able to do this motorically (given her low muscle tone) was the only silver lining in this episode. (It's amazing what the energy of fear and anger can do!) Running into her room after we heard her fall, we found her dazed and whimpering but apparently okay. By the next morning, however, she awoke with her neck tilted rigidly to the right. And we were off to Children's Hospital again, a place we'd come to know all too well.

The orthopedist called it "torticollis." His assessment was alarming: Esther probably had a slipped cervical disc. She might well need hospitalization and traction. A CAT scan was scheduled for the following Monday, and she was discharged for the weekend under our care.

"Be careful that she doesn't fall again," the good doctor said casually as we got ready to leave, "or she might have further neurological complications."

"Like what?" I asked, ever the one to know the possibilities.

"Like paralysis from the neck down."

Uttered with a disarming nonchalance, these careless words were a mainline of fear shot straight into the chambers of my heart. Had we come this far with Esther only to lose her to mundane falls that could make her quadriplegic?

I descended into a raw terror that would not loosen its grip for the next two days, a ragged zone of fear about Esther's fragility. When not with Esther, I paced the floor praying for her safety. Feelings this powerful often compel us to seek comfort, distraction, or oblivion. But these options seemed useless. There was no pill or drink or TV program strong enough to distract me.

After several hours of trying vainly for some relief through sleep, I saw that there was no escape. I remembered a bit of advice that my midwife had given me when I was in the grip of labor with Aaron: When you feel the pain coming, head straight into it. I decided to head straight into the fear, to make fear my meditation.

All night, I lay awake, experiencing a succession of physical and mental states that I tried to witness without flinching: a numbing cold in my extremities, my gut churning, my chest radiating with the sensation of hot dry ice. I watched my mind tell tragic tales about my life with a child impossible to protect: Esther paralyzed and unable to move, all her progress finished for all time. Esther in a wheelchair, immobile. Our lives in ruins. After a seemingly endless time, I noticed a shift: The fear felt less like a siege and more like an energy moving through me. I began to be more curious about it, to just notice it.

At four in the morning, the fear broke, like a fever. And my mind's agitation came to a full stop. I was thoroughly awake, in a state of wonder. Somehow, mysteriously, my heart had emptied itself and I was lifted up, in a state of inexplicable ecstasy. My face awash with tears of joy, I felt as though I could burst with it. Whatever this child brought me was going to be all right, I thought. At the same time, a warm energy coursed through my body, concentrating itself in my hands, which were now hot and tingling. A voice, quiet but insistent, said: *Go to your child.*

When voices like this insist, I do my best to listen. I got out of bed and followed directions, extending my hands over Esther's body in the darkness.

The energy seemed to stream out of my hands toward her sleeping form. After a timeless time, the voice said: *She's all right.*

Another voice—the doubting voice that hardly ever leaves me, despite my many experiences as a reluctant mystic—whispered in my head, *This is really nuts. You've finally flipped.* I decided to ignore it, since it seemed to have nothing constructive to say.

Returning to my bed, I saw the light begin to dawn, a rosy glow against the darkness. In my mind's eye, a book, open to the table of contents, appeared to me. Looking closer, I could actually see the chapter headings laid out before me: *Grief and gratitude, fear and joy, despair and faith.* I grabbed the pen and paper I always keep at my bedside and managed to scribble these words down before falling into a welcome, dreamless sleep.

When I awoke a short time later, I felt impossibly rested and calm.

We returned to the orthopedist on Monday, who declared with obvious befuddlement that Esther's CAT scan was normal. He wanted to do more tests, to see if there were some other "anomalies." We politely declined and took our daughter home. Esther's crooked neck straightened itself out and has not been a problem since.

Ever the scientific mystic, I wonder: was Esther's "healing" the result of some miraculous shamanic magic I'd stumbled into, or was this about an arrogant doctor's mistaken diagnosis? There is mystery here, but one thing is clear: There was an emotional alchemy that my life was teaching me, again and again. The heart heals itself when it's open to pain. The lead of suffering transforms into the gold of spiritual power.

In addition to the joy of this alchemy, two other gifts came with it. One was the energy work I spontaneously learned that night. In retrospect, having taken a course in Reiki, I can see that what I was doing has a strong resemblance to this healing art that is used by nurses, physical therapists, and laypeople. The practice came to me when I needed it most.

The second gift is the book you are reading—inspired in this moment of fear's alchemy.

## The Three Ways in the Alchemy of Fear

Since Esther's fall and its aftermath, I have tried to describe the alchemy I experienced in discursive terms. It was during this time that I began to think about what I have called the way of non-action, the way of action, and the way of surrender.

## THE WAY OF NON-ACTION

Being with fear in a state of awareness in which we don't avoid, cling to, try to fix, or even try to understand, but are simply present: this is the precondition that makes the alchemy of fear possible. Allowing your vulnerability to become the focus of your meditative intention, you practice the art of non-action. This is a process without a "goal" in sight. You are not trying to fix fear, make it go away, or to feel more "in charge," less vulnerable or helpless. You just watch and listen. This may feel impossible, but it isn't. It requires an intentional choice to regard fear as a kind of "meditation" and then to focus on it as clearly and openly as possible.

## THE WAY OF ACTION

When we master the way of non-action, we hear what fear is asking of us. Sitting in meditation and feeling the peristaltic movement of fear in her body, Evelyn befriended the energy. She saw the connection between her fear and her anger—how her anger masked the fear she couldn't tolerate. Then she could hear the call to pray for release from her anger and to speak fear to her husband directly. The way of non-action led to this action she had not taken before. In the process, she found a new way to make love, to open up and enjoy herself.

Listening to my fear after Esther's fall from the crib, I came to the practice of healing hands, a way of action I'd never dreamed of before. And this book arose in my vision, like the sun after a long, dark night.

In the alchemy of fear, listening closely, we find the right action, the action that fear asks of us. In the immediate alarm of fear, the action is often obvious. There have been reports of mothers exerting superhuman strength when their children's lives are at stake. But the right action does not have to be a brave, aggressive move. Sometimes the right action is a small one: speaking our fear, becoming vulnerable when we least want to. Sometimes the right action is extending our compassion to ourselves or others when we are afraid . . . or giving someone a hug. Political action is another form of right action. Working to change a policy of environmental recklessness is a balm against the fear of global peril. Spiritual service—serving others not for personal gain but because there is joy in being of use—is a right action, regardless of what kind of fear we're working with.

Sometimes the right action is going out and having as much fun as possible when you are most afraid—even being excessively silly. Patch Adams, the famous doctor played by Robin Williams in the film of the same name, cured himself of his own fear and despair by becoming an outrageous physician who put on a clown suit and entertained his sick and dying patients.

Knowing the right action comes from mastering the way of non-action. When we listen to fear, the appropriate action becomes clear. This is not always the action our rational minds would choose; it is the action that comes to us from the heart. We find the right action not because we are willful but because we are willing. When we are willing to accept the dark emotions rather than conquer them, we become warriors of vulnerability, and we learn the way of surrender.

## THE WAY OF SURRENDER

When there seems to be no way out of a fearful situation, there is still an action that can work to alleviate fear: prayer. Sometimes prayer is the only action possible. The wonderful thing is, it works! We may not always get exactly what we pray for, but we discover that fear does not have to be a barrier to joy; it can be the gate that opens into it. Prayer comes to us instinctively, almost despite ourselves, when we are afraid. It is an ancient practice in the art of surrender.

Unlike the Warrior's armoring and the Victim's self-limiting reactions to fear, the way of surrender is about remaining vulnerable and finding the power of no-protection. Surrendering to fear does not mean acquiescing to what scares us, giving in, becoming passive, or becoming cowardly. Surrender is the art of letting fear be.

It is popular nowadays to speak of "letting go" of "negative" emotional states. But no one can force a letting-go process. Forcing only makes letting go less likely. *Letting be* is what allows *letting go* to happen. Current "cures" for phobias are all based on facing into the fear and becoming more tolerant of how it feels. Whether using marvelous high-tech, virtual-reality cyberspace computer equipment, or just making fear your meditation as you go through your life, it all gets down to this: Face into your fear and it lifts!

The art of surrender to fear is the art of living. Our culture tells us that fear is irrational and that we must let go of it to be happy. But the truth is that when we can attend to fear, it lets go of itself.

My daughter Esther seems to know this alchemy by heart. She is the teacher in this area, and I am the rather slow student. Since her fall from the crib, she has fallen and fractured eleven bones. She is at risk for falling, breaking bones, dislocating knees. Her fear of falling is something she lives with, but she walks on. In fact, in her own unique way, she does more than walk: she dances—leg braces, back brace, and all. Every day she's alive, she finds something to be joyful about. Remembered joy is, in fact, one of her self-applied balms for fear. "That was a good day," she'll muse when confined to her bed or the house because of yet another dislocated or fractured bone. Esther could find the bright side of the moon on the darkest night—because fear doesn't stop her. Living with it daily, she always knows the right action, and keeps on surrendering. And living with fear for Esther every day, I can find, at least on the good days, the secret she seems to know instinctively.

The way of non-action and the way of action, when practiced, become the way of surrender. Fear calls us to act for the sake of life and to surrender to life; and this surrender itself brings joy. Happiness flows naturally. We don't have to go looking for it by consuming pleasure. It comes to us as a birthright.

Joyful living is not the same thing as living without fear. It's about living fully with fear. Joy is what we find when we act with our fear for the sake of life. Mindful fear moves us to act with courage and loving-kindness, in the service of ourselves and others. And these acts of compassion and service are the quickest route to dispelling fear. If you're afraid of illness, serve someone who's ill. If you're afraid of disability, serve someone who's disabled. If you're afraid of not having enough money, work for the poor. If you're afraid of death, volunteer at a hospice. If you're afraid of loneliness, work with the elderly shut-ins in nursing homes. Then you will discover the alchemy of fear.

Facing into our worst fears—of death, loss, pain, vulnerability, isolation, and chaos—takes as much courage as trekking in the wilderness in a snowstorm. The good news is that the more dreadful the fear, the greater the joy of facing into it. It turns out that our fears of loss, death, vulnerability, pain, chaos, and even helplessness are not intolerable. Finding the core of our fear, we find our way. Like the wilderness adventurer who makes it home through the storm, we are filled with joy.

## Fear in the World

In an interview in *Wildfire* magazine, Adam Trombly, the prescient director of Project Earth, had this to say about our current emotional predicament on earth:

> People aren't educated emotionally, spiritually. It's literally as if feeling has stopped in human culture. People are numbed, in

shock. It's like a body . . . . If you stick your hand into a fire, pain signals are sent to the brain. The human body, as it stands right now, is disassociated from its feelings, it doesn't feel the rainforest being cut down, the underground nuclear explosions. Yet I am convinced we do feel it! We might get sick and not know why we're sick. We may not know why we feel it but we feel it . . . So we've got to start realizing what it is we're feeling because the impulse has to get from the hand to the brain and to the heart, so we can pull the hand out of the fire; so we can take corrective action—do a different ceremony than we're doing. The earth has been profoundly destabilized by the withdrawal of feeling.[4]

Pulling one's hand out of the fire of environmental destruction that threatens to destroy the earth is perhaps the most urgent mission of our time. The fire of global disaster may seem small and contained now. It may seem that, with our antipollution legislation, the EPA, and other environmental watchdog organizations, we are taking care of it. We don't want to become alarmist and treat the small fire like a conflagration. Politicians are often quoted as saying that "we should not become alarmed by these reports" about global warming, ozone depletion, air pollution, cancer rates, and so on. Should we then stay numb? Or trust in the government to control the things that scare us? The government will not do the job for us. The small fire endangers us every day. With our hands in the fire and no sensation of fear to alarm us, we are at greater risk of harm.

Fear, in the context of our global predicament, is not the enemy. It tells us that we are in urgent need of finding a different ceremony. To do this, we would have to expand our experience of fear and tell a larger story: one that encompasses the fear of every human being on this earth who wants to live in harmony with nature and to see future generations flourish. Our beautiful planet calls to us, through our collective fear, to act for the sake of Life. May we heed the call.

## Emotional Exercises for the Alchemy of Fear

### STEP I. INTENTION: BEFRIENDING FEAR

Fear is a difficult emotion to tolerate because when you are afraid, you are impelled to "do something" about it—and fast! This propensity to action is part of fear's intelligence. But without the ability to mindfully experience fear in the body, the propulsion to action can be premature and destructive, designed more to banish fear than to listen to it.

Start with an intention like this: My fear is a human call to protect life. I can feel fear fully, with awareness. I can use fear's energy wisely, to find the right action.

### STEP 2. AFFIRMATION: THE VALUE OF FEAR

Befriending fear in a fear-negating culture is essential if we want to use this emotion wisely. To do this, we have to be aware of our negative, limiting beliefs about fear, and to reconstruct and affirm a new set of beliefs.

We can't be warriors of vulnerability if we think fear is a shameful, debilitating emotion. Think of fear not as a weakness but as information, a signal of unsafety, a usable energy, and a way of knowing. What fear tells you is that you are human. You are vulnerable. You are interconnected with others in the fabric of life. You can let yourself feel fear, breathe through it, and use its energy. You don't have to let fear become panic by avoiding it. You can feel it and let it be, and doing so can open the gates to joy.

These affirming statements about fear may seem dubious. Honoring fear and treating it like a legitimate emotion can be uncomfortable and feel "wrong." Affirming the value of fear requires a kind of revolution within, to transform the fear-negating culture we have internalized.

Try this: Write a list of fear-affirming statements and pin them on your bathroom mirror or some other place where you look often. Changing what you believe about what you feel is one of the most important ways to shift an old emotional pattern. Psychologists call this "reframing," and it's one of the important skills in the alchemy of the dark emotions.

The following questions might help you frame your fear-affirmations:

- What fears have you faced? What did you gain from facing them?
- If your answer to the previous question is "none," ask yourself: Why not? What got in the way of facing your fears?
- Think of a time when you felt paralyzed by fear. What kept you from moving through it? What, if anything, helped?
- Think of a time you acted in spite of fear or acted with fear. What happened?
- What did you learn?
- What fear(s) are you holding in now? What fears are you avoiding? What do you think would happen if you let yourself feel them?

Following this, try the following sentence completions:[5]

- If fear didn't scare me, I would use it to. . . .
- The resources and strengths I now have to use my fears creatively are. . . .
- When I view fear as teacher, I learn. . . .
- Something productive I can do with my fear is. . . .

Changing your shaming beliefs about fear creates an opening, a place in the heart where fear can live without wrecking your self-esteem and composure. The open heart can befriend fear and is ready for alchemy.

### STEP 3. BODILY SENSATION: LOCATING FEAR IN THE BODY
Fear is a pronounced bodily experience. If you're not numb, you can't miss it. The trick is to hang in there with it, without converting fear's energy into anger, aggression, violence, or any manner of acting out—and without resorting to alcohol, drug dependency, or other addictions to numb it.

Try this: Find a quiet space in your life where you can consciously experience your fear in your body and soothe it. (See exercises 6 and 7 in chapter 10.)

### STEP 4. CONTEXTUALIZATION: THE WIDER STORY OF FEAR
This step is one of the most critical to using fear's energy wisely. It is essential to know how to tolerate fear in the body and to affirm its value. But without widening the story of fear that we tell ourselves, we can easily be led to actions that are nonproductive or xenophobic. Fear tells a story not only about your own particular situation, but about the lives of others in your family, your community, your society, the world. In this day and age, and in this world, fear is an eminently relational emotion. Contextualizing fear in a wider emotional ecology takes some rethinking, because we tend to think of it as exclusively personal, subjective, and private.

Try going on a "train ride" of inquiry: probing the depths of your fear to the final stop or destination, and then widening fear's story from this end point.

For example: You are afraid of heights. You think this is all your own *mishegoss* (Yiddish for "craziness"). But ask yourself: What does this fear really get down to? If you're standing at the top of the Prudential Center and looking down at the antlike people below, and the cars that look like toys, what is that adrenaline pumping through your veins telling you?

Chances are that you're afraid of falling. Now keep going on this "train ride." If you're afraid of falling, what's that about? This is a no-brainer: You're afraid of ending up smashed on the pavement below. Unless you have a falling disorder, this is highly unlikely. So what's the fear of falling all about? Probably losing control, getting hurt, and dying. Okay. That's the last stop on this train ride of inquiry: You're afraid of chaos and uncertainty, not being able to control everything. And you're afraid of dying.

So you do have some choices here: You can avoid tall buildings and end up phobic. Or you can meditate on your fear of uncertainty, loss of control, and death. This probably doesn't sound too appetizing, but you'd be amazed at its power. Avoiding tall buildings will not lengthen your life span. You're much more likely to get hit by a car than you are to fall off a tall building. The damn thing of it is, none of us knows how and when we're going to die. So the pertinent questions are: Can you find some peace in the midst of uncertainty and not-knowing? Since you can't control the time and manner of your death, what *can* you control? What would you want your life to be like before you die? What would be most important to you if you died tomorrow? Are you doing what you want to be doing now so that you can die in peace? If not, why aren't you controlling what you can control—what you do with your life?

Use the energy of fear to help you meditate on these kinds of questions. Your fear of heights misinforms you: It tells you that death is imminent, right now. On the other hand, there is some truth to fear's information: Death is imminent—eventually! So fear is asking you to live life as though death was really going to happen to you—which it is!

Then go to the next step, widening the story.

Here's the deal: We're all on the same train, afraid for our lives. And we're all headed to the same destination on this train. We're all getting off at the same stop—but at different times. And none of us knows exactly when. So this private, subjective, personal *mishegoss*—your fear of heights—is just a tiny speck of fear in the huge mass of fear that humans feel in facing (or refusing to face) their own mortality.

Now take the train ride again: What would make you feel less afraid (besides never entering anything higher than a ranch-style house)? In the larger scheme of things, what would help all of us in this larger story feel less afraid? Uncertainty is one of the fears that haunts you, so I assume that if there were just a bit less random violence in the world, you might be somewhat soothed. (This is true for all of us.) A less violent neighborhood, a less violent society, a less violent world would go a long way toward helping us feel less afraid.

So here's the final question on this train ride: What could you do to help make your neighborhood, society, world just a little bit safer? Don't be over-whelmed by the question! Think of some simple, small thing that you could do, given the skills and talents you were born with, the kind of work you do, or the interests that you have. Think of one small thing you can do if you put this adrenaline-pumping energy to work to reduce fear in the world. (This is how the "larger story" leads directly to step 6, the way of action [see below].

The action may not come to you right away. You may want to meditate on your fear to get to it (see step 5, the way of non-action, below). But one thing is certain: widening the story of your fear can release you from the grip of feeling isolated and demeaned by your fear. Fear is not your exclusive problem—it's an integral part of the human condition.

## STEP 5. THE WAY OF NON-ACTION: BEING MINDFUL OF FEAR

*Witnessing Fear without Fear.* Fear-tolerance is not something we can find by ignoring our fears or avoiding them. It's what happens when we approach our fears mindfully. And this takes some serious, consistent practice.

Again, the practice of mindful meditation can be used specifically to focus and sustain awareness on your fear (or any emotion) and help you tolerate it with more equanimity. (See chapter 10, exercises 18 and 19.)

*Cultivating Fearlessness by Befriending Fear.* From Pema Chödrön's wonderful book *The Wisdom of No Escape*, I learned the practice called *tonglen*. This is a practice that cultivates fearlessness by befriending your fear. In *tonglen*, you are willing to feel the pain of life on each in-breath and to share the joy of life with each out-breath. In the Shambhala Buddhist tradition, the true Warrior is the opposite of the armed aggressor. The Warrior doesn't cover up or shield the most vulnerable part of herself. She doesn't fight an external enemy in order to conquer fear. She witnesses her own fear and suffering with equanimity.

This next exercise is a meditation practice based on *tonglen*: With each in-breath, acknowledge and befriend your fear, and the fear all around you in the world. Allow this fear to just be. Feel it wherever it lives in your body, and just breathe it through you. Then with each out-breath, focus your awareness on every bit of happiness and joy you have felt or are feeling, and give that joy to the world. Breathe in the world's sorrows and fears, and let them pass through you. Breathe out your accumulated joy and let it pass into the world.

You may notice that this practice is the opposite of many New Age guided meditations, in which you are encouraged to inhale the pleasurable emotions and exhale the painful ones. From a New Age perspective, this exercise may seem dangerous and foolish. Why would you want to take in all that suffering? And why give away all that good stuff? Wouldn't all that negativity get stuck in your body and make you sick? Wouldn't giving the good stuff away weaken and deplete you?

The problem is that many New Age meditations are stuck in what Chögyam Trungpa calls "spiritual materialism." Like any kind of materialism, hoarding good feelings and avoiding "bad" ones easily creates more fear, aversion, and grasping—and more suffering.

### STEP 6. THE WAY OF ACTION: DON'T LET FEAR STOP YOU

*Fear and Political Action.* Make a list of your three worst fears on earth. Decide on some act of a political nature that honors these fears. This can be as small as writing a letter to your senator or as large as selling your business and becoming a full-time peace activist. Whatever your political bent, find something to do with your fear and do it! But make sure you have developed your fear-tolerance before you decide what action calls to you.

*Fear and Spiritual Service.* How does fear influence your spiritual practice? Or lack of spiritual practice? How does the fear of fear influence your ideas about spirit? Do you avoid reading about things that would upset your peace of mind? Do you avoid conflict and disharmony rather than approaching it with openness? These are signs of the fear of fear.

Think of something in the world that upsets your equanimity and scares you. Then find a way to do some service that would put you in contact with your fear and open you to transformation. Volunteering with the sick and dying, finding a community project that interests you, let your fear open you to the world rather than cut you off from it.

### STEP 7. THE WAY OF SURRENDER

Surrendering to fear brings peace and joy, but only if it's authentic—that is, if you've looked fear in the face and made friends with it. Surrender happens when you're on good terms with yourself, not when you're at war with yourself. While you can't force surrender, you can help it along. Here are some ideas about how to do this with fear.

*Fear and Prayer.* Create a small ritual for honoring fear. You might try working with a "fear stone." Holding the stone to ground you, pray from the heart: Let my fear be acceptable and let me use it to help all beings who suffer. You will begin to associate holding the stone with surrendering to fear—letting it be.

Write a list of prayers that help you with fear and say them daily. These could be prayers for help and guidance, prayers of gratitude, and prayers of surrender.

A prayer for help and guidance: *Help me when I am afraid, to not be afraid of my fear. Help me to allow it to move me to an action in the service of life.* Or, if this seems out of reach, something simpler: *Help me find a way to soothe my fear.*

A prayer of gratitude: *While I know that I am afraid, I also know that others live in constant, daily fear in the world. I am grateful for my relative freedom from fear, for being able to speak my fear without danger of reprisal. I'm grateful that I am alive.*

A prayer of surrender: *May I accept my fear. May fear guide me to do the right thing.*

*Having Fun with Fear.* Sometimes we need a quick antidote to fear. If your child is hospitalized, your friend has cancer, your mother is dying, you don't necessarily want to communicate your fear to them. Or if you are ill, you don't want to be constantly connected to your fear. Sometimes, we are in need of a "positive distraction" from pain and fear in the interests of healing. At times like this, the quickest antidote to fear is laughter and play. This was the secret of Patch Adams's approach to medicine. Norman Cousins wrote a book about laughter as the best medicine called *Anatomy of an Illness As Perceived by the Patient: Reflections on Healing and Regeneration.* He was able to heal himself of a crippling, potentially lethal disease through an attitude of hope and lots of comic relief.

For laughter and play to work as a transformational practice, you have to be able to tolerate your fear. Then putting on a clown suit, doing comic improvisation, watching comic videos, and just plain getting silly become reliable alchemical practices rather than just avoidances.

See "Play and Silliness: Having Fun in the Dark," page 293, and exercise 33 in chapter 10 for how to do this.

# PART THREE

# *Emotional Ecology*

# 8  *We Live in the World and the World Lives in Us*

> An individual's harmony with his or her own deep self requires not merely a journey to the interior but a harmonizing with the environmental world.
>
> —James Hillman, "A Psyche the Size of the Earth" in *Ecopsychology: Restoring the Earth, Healing the Mind*

## The Self-in-the-World

> Our present ego feeling is only a shrunken residue of a much more inclusive, indeed, an all-encompassing feeling which corresponded to a more intimate bond between the ego and the world about it.
>
> —Sigmund Freud

RUTH WAS A PARTICIPANT in one of my workshops on befriending the dark emotions. She was a twenty-five-year-old woman who had been raised in an orthodox Lutheran family that was very involved with the church. Solemn and devout as a young child, she had felt secure in her large and close-knit family. But by the time she was ten years old, for reasons she couldn't name, she'd become estranged from her family.

When I asked participants to visualize a dark emotion that they wanted to work with for the day, Ruth reported being flooded with intense feelings of sorrow and fear. She saw herself as an eight-year-old, at the moment she first heard about the atomic bomb.

Describing her experience to the group, she said: "I couldn't put God as I had learned about Him together with the bomb. I needed to talk about it with my parents, and I even brought it up at church. But no one would talk to me. They sang hymns instead. From that time on, I stopped feeling. I became emotionally frozen."

Driven by an urgent need to know why human beings would make and use weapons of mass destruction, Ruth needed immediate attention, but her questions and emotions were ignored. She was traumatized twice: once by the news of the bomb and then again by the silence of her family and faith community. Their hymn singing, once spiritually uplifting, became a denial of the demons she was facing. In the community's silence, Ruth's emotions froze, and stayed frozen for the next seventeen years.

Instead of learning to honor her sorrow and fear for the world, Ruth grew up believing that she was "too sensitive." In the workshop, she was able, finally, to cry the tears she'd stopped crying as a child and to be respected for her "sensitivity." In being heard by a community of validating listeners, Ruth began to thaw from her long emotional freeze.

What do we make of this story? If Ruth's mother or father had been emotionally or physically abusive, we'd have no trouble attributing Ruth's long-held sorrow and fear, as well as her emotional numbing, to childhood trauma and bad parenting. But nuclear terror and community silence? Could these really be causes of Ruth's family estrangement and emotional deep freeze?

Many experts in psychology would have their doubts. Their training would lead them to search Ruth's past for some more personal, familial drama that was the real cause of her problems. Therapists don't generally ask questions like: What did you feel when you first heard about the atomic bomb? How do you feel about the state of the planet? When you think about the world your children will inherit, what are your fears? They ask questions like: What was it like being the youngest child? How do you feel about your mother? How did you feel when your parents divorced? We are not trained, nor do we think it makes sense, nor in most cases would we feel comfortable, to ask the former questions, which assume that our dark emotions are fundamentally connected to the world in which we live. Bound within the confines of our narrow psychological paradigm, we don't hear answers to questions we don't ask.

We think of emotions as existing "inside" us, in a realm that is removed from the world "outside." This way of thinking about feelings goes along with our culture's favored way of thinking about the self: as an atomistic ego, enclosed within its "boundaries," formed in the crucible of the nuclear family. Grief, fear, and despair, in this way of thinking, are remnants of a dim, familial past that haunts the present, rather than responses to the here-and-now life we live in this world. For more than one hundred years of Freudian and post-Freudian psychodynamic psychology, we have been deeply embedded in these ways of thinking about feelings—ways that are at best partial and at worst dangerously outmoded.

"In psychology," says Theodore Roszak, "theories are best seen as commitments to understanding people in certain ways."[1]

My commitment is to seeing individuals in a way that doesn't neglect to take the world into account. In this respect, I look for a different story about the dark emotions than the one our culture tells: a story not restricted to an inner child of the past but one that extends out to the connections between personal suffering and its larger context. I call this larger context "emotional ecology."

From the standpoint of emotional ecology, the individualist lens through which psychology sees its subject has made us myopic—unable to see beyond our own noses. By the microscopic norms of conventional psychological theory and practice, clinicians are accustomed to thinking about individual wounds that are inflicted in one's family of origin and transmitted in family legacies of pain. What we don't think about very well, if at all, is how these legacies are related to the historical, cultural, and environmental contexts in which they occur.

As much as it has taught us about our feelings, conventional psychology bears a large share of responsibility for what keeps the dark emotions pathologized, privatized, and disempowered. With the increasing popularization of a post-Freudian view of the psyche, the "inner child" whose sorrow, fear, and despair can be cured psychiatrically has become an accepted idea in the culture. Emotional pain is increasingly seen as a disorder that can and should be treated, if not through individual "talk therapy," then by swallowing a pill. This orientation has made it difficult, if not impossible, to see how the dark emotions we feel are shared throughout the human family, what they tell us about our relationship with the world, and how to heal ourselves through more collective means.

Like Ruth, when we are grieving, afraid, or in despair, we feel alone. We may think that we must nurse our wounds in private because they are in some sense secret, and should remain so. Often, the only person we permit ourselves to burden with these private dark emotions is a stranger, to whom we pay the going rate for a listening ear. But the loneliness of the dark emotions is not intrinsic; nor is it necessary. It is an "add-on" imposed by our social-emotional conditioning. What Ruth needed as a child was to be heard in community. She needed to know that she was not alone in her fear. We all experience fear in an endangered world and, like Ruth, we need to be accompanied in our dark emotions. Ruth didn't get this. Most of us don't.

It's hardly surprising that, as the twenty-first century opens, the faceless and anonymous cyberspace chat room has become the public forum and virtual community for millions of otherwise silenced, atomized, lonely people who sit in their enclosed cubicles with their unnamed, unspoken sorrows for themselves and the world. It's not a wonder that, for the most part, we experience the dark emotions in isolation and turn to individual therapy for their cure. This isolation can be, and often is, devastating, even if handled by a skillful psychotherapist. It is isolation that aborts the healing alchemy of dark emotions.

Most of the therapists I know who have worked for many years with victims of terrible injuries such as incest, child abuse, and domestic violence are aware that many seemingly "private wounds" are rooted in a damaged and damaging social environment. This is true for all of our emotional wounds, but not always in obvious ways. Therapy alone is not enough for those most damaged by the world. Being heard and held in community is something even the best therapist cannot offer. Yet the lack of such community is a source of terrible wounding to us all, therapist and client alike.

With the privatization and isolation of the dark emotions, they lose a great deal of their redemptive power. We learn little of what they have to teach us in the larger scheme of things. We don't learn that emotions are ways of knowing, informing us not only about a private, traumatic past but also about a troubled collective present or a threatened global future. We ignore the sacred dimension of the dark emotions, treating them as irrational and dangerous. When we hurt, we think of therapy, not community involvement, political action, or spiritual service.

It takes a prolonged period of economic decline, a community-wide tragedy in our midst, or a collective catastrophe such as a war to remind us that we are all emotionally interconnected. Suddenly, we are brought up short, facing the walls of our own egos. We realize that our emotions, seemingly purely personal states of mind, are actually connected to the actions of others in the world, and to the state of the world itself. To the extent that we are able to keep our illusions of separateness, we do so at the expense of our empathic connection to others in the world who suffer every day. And for most of suffering humanity, what's needed is not psychotherapy but food, shelter, justice, and world peace.

"Psychology, so dedicated to awakening human consciousness, needs to wake itself up to one of the most ancient human truths," says the psychologist James Hillman. "We cannot be studied or cured apart from the planet."[2] The intrapsychic paradigm, however useful it may be to the individual in the West, lacks the wisdom to understand the problems that beset us as a human family. In this era of global crisis, more than ever, we need to get out of the isolation of our bounded egos and heal not just the depths but the width of human suffering—to develop models of healing that include the world.

Our beautiful world, a place of magic and wonder, is also a place of poised weapons of mass destruction, perennial violence, ecological damage, and a baffling, often overwhelming collection of ongoing collective sorrows.

If grief is a signal of our interconnectedness, why wouldn't we grieve for such a world? If fear is an alarm that alerts us to protect life, why wouldn't we be afraid? If despair is a messenger that asks us to re-create the meaning of our existence, why wouldn't we feel despair for our world, which so urgently needs to develop a meaning-story compatible with its own sustainability?

And if we feel these dark emotions in relation to the world, what happens to them when, as in Ruth's story, they are unwelcome or unrecognized? Are we all encased and trapped in an emotional deep freeze we barely recognize, much less know how to heal?

## We Feel in Community; We Heal in Community

In the deep structure of emotion, there is an inescapable link between the self and the world. Thinking that our dark emotions are strictly personal and individual makes about as much sense as believing that onions grow in wrapped plastic containers in the supermarket. Dark emotions grow in the soil of a painful world. Just as an individual plant doesn't exist outside of its ecological surround, our individual emotions don't take place in a vacuum. We are never simply individuals; we are always connected to many systems—natural, social, and sacred—in which we exist in a state of interdependence. The dark emotions both grow out of and return us to a living matrix of relationships with others.

In the field of psychology in the past two decades, one important breakthrough has come from the work of the Stone Center at Wellesley College. The relational theory that has emerged there has challenged the concept of the self as an autonomous, bounded entity that develops through separation from others. In relational theory, the ego develops through "affiliation," embedded in relationship. In the words of the psychologist Janet Surrey, the self is a "self-in-relation."[3]

Emotions, too, are relational. As children, we learn about sorrow, fear, and other emotions only when they are recognized, named, and responded to empathically. As adults, we continue this emotional learning process in intimate relationships. Emotional energy flows between and among us. It doesn't stop at the boundary of the body or the imagined "boundary" of the ego. These "boundaries" do not prevent the unconscious emotions of the older generation from turning up in the dreams and unconscious of the younger. We feel one another's feelings—though, as with our own feelings, not necessarily consciously. Transpersonal feeling-with-others is built into our cells—an intuitive and powerful way of knowing if harnessed, a potentially destructive process if unconscious.

In search of healing, the victim of violence and other kinds of trauma must have the courage not only to enter her woundedness, but also to reach out and find connection to others, to some larger community of meaning. What helps her is not just an interior journey but a wider view of her problem—a sense that others have experienced this pain and that she is not alone in it. The single greatest barrier to her healing and transformation is not really the traumatizing events themselves but her isolation. This isolation, to my way of thinking, is not so much a failure of the individual to find connection as it is a failure of the human community to offer connection to the individual.

What's true for the victim of violence and trauma is true for all of us.

Feeling and healing are transpersonal events. The redemptive power of the dark emotions cannot find its full flowering until we can match the deepening of our awareness—a going-in, getting-deeper process—with the expansion of our awareness—a going-out, getting-wider process.

We are more than our atomized autobiographies. We are all connected, for better and for worse. In this interconnectedness lies the only hope for global healing and redemption. The pain of the world is carried in our bodies and hearts. Locked away, this pain can harm us—emotionally, physically, and spiritually. Consciously liberated in community, it moves us to a deeper sense of connection and compassion, helping us heal not only ourselves but our environment.

Look into the pain of the world and you find your own private pain writ large. Look into your heart and you find the broken heart of the world.

In the twenty-first century, psychology's view of human nature and behavior, if it is to have any relevance to what ails us, will have to contend with human suffering in a social context that is becoming more and more destructive and a planet that is in the process of being seriously damaged.

In this emotional ecology of our age, the following kinds of questions become paramount:

- How are our personal dark emotions related to a worldwide context of collective violence and environmental destruction?
- How do we begin to understand mass psychology in an age of global distress and terror?
- How must we change ourselves in order to meet the challenge of global crisis in the twenty-first century?
- How do we address the need for healing of the human family and the earth, rather than just the individual?

I don't have answers to these questions, but I do know that we need to ask them. This chapter and the next are meant to be a small contribution to the answers we so urgently need.

With these questions in mind, I start with the following assumptions:

The dark emotions are shared in the human family. Emotional energy is transpersonal. It's not "inside" any more than it is "outside." It flows through us and is transmitted intersubjectively. Grief, fear, and despair in the human family carry information that remains private and disempowered so long as we see it as "mine" alone.

We are all interconnected in social systems that are imbued with emotional energy, as individuals are. These systems include our families, workplaces, communities, states, nations, and the world. Like an individual, a system can be—and often is—unconscious of the dark emotional energy that circulates through it.

Unconscious dark emotions, whether in an individual or a system, are potentially dangerous. The tendency to act out of the unconscious emotional energies of grief, fear, and despair fuels acts of blindness and escalating violence. Our ability to work productively with emotional energy in a given system depends on our collective emotional intelligence—our levels of emotional awareness and emotional tolerance.

The most important single skill in working with the dark emotions within larger social systems is the capacity for empathy. It is in feeling with others in the human family that we find ways to heal ourselves and the systems in which we are embedded.

Our difficulty in empathically identifying with our fellow humans and with nonhuman life is one of the primary sources of the collective emotional dysfunction of the world as a "family system." The natural human capacity for empathy has been sundered at the root in patriarchy, leading to the erosion of emotional ways of knowing that are critical to the transformation of our social institutions and, ultimately, to the fate of the earth itself.

Patriarchy is a world system. The overall impairment of emotional intelligence in patriarchy is rooted in its characteristic splits in consciousness: between reason and emotion, spirit and nature, psyche and body. In particular, we suffer from the devaluation of emotion as a way of knowing. These splits in consciousness and this devaluation have fueled patriarchy's endemic tendency toward destruction and violence.

In the realm of emotion, these splits are manifest in two contrasting emotional styles, which I call the emotional "carrier" and the "bystander." These styles roughly parallel feminine and masculine gender socialization. Understanding these gendered styles of emotion and their potential social consequences is an important piece of gaining a wider comprehension of mass psychology in our time.

These are the premises that inform my way of thinking about dark emotions in a wider ecological context; they will be developed in this chapter and the next. Like all psychological theories, these ideas are commitments to seeing people in a certain way. My hope is that they can be of some use in re-visioning our emotional predicament as a species and finding our way through our dark emotions in an age of global distress.

## Sally and Joe: The Carrier and the Bystander

To begin to think about emotional energy systemically, think of a couple I'll call Sally and Joe. Their relationship has what therapists call a "dynamic," a manner in which emotional energy is communicated—consciously and unconsciously—in a relational system. The dynamics of this relational system are reciprocal and mutually reinforcing. What Sally feels and how she behaves affects what Joe feels and how he behaves, and vice versa. Sally may nag Joe when she's hurt. Joe may shut Sally out when he's fearful of being criticized. A change in one part of the system in the direction of more direct emotional communication (Sally stops nagging and discloses her hurt), can change another part of the system (Joe opens up to Sally). Ideally, the result is a more fluid, flexible, and intimate emotional dynamic (Joe and Sally feel more connected).

The metaphor of emotional dynamics makes sense to us intuitively. We all know that feelings, especially intense dark emotions, affect us intersubjectively. Little Rosie starts to cry, and all the babies in the day-care center join in a collective wail. We see someone weeping on stage or in the movies, and we tear up ourselves. Patrick goes into a panic about not having enough money, and his wife and children become very anxious. Hanging around with depressed Debbie gets to be really depressing. Similarly, when someone communicates joy, faith, or compassion, it lifts us up.

In the same way, when the world is hurting, we hurt—though we may not be aware of this hurt until a world crisis hits home. For better or worse, our emotional experience is responsive to others. This doesn't mean we can't "take charge" of our own individual emotions; it means that we must not lose sight of our emotional interconnections in the larger human family. And that healing, if it is to mean more than feeling better while denying the pain of the world, must be conceived of in collective as well as individual terms.

Let's return to Sally and Joe in couples therapy. Though both of them are concerned about their relationship, Sally is the one who cries. She's the one who voices her sadness, hurt, disappointment, and fear for the relationship. She emotes. Joe appears to feel little, if anything. He wants to do the right thing to make things better, but he leaves the feeling part to Sally. He detaches and stands by as Sally feels the dark emotions for the two of them.

In this couple system, Sally is the empath who feels what Joe doesn't. She is the emotional carrier. Sally's fear, hurt, disappointment, and sorrow are in some sense also Joe's fear, hurt, disappointment, and sorrow—the feelings that Joe doesn't let himself experience. Sally carries these feelings for both of them and, in some sense, for the couple as a relational system.

Joe doesn't know what he feels. He cuts himself off from the direct experience of emotional energy. Psychotherapy, which centers on the expression of emotion, is alien territory for Joe. He sincerely wants to do something to improve his relationship with his wife—so long as he doesn't have to feel anything in the process. Joe is the emotional bystander.

Sally and Joe are examples of two contrasting emotional archetypes in patriarchy. In real life, people tend to be more complex than Sally and Joe, less one-dimensional than this picture would imply. Often, one member of a couple carries the sadness and hurt, while the other carries the anger. Or one member carries the despair and the other the hope for the relationship. All psychological theories drastically reduce human experience and behavior. They make a one-dimensional drawing of the glorious, holographic, multifaceted human spirit.

With this proviso in mind, let me tell you that I've seen dozens of Sallys and Joes in couples therapy over the years, and, with few exceptions, the Sallys are the carriers and the Joes are the bystanders.

This is because emotional styles in patriarchy are socialized by gender. Women are socially designated to carry emotions and men to conquer them. Women are culturally set up to be carriers and men to be bystanders.

## Men, Women, and Dying Ducklings: Female Carriers and Male Bystanders

On a glorious Saturday in early spring, I strolled around Jamaica Pond. The sun was shining, the trees in bud, and everyone who could walk, crawl, or bike was out in full force. As I rounded a curve of the pond, I saw a man and two women standing near the water, hovering over a duckling. The baby duck was in distress, if not close to death. Its body floated in the water like a lifeless twig, its head to the side and eyes barely open. Every few seconds, it would open its eyes, try to move its little fuzzy body, and then drop its head back down again.

The two women were clucking over the duckling and talking about how they could help.

"Should we take it to the boathouse and see if someone there can revive it?" the first woman wondered.

"I don't know that taking it out of the water is a good idea," said the second. "I think that might make it worse. Maybe the mother duck will come by and take care of it."

"It's survival of the fittest," said the man, ending the conversation. Nudging his wife, who seemed reluctant to leave, he took her by the arm and off they went.

The first woman remained, overcome by maternal feelings for the baby duck. We stood together for some time, pondering the duckling's future, and came up with a plan: She would call a nearby animal hospital on her cell phone and see what they had to say.

"There's a tiny duckling here that seems to be dying, and there's no mother duck in sight. Is there anything we can do?" she asked the man on the line.

"It's the way of nature. Just leave it where it is," he said. And he hung up.

By this time, another bleeding-heart female had arrived on the scene. We were now a three-woman vigil. Finally, after staring at the duckling for about five minutes, we realized we could do nothing but leave it in the water.

"Okay," said the young woman with the cell phone. "I'm just going to pretend that the mother duck is coming by any minute, because that's the only way I'm going to tear myself away."

We all agreed that, on the count of three, we would brace ourselves and move on. And so we did.

The two men in this story—the one at the pond and the one on the phone—weren't necessarily heartless; they just had a more bystander response to a suffering critter. They were not empathically connected to the duckling. They were probably right about survival of the fittest in the wilds of Boston. In the end, the female carriers, whose heartstrings were pulled by the duckling's plight, did no more for the duckling than the male bystanders did. But it was a whole lot easier for the male bystanders to detach and move on than for our little circle of female carriers.

In patriarchy, men are systematically trained to become bystanders to their emotions and the emotions of others, while women are socialized to feel and express not only their own but others' emotions—including the emotions that men don't feel and express. Girls learn early to be little empathic emotional connectors, boys to be masters of the emotional cutoff.

At the same time, the bystander archetype is the norm in male-dominated culture. This puts women in a profound double bind: expected to carry emotions for the culture in order to be "feminine" and, at the same time, devalued for it. As we shall see, this creates a host of problems unrecognized by the culture.

Take, for example, the issue of crying at work. I once read a magazine piece in which it was reported that people who cry at work are viewed as incompetent and unstable, thereby losing respect and power. The criers—no big surprise—are women, who cry not only when they are sad but also when they are angry. (Since exhibiting anger is still by and large socially prohibited for women, crying is often a feminine expression of anger.) If they want to get ahead in the workplace, said the author of this piece, criers should wait till they get home to show their emotions. In other words, women who embody the carrier style of emotional expression at work have to develop a more culturally masculine bystander style of emotional suppression, or suffer the consequences. It never occurred to the author to suggest that the workplace itself could use an emotional-intelligence overhaul.

Crying is a carrier behavior for which we are shamed in a bystander culture. (A typical symptom of the shame of the carrier is the habitual, automatic apology people utter when they begin to cry.) While it may feel humiliating, the emotionalism of the carrier can be a potential source of information that the system needs to balance itself. The woman who cries at work because her boss devalues her has a legitimate complaint that may not get aired so long as she is ashamed of her tears and sees them as a sign of her own weakness or inferiority (or is viewed this way by her boss). In this way, emotional information that could transform the system ends up being internalized by the carrier.

The bystander in a bystander system, on the other hand, is generally rewarded for his "cool," regarded as more objective than the carrier. The emotional cutoff is seen as a sign of rationality, intelligence, and calm. Sometimes, being emotionally withheld is just what the situation warrants. But emotional disconnection can also be unhealthy to the bystander, the carrier, and the system. It can render a system quite inflexible and keep everyone stuck in denial.

Yes, men are from Mars and women are from Venus. And certainly, it is helpful for Martians to learn the language of Venusians and vice versa. But there are larger social implications to the gendered emotional styles of men and women that John Gray, author of the best-seller *Men Are from Mars, Women Are from Venus*, doesn't address. The gender polarization of emotional styles may seem rather inconsequential, as in the duckling story. But the social consequences of this polarization on a large scale are often anything but benign.

Men who are socially conditioned to compulsively control the energy of the dark emotions often cease to experience them altogether. At the same time, they are socially allowed, if not encouraged, to feel and express anger—a more active, and therefore more culturally masculine emotion. This particular mix, by which the energy of unfelt grief, fear, and despair is funneled into anger, can be destructive and dangerous. Men who are unable to identify their own woundedness and who armor themselves against it through compulsive control and dissociation, while allowing their anger full sway, tend to have severe relational impairments. They also tend to act out in aggressive and violent ways. This is true on an individual as well as a collective level. The result is trouble for men, women, and the planet.

Women, in the meantime, carry the dark emotions of grief, fear, and despair for the human family as a whole. They carry emotional information that the system tends to deny. The result of all this is also far from benign. Female carriers are at high risk for feeling emotionally overwhelmed and depleted; for high rates of depression and mind/body ailments; and for being psychiatrically diagnosed, trivialized, or punished by larger systems steeped in emotional denial.

To generalize with a very broad stroke, it's men's lot in patriarchy to have their capacity for emotion damaged or broken, and it's woman's lot to carry the accumulated sorrows of the systems in which they live, while being devalued for it. It's hard to say who is more wounded by this division (not to mention the suffering of those who don't fit neatly into these gendered emotional styles). When it comes to emotional wholeness, we are all the walking wounded in need of healing.

## Systemic Problems for Carriers and Bystanders

When the carrier is conscious, she feels emotional energy somatically and is attuned to the information it brings. This makes her an expert intuitive, wise in the ways of emotional knowing, even gifted in the prophetic power. But the carrier can also be unconscious of what she's carrying. Without awareness, the density of dark emotional energy gets stuck. Alchemy can't happen. The carrier easily gets bogged down in toxified dark emotional energy. This sets her up for a host of mind/body ailments, including migraine and tension headaches, gastrointestinal disorders, and PMS. Carriers who are not centered in their bodies easily become anxious and depressed when they are emotionally overwhelmed.

An example of the carrier is the empathic psychotherapist. Therapists new to the practice of psychotherapy often have to learn to be more conscious of how they empathically carry their clients' emotions. When I first started my clinical practice, I had various aches and pains in sessions with clients that I sensed were not "mine." I began to use these bodily signals in the work of therapy. Almost invariably, I found that they were vehicles of emotional information I was receiving from the client. Sometimes there were direct correlations: I would get a headache if my client Sandra came in with one. Or I would experience a tightness in my chest when Jenny was on the verge of tears. As soon as Sandra began to speak of her headache and its relation to the stresses in her life, my headache would disappear. When Jenny cried her tears, my chest would relax.

Sometimes, these physical signals had a more symbolic meaning. One time, I felt almost frozen to my chair with a client I'll call Deborah. I remember saying, "I'm getting a physical feeling of being bound up. Does this make any sense to you?" Deborah broke into tears and told me that she had memories of being sexually abused by her grandfather, who had tied her hands when he assaulted her. Later on, Deborah asked her parents about her grandfather and discovered that they had been suspicious of him as well, but didn't want to believe that he was capable of sexual abuse.

In these early days of my practice, using my odd bodily signals in the work of therapy was helpful—but at a steep cost. Working this way was very depleting. I would come home wasted.

It took me some time as a practicing therapist to learn that I didn't need to actually feel my clients' pain in order to be empathically and intuitively attuned to them. I found ways—such as staying centered in my breathing or visualizing my clients' emotional energy moving through me—to prevent the dark emotions from sinking into my body and coalescing into bodily held clumps of pain. I learned to take care of myself as a carrier without constricting the openheartedness that I believe is essential to any good therapeutic relationship. No longer depleting, the work of therapy then became energizing.

Bystanders don't have these kinds of problems. In contrast to the carrier's intuitive, emotional ways of knowing, the bystander operates from a more emotionally detached mode that our culture calls "objective." In many situations, being emotionally detached is necessary. The soldier's ability to detach from emotion is what allows him to fight for a cause and put his body on the line for it. The surgeon, the firefighter, the emergency room staff, the news reporter on the job in the event of a catastrophe—anyone dedicated to doing work that is potentially traumatizing requires the ability to "put feelings aside" until the work is over.

But internal disconnections from emotional energy are not always a matter of conscious suppression and control. They can be automatic and unconscious. This is when emotional bystanding becomes a problem. The bystander protects himself by minimizing empathic connection rather than by working with the energy of the dark emotions. The resulting emotional detachment is not necessarily equivalent to rationality or objectivity. Emotional energy affects the bystander as much as it does the carrier, but the bystander tends to be unaware of it. And being unaware poses at least as many dangers of irrationality as overt emotional carrying does.

Being unable to receive information empathically or intuitively is, in fact, a great hindrance to emotional intelligence. Limbic, intuitive ways of knowing are necessary to our ability, both as individuals and as a species, to respond to life-and-death situations. Ecologically speaking, we are all currently living in the midst of a global situation of this kind.

Furthermore, unalchemized dark emotions in the bystander put him at risk for some form of destructive or violent acting out. Releasing pent-up emotional energy in violent bloodletting is an all-too-common path in someone who is socialized in the macho bystander mold. In the extreme, the bystander is so numb to his own pain and/or the pain of others that his moral sense, which is intimately related to the ability to feel, is profoundly impaired. The bystander can so thoroughly lose a sense of a vital, emotional core that he becomes prey to any charismatic leader or figure who stirs up his dark emotions, turning them into a rageful passion that can turn deadly. Perhaps the most extreme example of bystander consciousness is the terrorist who has absolutely no empathic connection to the pain he inflicts on the innocent, while acting out the dark emotions that are whipped into a furious rage by the "cause" with which he identifies.

If you're more of a carrier than a bystander, you need to make an intentional effort to take care of your own needs for emotional, physical, and spiritual sustenance. You need to learn to put self-care on the top of your list of priorities and find ways to retain your center of awareness (my preferred term for "boundaries") rather than get lost in the emotions of others. At the same time, you need to recognize and honor the emotional information you carry.

If you're more of a bystander than a carrier, you need to make an intentional effort to reclaim emotions in your body, to put emotional recovery at the top of your list of priorities, and to befriend emotional energy rather than automatically cut off from it. You need to value your emotions and give yourself the gift of being emotionally alive.

Carriers and bystanders, however, are not absolute "types." Rather, there is a carrier and bystander admixture in most of us, as there is within the larger communities in which we live. Sometimes we are split into a carrier persona and bystander persona. The carrier persona, when it feels overwhelmed, may shift into the bystander persona. The bystander may keep it together all day, then come home and hand emotions over to the carrier, who promptly experiences and exhibits the dark emotional energy that has been split off from consciousness in the bystander persona. Your carrier, if kept under the thumb of your bystander, may show up only when you're under the influence of a substance and you begin to cry into your beer.

Though none of us are "pure" archetypes, most of us are imbalanced in a particular direction. And there are large-scale groupings of carriers and bystanders.

After women, the most common group of carriers are children, especially those called "sensitive." Sensitive children carry the denied or unvoiced pain of their families, and of larger systems in general. As children, sensitives tend to be the "identified patients" in the larger dysfunction of their families. As adults, they appear in therapy offices in great numbers—self-referred when their pain has become unbearable. Bystanders, on the other hand, are found in great numbers in almost any group of male professionals trained in Western norms of rationality, science, and expertise.

In the opening story, Ruth, as a child, was an emotional carrier. In her community, Ruth was the one who felt sorrow and fear for the world. These feelings affected her parents and other church members as well, or they wouldn't have avoided speaking about them! But the community did not confront these emotions head-on, in the way that Ruth did. Ruth's family and community embodied bystander consciousness. Their way of ignoring Ruth's dark emotions was typical of the bystander's denial. Ruth was shamed for what she felt and wounded by the community's inability to carry these emotions with her. The community kept going, its customs unaffected by the carrier's pain and her need to share it. This, again, is a typical carrier-bystander dynamic. Had Ruth's terror and sorrow been heard by her parents and the church, the resulting experience of interconnectedness would likely have been healing for Ruth. It would also have helped unite her community religiously to face the darkness in the world together.

We must beware, however, of simple dualisms or absolute assignations of moral value. Neither the carrier nor the bystander is purely good or bad. Carriers, while generally more empathic than bystanders, can easily become overwhelmed by emotions and get lost in themselves, becoming narcissistic, selfish, and solipsistic. They can be so overcome by the emotional energy they carry in an unconscious way that they act out against themselves or others. And bystanders who are more aware of themselves, while they do not easily experience emotion or express empathy, can be motivated by great compassion for others and be steadfast, courageous, and noble.

Both carrier and bystander consciousness have strengths and weaknesses. The question is how they are balanced or imbalanced in the individual, as well as in the world as a family system.

In patriarchy, social institutions polarized by gender are unbalanced in the direction of male power. This system of power rests on a bystanding style of emotion. In the larger, collective dynamic of patriarchal culture, carriers and bystanders coexist in an uneasy equilibrium. The more that bystanders deny the dark emotions in the system, the more carriers must carry. Both carriers and bystanders must contend with the damages of an emotionally unbalanced system.

In the human family, dense emotional mushroom clouds of unredeemed grief, fear, and despair daily contaminate our world, affecting us all in ways that we don't see through the individualist lens of psychology. It is largely the female carrier who feels these energies. But we are all deeply affected by them. The gendered polarization of carriers and bystanders in the world family system has profoundly unbalanced our emotional intelligence as a species. We have trouble rallying our emotional resources together and using the energies of grief, fear, and despair for social as well as personal transformation.

## Worlds of Pain: A Carrier Story

> I am beginning to believe that we know everything, that all history, including the history of each family, is part of us, such that, when we hear any secret revealed . . . our lives are suddenly made clearer to us. . . . For perhaps we are like stones; our own history and the history of the world embedded in us, we hold a sorrow deep within and cannot weep until that history is sung.
>
> — SUSAN GRIFFIN, *A Chorus of Stones*

I learned the rudiments of what I know about emotional ecology as a child growing up in a post-Holocaust refugee camp in Germany and, later on, in the South Bronx. While the world I experienced as a young child is not universal, we all live in the world, and the world lives in us. We are all embedded in some known or unknown history larger than our own autobiographies. I tell my story in the hope that it will shed some light on what it means to be an emotional carrier of large-scale historical events, and on the ways in which our private sorrows are deeply rooted in the world.

My birthplace and first home was a Displaced Persons Camp in southern Germany for the remnants of Hitler's war against the Jews. It would be many years before I learned how I came to be born in this place or what was happening to my parents just before my birth. The Holocaust was not a story for children, and my parents, hoping to protect my innocence, kept it well hidden.

My father grew up in a shtetl in central Poland, with cows, goats, and chickens at the door. My mother was a city girl from the teeming industrial city of Lodz. They met in a circle of young, idealistic, socialist Jews who dreamed of a better world, a workers' paradise, freedom for the oppressed. Married in August 1939, they honeymooned on the run from Hitler's invading army. Escaping from Lodz into the Soviet-occupied eastern zone of Poland, they met the reality of the Soviet Union's brand of "socialism." All refugees here were asked by the authorities whether they wished to return to their homes in Poland after the war or become Soviet citizens. Those who indicated a desire to return were thereafter considered enemies of the state and shipped immediately to gulags in the northern Siberian forests.

In these camps, prisoners died of hard work, cold, and starvation, rather than the industrialized mass death of the Nazi concentration camps. My parents survived two years in such a place, where their beds were wooden planks on the floor and their rations not much different from the watery soup and crusts of black bread served at Auschwitz. For almost four years following their liberation from this camp, they wandered in Astrahkhan and Uzbekistan, searching for food and shelter, before wending their way back by cattle car to their destroyed world in Poland.

After the war, my father, one brother, and a sister were all that remained of a large clan of eleven children and twelve grandchildren. My mother was the sole survivor of her family of five. Locked out of their homes—which were occupied by Poles who delighted in their inheritance of stolen Jewish property—my parents lived in a purgatorial world.

In defiance of Hitler's mission and a world still bleak and venomous, my parents chose to live. I was their commitment to life, conceived in 1946 in the gardens of Bad Reichenthal, Hitler's former playground in the German Alps—a temporary stop on their way to the Displaced Persons Camp where I was born. Rejuvenated by the alpine air and majestic scenery, in a rare moment of relaxation, my mother became pregnant at once. Of the generation of Jewish women of childbearing age just after World War II, the highest birth rates occurred in Holocaust survivors living in DP camps. I was one of this post-Holocaust baby boom, born like a phoenix from the ashes and set up by history for my role as the emotional carrier of my parents' suffering.

After almost four years of refugee camp life, we got our visas to America. But our move to the South Bronx, from my child's-eye point of view, wasn't much of an improvement. The Bronx streets were scarier than the refugee camp in the Bavarian mountains. This was a world without green—all hard edges, gray cement, and grime. A sense of unsafety and foreboding filled the air.

Like most children, I was inducted into the culture in large measure through watching television. On TV, I saw images of family happiness, conviviality, and lightheartedness; of order and abundance, neatly cropped lawns, lemonade in the summertime; happy-go-lucky sons and daughters in sunny families who sang their way through the rough times, like the Nelsons on *The Ozzie and Harriet Show*. Television people lived in cute little white houses surrounded by bushes and white picket fences that looked nothing like the soot-stained apartment houses on Westchester Avenue. Beaver's mother seemed to spend most of her day dusting the furniture. My mother sat in the shadows remembering her dead. Whereas Father always knew best how to set everything aright for his darling Princess, I barely saw my father, who worked a sixteen-hour day, six days a week, in a factory in lower Manhattan. I knew for sure that I was no princess.

Nothing bad ever happened to these television people, whereas all the bad things that happened to my family had already happened before I was born; and though I felt these bad things in every cell of my body, I had no idea what they were. We shared our home with the ghosts of my parents' murdered families and friends, their annihilated world. My childhood world was supercharged with powerful emotional energies, traces of this lost world. I knew that my mother was unbearably sad, though I didn't know why. I knew that my father, a sweet, compassionate, and gentle man by nature, occasionally flew into terrifying rages that descended on me but were not about me. I knew that there was a shadow world of sorrow and fear that they inhabited that I could not enter, but that had entered me.

A drama as real as my life lived itself out in my parents' memories, an unnamed, unspoken parallel reality. Nothing I saw at school or on the streets was as compelling as this shadow reality I lived with at home. I was a carrier of ghost stories—stories I couldn't tell because they weren't told to me; a repository of the emotional information attendant on genocidal trauma.

It is possible to listen so closely to silenced suffering that the stillness itself speaks. For me, it spoke in dreams. I dreamed my mother's life, the rudimentary story of her escape and survival, before she told it to me. In the dream, recurrent in differing forms, I had to pack my bags and flee before the Unnameable happened. The emotional undertone was of an almost choking terror and dread. I had to board a train before it was too late. I tried in vain to rescue others who were in danger. When the dream ended, I always stood alone.

What I dreamed, my mother lived. She and my father packed one rucksack each before escaping from Lodz and fleeing Hitler's invading army. The Unnameable happened. No one in my mother's family was rescued.

How could my dreams record a reality I hadn't personally experienced or known about?

It is not unusual, as it turns out, for children of Holocaust survivors to know things they were never told. Wired for survival, many are exquisitely attuned to the nonverbalized force of dark emotional energy. Psychologists would explain my ways of carrying my parents' dark emotions as "vicarious traumatization"—a secondary post-traumatic stress disorder, intergenerationally transmitted to the offspring of direct victims.

In its clinical tone, this terminology speaks of the contagion of the dark emotions. We all know that witnessing a horrific event can traumatize the witness, even if he or she is not a direct victim. It seems that one doesn't have to actually *see* such events to *feel* them. The reality of any historical trauma, even if not seen or spoken, can be felt in the bodies of the descendants of the victims. My parents had hoped that in not speaking to me of the Holocaust, they would spare me suffering. But the transmission of these collective dark emotional legacies is not averted when the traumatic stories are silenced. In fact, it may be that the dark emotions, for both the bearer and the carrier who is "vicariously" traumatized, are much harder to heal when they can't be spoken aloud.

My parents' stories were not known to anyone but a few select others like themselves, refugees who came from the same town. The larger context for my parents' dark secrets and silences was a world traumatized by a war that had just ended, and now caught in the grips of a new "Cold War." In this larger context, my parents feared that if the truth about their imprisonment in the Soviet Union were known, they might be refused entry into the United States, or even be locked up again.

If my parents were "paranoid," their paranoia was not a divergence from, but a direct result of, the larger paranoia and persecution in the world—both in the countries that had hunted them and locked them up, and in the country to which they emigrated. This was the American era of Joe McCarthy and the House Un-American Activities Committee, of a rabid, hysterical anticommunism, of high-level Nazis working for the FBI to gather secrets against the Red Menace. Jewish and other refugees who had spent time in Soviet labor camps were tainted with the suspicion of being communists. My parents had already been imprisoned by the government of one country while the government of another decimated their families and their people. In such a world, it made sense to keep their silence.

Silenced stories of suffering are not unusual. Many, if not most, victims of large-scale trauma know what it's like to be unable to speak the truth about their experience, not because they are incapable of doing so, but because there is no one who will listen. The resounding silence that greeted Holocaust survivors in the immediate aftermath of World War II is well documented. Landing in the United States, survivors who told their stories to anyone but other survivors were generally greeted with incredulity, avoidance, or exhortations to "leave the past behind" and "start a new life." Many were told: "These things could not have happened. You are making them up. You must be crazy." Survivors who talked to psychoanalysts about lying in their own shit in Auschwitz were told they were "anally fixated." For many Holocaust survivors, the inability of others to listen to them proved to be the final seal on the trauma of genocide, locking in a permanent sense of isolation from the human family. Having suffered Job's fate, they were left to endure a world without Comforters.

In this larger world context, like many "sensitive" children, I became, or tried to become, my parents' comforter. I carried their suffering in my body, trying to heal the harm the world had inflicted on them. I carried their dark emotions as a way to soothe them, to make them feel less alone. I carried their pain to relieve them of the intolerable weight of their grief. In this way, I was also trying to heal them, so that they would leave their ghosts behind and live in the present with me. I made their story my own, and, in some sense, it became my mission to balance the energies of light and darkness in my own body.

The fact that this self-appointed mission was unconscious and impossible made it no less compelling. In some larger sense, I carried my parents' emotional information as an unconscious protest. By recording their story in my body and in my dreams, I tried to rectify an evil, to make up for what the world couldn't provide, to balance an unbalanced world.

However we may explain it—whether as a form of transmitted trauma or as a particular spiritual destiny—what I got from my child-of-survivors mission was a gift that became the ground of my work as a psychotherapist as well as the core of inner guidance that has helped me through the hard times in my life: an abiding faith in the wisdom of the heart in darkness. In the inarticulate, heart-centered way that children know things, I knew that emotional pain had a story to tell that needed to be heard. And I knew that, from knowing this story, something good would grow, like the trees that sprouted from between the cracks in the South Bronx sidewalks.

## The Dark Emotions As Transpersonal Ways of Healing

> We must serve as carriers of empathy, as watchpeople
> for the vulnerable.
>
> —ANNE ROIPHE, A Season for Healing

Each of us has a story of suffering that we are handed at birth through the transmission of emotional energies in our families. We then develop our own stories, which always include more suffering. When we search for healing, the full expanse of these sufferings is involved.

I spent many years as a child and young adult with isolated trauma before I could do the work of healing. The work took decades and continues in different forms to the present day. Individual therapy, meeting with other children of survivors, meditation, spiritual practice—all of these were helpful. Creative process has been an important part of this work. For me, as for many survivors of trauma, this has always involved searching the story I have been given for what it has to teach me and what it has to teach others. I know both from my own personal story, and from my work as a psychotherapist, that all stories of suffering bear lessons that the world needs to hear.

The dark emotions are the vehicles of these lessons as well as ways of healing. Carriers carry a story that needs to be known until that story is ready to be revealed. They get information from emotions suppressed or denied by others, and, when they are conscious of it, they can then bring this information into the light of day.

An example is the incest survivor who has no memory of early sexual abuse but recovers memories through the emotional information in her body. While recovered memory has become a controversial issue in the world of psychology, I have no doubt that it is a real phenomenon, and that it is guided by the dark emotions that are held in the victim's body until the moment that it is safe to tell her story. Incest, like many other dark legacies, often runs in families. I have seen this happen: When an incest survivor begins to enter the emotions held in her body, she may recover not only the memory of her own violation, but the transmitted memory of a mother who allowed the sexual abuse of her daughter to go on because she was in denial of her own sexual abuse as a child. The incest survivor viscerally knows the truth that will set her free; and that truth has wider implications than her own particular wound.

The story that suffering tells is always larger than the individual sufferer. Silenced or denied emotional legacies are transmitted from generation to generation. The younger generation inherits the hidden, intolerable emotions of the older. The hidden emotional legacies of violence, incest, alcoholism, mental illness—all kinds of muted griefs without a name—are transmitted in this way. Dark emotions vertically transmitted from generation to generation carry the hidden depths of the collective pain of families, of nations, of the human species itself.

Similarly, dark emotions are laterally transmitted in the world. In the present global context, collective dark emotions haunt us in ways that we barely recognize.

The transmission of emotional energy through the generations and within the human family may seem burdensome and discouraging, but it actually reflects an innate healing tropism—a movement from darkness toward conscious awareness, for the purpose of healing. The human organism wants to heal itself; and the dark emotions that spring from woundedness and turn up in the human family are the vehicles of that healing. This is why they keep on living in the body until their truth can surface.

## The World Family System

Family therapists in the 1970s were the first to speak of the family as a relational "system" with its own dynamics. One of the major contributions of this model was the idea that the person who comes to therapy for help is the "identified patient" of the larger system, which itself needs healing. The patient, in other words, is the emotional carrier of the family system. Unlike the individual therapy model, in family systems thinking, the patient can be healed only if the whole system is attended to.

Think of the world as one huge family system: a clan so vast and so intricate that it is very hard to track, and so dysfunctional that it is in the throes of destroying itself. What one member of the family feels and how he behaves affects how the others feel and behave.

Within this vast clan, nations, like individuals who are enclosed in a rigidly "bounded" ego, have relationships with other nations that are based largely on self-interest and a narrowed sense of connection. There are competitions for economic, political, and cultural power; alliances that change as these power dynamics change over the course of history. Powerful nations rule and oppress less powerful ones. There are huge schisms: some family members have been stripping others of their resources and dignity for centuries. Unequal groups based on sexual, racial, ethnic, religious, and economic divisions are kept in force through violence and the threat of violence. There are ongoing quarrels between members who fight and kill each other, often in the most horrific ways. Shifting alliances bring war and the threat of war. Presently, powerful "haves" are "globalizing"—joining with other members in order to gain more economic and social power, to satisfy their greed for control, privilege, and creature comforts. Other groupings are engaged in attack and counterattack for which they always feel justified, in which massive numbers of innocents are terrorized and killed.

In this world family system, some individuals are just going along ignoring all the strife and trying to cultivate their own gardens. Others barely notice what's happening. Increasingly, many individual family members are unable to function without a fix of alcohol, drugs, prescribed medications, entertainment, or computer techno-games. Some in the family are barely holding it together. Others are actively trying to get the family to change.

Carriers in the world family system abound in groups that are subordinated and disenfranchised: women, people of color, the poor, homosexuals, the elderly, the disabled. Bystanders tend to keep the system going, creating a long shadow that the society prefers to ignore—until some group stands up and says: "Look! You call this a democratic society of equals? You haven't been feeling the pain of women, people of color, the disabled." These uprisings are guided by the dark emotions of despair, fear, and grief, as well as anger—emotions that demand that social conditions change to create a more livable, less pain-inflicting environment.

In the world family, grief, fear, despair, as well as anger, are always circulating somewhere in the system. Because emotions are energies, they are passed on—from person to person within families, from generation to generation, from whole groups of people to other groups. Social events and conditions awaken emotions that, especially when they remain unacknowledged or unexpressed, are passed along in various forms of collective experience and behavior. Social conditions of victimization as well as particular historical events traumatize and wound whole classes, races, and ethnic groups who carry dark emotions, often in masked or displaced forms. Traumatized groups often act out in destructive ways, perpetuating cycles of vengeance and violence. All of us in the global human family, especially in this age of instant electronic media, are affected. Dark emotions in the world create large clouds of emotional energy that have traumatic effects for all of us, effects especially experienced by carriers.

## CARRIERS AND BYSTANDERS ON THE WORLD STAGE

I once spoke to a woman with serious, life-threatening allergies to a number of everyday substances, some known, some unknown. She became so ill that she had to move to a small, environmentally controlled house in the middle of the desert in California. Environmental illness, at the time, was still denied by most of the medical profession. (It has yet to be widely understood and treated.)

When I asked her what she thought was going on in her body, she told me: "I believe that my body has been toxified by the level of pollution in the world. I believe that the pain I feel is the pain of the earth."

In the past decade, in my therapy practice and in my community of friends, I have spoken to more and more women who feel, in their bodies, the connections between the harming of the planet and their own emotional and physical ailments. These connections are barely recognized by conventional medicine. Stating these kinds of connections aloud can get one diagnosed as hysterical or delusional. The expertise of carriers in making these kinds of connections between "outer" and "inner" events goes unrecognized and is pathologized.

In a bystander system, carriers are at risk for being dismissed, pathologized, and marginalized. For many years, incest survivors who spoke of their pain were told they were making it up. Battered women who complained to their priests were told that they weren't good wives. Bystanders refused to take in the emotional information of these female carriers. The environmentally ill were told they were mentally ill. Think also of the fate of peacemakers, who carry grief, fear, and compassion for the world and are derided for being wimps and cowards.

In the case of incest survivors, my own profession has historically contributed to large-scale bystanding in the field. Sigmund Freud was unable to sustain his emotional tolerance of the shocking information he was receiving from his female patients about the pervasiveness of incest and sexual abuse in Victorian society. Instead, he came up with the lively idea that women who reported sex with their fathers are not remembering, they are wishing. It took the "second wave" of the women's movement in the 1960s and 1970s to listen to stories of incest and take them at face value, thereby surfacing the truth.

The devaluation of the carrier is related to the fact that she often carries taboo information that is denied in a bystander system. This is not just a matter of unconscious denial on the part of individuals but of the system as a whole. The emotional information of the carrier is not welcome because it has a potentially destabilizing effect on the social order. And social orders have their own forms of resistance to the emotional knowledge of those who carry dark histories. What Jung called the "shadow" of our society is thereby neatly enclosed, like a cyst, within the heart of the emotional carrier, where it will not disrupt the workings of the social machine.

In contrast to the fate of carriers, think of the elder President Bush in 1991, declaring to the press that he felt "serene" about sending thousands of

young men off to war in the Persian Gulf. Even if he thought a war was necessary, "serenity" seems an odd emotional state for mobilizing it—a state
most psychologists would call inappropriate. Perhaps President Bush
meant to say that he was resolved to go ahead with war because he thought
this was the right thing to do. But why not say he felt compassion and sorrow in sending soldiers to a war that would kill many innocent civilians? Sorrow and compassion don't mitigate resolve; nor do they indicate "weakness."

In a bystander system, President Bush would not have gotten very far if
he'd talked about emotions like these, assuming he was capable of feeling
them. He would have been made a laughingstock. His "serenity," on the
other hand, suggested to the media hounds (who'd been going after him for
being a wimp) that perhaps he was man enough to be president after all.

Years later, I saw an interview with President Bush on TV in which the
interviewer asked him how he felt now about sending soldiers to the Persian Gulf. The former president sat in silence. After what seemed like a
long time, two lonely tears trickled down his face! Were these the tears he
never shed at the time? Guilt and regret for his decision? Grief for the soldiers who died? We'll never know, because the interviewer quickly changed
the subject.

The media that went after President Bush for being too "soft," the president who was serene about ordering a war that killed thousands of innocents, the population that saw his serenity in launching a war as a quality
that made him more "presidential," the interviewer who turned away from
the president's tears: these are all examples of bystander consciousness.

The bystander system perpetuates itself through a kind of unconscious
collective consensus: to avoid and deny the emotional truths that would
threaten or destabilize the system. And so the world keeps turning, even if
the manner in which it turns is bound to end in global disaster.

The mourners carry the casket of a young man to the burial ground. The
sharp keening of the women, the raised shouts of the men build into a
crescendo of chanting: "Down with the olive branch! Long live the rifle!"[4]
The young men and boys run to pick up stones that the women have gathered, hurling the intolerable weight of their grief, despair, and rage at the
young men in uniforms who police their world. These soldiers then aim at
the crowd and unleash a hail of gunfire. At the end of the day, the dead are
counted on both sides.

As I write, a pogrom of sorts, spearheaded by Jews and aimed at Arabs in
the town of Nazareth, is reported. Two days later, the lynching and mutila-

tion of two Israeli soldiers by a Palestinian mob on the West Bank is captured on videotape, then played and replayed on television.

Carriers and bystanders are easy to spot in areas of the world characterized by chronic, unending, violent conflict that spirals into larger and larger conflagrations. The most obvious example, as I write, is in the Middle East, where a tragic conflict of emotional carrier and bystander—both within Israelis and Palestinians—daily unfolds, destroying all possibilities for a lasting peace in this grieving and despair-ridden part of the world family system.

Every racial, religious, or ethnic group carries a set of dark emotions transmitted over the generations. The Jews carry their history of anti-Semitic persecution, expulsion, and genocide; the Palestinians their history of displacement and oppression. The fact that many of the recent clashes between these cousins in the human family have a kind of "ritualistic" character following Palestinian funerals is an example of how toxified grief is converted to angry violence—especially because currents of dark emotional energy in this part of the world have been building intensely for nearly a century. Jews carry their history of trauma, and Palestinians theirs; but they can be bystanders to the grief, fear, and despair of the "Other." Ritualistic cycles of vengeance are a way to exorcise the force of these collective dark emotions through violent bloodletting, a way that has become deeply ingrained in Israelis and Palestinians, as well as among people in many other areas of the world, including Bosnia, Rwanda, Ireland, and Malaysia. The explosion of emotion following the deaths of Palestinians and Israelis is fueled into acts of violence that, in an increasingly deadly cycle, become the occasion for more violence from both sides. The cause of the violence is always attributed to the Other. Each bystander to the Other's fear, grief, anger, and despair takes no responsibility for the darkness he contributes to the system. Rather, they both perpetuate the ongoing dynamic of an eye for an eye—on and on and on, until, as Gandhi said, "the whole world is blind."

Partisans for each side around the globe engage in the same sort of exchange on another level. The communications of those who demonize Israel and those who demonize the Palestinians are fraught with a similar carrier-bystander dynamic. Those who see Israel as the sole source of evil in the Middle East are emotionally empathic with the Palestinians and unempathic bystanders to the dark history of Jewish persecution and anti-Semitism in the Arab world. Those who see Palestinians as the sole source of evil are generally empathic to the unending sorrows of Jewish history while unempathic bystanders to the occupation and oppression of Palestinians by Israel. Violent debates, irreconcilable differences, even death threats have been the recourse of many who are passionate about the Middle East but cannot mindfully tolerate their own vulnerability, helplessness, grief, and despair. Rhetoric about the conflict, like the conflict itself, is characterized by a kind of bystander consciousness about the pain of the Other. The carrier-bystander dynamic is maintained at the expense of mutual understanding and compassion, which, in the end, is the only pathway to peace.

Whole groups of people carry the collective wounds of a civilization unbalanced by vindictive bloodshed, cruelty, and oppression. People of color carry the history of racism. Women carry the wounds of patriarchy. Jews carry the scars of anti-Semitism. Kurds carry the history of oppression and exile. Bosnians. Serbs. Hutus. Tutsis. Cambodians. Muslims. Christians. Jews. How many people in the world have been spared a history of blood and tears?

Looking at the world as a family system, we don't have to be Sigmund Freud to observe what a royally messed up family it is! The rupturing of our capacity to feel and honor dark emotions in ourselves and others is a symptom of our global emotional illness. We are all embedded in the web of dissociated emotional energy that is harming our souls as surely as pollution is toxifing our bodies.

We live in a bystander system that relies on emotional dissociation—the separation of empathic emotion from awareness and action. We live in a world stuck in the confines of bounded national egos in competition for resources, status, power, and wealth. We live in a world in which one member of the human family continually denies the pain of another member—and as a result, conflict is generally dealt with by generating more conflict.

Denial, at its root, is an insistence on fragmentation of awareness. Because we cannot maintain our awareness of the suffering of others, or the world as a whole, we feel righteous in our own pain and its justification for any and all acts of cruelty we add to the human family system. Emotional dissociation from the dark emotions within ourselves and/or others maintains the unhealthy status quo of the world in which we live, and prevents its healing.

More than ever, healing must be seen in relation to the whole: an integrity that opposes the insistence on fragmentation that is the essence of bystander denial. In the end, only an expansion of awareness to include the dark emotional history of the Other has the potential to redeem human suffering. In understanding that the pain of the Other is, ultimately, my own pain, we find a way to bring compassion to a world in urgent need of it.

## Bystanders and the Problem of Evil

> There are many ways we have of standing outside our-
> selves in ignorance. Those who have learned as chil-
> dren to become strangers to themselves do not find
> this a difficult task. Habit has made it natural not to
> feel. To ignore the consequences of what one does in
> the world becomes ordinary.
> — SUSAN GRIFFIN, *A Chorus of Stones*

In *The Roots of Evil: Genocide and Individual Responsibility*, Ervin Staub writes about people who look on as others are attacked or killed. He calls such people "bystanders." He is not speaking here of an emotional style, but of social passivity in the face of large-scale, collective violence or mass murder. Staub is describing a social bystander, a witness to the perpetration of evil—as opposed to the emotional bystander who detaches himself from his emotions. However, the relationship between the first kind of bystanding and the second is clear. "People tend to inhibit expressions of feeling in public," says Staub. "In an emergency, the fact that all bystanders are hiding their feelings may lead them all to believe that there is no need for concern and nothing need be done."[5] I would add: It's not just that the bystander doesn't want to express emotions in public, but that he doesn't want to feel them. He removes himself from active involvement in mass violence against a vulnerable populace to avoid the pain of empathic identification with the victims. In other words, emotional bystanding easily results in social bystanding.

The social bystander's passivity, according to Staub's research, confirms the perpetrators' faith in what they are doing, and encourages escalating acts of aggression. Passive social bystanders are key players in the perpetration of mass evil. (On the bright side, when bystanders rally themselves, they can help avert acts of mass violence.)

Some of the great psychologists of all time have wrestled with the problem of evil. Freud spoke of Thanatos, the instinct toward death and destruction. Jung spoke of the Shadow, Rollo May of the daimonic. Otto Rank saw the fear of death as the pivotal source of the problem of evil. Wilhelm Reich believed that a great deal of human suffering and misery comes from man's denial of his animal nature. What they didn't write about was the relationship between evil and social bystanders to evil.

In the words of Edmund Burke, "the only thing necessary for the triumph of evil is for good men to do nothing." The emotional bystander is easily conscripted to larger forms of social bystanding. There are more pas-sive social bystanders in the world family system than there are perpetrators of evil. But the social bystander's propensity to "do nothing" is what allows evil to flourish.

I cite a few instances of the dangers of emotional and social bystanding in the world family system. For a broader array, consult the daily news.

## THE COMMUNITY AS BYSTANDER

An entire community can develop bystander consciousness.

Adam Enos was murdered in full view of his friends one summer night in 1991, shot in the back several times while standing in the doorway of a hous-ing project. Everyone knew the killer, yet the killing remains "unsolved." People talked to each other about it; but they wouldn't talk to police.

This is just one of many such stories in Charlestown, a suburb of Boston. Charlestown has a significantly higher percentage of no-arrest murder cases than the rest of Massachusetts. The town is known for its open-air murders in full view, which are never brought to trial because no one will identify the murderer. This is referred to as the Charlestown "code of si-lence." Residents hear gunshots, see the murderer fleeing, and gather round the corpse. The word spreads about the murderer. Everyone knows; nobody talks. They call it "Townie Pride."

Reverend Ron Coyne, a pastor in a local Catholic church says: "So what you have is children growing up in a community where murder is accept-able behavior." He explains that while residents in other communities may become "jaded" to drugs and delinquency, in Charlestown, they are jaded to murder: "People might feel badly, but they're not shocked anymore. It happens, and then it seems you just go on with your life."[6] The normal emo-tions evoked by witnessing a murder are revulsion, horror, fear, outrage, and grief. When these are numbed and muted, they lose their power to bring needed information to the community. In this way, justice and heal-ing for the victims and their families, indeed for the entire community, are derailed.

## BYSTANDERS IN HIGH PLACES

In the annals of sex abuse offenders, one of the most notorious in the past decade was the story of Father Porter.[7] A Catholic priest in the Fall River/ New Bedford area of Massachusetts, Father Porter was indicted in 1992 on forty-eight counts of sexual assault and molestation when a large group of his victims came forward and revealed their ordeals as children in the churches in which he served in the 1960s. Porter later admitted to molesting and raping between fifty and one hundred children, using his entrusted priestly role as a shield.

Two of his accusers reported that another priest walked into the room in which Porter was in process of raping a boy, left the room, and took no action. Perpetrators of pedophilic sexual assault like Father Porter are no longer seen as moral monsters; they are diagnosed with mental illness and sex addiction. But what of the bystanding priest? He didn't rape the boys; he just looked the other way when he saw it happening. What diagnosis does he merit? From what emotional sickness does he suffer? There is no diagnosis for bystanding in the DSM-IV.

The behavior of the bystanding priest, it turns out, was not dissimilar to that of the Catholic church itself. Despite the repeated allegations that cropped up about Father Porter, no one from any of the eight churches in which he served reported his behavior to authorities or to the parents. He was quietly moved from church to church, sent for treatment, and allowed to continue until he was caught again, then sent elsewhere. Neither the Vatican (which was aware of his actions because Porter wrote to the pope requesting to leave the priesthood) nor the bishops and other Catholic officials aware of Porter's criminal acts thought it necessary to inform the parents of victimized children.

Again, when one witnesses or hears about violence done to children, it is natural to feel disgust, outrage, fear, sorrow, compassion. These feelings have to be suppressed and their information denied in order to maintain a bystander consciousness. The resulting crimes of silence are not prosecuted because they are not against the law. Bystanders in high positions of authority frequently handle the dark emotions in themselves and others by silencing them—contributing to the kind of institutional psychic numbing exhibited by the Catholic Church in the case of Father Porter, as well as a host of other institutions. Victim-carriers of violence are then left to deal with their grief, fear, and despair in isolation.

## BYSTANDER DENIAL

Susan Griffin, a brilliant analyst of patriarchy and culture, has commented on the paradoxical relationship between denial and the psychological feeling of safety: "It is the system of denial which threatens life on earth today that has helped to fabricate a feeling of safety in the European psyche. What is lost to public awareness is a strong visceral reaction to environmental disaster, the bodily intelligence necessary to survival."[8]

The bystander—whether as an individual, a community, or a nation-state—relies on denial and psychic numbing as illusory ways to feel safe. Psychic numbing and denial on a large scale result in mass acting out of toxified dark emotional energy, posing grave dangers around the globe and contributing to the perpetuation of mass violence in all its myriad forms and levels—from individual workers who numbly kill coworkers, to high school students who are numb to the humiliation and harassment of their fellow students, to terrorists who engage in "suicide attacks" against innocent civilians. Whole communities lost to psychic numbing exist not only in Bosnia or Rwanda but in our American high schools.

Denial is a critical element in how systems that perpetuate social domination and inequality maintain themselves. It's more than an "intrapsychic" mechanism; it operates as a palpable emotional force within a given system, a force that is difficult to oppose. Denial is always about keeping consciousness fragmented.

None of us are immune to the dangers of bystander denial, even spiritual communities whose aim it is to cultivate enlightenment and compassion. There exists, in fact, a particular form of bystander consciousness in communities that put a premium on devotion to a guru who stands outside of the ordinary frameworks of morality. Spiritual communities of all types and denominations—Buddhist, Hindu, Muslim, Christian, Jewish—have known sex abuse by a teacher, leader, guru, or "awakened" soul that has gone on because the community tolerated it and stood by, separating their "ordinary" emotions from the event because they ascribed a "higher" purpose to the behavior.

One of the strongest forces influencing the increasing bystander consciousness of our society is the ever-more-powerful media industry. Statistics tell us that the average child watches forty hours of television per week. Every airport has a TV in every lounge. College students take their sets with them to school. TV, for many, is more a member of the family than the human members. The more we watch television and play video games, the more we lose our capacity to feel authentically and to discern reality from illusion. Everything is leveled by the "remote control" (an apt term for bystander consciousness!): one click and we go from an image of a child starving in Africa or dying in Boston to children who are threatening to take over the world in some sci-fi thriller. From sex-and-violence music videos to news reportage about another rape. It all becomes spectacle. Illusion is reality. Reality is illusion.

In a bystander society, the addictive quality of media fuels our emotional numbing and denial. It erodes our moral and emotional capacity to feel authentically the real problems of the world, feeding the bystander in our children and in the culture as a whole.

Finally, a word must be said about the large-scale carrying and bystanding in an age in which the earth itself can aptly be described as a victim of ecocide. The world's dark emotions in the context of our current environmental crisis are so overwhelming that we all rely on bystander defenses that further erode our emotional tolerance for the dark emotions circulating in the world. We all share some degree of "compassion fatigue" and psychic numbing in the face of the enormity and pervasiveness of the world's ongoing suffering. It's difficult for any of us to feel our way through the dark times in which we live, to maintain the mindfulness we need to experience our sadness, fear, and despair about terrible world events; and to use our dark emotions wisely in the interests of social transformation and planetary survival.

Emotional alchemy, in this wider emotional ecology, becomes less and less possible as a strictly individual process. We need each other's help in learning to find collective ways to carry the dark emotions consciously and use them to guide us to a saner way of life for the world family.

## *Empathy and Compassion: Essential Gifts in the Alchemy of the Dark Emotions*

> Can I see another's woe,
> And not be in sorrow too?
> Can I see another's grief
> And not seek for kind relief?
> —WILLIAM BLAKE,
>     "On Another's Sorrow"

> A human being is a part of the whole called by us "Universe," a part limited in time and space. He experiences himself, his thoughts and feelings as something separated from the rest, a kind of optical delusion of consciousness. This delusion is a kind of prison for us, restricting us to our personal desires and to affection for a few persons nearest to us. Our task must be to free ourselves from this prison by widening the circle of compassion to embrace all living creatures and the whole of nature in its beauty.
> —ALBERT EINSTEIN

Fortunately, the gifts that come to us through the alchemy of the dark emotions are good antidotes to the dangers of denial and numbing in the human family. As we become more aware of our own dark emotions and able to tolerate them, we become more aware of the suffering of others and more empathic. We loosen the constrictions of isolated pain. We open our hearts to the world. We grow in compassion.

Empathy is not some mushy activity that women practice when they have coffee together. It is encoded in our brains, part of our natural equipment for adapting to our environment. I have often thought of how different my parents' lives, and mine, would have been if Holocaust survivors had had empathic listeners to greet them after the war. How much this would have lessened the traumatic impact of genocide. Imagine what might happen if Palestinians and Israelis, Serbs and Croats, Tutsis and Hutus, Muslims, Jews, and Christians were systematically trained in empathy for the history and suffering of the Other.

In cultivating our inborn capacity to feel with others their pain and pleasure, happiness and sadness, love and fear, desire and despair, we are protected from the potential harm of bystander denial and its transgressions. We walk a path toward global compassion, healing, and peace.

The practice is deceptively simple: Speaking from the heart and listening with compassion, we heal ourselves and each other. In its variant forms, this is the work of alchemical transformation—from individual psychotherapy to the highest levels of international diplomatic negotiations and conflict transformation.

Healing comes when we know how to do this well.

When we really get it that everyone alive experiences sorrow, fear, and despair, when we can tolerate these dark emotions in ourselves and others, they transmute to gratitude for life. They remind us of the exquisite fragility of life and our need to protect it. And they open us to a meaning system in which empathy and compassion are elevated to their true importance for ourselves and the world.

Through these gifts, we expand our consciousness of suffering, release ourselves from the "I-me-mine" prison of ego to an awareness of suffering as a universal condition. We are no longer isolated in "my" problem or "my nation's" problem but can move out into an enlarged, interconnected sense of Self or of universal consciousness.

Many spiritual traditions speak of a larger sense of Self connected to the Divine. We can realize this Self as we grow in compassion through the alchemy of the dark emotions. This Self sees the larger picture and knows that compassion, the highest form of love, is the greatest healing balm for universal suffering. This kind of love is the Divine at work in the lives of humanity. Compassion is the gold in the accumulated sludge of humankind's sorrows. It is the best medicine for what ails the human family.

# 9 Global Healing in a Brokenhearted World

There's a crack in everything;
That's how the light gets in.
—LEONARD COHEN,
"Anthem"

STARTING IN THE YEAR 1992, I began to research emotional ecology by reading the news. I was looking at how large emotional currents move through world events; how the environmental crisis and mass violence affect our emotional lives; how emotions were reported in the media. Every morning, I read everything I could find about the kinds of events in the world that inspire the dark emotions of fear, grief, and despair. My family got used to seeing me reading while eating breakfast, marking off important articles with my red marker, shearing through the newspaper with my scissors.

I accumulated dozens of articles and organized them roughly into labeled folders: carriers and bystanders in the news, patriarchal violence, wars and civil strife, racism and hate crimes, worldwide poverty, dark emotions in the headlines, biomedical crimes, and ecocide.

After a while, I began to feel like the protagonist in Doris Lessing's *The Golden Notebook*, whose nervous breakdown was marked by her increasingly frantic clippings of dark news stories into a series of notebooks. I kept this up for a year, at which time I had a kind of breakdown of my own—more physical than mental. But clearly there was a mind/body relationship here. For months, I'd been experiencing increasing stomach pain. I paid it no mind and continued my obsessive vigil of world events. It wasn't until I was literally on the floor in intractable pain that it occurred to me to have this thing looked into.

A series of tests told me that I had an acute inflammation throughout my gastrointestinal tract. I could no longer eat without pain. In fact, I was in pain most of the time, but particularly just before, during, and after a meal. I became averse to eating. What little food I did take in was poorly absorbed, so I grew weaker. My energy level declined alarmingly until I could barely walk to my beloved Jamaica Pond and back (a distance of less than half a mile), much less the two-mile walk around it. Soon, walking two city blocks became a strain. I was well on my way to some kind of chronic fatigue syndrome, if not already in it.

Somewhere in the midst of this project, I'd forgotten the first and most essential skill of emotional alchemy: attending to emotional energy with awareness. As a result, I lost my balance. Along with my cereal, I imbibed the tears and blood, loneliness, misery, trauma, and horror that is daily life for millions of people on the planet. In the telling language of body-metaphor, I "couldn't stomach" the pain of the world. I was not alchemizing the dark emotions, I was swallowing them whole.

It took me about a year to recover my health: a year of exacting attention paid to my diet—not just to what I ate and when I ate but how I ate. I had to retrain myself to eat calmly, to be in the present moment, to enjoy food again, and to give it time to digest properly. I did yoga, saw an acupuncturist, and returned to my lost meditation practice. I initiated a new family custom: taking three long breaths before eating each meal.

In the laboratory of my own body, I learned what happens to a carrier who ingests the globe's bad news and its attendant emotions with breakfast and doesn't circulate the energy through the heart, but lets it sink into the guts and stay there. The result was a fire that swept through my innards and left me weak as a dishrag. Everything that I wrote about in chapter 3 happened to me: grief devolved into chronic anxiety and a leaden, physical depression. Fear got lodged in my guts. Despair for the world sank me, body and soul.

After I got sick, I had to put away all thoughts of the world for some period of time, except when I held the world in my prayers. I'm more aware now of the merciful nature of emotional numbing and denial. I can see the compelling appeal of the fantasy of innocence: I want to believe that we can cultivate our own individual gardens at a distance from the world and live the good life. I wish that this were possible. I'm aware of my own need to screen out reality and live with blinders on. I'm aware that my capacity for emotional alchemy is sometimes quite limited. I'm aware of how much all of us, the wounded, the healers, and the wounded healers, need each other's help, support, and guidance. We must be humble and learn from one another.

In the end, I threw all my news clippings away. I realized that there was no further need for more facts about how we are living in an age of global distress and terror, or how the human species is committing ecocide. We know this viscerally. Our bodies know. Our hearts know. And our souls know.

Years ago, when the hole in the ozone layer over North America first became front page news, I was taking a yoga class. We started each class with a silent meditation, not unlike the silent meetings of Quaker custom, in which people speak from the heart if so moved. Many prayers had been spoken in the circle, mostly for health, well-being, and inner peace.

This particular morning, I had just read the news about the hole in the ozone, our protective atmospheric skin, which was now seriously, perhaps irremediably, damaged by human tampering. The wounded world was the focus of my meditation, and I found myself uttering a prayer for the health of the planet.

To my surprise, the yoga teacher broke the usual decorum of silence to reassure me: "Just meditate and pray, and you will be okay."

I wasn't worried about being okay; I was concerned about the fate of the earth. I wasn't looking for reassurance, nor did I take any from the idea that I would be personally protected by meditation and prayer.

Somehow, my prayer for the earth had pierced the "serenity" of the yoga class. After the meditation, one of the students reprimanded me: "I don't know why you're bringing all this external stuff about the world into this room. It doesn't belong here."

This idea—that the world is not in the room, or its reverse, that the room is not in the world—is a clear reflection of how dissociation works. From this split of self and world, we derive a false sense of security. Perhaps that was why the yoga teacher tried to comfort me. My prayer for the earth, implying that we are connected to its fate, had punctured the denial. The teacher was comforting everyone, and perhaps himself as well, by trying to return to the split consciousness that defends us from our fear of vulnerability. His message was: If you take care of yourself, you don't have to take care of the world.

The truth is that the world is in the room in which we sit and pray, as much as the room is in the world that is being damaged and destroyed. And while I believe in the power of prayer, and in the miracles that can happen when that power is enlisted, I also know that the protection prayer affords is not quite the kind you get from a weight-loss-product sales pitch: Say this prayer and your life is guaranteed, or your money back. Nor do I think that self-care can be neatly divorced from care of the world. I believe that the world needs care and that all of us are called to that care by the grief and fear we feel when we allow ourselves to know in our hearts and guts how much the world is hurting.

It's hard to accept the truth that none of us are "protected"—whether by sunscreen or by prayer— while the earth itself is sick. If cells in the body are cancerous, the problem is not restricted to the tumor—the whole body is ill, and its survival is threatened. We are cells of one body, and that body is daily afflicted, tortured, scorched, toxified, rendered waste.

Like Ruth in the preceding chapter, we all carry fear not only about our own personal future, but also about the world's continuity. We are all to some degree emotionally frozen in dissociated dread of the prospects that haunt us: nuclear menace, chronic violence, epidemics of disease, the specter of biological and chemical warfare, environmental destruction. We live in a social world that in many ways, large and small, denies these terrors and goes on with business as usual.

We are all in need of communities in which to face the dark times in which we live, to speak and listen to our pain for the world. We need to learn together how to use the energy of our fear and sorrow to mobilize ourselves to protect the earth.

## A Collective Dark Night of the Soul

> In acquiescing to nuclear weapons we have deliberately anesthetized the normal feelings, emotions, anxieties and hopes that alone would bring us to our senses.
>
> —LEWIS MUMFORD

It is fear that alerts us to threat, grief that tells us of our loss, despair that asks us to change our ways or remain hopeless. No one in his or her right mind should be entirely fearless in an age of global danger.

Like many parents today, my worst fears are for my children.

My youngest child, who suffers from asthma, is a weather vane for our polluted air. Her chronic cough tells me how toxic a day it is. Asthma is now the leading chronic childhood illness, affecting almost 5 million children in the United States alone.

I cook for and feed my children and wonder: How carcinogenic is this carrot? Is this soy genetically modified? I grew my own vegetable garden until I had the soil tested and found out that it had a high lead content. The day we gave up growing carrots, my children cried.

I grieve for my children's loss of innocence.

When my older daughter was six years old, a political activist sporting a "Ban the Bomb" button rang the doorbell seeking a donation. Anna greeted him and asked him what the button meant. He took it upon himself to break the news of the atomic bomb. Before I had a chance to clamp his mouth shut, he'd already mentioned Hiroshima. After he left, Anna asked me a million questions, including, "Why would anyone bomb people who haven't done anything wrong?" and "Is there a lot of blood?" and "Does anyone live, or is everyone killed?"

Several years later she asked me, "Can you get breast cancer if you don't have breasts?"

I'm afraid of what the world will be like for my children when I am gone. When I think of how they will have to mop up after us adults, who have so ruinously dealt with the beautiful earth we've been given, I am ashamed.

I know I am not alone in these thoughts and feelings.

"To be conscious in our world today involves awareness of unprecedented peril." These are the prescient words of Joanna Macy. In *Despair and Personal Power in the Nuclear Age*, she wrote about the mass psychology of living in a nuclear age:

> Until now every generation throughout history lived with the tacit certainty that other generations would follow. Each assumed, without questioning, that its children and children's children, and those yet unborn would carry on, to walk the same earth under the same sky. Hardships, failures and personal death were ever encompassed in that vaster assurance of continuity. That certainty is now lost to us. That loss, unmeasured and immeasurable, is the pivotal psychological reality of our time.[1]

While New Agers speak of the Age of Aquarius, Hindu scripture and yoga philosophy say that we live in the Kali Yuga, an age of darkness and spiritual decline. Buddhists also speak of the "dark age" when the sacred dharma of enlightenment is not recognized, materialism is worshiped, and unredeemed suffering is the basic state of the planet.

In this age, we have entered a global dark night of the soul.

Our bodies, hearts, and souls carry the news of our endangered earth. Our emotions, when we allow them to, bring the earth's cries to us. Because we are all interconnected in the web of life, and because that web is poisoned and threatened, the wounds of the earth are our wounds. We carry them in ways that we don't necessarily recognize or connect to the state of the earth. But if we listen, we can feel the earth's voice within us. We are called to listen.

We are called by our fear to defend and protect our earthly home. We are called by our grief to join with others who grieve in a communal uprising against the status quo. We are called by our despair to descend together into our collective dark night of the soul and renew ourselves, to emerge with a sense of meaning that is compatible with peace on a healed planet.

*Take two minutes and close your eyes. Breathing deeply, allow yourself to feel one or more emotions about the state of the world at this time. Don't try to fix or change what you feel. Just let it be. Notice where the emotion is in your body and breathe through it. Listen to its message. Can you hear what it is telling you? Asking of you?*

## Mass Emotional Disturbances in a Troubled World

Living in an endangered world ecology affects and alters human psychology.

This seems obvious enough, but it is still largely overlooked by conventional psychology and almost all quarters of the helping professions.[2]

We all know people who have died or are dying or will die of cancer. Most of us know someone who has suffered from chronic fatigue syndrome or environmental illness. We all know, deeply, that our health and our children's health is threatened in a polluted world. We know that future generations must grow up in a world of silenced terror.

We keep our fingers crossed while trying to keep our fears and sorrows at bay, many of us relying on defenses that are used by survivors of trauma: psychic numbing, dissociation, emotional constriction. These are punctuated by bouts of anxiety and even panic. Millions of people go to bed each night unable to sleep without some form of pharmaceutical help.

Sometimes, the vulnerability of living on an imperiled planet hits close to home—your mother, daughter, or sister is diagnosed with breast cancer. Your father, son, or brother is diagnosed with prostate cancer. Or you yourself have cancer. Your child is contaminated by an unknown toxin. Your friend has skin cancer. When these things happen, we are plunged into the terror, grief, and despair we've managed to suppress.

But even those who are not personally touched, in increasingly large numbers, are suffering from depression, sleep disturbances, intrusions of nightmares, unexplained anxiety or panic. Still others wonder: My personal life is going well. I have a husband and two wonderful children. My health is good and I have a job I love. So why am I so uneasy?

More than most, the current generation of adolescents is suffering the symptoms of a deranged world: depression and anxiety, attention deficit disorder, violent behavior, addiction.

Emotional constriction and explosion, depression, sleep disturbances, nightmares, anxiety. Constellations of symptoms such as these are often diagnosed as post-traumatic stress disorder (PTSD). In an imperiled world, we all suffer from some measure of PTSD—not *post-*, but *pre-* or *present-*traumatic stress disorder, a psychological condition related to the traumas of everyday life in the present and those we dread in the future. This doesn't mean we're all mentally ill. It means we're all connected to the state of the earth.

Several other features of the mass psychology of Westerners seem noteworthy. The first is what I call *frantic individualism* or the "I'm Too Busy" syndrome (applicable to many professional clinicians, this is not a diagnosis you find in the DSM-IV). I'm too busy to play with my children. Too busy to call my mother. Too busy to have lunch with an old friend. Too busy to play. Too busy to breathe. Too busy to be.

We're too busy to feel. This is the zeitgeist, the spirit of the times. The mantra *I don't have enough time* keeps us from feeling much of anything. Self-enforced workaholic numbing, in the past decade, has become epidemic. I see it in my clients, colleagues, friends, and myself. More than an individual aberration, it's a symptom of the mass psychology of living in an age of global distress.

Then there's what I call *pseudo-rationality,* in which rationalization masks dissociation of emotion from awareness and action. In a context of benumbed emotional responses, we tend to rely on rationalization and to put our trust in the "facts." It's not so bad, we think, because someone who knows more than I do tells me not to worry. The facts can only be determined by experts with a Ph.D. or M.D. after their names—or, in another context, by the government, the CIA, the corporate world. We hand our responsibility over to these authorities and hope that somehow they will take care of the world for us. Let them do it. I'm too busy.

William G. Hyland, former deputy director of the National Security Council, said, "If you allowed the emotion of nuclear war to enter the Defense Department, you'd end up totally paralyzed." He was saying that having emotions like fear or grief about using nuclear weapons was irrational, since these emotions would prevent us from using them! When my daughter first heard about the bomb, she asked me: "Why would anyone use a bomb on people when they haven't done anything wrong?" She was too young to understand nuclear attack as "defense."

So who's more rational—William Hyland or the six-year-old girl? Guided by fear, the emotional child is wiser than the pseudo-rational adult. She knows what he doesn't (as the young are always being told by adults): Violence is not the answer! If everyone took this six-year-old wisdom to heart and refused to use or develop weapons because they were afraid, we'd live in a much more rational world. But pseudo-rationality has taken us far afield from the wisdom of children.

Another sign of living in an era of global terror: our escalating array of addictions. Alcohol, tobacco, and drugs have become a routine part of youth culture in a way that outdoes the 1960s. Most colleges have essentially given up on any serious attempt to grapple with the use of addictive substances by a large percentage of their student population. Television, cyberspace, and compulsive entertainment are addictions in another guise. Our civilization's addiction to technology is the biggest one of all.

Whatever else they are, addictions are ways to numb pain. They rise as the world's collective grief, fear, and despair rise.

So does violence. The new and growing diagnosis of "oppositional defiance disorder" is psychiatry's label for children who are increasingly out of control or violent, utterly defiant of adult authority they neither trust nor respect. Violence among teens has moved from packing a knife to stockpiling an arsenal of guns, rifles, and machine guns and using these in acts of mass murder.

Traumatic stress disorder. Anxiety and panic. Depression and sleep disorders. The "I'm Too Busy" syndrome. Wide-scale addictions. Pseudo-rationality. Increasing violence. These are some of the emotional disorders we suffer as world citizens in an age of global terror and environmental degradation. I'm sure there are many others I haven't chronicled.

Yet not one of the approximately 360 diagnoses in the DSM-IV makes a connection between our emotional states and the state of the earth. This is part of the massive denial of our time, and sad to say, my profession has contributed to it. We would have to rewrite the entire DSM-IV to take our current emotional ecology into account, or chuck it altogether. The distinction between the sick and the well falls away in this larger context. We all come to the barrier, the brick wall of our inability to feel through what we are actually living through, because it's simply too much to bear. Denial, social powerlessness, and toxified emotions keep us from acting on the information that our fear, grief, and despair would bring us about the need to reshape the social order for the sake of the earth.

## Rebalancing the World's Emotional Ecology

The normal psychology of our species has brought us to a state of affairs in which the very life of our planet is endangered. This is the context in which our "normal" lives are lived. The normal ego in patriarchy is the bounded self—with its emphasis on control and power-over, its qualities of competitive self-interest and mastery over nature, its profound cutoff from others, from the earth, and from the power of the feminine.

This ego is what has to change if we are to avert a global dead end.

Many social critics have written about the disastrous consequences of our profound alienation from nature, from the feminine, from each other, and from ourselves. Our heads and hearts are in different places; our bodies, minds, and spirits have their own separate compartments; our gendered emotional styles keep us at war with different parts of ourselves. We don't know what we feel, or feel what we know. As a species, we don't know how to live with each other without hierarchy, strife, and war.

What's needed is a shift in self-definition—an evolutionary leap in consciousness from a patriarchal ego to something larger: from a patriarchal meaning system, with its devotion to hierarchy, military power, and death, to a more archetypally feminine meaning system, in which the nurturance and care of others is not devalued as second-order business but elevated to its true importance; and in which care for the world is seen as an extension of our care for ourselves.

In Hindu myth, the dark goddess Kali sprang from the head of Durga in order to overcome demonic male power in a world overrun with masculine force. We need the strength and courage of the dark goddess now if we are to even imagine what global recovery from patriarchal abuses might look like, much less how to bring it about. In recovering the feminine force once called Goddess and reclaiming its power to change our minds, hearts, and institutions, we contribute to rebalancing our civilization. The alchemy of the dark emotions is part of that reclaiming and rebalancing.

But so long as it remains an isolated journey disconnected from the world, we will find it wanting. We will become junkies for the next shot of healing—the next psychotherapy, self-help book, celebrity guru, behavioral technique, talk-show hostess, what have you. People in most parts of the world know what we individualist Americans have such a hard time getting: Healing is more than a solo flight.

Our fear can move us, as it did the mothers in Love Canal or in Woburn, to take action against those forces in the world that would poison our children. Our grief for the earth can move us to join hands with others to create what Adam Trombly calls a "different ceremony." Our despair can move us to reroute our lives, to break the numbed cycle of business as usual and find a path toward greater peace within and without.

In doing this work together, we are empowered to make the necessary shift—from the denial and subjugation of the dark, of emotion, of the feminine, of the body, of the earth, to a transformed consciousness and social order. We can then come to know our place as a cell in the larger body of the earth while honoring the particular light that we bring to a darkened world.

*Take a minute and recall the emotions about the world that you felt earlier. What if you honored these emotions and listened to their message? What actions would they lead you to? What is the particular gift you can give to the world?*

This all sounds very grand—a vision of what could be. We could all get it together and do our healing work and heal the world. Many of us have had this vision, in one form or another, since the 1960s.

Nowadays this vision seems just a bit harder to come by. Repeated genocides, governmental irresponsibility for environmental abuse, chronic and escalating violence all over the globe, disastrous corporate globalization, all these and more are terribly disheartening. We humans seem to learn through pain, and so the dark emotions are and will be our lot for the foreseeable future. All signs point to the prospect of a lot more global pain before we change our ways.

While it is possible to heal through the dark emotions and live with gratitude, faith, and joy, we must get over the idea that we can do this consistently and perfectly in an unbalanced world. Emotional alchemy is a possibility that needs encouragement and needs to be embodied in some kind of ongoing practice. This is why I have included an extensive home course of exercises (in part four) to share the practices I have found helpful in my professional and personal life. My hope is that these practices can be done more communally rather than simply with an individual psychotherapist, so that we can expand our abilities to alchemize our pain and grow in the ability to act with compassion, to heal ourselves and one another.

Does this mean we should give up the idea of individual healing? Of course not. No more than we would give up on helping someone who is bleeding in the street. Helping others in need of healing is my life's work and my love. There is great joy in helping someone heal from a life of trauma, illness, or loss. From this work, I know that even the most profound losses and traumas can be healed, sometimes in very unexpected ways. I also know that a great deal of healing takes place without the help of a therapist, and I believe that at this point in time we need to develop these more collective, world-related models. Individual and world healing can build on each other dialectically. We mustn't neglect ourselves in a frantic compulsion to save the world. We need to take care of our own broken hearts in the midst of a brokenhearted world.

## The Silence of Majdanek: A Healing Story

> If a way to the better there be,
> it lies in taking a full look at the worst.
> —Thomas Hardy

This is a story of individual healing, my own, that took place in a concentration camp.

In 1993, my father asked me to join him and my mother on a pilgrimage to the towns and concentration camps in which his family had perished. He wanted, by his presence in these places, to place a symbolic stone at their nonexistent graves, and to say the Kaddish, the Hebrew prayer for the dead. He had just turned eighty. "This would be a way to heal before I die," he said.

It was startling to hear my father speak of "healing," a word he'd never used before, and certainly not in relation to the Holocaust. What healing we would find in Treblinka and Auschwitz, I couldn't imagine.

And so for seven days in April, on the occasion of the fiftieth anniversary of the Warsaw Ghetto Uprising, we sojourned together on a tour of Polish ghettos and concentration camps. We traveled in a small group, in a tour van provided by the state-sponsored Polish tourist agency. Of the eleven of us, ten were Holocaust survivors. I was the only member of what, in survivor circles, is called "the second generation."

Toward the end of this trip, after Treblinka and before Auschwitz, we arrived at Majdanek, a lesser-known death camp built in 1941 near Lublin. Some 360,000 women, men, and children died here, mostly, but not all, Jews. With its watchtowers and barbed wire, six barracks, three gas chambers, and crematorium left almost exactly as they were, Majdanek is the only standing, intact death camp.

Entering the gates of Majdanek, I am struck at once by the silence—as though a time-defying horror has frozen everything in place. We tramp through the rain-soaked mud, the watchtowers peering at us. The enlarged photographs of Jews in various phases of their extermination that are hanging on the walls, and the organized piles of human hair and shoes from the victims, are the only museum artifacts. All else is now as it was then: The barracks with their wooden bunk beds. The shower room where inmates were sent before being dispatched to the gas chambers. The three gas chambers with their blue-tinged ceilings—a residue of the deadly Zyklon-B gas. The small storage room piled high with remaining Zyklon-B canisters, with its window through which the inmates could be watched in their last moments.

Still as a tomb and yet vibrating with the sounds of the dead, this place has a dreadful eloquence. As we walk and look, the silence gathers, making the air dense.

We enter a small room where a flat slab of wood on a frame is labeled "dissecting table." Here the bodies of the dead were plundered for valuables—gold teeth and hidden jewels. Next is the "bone room" where human legs, arms, skulls are exhibited under glass. From here, we come into a much larger space, a room oddly illuminated with light that streams through the small windows near the top of the building onto the dark black twin crematorium ovens that stand in the center. There is nothing else in this room but these ovens. And it is here, at their gaping mouths, that we come to a full stop.

Five or six large candles burn at the entrance to each oven. Someone has left a bouquet of flowers, their pale pastel colors startling against the blackened steel. There is another tour group here, huddled together as the leader, a rabbi, recites the Twenty-third Psalm. *The Lord is my shepherd; I shall not want. He makes me lie down in green pastures. He leads me beside the still waters, He restores my soul. He guides me in the paths of righteousness, for His Name's sake.*

As I stand and listen, the silence is humming. It gets louder and louder until there is nothing else but the silence. The rabbi's prayer, the muffled sobs of these pilgrims in search of whatever secrets one can distill from standing here, in the midst of this oddly illuminated darkness, my own thoughts and feelings—everything recedes, imploding into the vortex of silence.

I can't really "explain" the silence of Majdanek. I believe it was the most profound and prolonged meditative state I have ever experienced. Beyond thought and emotion, I was just present.

After Majdanek, returning to the hotel at Lublin, I felt curiously light and buoyant. Passing a mirror in the lobby, I was startled to see my own face. It looked ruddy, healthy, alive. I was in some kind of altered state that reminded me, oddly, of how I felt on my one venture into LSD in my youthful days: Looking at the trees, birds, plants, and insects, I could see the life flowing through them. I could feel life flowing through me. And now, after standing at the crematorium, I felt that same life force and saw it in my face. Perhaps what happened to me in Majdanek is this: the Holocaust became, finally, an event of the past. And because I could let it be past, I felt alive in a new way.

That night, I met Shmuel. He was traveling with another larger group of survivors. I introduced myself to him after dinner at the Lublin hotel, drawn to his radiant face and shock of white hair as though to an angel. He told me he was an Australian citizen, on a journey of remembrance. He'd grown up in Warsaw, where, as a fourteen-year-old boy, he daily climbed over the walls of the ghetto to the Aryan section, risking his life to steal food for his family. One day he returned to find his parents and six siblings all gone, taken to Treblinka. After this, Shmuel told me, he was no longer afraid of death, because he had nothing to live for. Yet, despite his longing for death, he resolved to stay alive, to tell his family's story.

One day, his longing seemed to be answered. He was picked up by the Nazis and lined up against the wall to be shot, along with a few other Jews. In what he took to be his last moments, as he stood with his face to the wall, Shmuel saw his grandfather, who had died when he was a young child. *Don't give up! You will live!* he heard his grandfather say. At that precise moment, the Nazi in charge told the gunman: "Take him out. He will die later, along with everyone else." Shmuel was spared.

He was then sent to Majdanek and, afterward, Auschwitz, where he awoke each day knowing that he would live. From the moment of his grandfather's visitation, this inner conviction of his survival never left him.

A large man with a wide face, blue eyes, and an aura of radiant health, Shmuel, in deference to my work as a psychologist, asked me what I made of his story. I answered: "The angels must have been very busy during the Holocaust."

We can and must heal from the wounds of history. We are all situated in history, perhaps not as evidently as in my story, but always the frame of history surrounds us, or, rather, we live in its ground. We may be African American descendants of an enslaved people, or descendants of the Irish famine, or of the Puritans; but whoever we are, we are always a link in a long chain of people whose stories we carry in the color of our eyes, the curve of our lips, the cast of our temperament, the way that we think and feel about the world, the transhistorical traumas that live in our bodies.

To heal through the dark emotions, in one sense, is to recover from one's history. And to do this, we must first fully reclaim it. Knowing the story, intimately, we can arrive in the present, like a newborn child.

My father didn't exactly heal from the Holocaust on his visit to Europe, but he found a greater level of peace, which is perhaps the only healing possible for someone with his life experience. Unexpectedly, this same pilgrimage, for me, was a decisive healing moment. Though I had no personal connection to Majdanek (my relatives were killed in Auschwitz and Treblinka), my visit there did what years of talk psychotherapy had never accomplished. I shed a skin l didn't know I still had. The sign of healing was somatic as well. On a physical level, something happened that I could not explain. When I started this trip, I was sick with a pelvic infection that I worried would get worse in Poland. After Majdanek, I was well.

I did not lie down in green pastures, I stood at the mouth of a crematory oven, and yet, mysteriously, as in the psalm, my soul was restored and my life flowed more freely. It seems that healing is possible not only by resting in the arms of a benign and comforting God, but in a silent, unflinching presence to human evil.

When we enter the healing power of the present moment, the body sheds an old skin; the cellular composition changes. The clouded tissue of the past is transmuted; a biochemical shift occurs; we are renewed. By being fully present to the darkness, without resorting to our usual obstructions to full awareness, healing is possible, even from the worst.

At the same time, I do not confuse my own "healing" with the world's. I don't believe that my personal healing has made the world one bit more habitable for the millions whose daily suffering is unredeemed. Knowing this, I remain an undisguised wounded healer. A sadness rests at the periphery of my consciousness, an old and intimate companion, and will remain, so long as I am connected to this world. While it does not obscure my capacity for joy, it coexists with it.

The awakened heart, said Chögyam Trungpa, is characterized by a special kind of sadness. "If you search for awakened heart," he says, "if you put your hand through your rib cage and feel for it, there is nothing there except for tenderness. You feel sore and soft, and if you open your eyes to the rest of the world, you feel tremendous sadness."[3]

Joy and sorrow are not antagonists; they are both a part of being fully alive. Each day, the world gives us cause for both. Shmuel's angel, glimpsed as a Nazi held a gun to his head, is just one story of the sacred at work in the daily lives and events of this world. And yet, the three men lined up against the wall with Shmuel were shot dead on the spot—three of millions. People are tortured and murdered every day on the planet. And yet, events that appear utterly unredemptive are pregnant with moments of undying love, heroism, and miracles.

Knowing this, we are both sad and joyful. Healed and unhealed.

## Individual and Global Healing Together

> An unhealed life is a statement of our need to work together to heal the whole. It is an opportunity to refrain from turning away, separating our reality from the reality of others.
>
> —YAEL BETHIEM, *The Unhealed Life*

As our individual healing progresses, we are more and more able to give ourselves to something larger. And as we give ourselves to something larger, we are more and more healed ourselves. This is the dialectic of personal and global healing that I have seen in survivors of trauma. The dialectic applies to all of us.

Once, in a dream, I heard this voice: *We are not here to get our needs met. We are here to serve the world.*

At the time, I found this voice rather harsh. Then I thought about it. The trauma survivors I work with who are consumed with getting their needs met are generally the most miserable. The ones who find their way through their trauma, in part, by giving something back to the world are generally the happiest, the most grateful for what they have, the most able to enjoy their bodies and their lives. They are the ones who live with faith despite their histories of pain.

We each have something to contribute to the global healing process, a particular gift or vision, skill or song. Individual healing has a lot to do with finding this gift and using it for the world's sake, finding our song and singing it. In the process, a largeness of self breaks out of the chains and prison of the ego's isolation. This brings balance and compassion, which are the major ingredients of healing.

When we find a way to manifest our gift and give it to the world, no matter how small or large it may seem, we are made whole. We find a way to be a channel for the dark emotional energy in the world, a channel that balances the dark and the light of existence. And in so doing, we become fuller, we fill up with compassion; we become so full that we want to spill over with it, to extend it. We find that compassion, though not always about pleasure, is a good way to live, a way that keeps us connected to others, to life. And in our connectedness, we find wholeness. This, to me, is what individual healing is all about.

At the same time, the world cries out for a rebalancing of its emotional ecology. We are called to see into the darkness of our brokenhearted world, to recover our capacity to feel and know with our hearts, and to act collectively, from this place of compassion. In harmonizing our culture's dissociative splits between head and heart, mind and body, spirit and nature, self-interest and the collective good, we come to an understanding of healing that goes beyond the individual and beyond the facile appeal of a spiritual bypass of the dark.

A healed life is always a work in progress, not a life devoid of all traces of suffering, but a life lived fully, deeply, and authentically, compassionately engaged with the world.

## GLOBAL YOUTH CONNECT

The collective alchemy of the dark emotions may seem like a distant dream, but there are those who live it and show us the way. One group of these torchbearers is called Global Youth Connect.

Every year, more than one hundred thousand victims of political violence find safe haven in the United States. Many are children. Some have experienced large-scale governmental or military terror and violence. Others have seen their relatives murdered or taken away in civil wars. All have suffered trauma and experienced the most intense forms of grief, fear, and despair.

A group of these survivors founded an international human rights organization for young people called Global Youth Connect. This happened when Dr. Frank Ochberg, a psychiatrist specializing in trauma, approached Judith

Thompson, an American who had worked with children from war-torn countries who used their experiences to spark social activism.

Members of Global Youth Connect come from all over the world, including Cambodia, Liberia, Guatemala, Serbia, Nigeria, and Brooklyn. They train young people from around the world here in the United States to develop youth leadership, rebuild communities, take action on human rights issues at home and abroad, and do the work of peace.

Here are some voices from Global Youth Connect:

Eva Morales, thirty, is from Guatemala, which was torn by civil war for thirty-six years. More than one hundred fifty thousand people were killed in this war, fifty thousand are still missing, and more than a million were driven from their homes:

> So many people, young and old, have grown up with so much horror and so much fear that they are frozen inside, like I was. When millions of young people are closed up because of what they have seen and endured, there is no chance for freedom to come to a whole society. Talking about my experiences with the group, becoming free, has made me want to do it for people back home."[4]

Hafsat Abiola, twenty-four, is from Nigeria, which has been ruled by the military for twenty-eight years. Her father, the elected president of the country, was imprisoned in 1993 after a military takeover. He died in prison. Hafsat's mother was shot dead by military agents. At least seven thousand political prisoners in Nigeria have died:

> We want to use the power that grows among us for others too. We want to spread the spark of healing and encourage acts of courage. The world needs that so badly. It's so easy to be a bystander, to watch things from afar, to wish they were better but do nothing about it.

Arn Chorn-Pond, thirty-one, is from Cambodia, where the Khmer Rouge murdered 1.7 million people—a quarter of the population—between 1975 and 1979:

> The Khmer Rouge killed my friends and family without warning. To the Khmer Rouge there was no excuse for crying. I watched children my own age being taken to work fields and executed

when they cried. I learned how not to cry when I saw those horrible things happen. If I had cried, I too would have been executed. My big job has been to learn how to cry, to get my feelings back, to get myself back, to be with others. Somehow sharing the pain has been the way in which I could find myself again and commit myself to the world.

Arn Chorn-Pond worked with a group of Cambodian orphans and prostitutes and built an organization called Cambodian Volunteers for Community Development. It now has more than fifty thousand members rebuilding their communities. He has also worked to recover Cambodia's culture of art and music. Eva Morales organized a group of twenty Guatemalans in their late teens and early twenties, which has now grown to one hundred and spread to other parts of the country. Others in Global Youth Connect have worked in a number of peacemaking projects in different parts of the world.

What these young people found together was a collective alchemy of the dark emotions. As they worked with others wounded by the world, sharing their tears and pain, they healed themselves and became the agents of others' healing. Carriers of the dark emotions of their nations, they journeyed deeply within themselves by moving out into the world, and they moved out into the world by allowing their dark emotions to be spoken and heard in community.

This collective emotional alchemy has made them wise in the ways of peace. Their spiritual strengths shine forth like a light in the darkness of our world: gratitude for life despite monumental losses, faith in the world despite experiencing the worst of human evil, compassion despite being profoundly victimized, and courage for personal and global change.

These men and women inspire us all to find creative ways to heal through the dark emotions together.

## Global Suffering and Redemption

> God is waiting for us to redeem the world.
> —ABRAHAM HESCHEL,
> *I Asked for Wonder*

> The redeemer comes a dark way.
> —THEODORE ROETHKE,
> "The Shape of the Fire"

The loss of connection to nature in Western post-industrial society and the devastation of our environmental resources are the largely overlooked global contexts that trigger and complicate the dark emotions in our time. In this global crisis of our age, the dark emotions are inevitable responses. Affective markers of our collective fate, they carry information our conscious minds would often rather deny or avoid. They are the repository of this information, the conduit of our moral responsiveness to the world, and the unrecognized vehicles of an urgently needed worldwide social and spiritual transformation. The emotions we most dread offer essential information that humans need in order to survive and evolve, and to live in balance with nature. If we ever needed the wisdom of the dark emotions, we need it now.

For some, the yearning for global healing may have religious overtones. If God, as Abraham Heschel says, is waiting for us to redeem the world, then we are making God wait a very, very long time. No doubt, God is patient. But when will Messiah come?

In my faith, Messiah will arrive when the world is made whole—a process called *tikkun olam*, repair of the world. To willingly and consciously take on the world's suffering and transform it is the messianic hope and challenge of our time. In Christian theological terms, it could be said that we must all become as Christ—who, in taking on the pain of the world, transforms and redeems the sins of humankind. (Hopefully, we won't have to get crucified to make this happen!) Global redemption will come when we bring Messiah into the world through our actions.

Imagine a society in which every child learns to value and honor herself and others because she knows that we are all connected emotionally. Imagine a society in which the emotion-norm is one of empathic connection, and where acts of compassion are a widespread, socially encouraged practice.

Imagine a world in which emotional wisdom is thought to be critical to our mental health, our national security, and the health of the planet. Imagine a world in which national leaders are trained in emotional awareness and tolerance and use their wisdom to help heal the conflicts between nations through peaceful means. Imagine.

This is a utopian vision. And yet it's not impossible to bring the alchemy of the dark emotions into the public sphere. A small start are the classes in emotional intelligence that are now being taught in a few (too few) grade schools throughout the country. The education of large segments of the population and perhaps even world leaders (who seem to need it most) in models of conflict transformation that highlight the importance of speaking and listening to each other's emotions empathically is a possibility toward which we must devote our intentions and actions. This kind of education grows in importance the more strife-ridden our world becomes. Models of emotional wisdom on a community-wide basis are available to us if we look for them. Peacemakers work among us and would teach the ways of peace if we financed them. Many religious organizations today are grappling with the question of what it means to be a person of God in an age of global threat. A cornucopia of political organizations exists to help bring about peace and justice and to protect the environment.

There are many paths to healing in a brokenhearted world.

There is yet hope that we humans will learn to live mindfully with the shared pain in the global human family, and that we will recover the wisdom and power of the dark emotions. In so doing, may we heal ourselves. May we rejuvenate the healing energies of our communal connections to one another. May we redeem the soul of the world.

# PART FOUR

# A Home Course in Emotional Alchemy

# 10 *Thirty-Three Emotional Exercises*

> Emotion is the chief source of all becoming-conscious. There can be no transforming of darkness into light and of apathy into movement without emotion.
>
> —C. G. JUNG, *Psychological Aspects of the Modern Archetype*

THE SO-CALLED NEGATIVE EMOTIONS have tremendous power. Emotional alchemy is not about taming or transcending this power but about befriending it and using it for the good of ourselves, others, and the planet. Tapping into the powerful energies of the dark emotions takes skill, patience, and faith. This "home course" in emotional alchemy is designed to help you develop these skills and to cultivate patience and faith in your ability to be a shaman of dark emotional energy.

These are the words of Brooke Medicine Eagle, a North American Nez Percé Sioux medicine woman:

> In the philosophy of the true Indian people, Indian is an attitude, a state of mind . . . a state of being, a place of the heart. To allow the heart to be the distributor of energy on this planet; to allow your heart, your feelings, your emotions to distribute your energy; to pull that energy from the earth, from the sky, to pull it down and distribute it from your heart, the very center of your being—that is our purpose.[1]

These words may appear strange to those who are centered not in the heart but in the head. But the words are a great description of emotional energy, when it is in balance with the world and used for alchemical transformation. Brooke Medicine Eagle describes emotional energy as a palpable force that can circulate, like blood, throughout not only a person, but an entire field or environment.

We may think of the "place of the heart" as a metaphor for the center of emotion. But recent research indicates that the heart is more than a blood pump; it is a complex organ with biochemical resemblances to the brain. Like the brain, the heart can influence our entire body. Furthermore, it appears that emotions can alter the heart's electrical field, affecting not only our whole bodies but also the space around us.[2]

Science is affirming what the Sioux Indians and other indigenous peoples long ago knew to be true: emotional energy is real and is centered in the heart. It can be communicated to others, distributed in a transformative alchemical process that is healing for oneself and the world.

The following program of thirty-three exercises is designed to help you locate and befriend your heart's emotional energy and use it for transformation. Many blessings on your heart's alchemical journey!

Emotional exercise is very different from aerobic exercise in one crucial respect: You have to slow down rather than speed up in order to do it right! Relax your mind and body, slow down your thoughts and brain waves. Breathe deeply, find a slow groove, and you're ready to go!

This is an entirely fluid, nonlinear, heart-centered process, not a static system or set of standardized steps that you follow in an orderly progression. The seven steps of the emotional alchemy process don't need to be done in any particular order. Do some, skip others; by all means, play around with them! While it's helpful to consolidate the right and left hemispheres of the brain and have a map of the journey through dark emotions, fruitful detours are often very rewarding. No one is the final expert on this process but you.

Remember, your heart will find its own ways of healing through the dark emotions if you set out with a strong intention and cultivate emotional tolerance. Keep an emotional alchemy journal to write down any part of this program you're practicing and see how your capacity for emotional alchemy grows.

# Step 1. Intention: Focusing Your Spiritual Will

### EXERCISE 1. THE POWER OF INTENTION
What is your best or highest intention with regard to the grief, fear, and despair in your life? Sit and meditate on this question. Listen to what your heart is telling you. Frame your intentions carefully and write them down. Affirm your intention each day as you wake up and as you lie down to sleep.

If you're having a hard time with this one, try this: Take a page and divide it in half. On one side of the page, write "Personality" and on the other side write "Spirit." Now describe the attributes of your personality on one side and the attributes of your spirit on the other. When I do this with clients, there are often striking contrasts in these lists. For instance, your personality might be impulsive, impatient, type A; while your spirit may be patient, loving, tolerant.

Now think again about the intention question, only this time addressing it to your spirit rather than your personality. What is your spirit's intention with respect to your grief, despair, or fear? Keep the answer posted in your awareness.

## Step 2. Affirmation: Developing an Emotion-Positive Attitude

There are two parts to this step: (1) identifying your beliefs about your dark emotions, and (2) changing your beliefs about your dark emotions.

### EXERCISE 2. IDENTIFYING YOUR BELIEFS

This is a sentence completion exercise to be done for each of the dark emotions in turn. You can also do this exercise with anger or any other difficult emotion. Write down these sentence fragments and then complete them. The trick is not to think about it too much. Just write whatever comes into your head. Don't censor or doctor or try to prettify your thoughts—just get them down.

- I think of (grief, fear, despair) as . . .
- What my (grief, fear, despair) says about me is  . . .
- If I fully experienced my (grief, fear, despair), I would  . . .
- What I'd most like to do with my (grief, fear, despair) is  . . .

Notice the negative beliefs. Also notice the positive beliefs. Try to eliminate the negative and accentuate the positive. By eliminate, I don't mean hate yourself for thinking this way. Simply notice that you have some negative beliefs and try to replace them with positive ones. (See the next exercise.)

### EXERCISE 3. AFFIRMING EMOTION-POSITIVE BELIEFS

Write a set of affirmative beliefs to counter the negative beliefs you uncovered in the previous exercise.

Here are some examples of affirmative beliefs about dark emotions:

- I think of grief as a process of healing from hurt and loss.
- I think of fear as a signal to pay attention to something important or urgent.
- I think of despair as a call to transform my sense of life's meaning and to renew my faith.
- What my grief says about me is that I am open, tender-hearted, and loving.
- What my fear says about me is that I am human.
- What my despair says about me is that I need to take care of myself and attend to my soul.
- If I fully experienced my grief, I would feel more fully alive and grateful for each moment.
- If I fully experienced my fear, I would be able to enjoy my life more.
- If I fully experienced my despair, I would renew myself and have more integrity and meaning in my life.
- What I'd most like to do with my grief is use it to grow in compassion.
- What I'd most like to do with my fear is use it wisely to serve and protect those I love.
- What I'd most like to do with my despair is learn from it how to see clearly and live fully in the light and dark of existence.

EXERCISE 4. LEARNING FROM YOUR DARK EMOTIONS

Complete each of the following sentences with what you would ideally want to believe about your dark emotions.

- Out of knowing and being with my (grief, fear, despair), my task is to . . .
- When I view my dark emotions as teachers, I learn . . .
- Instead of avoiding dark emotions, I can use them creatively by . . .

EXERCISE 5. ERASING NEGATIVE BELIEFS

Often, it is difficult to get rid of negative thinking about our feelings. We are haunted by negative thoughts that we can't stop. Our negative thoughts about our dark emotions reinforce the emotions. For example, if every time you feel depressed, you think to yourself, "Here I am depressed again. None of my friends can stand me anymore. I'm weak and inadequate," this thought pattern will further reinforce your depression.

If you have thoughts you'd like to stop, you must first know how to locate or "catch" the thought as it's happening. (See exercise 18 on mindfulness meditation practice to help you cultivate the ability to be more aware of your mental processes.) Once you can locate your thoughts as they happen, you can put any thought on your "mental screen" and cross it out. Visualize the screen (a blank square, a computer or television screen) at mid-forehead, just above eye level. When you catch yourself thinking, "I'm weak and inadequate" (or any other thoughts you'd prefer not to have), immediately shift the thought to the screen and put a big X through it. See the X very clearly in a particular color that works: red, black, or white. This X is large enough to encompass the entire thought and cross it out. As soon as you've written the X on the screen, the thought disappears.

In the computer age, another way you may find effective is this: Instead of crossing out the thought, drag it to the trash and then empty the trash.

## Step 3. Bodily Sensation: Soothing, Sensing, and Naming Emotions

### Soothing: Conscious Breathing

EXERCISE 6. THE SOOTHING BREATH
The simplest, easiest, most efficient, and least conspicuous way to soothe yourself is conscious breathing. You don't have to sit in the lotus posture, study t'ai chi, or become adept at visualization (although all of these are useful) to soothe your emotions: You just have to know how to breathe.

I know a friend who runs to the bathroom and locks herself into a toilet stall when she's feeling stressed at work because she wants to be able to breathe deeply without looking odd. Whether you do this on the toilet or at your desk, as part of a morning routine or as needed, your breath is your first and best friend in the art of emotional alchemy. It is always there and will never let you down. It's your body's lullaby singer. Regardless of ability, disability, personal history, or social circumstances, we all breathe! So long as you can take a breath, you can soothe your grief, fear, and despair.

The soothing breath that I use and teach is a version of the long, extended breath I learned almost thirty years ago when I first took a yoga class. I'm convinced that this breath has helped me get through many moments of adversity in my life. (You don't have to do yoga to do the breath—but it helps!)

Put yourself in a comfortable place, sitting or lying down. Start with your normal breath and then consciously slow down and elongate your breath. Breathe deeply into your body, feeling the breath enter at your abdomen and then fill your chest, all the way up to your throat, feeling your diaphragm expanding and your chest opening. Breathing in, focus all of your attention on the in-breath.

Then, as you exhale, feel your breath leaving your throat and chest, and then your belly. Flatten your belly a bit at the end of the exhale, to expel any remaining breath. Breathing out, focus all of your attention on the out-breath. Allow a sound to emanate with the breath, if you're so moved.

As you breathe, it helps to visualize your breath as a cycle of renewal and cleansing: breathing in a fresh, rejuvenating energy; breathing out whatever is stale and tense. You might want to see your breath as a color or texture. Do whatever works. The main thing is the quality of your attention.

*Alternate Soothing Breath.* If you are feeling particularly stressed out and in emotional turmoil, do the soothing breath exhaling through your mouth rather than your nose. This is the quickest way to relieve the tension you are holding around emotions and settle into them more mindfully.

## Sensitivity: Listening to the Body

To feel and befriend your dark emotions, you must know how to listen to your body. You might need a listening aid to develop the skill of emotional sensitivity. Luckily, we all have one: the conscious breathing of the previous exercise. Breathing into the body helps soothe our sorrows, fears, and despair. It also helps us locate our sorrows, fears, and despair. Conscious breathing helps us tune in to the numbness we've used as a substitute for soothing, when we don't know how to authentically soothe our pain.

EXERCISE 7. ATTENDING TO YOUR BODY'S EMOTIONAL SIGNALS
THROUGH CONSCIOUS BREATHING
Sitting or lying, take a few moments to listen to your body. What are you feeling? Where in your body is this feeling located? Get acquainted with your body's particular signals for sorrow, fear, despair, or other emotions. There are certain common locations and sensations for these emotions.

Many people experience grief in the chest. (In the Chinese medicine system, the lungs are the organ system linked with grief.) Many people experience fear in their gut. When fear is very acute, you might feel your intestines churning or get a stomachache or diarrhea. Despair tends to be more of a full-body experience, with a kind of numb hollowness as a primary sensation. However, your own particular locations and sensations of emotion can be quite idiosyncratic. Don't rely on anyone's "system" of bodily felt emotion. New Age literature is full of ideas about where emotions are in the body or what physical ailments correspond to which emotions. These are all fine as evocative suggestions, but you need to do your own work and cultivate emotional sensitivity in your own unique bodymind.

Just as breath is the medium of soothing, it is also the medium of awareness. Once you have located a dark emotion (or more than one) in your body, use the long breath of exercise 6. Bring the long breath to the emotion in your body and breathe through it. Breathe through the sorrow in your chest, the fear in your gut, the despair in your heart. There is no effort here. You are not trying to change how you feel; you are simply bringing awareness to how you feel, through the breath. Breathing into the emotions-in-your-body, you become more mindful and tolerant of these energies.

EXERCISE 8. BODYTALK

If you are having trouble locating emotions in the body, try this: Sitting or lying down, do a full body scan—moving the focal point of your attention from the tips of your toes to the top of your head, going through each part of the body in turn: toes, feet, ankles, lower legs, knees, thighs, genitals, pelvis, lower back and belly, midback and midtorso, upper back and chest, shoulders, upper arms, elbows, lower arms, hands, and fingers. Then moving to throat, jaw, face, ears, eyes (and the area around your eyes), forehead, and scalp.

Note any places where there are particular knots of tension or discomfort. For the purposes of this exercise, assume that every tension point in the body has an emotion-correlative. That is, the places you are tense are also the places where you are holding unexpressed emotion.

Now choose one particular site of tension or discomfort in the body and bring your full attention to it. Imagine that your body has a voice, and allow this voice to speak—in the present tense, using the pronoun "I." For example, you might find a chronic knot in your stomach area. Free-associate from this area of the body; say anything that comes to your mind, while staying focused on your stomach and breathing: *I'm all knotted up. I can't relax because if I do, something terrible will happen.* This is the voice of your body's fear. Or you may find a tight area in your chest that says: *I want to cry but I'm afraid I'll never stop.* This is an old grief. Or you may find a clenched jaw that says: *I'd like to scream, but I'm used to keeping everything inside.* This is suppressed anger

You can do this bodytalk with one or more sites of bodily held emotion. The aim of this exercise is not to get lost in your emotion but to locate it in your body with awareness. Once you have done so, you are ready to practice more of the steps. Write down everything your body tells you in your emotional alchemy journal.

### EXERCISE 9. CHAKRA BODYTALK

As we know, emotions are energies. When they are mindfully experienced and allowed to flow freely, they bring vitality, passion, and color to life. When they are held back or held on to, denied or ignored, they become "stuck" in the body, contributing to the imbalance of *prana* in the system. This is why certain emotions have been found to be implicated in bodily conditions such as heart and cardiovascular disease, immune system disorders, and cancer. *Chakra* in Sanskrit means "wheel." The chakras are variously described as revolving wheels of light, energy, and color. They draw energy, which the Hindus call *prana,* into the body. Well-being is a state of balanced energies, while disease or disorder is an imbalance or blockage of *prana.* Turning your attention to the chakras is a good way to train yourself to be more aware of emotional energy. Mindfulness of the emotional energy that can block the balance of the chakras and of life force in the body is a critical skill for maintaining both physical and mental health.

In this body scan, you focus your attention on each of the seven chakras or centers of energy in the body in turn. Start by envisioning each of the seven chakras as wheels of light and energy:

1. the first or root chakra at the base of the spine
2. the second chakra at the genitals and abdomen
3. the solar plexus chakra, just above the navel
4. the heart chakra, at the breastbone
5. the throat chakra, at the base of the throat
6. the "third eye" chakra, just above eye level in the center of the forehead
7. the crown chakra, at the top of the head

It may be helpful to visualize the colors with which these energy centers have been traditionally associated: red at the root chakra; orange at the belly chakra; yellow at the solar plexus; rose or green at the heart; light blue at the throat; indigo or dark blue at the third eye; violet or purple at the crown.

It may also be helpful to know that each of the chakras is associated with a particular set of skills or attributes: the root chakra with survival; the belly chakra with sexuality and emotions in general; the solar plexus chakra with power and will; the heart chakra with love and compassion; the throat chakra with speech, communication, and creativity; the third-eye chakra with intuition and direct knowing; and the crown chakra with peace and connection with the Divine.

In the same way that you allowed the voice of your body to speak in the last exercise, now allow your body to speak from each chakra. For example: Focus your attention at the heart chakra and listen closely to hear its message. The message may be: *I am constricted from years of not letting myself be loved.* Or, at the throat chakra, you may hear: *I am afraid to speak my truth, so I swallow it instead.*

The dark emotions held in the chakras tend to be deep accumulations of emotional energy from the past. This exercise can help you identify these accumulations—the grief, fear, despair, or anger you're carrying around with you.

Again, write down what you learn.

If you are not used to using your intuition and imagination or trusting the wisdom of the body, bodytalk may feel, at first, ridiculous or nutty. Try to ignore these evaluations. Think of a five-year-old playing the Bodytalk Game. If you asked a five-year-old to play a game in which you each took turns letting your hearts speak, do you think he or she would say, "That seems ridiculous to me"? Let yourself be as open as a child to what you might discover through the power of imagination.

Then, when you're done, close your journal, do a long cleansing breath, and move on.

## Literacy: Name That Feeling

### EXERCISE 10. EXPANDING YOUR EMOTIONAL PALETTE[3]

Remember having a pack of eight jumbo crayons as a child? You could draw vivid pictures, but subtlety and nuance were limited. Now remember your first box of forty-eight crayons? There's so much more that you could do with burnt sienna than with brown. This skill of the emotional alchemy process is about developing the colors and shades of color on your emotional palette—moving from a box of eight to a box of forty-eight colors.

In this exercise, you become more acquainted with emotion-terms and how you use them, and more familiar with the process of identifying bodily sensation with certain emotions.

First, ask yourself: How do you use the words *grief*, *despair*, and *fear*? The words *sadness*, *anxiety*, and *depression*? Notice in what contexts you're likely to use the word *anxiety* as opposed to *fear*. (Do you ever use the word *fear*?) The word *sadness*, as opposed to *depression*? When and how do you use these words? How do you feel about acknowledging that you're sad, despairing, or depressed? Try moving the words around a bit. For example, try using the word *despair* instead of *depression* and see how you feel when you use these two very different terms. Does anything change? Try using the word *sad* where you would use the word *depressed*. Does anything change?

Next, try naming certain bodily sensations in emotion-terms: for instance, *this feeling in my chest when I feel like I can't breathe is fear.* Or *this churning in my guts is fear. This heat in my chest is anger.* Or *this clenching of my fist and tightening of the muscles in my arm is anger. This hollowness in my heart is grief.*

Try also noticing how you may be unconsciously converting emotions that shame or scare you by keeping them unnamed and moving their emotional energy into less shaming emotions or actions. For instance, when you feel and show anger, is this because anger is less shaming or scary to you than sadness? Or, when you find yourself eating a pint of Ben & Jerry's Cherry Garcia ice cream at one gulp, are you running away from your despair?

Don't forget to write what you learn in your emotional alchemy journal.

### EXERCISE 11. YOUR DARK EMOTION PORTRAIT

Think of the primary dark emotions as colors on a palette. Note which of the primary dark colors are most prominent in your emotional portrait—grief, fear, or despair. You will want to include anger, since we often convert our dark emotions into anger. Ask yourself: Do you tend to be more angry than sad, or vice versa? Are there certain dark emotions that you use to cover up others? For example: Do you cry when you're mad because sadness is more acceptable to you than anger? Does your anger cover your fear? Does your despair numb your grief?

Write it down. Use this emotion portrait as a touchstone for future awareness of your dark emotions.

## EXERCISE 12. I FEEL . . . I KNOW

In your emotional alchemy journal, start a page each day with the words: "I feel . . . I know." Then just free associate: "I feel . . . mad and irritated. I know . . . that these feelings are a cover for feeling vulnerable, sad, and scared." Or: "I feel sad . . . I know this is because I haven't been able to talk to my husband about what's on my mind and now I feel lonely." Or, "I feel scared . . . I know I usually cut myself off from people when I feel this way."

Keep to this practice every day. You will become friendlier with your dark emotions: more proficient in sensing and naming them, listening to what they tell you, and learning about what you do with them.

# Step 4. Contextualization: Telling a Wider Story

Contextualization is about enlarging our personal story of suffering. Imagine changing your self-viewing instrument from a microscope to a telescope. You're still in the picture, but the picture is larger.

Enlarging the story doesn't mean ignoring yourself. It means connecting your personal story of grief, fear, or despair to a larger story of grief, fear, or despair in the world.

To start with, it is helpful to locate your core-defect story with some self-compassion. (Return to chapter 4's introduction to step 4, page 83, for more about contextualization and the core-defect story.)

## Narration: Telling Your Core-Defect Story with Self-Compassion

### EXERCISE 13. TELLING YOUR CORE-DEFECT STORY

In this part of the emotional exercise, you become acquainted with your core-defect story. What do you think is your deepest, most intolerable flaw?

Begin with the words "What's wrong with me is . . ."

For example: "What's wrong with me is . . . I'm selfish." Or "I'm stupid." Or "I'm basically unlovable." Core-defect stories are absolute and dogmatic. We all tend to have one, so in this part of the exercise the idea is to tell it like it is.

Write down the first line of you core-defect story and as much of it as you find useful.

### EXERCISE 14. TELLING A WIDER CORE-DEFECT STORY

In retelling your core-defect story, you allow yourself to loosen the grip of your self-condemnation by stepping back and telling the story from a wider angle of vision. Look to your mother's or father's story, or even further back. If your story is "I'm selfish," for example, think about how you got this idea. How did it get implanted in your heart's brain?

Then, widening your "I'm selfish" story, tell a story of how you developed the belief that you're selfish. Such as: "I grew up thinking I'm selfish because my mother's message was that if you ever put yourself before others, you're selfish. She was never allowed to put herself first because it was her job, as the oldest girl in a large Catholic family, to take care of all the others. Any sign of self-development on my part was labeled 'selfish.' This was the cultural legacy for girls in my family, especially if they had any ambitions of their own."

Or, widening your "I'm stupid " story: "My father always felt stupid because he never got beyond the fourth grade. We grew up poor, and all he cared about was that I get a trade. He laughed when I took books home from the library. 'What are you doing, Mr. Einstein?' he'd say, 'developing your genius?' He could have been somebody, if he'd had money, but instead he mocked my attempts to learn. Poverty and a lack of educational opportunity bred in him—and me—a sense of stupidity."

Or, widening your "I'm unlovable" story: "I first concluded that I was unlovable when I was four years old. Being parented by two alcoholics, I basically had to raise myself—and take care of them, as though I were the parent and they the children. Neglect taught me that I was not inherently lovable. My parents were themselves neglected emotionally by their own alcoholic parents. Generations of alcoholism have bred this core sense of unlovability in our family."

It is not always easy to get at the larger stories in which our own personal core-defect stories are embedded. This step entails an empathic leap into the stories of others in your family and beyond. But the effort is well worth it. If you don't know your parents' or grandparents' stories very well, this step is a good reason to find them out. The more you understand the larger context, the more likely you are to find a compassionate view of yourself and others.

### EXERCISE 15. CULTIVATING SELF-COMPASSION

Imagine that your core-defect story is the story of your child or spouse or best friend—anyone you really love. What would you want to say to this person? Often, we are willing to extend compassion to others more than to ourselves. Seeing your story in this "third person" way sometimes helps you dip into the well of compassion for yourself.

Know that you are as worthy of compassion as those you love. Imagine that you can breathe compassionate, loving energy into all the parts of the body that you located in the bodytalk exercise, especially the parts where you found tension; and into all the chakras, especially where you found stuck dark emotions. Breathe the healing energy of compassion through all these parts of your body. Through all seven chakras. Through the particular emotions that shame you.

Say these words or any others that affirm your inherent worth: May compassion bless my spirit and the spirits of all those who suffer. May I be at peace with my pain and not blame myself for it. May I know that I am worthy of love.

## Making Meaning

Transforming your dark emotions entails making meaning of your suffering. The meaning may or may not be intrinsic to the experience. Thinking that painful events have intrinsic meaning is just another meaning-story. Do things happen for a reason? Or do they just happen and we make up the reasons afterward? The answer to this depends on your theology and the kinds of meaning-stories you prefer. My answer is this: Whatever meaning I make out of suffering, I want it to be one that makes me feel more open to life, not less; more authentic, more loving, and more compassionate. I want it to build, not diminish, my integrity. If the story helps me do these things, it's a good story. If it doesn't, then I must go back and keep walking the old existential ground till another meaning story emerges.

"Your child died because it was his time to go." People said this when Aaron died, and I thought: This story may make them feel better, but it doesn't do much for me. I had to find the meaning myself.

One thing I know: It's never skillful to tell someone else the meaning of their pain (which is why I don't think that the conventional psychoanalytic trick of interpreting the patient's words is very helpful). Your husband was mangled and crushed to death by a threshing machine because the moon was in Capricorn. Your wife was raped because she needed to learn humility. Your chose your cancer so that you could learn how to love. Your child died because you were chosen by God to have a little angel of your own. Stories like this drive me crazy when they are told to people who are in the throes of grief, fear, and despair. Forget telling others the meaning of their pain: Just make meaning of your own!

As I see it, we're all putting frames around the inherent Mystery of existence. Basic existential questions like *Who Am I? Why do the good suffer? Is there a God? What does He or She have in mind? What's the meaning of my suffering?* are not and cannot be easily answered. It's the asking that's important. Beware of cheap philosophies that reduce the mystery to a Hallmark card.

Still, I can't help but put in my two cents in the Hallmark card department: When you are open to Mystery, there is magic even in the midst of pain.

Send this card to yourself and read it on the rainy days.

### EXERCISE 16: TELLING A USEFUL MEANING STORY: HOW MY DARK EMOTIONS HAVE MADE ME STRONG

Write a story of your dark emotions that highlights how your particular experiences of grief, despair, and fear have molded you for the better: What strengths have come to you through your pain?

Know the difference between why, how, and what. You may not know why you've had to cope with so much grief, but you can say how the experience of grief has transformed you. Same for fear and despair. And anger. Or you can say what the experience of these emotions has helped you discover about yourself and your life. Try to see the connections between your dark emotions and your spiritual strengths: gratitude, lovingkindness, courage, empathy, compassion.

## Getting Larger: Connecting Your Own Pain to the Pain of the World

In making meaning of suffering, it's always wise to find a way to see your own ego's pain in connection to the pain of the world. When you can see your pain as part of a much larger story, this connection helps you surrender your attachment to your own suffering while building your compassion for yourself and others.

### EXERCISE 17. DARK EMOTIONS IN THE WORLD

This exercise is adapted from the despair and empowerment work of Joanna Macy. It can be done alone or, preferably, in groups.

Start by placing an object in the four corners of the room to symbolize the grief, fear, despair, and anger in the world. When I do this exercise in groups, I place an autumn leaf in one corner, symbolizing the grief of the world; a rock in another, symbolizing the fear in the world; a stick in the third corner, symbolizing the anger in the world; and a crystal in the fourth corner symbolizing the world's despair.

Now, sitting quietly, take a moment to contemplate each one of these corners. Starting with grief, close your eyes and contemplate the grief of the world at this moment in time. The various areas of the globe where people are in chronic states of ongoing sorrow. Think of the news stories you've read and seen on TV of people in various postures of grief: holding their hands over their eyes, weeping, bent over with sorrow, or embracing one another. Now think also of the grief that you have in your heart for the world, its unending strife, conflict, violence, the degradation of the human and the nonhuman. The waste of human life, human potential, and the descent of the human spirit to the underworld of evil.

Now open your eyes and, if you are alone, write or create something out of your pain for the world. Then pray and ask for help or guidance in what you can do to consciously act for the amelioration of the world's grief.

Do the same for fear, despair, and anger.

If you are doing this in a group, have each person speak from the heart about his or her dark emotions in relation to the world. Speak your emotions aloud with dignity, not shame. Allow one another to hear how deeply we feel this pain; how much it goes to the core of our being; how much of our own seemingly individual pain is connected to the larger pain of the world. Write about this connection in your emotional alchemy journal.

Pray aloud with one another: May the world be liberated from its suffering. May I use my own pain to grow in compassion. May we learn and help one another learn how to heal and redeem the world's suffering. Amen.

# Step 5. The Way of Non-Action: Befriending What Hurts

## Mindfulness: Focusing and Sustaining Awareness

### EXERCISE 18: MINDFULNESS MEDITATION PRACTICE

The practice of meditation has become more widespread in recent years as people begin to realize its many physical, mental, and spiritual benefits. The simple practice I teach comes from the *vipassana,* or insight meditation, tradition of Buddhism.

In this practice, you bring your attention to your breath as you inhale and exhale at your normal rhythm. Focus on the place where you are most sensitive to your breath—your nostrils, chest, abdomen, or all three—and let your awareness encompass this area of your body as you inhale and exhale. Be aware of the space between breaths, as well as the breath itself.

Alternatively, you can count your breaths from one to ten, counting on each exhale and then returning back to one. If your attention wanders and you lose your count, just return to one and start again.

Many people think that to meditate you have to wipe out your thoughts. Then they get discouraged, because they can't do this. But when you practice mindfulness meditation, you don't try to wipe out anything. This is a gentle, nonjudgmental process. When you find yourself thinking, or when you are distracted from your breath by an emotion or physical sensation, this is not a problem. Just allow the thoughts, feelings, and sensations to move through, without trying to stop them or understand them. See them passing through, like clouds moving through the blue sky of your awareness. And gently return to your breath.

That's it. Meditation practice is the best form of emotional exercise I know. If you want to build your emotional muscle, practice it daily. Just as ten minutes of aerobic walking is better than none, five minutes of insight meditation is better than nothing. If you practice it daily, meditation will build the muscle of mindfulness necessary for tolerating the often turbulent energies of the dark emotions when they arise.

The main thing about meditation practice is practice. Practice, practice, practice. In the midst of crisis, meditation goes straight out of your head. When you most need to meditate is when you mostly can't find the *zitzfleish* (Yiddish for "patience"—literally, the willingness to sit for long periods) to do it. Every day that you meditate, you build the foundation of emotional tolerance that will see you through whatever crisis may come along.

EXERCISE 19. EMOTION MEDITATION
In a variant of the meditation practice above, begin with five to ten minutes of breath meditation and then allow your attention to come to a place of emotion in the body. Just bring your awareness to this emotion, without trying to do anything to it: Don't soothe it, fix it, or try to make it go away. Allow your awareness to befriend the emotion—whether it is sorrow, fear, despair, anger, some combination of these, or any other emotional state. See what happens when you bring your awareness to emotional energy in this way. Does the emotion intensify? calm down? does it change in any way? Watch as the emotion comes and goes.

Be aware of the "story" that your mind tells about the emotion. Example: You may feel a heavy feeling, like a stone in your heart. In the practice of mindfulness, you don't need to even name this feeling. Instead, just witness or observe it. Witness as well the difference between the feeling itself and your mind's chatter about it. For example: *Here I am sad again. What a drag! I'll never get over this.*

Try to discern as well the difference between the energy of the emotion in your body and your reaction to it: the panic, desire to run away, to eat, to drink, etc. Notice these reactions without judgment—just observe them, as you would any interesting event.

### EXERCISE 20. TONGLEN

In the Buddhist practice of *tonglen,* you invite in all the pain that you've been trying so hard to avoid or to shield yourself from. With each in-breath, you invite into your heart all of your own suffering and the suffering of the world, and you willingly feel it. You allow yourself to feel the discomfort, to open to it. And then, with each out-breath, you exhale your joy, well-being, peace, and happiness, spreading these energies to all the world.[4]

*Tonglen* practice helps you to remember the universality of pain and pleasure, to stop running from pain and to share your happiness with others. This is a wisdom practice that can have profound effects on your life if you practice it routinely. (Note: if you're feeling very depleted and depressed, you may wish to start with more soothing exercises before practicing *tonglen.*) See page 201 for more about *tonglen.*

## Envisioning Emotional Energy

"Your vision will become clear," said Jung, "only when you look into your heart." Another wonderful way to befriend your dark emotions in the way of non-action is to be able to see them clearly, to envision them. The following is an exercise I have done in groups. It can also be done on your own or with a partner.

### EXERCISE 21. VISUALIZING YOUR DARK EMOTIONS

Lie down and get comfortable. Start with the soothing breath and body scan, just noticing where the emotion knots are in your body. Then take yourself on a guided meditation to go deeper down into the part of your brain that knows intuitively rather than rationally. Go into the following guided visualization with the intention of meeting your most feared dark emotion(s). Choose one emotion, or simply open yourself to whatever emotion may come in the course of the exercise.[5]

See yourself in a safe place indoors or outdoors. Then see just in front of you that a door is opening, and behind it another door opens as you walk through the first door, and you find yourself in a dark shady forest, at the top of a hill.

Walking down this cool, shady path, you are going deeper and deeper into the forest as you walk slowly down the hill. Going down and deeper as you walk a step at a time, seeing small patches of sunlight among the trees, smelling the deep, cool breath of the forest as you go on deeper and deeper, until you reach the bottom of the hill to stand under overhanging trees by the edge of a dark cool lake, with water lapping against the shore.

There is a small boat there, and you untie it and step in, sitting or lying down at the bottom of the boat on blankets. And now the boat is setting off into the water, adrift and floating, rocking gently from the motion of the water, back and forth, and rising and falling, gently rocked as the boat drifts, as you feel only this gentle rocking, listening to the lapping of the water, and passing from under the trees into the warm sunlight.

Still floating, feeling the sunlight and the soft breeze that passes over you, as you drift . . . you can hear the birds singing, and you can feel the sunlight on your body as you drift on and on, feeling a great contentment, drifting drowsily down and down, down and down, with the gentle rocking. Feeling at one with the environment, the movements, the warmth, the sounds. Enjoying, taking pleasure in all this, as completely as you can. Just being in harmony with your surroundings, being at one with all that is.

Continuing to float, to rock, gently, drifting deeper and deeper, until your boat approaches the shore and runs smoothly aground at the edge of a meadow. Leaving the boat now, and walking through the meadow, the grass against your legs, the breezes on your body, rabbits in the tall grass, the smell of flowers all around, of birds singing in the trees, feeling the movement of your body as you walk. Now approaching a large tree, which, as you see it, you know is your tree, you sit down beneath it, in its shade.

This is the place of inner vision and alchemy. In this place you are perfectly safe. This is your sanctuary, a place where anything is possible.

Now greet whatever spirits or guides you have in this place. This could be someone you know who has died or someone who is living. It could be an animal or a color, or a nameless sense of communion with spirit. Whatever guides you, let it be present with you here.

And from this place under your tree, with the presence of your helper(s) around you, welcome and greet the dark emotion that you wish to befriend. See the shape of your grief, fear, despair (or anger). Welcome this emotion into your space under the tree. See it very clearly. What does it look like? What is its color? Describe its energy. And speaking clearly to it, from the heart, ask whatever questions you wish of this emotion. Ask: *What do you want of me? What information do you have for me? What do you wish me to do with you?* Each of these questions may engender other questions. Just keep going, until all of your questions have been asked. Listen very closely to the answers.

When you are finished with your questions, know that there is a gift that each dark emotion has for you. What is this gift? What does it look like? What color is it? What is it for? See this gift very clearly now, and receive it.

Now see yourself with the dark emotion, dancing. You are dancing a dance you've never danced before with each dark emotion. You are dancing with abandon, surrendering to the dance until it is completed.

Now, honoring your dark emotion, say thank you. And thank your guides and helpers for their help in this exchange. Return to your seat beneath your tree and sit. Know that you may return to this place whenever you wish and do whatever work you need to do for yourself, for others, and for the earth.

And now see yourself saying good-bye to the tree, for now. And feel yourself returning to your body on the floor. Feel your body as you lie on the floor, feeling each part of your body coming to life, from your toes to your head. Wiggle your toes and stretch your arms, returning to your usual consciousness. Count to five and tell yourself that at the count of five you will open your eyes and you will be completely relaxed and alert. You will remember everything of importance from this vision.

It's helpful to do this with a good friend. Have your friend guide you through the visualization, and then change places with him or her. This visualization can be very powerful, so allow enough time, and be in a safe and uninterrupted place when you do it.

When you are done, record everything you remember in your emotional alchemy journal.

Another way to extend the benefit of this exercise is to draw from your visualization: your tree, your helpers or guides, the dark emotion(s) you encountered here, the gift or gifts you received, the dance you danced. When you draw, draw from your heart—allowing your heart to guide your hand, and not worrying about the "product." You may draw exactly what you saw, or, if you feel that this is not possible, just draw the colors and shapes, the energy. Remembering the energy of the visualization, allow that energy to guide your hand, and forget about what it looks like.

Take a separate page to draw the gifts received. Drawing and other creative expression is a useful way to realize the gifts of the dark emotions. (See exercises 25–28 in step 7.)

## Dreaming: Seeing in the Dark

"The dream is the small hidden door in the deepest and most intimate sanctum of the soul," wrote Carl Jung, "which opens into that primeval cosmic night that was soul long before there was a conscious ego and will be soul far beyond what a conscious ego could ever reach."[6] As far back as I can recall, I remembered my dreams. They were not always pleasant, given the circumstances of my birth. Often, they were nightmares. But they were always vivid, interesting, compelling. They had a force and energy that seemed every bit as rich as my everyday waking life. My father encouraged my dreams by asking me about them and treating them seriously, as sources of information. By the time I was in high school, I had so many vivid dreams that I began to keep a dream journal. I wrote my dreams down because I felt, intuitively, that knowing my dreams would help me navigate my life.

Your dreams can do this for you.

Dreaming is the way that our souls help us see in the dark. Every night, we are given these gifts, but unfortunately, many of us barely remember that we dream at all, much less what we dream. Alarm clocks, a hectic pace of life, the information revolution, too much to do, and insufficient darkness due to too many streetlights—these are threatening to make dreaming an archaic process. Don't lose your dreams! As Jung knew, individual dreams often come from the place of the collective unconscious, giving us information pertinent to every facet of how we live. They shine a flashlight in the dark and say: Look here. This is what you need to know and see. They give us a way of seeing in the dark.

### EXERCISE 22. DREAMING THE DARK EMOTIONS

Start with a dream journal. Keep it at your bedside, with a pen. The basic way that dream journaling works is this: Before you go to sleep, do a soothing breath, followed, if needed, by some form of bodily awareness exercise: the body scan or chakra scan. Then give yourself this subliminal message: *I will dream tonight, and I will remember what I dream.*

Then, when you awaken, before you are fully awake, grab the pen and journal and write from your dream. It's best to do this in the state between sleep and waking, with your pen just gliding over the page as you write, not even looking at the page, just looking at the dream images as they appear to you before they elusively slide away, which they invariably do. Write down everything you see in the dream, all the details. The power of the dream is in the details. Also write down the colors and energies of all the dream images—for example, not only that you are in a hallway but the color of the hallway, the texture of the hallway, what the hallway feels like energetically. Finally, write down your feelings—both the emotions of the dream and the emotions you have waking up from this dream. Write down as carefully as you can each emotion, naming it precisely and writing down everything that you associate with the emotion—whether that association is in the dream or not.

This dream process doesn't necessarily work right away if you are not used to remembering your dreams. Obviously, there are many mornings that this dream journal process will not be possible, given how we live. But keep at it and see what happens!

### EXERCISE 23. LUCID DREAMING

This exercise is for masters of the dream. I freely admit, I've only been able to do it once. But my daughter Esther can do it at will. She can program herself to have any dream by simply thinking about it before she goes to sleep. So I know this is possible. In lucid dreaming, unconscious dream images can be influenced by and are available to the conscious mind.

Tell yourself as you go to sleep that you will have a dream about the most critical dark emotion in your life at this time. You will receive a message from or about this emotion that will help you in your life. And you will receive a gift in the dream.

For inspiration, I think of the Senoi people of Malay peninsula, who instruct their children in conscious dreaming from the time of their first reported dream. They teach them not only to remember their dreams but to transform them. For instance, it is expected that a child will have a falling dream. When the child reports such a dream, he or she is instructed to go back into the dream the following night and turn the falling dream into a flying dream! Children are also taught how to listen to their dreams for particular songs, dances, chants, or other gifts that are then brought back and become part of the waking culture of the tribe. Dreams are serious business for the Senoi, who believe that a bad dream about someone is something that you must attend to in waking life. For instance, should you dream that someone has hurt you, you must tell that person of your dream, and it is his or her responsibility to apologize for hurting you in the dream!

Because our culture is far less sophisticated when it comes to dreaming and emotion, we will never be as competent as the Senoi Indians are in the dream world. But we can still cultivate the power of the dream for emotional alchemy. If you can do this exercise, you are a master! Emotional alchemy should be no problem for you.

## Step 6. The Way of Action

### EXERCISE 24. SPIRITUAL SERVICE AND SOCIAL ACTION

I no longer make much of a distinction between spiritual service and social action. Acting for the transformation of our world in the direction of peace and justice, as I see it, is an act of spiritual service, whether or not the person doing it defines it that way. And spiritual service has social consequences for others. Whether you're volunteering at a children's hospital or working to reduce environmental toxins, acting with compassion is a powerful way of transforming the dark emotions. Use your experience of fear as a motivating energy to help someone who lives in fear: Volunteer at a battered women's shelter or a rape crisis center. When you're sad and lonely or in despair, volunteer at a food pantry. Get your hands dirty, so to speak, working with the emotion that scares you.

Who said "Don't get mad, get organized!"? Social action is not just a great way to use your anger; it's a way to find hope in despair, to find connection in a shared grief, to discover the joy of working to create a less fearful world. Find your emotional action, however small, and do it!

## Step 7. Transformation: The Way of Surrender (Flow)

*Creativity: Sing, Dance, Draw, and Write from Your Dark Emotions*

Creativity is the great healer. I'm convinced that many of the millions of people diagnosed as clinically depressed are soul-sick because they have no creative outlet. All of us need one, regardless of how "creative" we think we are. Creativity is not just for the talented few. It is a gift that all of us can use to enhance the flow of emotional juices and bring a healthy vital energy to our lives.

I use art materials in my office to help tap into the power of creativity for emotional flow. People who would be shy about dancing and singing are more likely to draw. I ask people to draw from the heart of their sorrow, fear, and despair, as well as anger. The drawing connects them to the energy of their emotions in a much more immediate way than talking.

Singing, chanting, and dancing are all forms of creativity that we can use to surrender to the flow of the dark emotions. Drum your anger, letting the beat release it. Sing your sorrow, letting the melody release it. Dance your despair, finding solace and new energy. Sculpt your fear, letting the emotion take shape in the clay. All of these creative outlets teach surrender to emotional flow, energize the bodymind together, and can be great fun! Creative flow is emotional surrender.

If you want to learn the art of dancing and singing for the purpose of emotional transformation, there's no better book to read than Gabrielle Roth's *Maps to Ecstasy*.[7] The following exercises on creative flow are adapted from it.

### EXERCISE 25. SING YOUR HEARTSONG

Singing and dancing gets this flow-through process to happen not only with feelings in the moment but with feelings long stuck in the body from the past.

To start, find songs that help you feel your sadness, fear, and despair and just sing along. If you feel like you can't sing, Roth suggests that you start by humming and then break into song when you feel like it. The idea is to get familiar with your voice, the voice of your heart.

Once you're more comfortable with your voice, find your own song and sing it! Belt out your anger, sing your sorrow and fear, dirge your despair. Let the song come from your guts and your heart, and don't try to "create art" out of it—just do it! Your song can be pure melody, or you can make up the words as you go along, just allowing the words to fill your throat and come out without censoring anything—a free-associative song straight from the body of your emotions.

Another variation of the heartsong is chanting. You don't need to "carry a tune" to chant. Chant with sounds or with words or both. Grunts and groans, shouts and whispers can all be part of the chant. End with a prayerful sound or word, like "Shalom," "Peace," "Om," or any sound that is calming.

### EXERCISE 26. DANCE YOUR HEARTDANCE

If singing is not your thing, try dancing! Same idea here: Let the dance arise from your body and your heart, with no conscious "choreography." You can do this to music that connects you to your grief, fear, or despair. (Gabrielle Roth's CDs and videos provide wonderful music to dance to.)

EXERCISE 27. DRAWING FROM THE DARK EMOTIONS

Drawing is the quietest form of creative expression, but unlike writing, it gets us beyond words and into the more emotional part of the brain. Purchase a large box of oil-based pastels, and draw from your dark emotions. Start with the intention: I will connect to my sorrow (fear, despair, anger) and draw it. See what comes out. Don't even try to make sense of it, unless the sense pops out at you. Emotional surrender is a non-rational process, but it has its own coherence and purposefulness. Discover how it works through practicing some form of creative expression as often as you can.

After you draw, write down your thoughts about the process on the back of your drawing or in your emotional alchemy journal.

EXERCISE 28. WRITING FROM EMOTION

Writing is a lifesaver, as we can see from all the recent best-sellers about it. In befriending the dark emotions, we write *from* emotion, not about it. This is an important distinction. Because of the prevailing models of psychology and psychotherapy that have permeated the culture, many people now confuse endless analytic self-scrutiny with direct emotional experience and understanding. This emotional exercise is designed to help you know the difference. When you write from the emotional energy, you don't analyze it or deconstruct it or ruminate about it. You just write it.

For example: Write from your sorrow, fear, and despair in "freewriting" style. That is, put your hand to the page and don't stop for ten minutes. Start with a lead sentence about the emotion and keep going until ten minutes are up or you're done. A lead sentence might be: "I'm trying not to cry . . ."

Remember, no one gets to read this but you. The idea is to just write from the emotion rather than about it. And then, when you close the journal, just let it all go.

## Heartflow: Heart Meditations for Surrender

By "heartflow" I mean the flow of emotions when we attend, befriend, and surrender to their energies. Each exercise in this home course is intended to contribute to heartflow. The following two exercises are particularly geared to emotional surrender and transformation.

EXERCISE 29. HEARTFLOW MEDITATION

The use of meditation for emotional surrender is very powerful, once you've got the hang of meditation basics. A simple way to exercise your capacity to surrender to the flow of emotional energy is to meditate on the heart chakra. Simply sit with your back straight, whether in a chair or on the floor, and focus your awareness around the heart. Now inhale and exhale through the heart. Be open to whatever images, colors, messages, or sensations may come as you do this.

You may also want to ask questions of your heart and listen to the answers. Write down what you learn.

EXERCISE 30. THE OPEN HEART CIRCLE MEDITATION

In a long-term women's group for befriending the dark emotions, I began to experiment with less individualistic forms of meditation practice that honor our ability to see deeply into our own hearts while at the same time opening our vision to the larger world. This is what I call going deeper and getting wider at the same time. If you have a trusted friend or several to practice this with, you can multiply your ability to surrender to the dark emotions.

Sit and focus your attention on your breath, as in the basic form of insight meditation. Now, when you have done this for a few minutes, reach out and hold hands with others in the circle. Focus your attention on your breath. Breathing in, you are taking in the forces of love in the universe; breathing out, you are letting go of emotional constriction and holding. Each breath is a cycle of renewal and cleansing, rejuvenation and surrender.

Now continue to breathe, and this time, breathing into your heart (as in the previous exercise), taking in the energy of love, the Divine (or whatever you wish to call it) in the universe; breathing out, you are moving that love through your heart and into the person on your left. (I learned from experience to specify the direction of the energy or it may actually collide unharmoniously in two different directions!) Continue this heart breath until you feel continuous heart energy moving through the circle. Breathing in love from the cosmos, breathing that love into the next person on your left, your heart becomes a kind of emotional energy distributor. See if you can focus not only on sending the energy but also on receiving it from the person on your right. Experience what happens to this circulating energy as it builds a momentum around the circle.

Now the next step: Imagine yourself expanding out from the ordinary boundaries of yourself, out into the larger world. Feeling your heart energy circulate now through the circle and out into the world. Up until this time, you have been holding hands in the circle. Now drop your hands and let yourself experience yourself in this expanded way, as though your heart were a central pumping mechanism for moving heart energy out into the world.

From this place of depth and expansion, allow prayers or affirmations to arise within you. Create a "soup" of collective prayers and affirmations by sharing them out loud with those who sit with you in the circle. Mix up the soup. Inhale its aroma. Nourish yourselves with it!

Now from this place, return your focus to your body seated on the floor. Keep a sense of expanded self, but ground it in your body in this place and time. When you are ready, open your eyes and return to your normal waking consciousness.

To surrender to emotional energy, you must be grounded in your heart and trust your heart. Among other things, this exercise helps you trust. But it is also a way of beginning to experience the soul, which, in my view, is not an individual entity but an energy that we experience when we can open ourselves and expand our sense of who we are. It is in the heart and soul that the work of emotional alchemy takes place; and this exercise helps you become adept in these realms: to experience the energy of your heart and how it connects with the energy of other hearts, to see yourself as larger than your ego.

If you do not have a group with which to practice the open heart meditation, do it yourself, sending and receiving love in an imagined circle that includes anyone you want to do this with. See what happens and write it down.

### Prayer: Inviting the Spirits In

EXERCISE 31. THREE BASIC PRAYERS
If you can say *Help me, Thank you,* and *I surrender,* you can pray. These are the three basic prayers.

1. *Help me* is the automatic prayer of every heart in trouble. When life brings you to your knees, you say, *God help me.* Or you learn that if you can't say *Help me,* you devolve into bitterness, hopelessness, isolation, or addiction. When you are afraid, grieving, or in despair, pray for help.

In my experience, the *Help me* prayer is almost always answered. When Esther was a baby and had next to no muscle tone, there came a point when carrying her became very difficult for me. She couldn't walk until she was almost three, so a lot of carrying was necessary, and I'm only five feet tall and not exactly Arnold Schwarzenegger. Lifting Esther during this period was literally dragging me down. But then I noticed something: Whenever I said, "God help me," just before lifting Esther, I could do it with greater ease. I could lift and carry her, and there was no pressure on my back. This prayer never let me down. It was always immediately answered. It's simple. Say: Please help me. And then be patient and listen for the response. It doesn't matter if you address your prayer to God, Goddess, Higher Power, Holy One, angels, spirits, inner resources, or the Great Emptiness. Absolutely no theology is required to pray for help. Just knowing that you can't go it alone is the prerequisite for this form of prayer. Ask for help with something specific: Help me be more patient, more loving, more open. Help me be nurturing to myself. Help me surrender to Your Will. No matter what shape you're in, you can ask for help.

2. *Thank you* is the second basic prayer. "The world is full of miracles," said the Baal Shem Tov, "but we put our fingers in front of our eyes and refuse to see them." Gratitude for life's miracles is one of the best ways to open your heart and surrender to what is. With an open heart, the dark emotions do their alchemy.

Even in pain, you can notice and be grateful for what you have. In fact, in dark times, *Thank you* is often the prayer you most need to pray. Thank you for my body, my eyes, these flowers, this tree outside my window, this moment. There is always something to be grateful for, and expressing that gratitude helps take you out of the drama of the ego's suffering and into a place of enlarged vista.

3. *I surrender*. Sounds wimpy, but it's one of the most powerful prayers I know. In Thy Will be my peace. This is the prayer most of us have the most trouble with, because it states, directly: "I am not in control here"—a fact most of us would prefer not to contemplate.

Each morning, when Esther goes to school, I say this prayer: *Goddess, I release this child into your care, and I pray that you guide and protect her.* Then I surrender to the fact that I cannot protect her. No matter how vulnerable she may be, no matter how prone to broken bones, dislocations, and falls, there is nothing I can do to help her through her day but pray for her and then surrender my need to control her movements.

When you pray for surrender, keep the focus on your heart and notice how it doesn't want to do this. Notice the constrictions, the contractions, the NO WAY AM I GOING TO RELINQUISH CONTROL feeling in your chest. Then see your heart as a tightened fist. Feel all the pain of holding it this way—and let the fist open up, the fingers of your heart spread out. Ah! What a relief!

## Energywork: The Transformational Flow of Emotional Energy

In this exercise, you learn how to work with the energy of the dark emotions and transform it to healing energy. To do this, you combine two skills you've already learned—body awareness and visualization—with a new skill: energy sensitivity.

Using Barbara Brennan's *Hands of Light* or any other book on transpersonal energy, become familiar with the idea of energy fields and how to see, experience, tap into, and use energy for healing. Reiki is another simple system for experiencing the healing energy available to us in the universe. When you feel comfortable with some form of energetic awareness system, you are ready to do emotional energy transformation.

### EXERCISE 32. EMOTIONAL ENERGY FOR HEALING

This exercise can be done alone, with a trusted partner, or in a group. Start with a simple meditation practice or soothing breath. Now, sitting or lying down, allow yourself to experience the energy you call sorrow, fear, or despair in your body. Locate any particular places in the body where this emotion is held. If you don't feel it, summon an image of the emotion.

The next step is the reverse: Having summoned and named the energy you call sorrow, fear, or despair, let go of the label. Simply be present to the energy as image or sensation in your body without calling it anything in particular. Breathing in and out through your solar plexus, breathe this energy—no longer sorrow, fear, or despair, but just an energy—through your solar plexus, allowing the energy to be breathed through you and out into the universe. Feel your center growing more and more energized with the power of this energy. Breathe into the solar plexus and out into the universe, passing the energy through you and out again.

Now begin to feel your whole body awakening to this flow of energy, which is a powerful source of healing both in the universe and in your body. Let yourself experience the energy in any way that it comes to you—as light, warmth, image, color. Now circulate this energy another way, feeling the energy coming in through the crown chakra on top of your head and into your center, then radiating out from your center and into your arms and hands. Your hands are beginning to feel warm and tingly.

If you are doing this exercise alone, place your hands on the spot(s) where you first located the emotion, or anywhere else on your body. If you are doing this with a partner, place your hands near the body of your partner, not touching but a few inches from the body's edge, and allow your hands to move to wherever they are drawn to go. Allow the energy in your hands to be extended with your heartfelt prayer for your partner's healing—and your own.

## Play and Silliness: Having Fun in the Dark

There is a Zen story about a man being chased by a tiger. The man is running, the tiger close upon him. He can feel the tiger's breath at his back. He runs and runs until he has nowhere to go: He has reached the edge of a cliff. He begins to descend the cliff, holding on for dear life. Above him is the mouth of the voracious tiger. Below him is the free fall from the cliff. Just then, the man sees some ripe red berries growing near his hand. He reaches out and plucks one, then tastes its sweet juice. Ah! Delicious!

I had two thoughts when I first heard this story: First, this guy's not too swift. And second, what if there aren't any berries? (I wasn't in the greatest mood at the time.) But on closer reflection, I see the merit in the story: Between the dark passages of birth and death, we are offered the juice of life's sweetness. Even in the valley of the shadow of death, we can always pluck the ripe berry and enjoy.

I once met a woman who was born with all sorts of disabilities. Her feet were deformed, so she walked slowly and with great effort. She had chronic rheumatoid arthritis and was in constant pain. To top it all off, she was blind. Yet she was one of the lightest people I ever met. She had an aura, an energy of peace and tranquillity that was palpable. I sat and talked with her about my daughter Esther's multiple disabilities, her unknown condition and unknown future. Of the many wise and amazing things she said, I remember this one most clearly: Get silly. She told me that when she was in a bad mood, she put on a gorilla mask and wore it when her friends visited. Now, this was one dignified lady, and it was next to impossible to imagine her in a gorilla mask. But she knew the value of not taking herself too seriously.

When it feels like life offers you no berries, you can always pretend. Like Marcel Marceau, eat them out of thin air! Even the Warsaw Ghetto had its clowns. And they were part of what kept people alive. Even in the concentration camps, people told jokes. (Did you hear the one about the Nazi and his glass eye? "Look into my eye and tell me which one is false," he says to a Jewish lady. She picks the right one. "Yes! How did you know?" he asks her. "Easy," she replies; "the right one has the human look.")

EXERCISE 33. HAVE FUN!

Don't skip the good parts of your life, no matter how much sorrow, fear, or despair you're in. Take a walk and smell the flowers. Play more with your children. Get silly! Gorilla masks aren't everyone's cup of tea. Find yours. Risk embarrassment. Think of two or three ways to take yourself less seriously and practice them weekly (if not daily).

Humor preserves us in a time of trouble. Tell jokes and funny stories, watch funny videos. Laugh and cry at the same time. This is emotional surrender.

Go out and find the ripe berry and pluck it! Taste and smell it, then eat it! Let the juices run down your chin! Enjoy!

# *Epilogue*

## Dark Emotions in an Age of Global Terror

> "My name is Ozymandias, king of kings:
> Look on my works, ye Mighty, and despair!"
> Nothing beside remains. Round the decay
> Of that colossal wreck, boundless and bare,
> The lone and level sands stretch far away.
> — PERCY BYSSHE SHELLEY, "Ozymandias"

> Traumatic events destroy the sustaining bonds between the
> individual and community. Those who have survived learn that
> their sense of self, of worth, of humanity, depends upon a feeling
> of connection to others. The solidarity of a group provides
> the strongest protection against terror and despair, and the strongest
> antidote to traumatic experience.
> — JUDITH LEWIS HERMAN, *Trauma and Recovery*

> In turbulent times, the best protection is peace of mind.
> — THE FOURTEENTH DALAI LAMA

THE IMAGES ARE INDELIBLY ETCHED in our collective consciousness: the monumental World Trade Center aflame. The jumbo jet crashing into one of the twin towers. The fireball. The billowing gray smoke. People hanging off the side of the skyscraper, falling and jumping to their deaths. And then the slow-motion collapse in that infernal cloud of dust, bringing with it the collapse of all of our dreams of safety. People running in the streets, the dust cloud chasing them.

The aftermath, described by some as a kind of "nuclear winter." The darkness, the piles and piles of gray dust. Debris fields fifteen stories high. The rescuers and volunteers digging through the rubbled landscape. The survivors, relatives, and friends of the victims, holding up photos of their husbands, wives, sisters, brothers, children, coworkers. Praying and weeping in front of the television cameras. Hoping that in the piles of melted steel, among the rubble of body parts, their loved ones would be resurrected.

I've spoken in these pages of "mushroom clouds" of grief, fear, and de-spair that daily affect our emotional states, usually below the level of con-sciousness. On September 11, the mushroom cloud became horrifyingly visible, and we all became conscious. America woke up to its vulnerability.

In a concentric ring, starting from "Ground Zero" and moving out, we are all trauma survivors now. Of course, civilians are killed every day, by terror-ists, by their own military governments, by war, in countries far away. These events leave concentric circles of trauma in the human family, just as did the events of September 11. Now, this truth has been brought home, and it has left us raw, trembling with heightened awareness of the immediacy of sudden, inexplicable death for everyday people. We had our plans for ter-rorist attack, our city officials schooled in the possibility, run-throughs in every major city in America. But we didn't think it could really happen here.

Losing an illusion is devastating. We hurt. We're frightened, if not pan-icked. Anxiety about worldwide terrorism, biological warfare, and nuclear menace will sound a permanent note in our psyches from now on. A cloud that we hadn't seen before now appears over us, moving as we move. The media speaks of new mass psychology following "the defining event of our time." In this mass psychology, the dark emotions are raised to a new prominence.

We want to be angry, to find a target for our global anxiety and terror. Anger feels less helpless than fear, more energizing than grief. Certainly there is a place for anger in all of this. No one with a heart could behold the hell on earth wrought by so-called men of God and not be outraged at the utter madness of human beings intent on arriving in heaven by using them-selves and others as bombs. But our anger, if it becomes a shield against our more vulnerable feelings of fear and grief, can easily shift from moral out-rage to righteous hatred and irrational vengeance. It can move us to destroy something—anything—in order to produce a feeling of safety, however fleeting. But there is danger in this way. Ultimately, you can't kill fear with weapons of war.

Blind nationalism and blind religious fervor, in the United States or in the Muslim world, or anywhere else, is not likely to make the world safer. These narrow passions are part of the problem. No doubt these passions will be raised to a new crescendo now, in the aftermath of September 11. But the only authentic transcendence possible in a world of global terror is that which comes from expanding ourselves, beyond the nation-state, be-yond religion, beyond race—to what we share in common as human beings.

To shift the world's current emotional ecology, we humans would have to open ourselves to an enlarged understanding of the grief, fear, despair, and anger of the Other. It is this suffering, and the desire for something better, that we have in common. This is not a time to proclaim that God is on our side no matter what or to wave our respective flags. It's a time to find a way to extend our commitment to life beyond the ego of national and religious boundaries. Because now more than ever before, it is clear: No one is safe unless we are all safe. Our only hope for lessening fear in the world is to rally together as a family of nations to make the world safer for everyone.

Out of the carnage of September 11, this hope for a saner world order, the seeds of which are fragile but present, is what sustains many of us in this terrible time. We share an opportunity to understand ourselves and the world in a new way. At moments like these, we can discover what's truly important, what we want to live for.

And we can discover the value of fear. Fear is a very powerful emotion. When you feel fear in your body, it's helpful to relate to it as an energy that can be mobilized for life. It may feel like a constriction in your chest, throat, or abdomen. Breathe through it without judgment and allow yourself to feel it as a very strong force. If you pray for help, you can begin to expand this energy we call "fear" and use it for healing and transformation.

In this regard, we can take our model from the heroes of flight 93 who, realizing that they were bound for death, stormed the plane and brought it down without hitting a civilian target. One cannot even imagine being able to do this without fear. Fear for the lives of others was the energy that mobilized them to do something meaningful with their last moments of life. Some of these people said good-bye to their husbands and wives and wished them happiness before they left this earth. They had found some peace in their last moments, peace in the midst of turbulence. And they found it through their last wish, which they heroically put into action: to help others live.

Perhaps there is nothing that can redeem the dead but our own actions for the good. This is the time to find out what we want to do for the world and do it. And, as every trauma survivor knows, this is also a way to make meaning out of pain, perhaps the most effective way: to draw something good out of evil. The heroes of September 11 point us to the choice we each have: to help create a state of global peace and justice that we, like they, will not see before we die. It is in giving ourselves to this vision, out of love for this world that we inhabit together, that we stand a chance of transcending the human proclivity to damage life. And that we honor those whom we have brought into this world and who must inherit it.

What is most important to you now? Does it further life? Does it have meaning when you think about how fragile life is? Do you give it any energy? Do you let it guide you? Listen to your heart, find out what connects it to the world, find out what actions you can do to help the world, and give yourself to that connection, to those actions.

Most trauma survivors know that there is no healing without reestablishing the connection to community that has been broken by violence. We mustn't lose hope in the possibility of global community. We mustn't lose hope that one day the nations of the world will find a way to be more than a collection of self-interested entities that give most of their resources to military warriors. The seeds of that hope are in the international coalition to fight terrorism. If we can combine emotional wisdom with our intention to rid the world of terror, if nations can look at their own records of terror, and not just at the records of others, there is a chance that one day we will study war no more. That we will become moral warriors; that we will become (in the words of my daughter at eight years of age) heroes of peace. As hard and unlikely as that way may appear, there is always a peaceful way. It may be a long way, but, in the long run, it's the only way.

Paradoxically, peace can come through a deep and abiding awareness of our collective vulnerability. It's hard to see what possible power there could be in our collective feelings of helplessness, fear, and grief. If there is a power here, it's not about enduring being defenseless in the face of horrific violence. This is where the necessity to see the wider emotional ecology of our dark emotions becomes paramount. We are more than individually vulnerable— we are *intervulnerable*. We are vulnerable to one another. What happens somewhere in Afghanistan, halfway around the globe, is suddenly right here, in our living rooms, in our office rooms, in our streets and in the innermost chambers of our hearts. We are vulnerable to some clandestine madness hatched in the minds of desperate men who believe that heaven and mass horror are simultaneous. And the people of Afghanistan who have endured unspeakable crimes against them are vulnerable too—they are vulnerable to us! They are looking up at the skies as I write, as the bombs reign down on their already bowed heads. Everyone in the world is vulnerable to whatever realignment of power comes from this new age of twenty-first-century war. Because we are all vulnerable, we are all in the same global boat.

Now we must find a way to say "our" safety, rather than just "my" safety first.

Now is the time to break through the bounds and confines of old, patriarchal forms of thinking, acting, and feeling. The old "U.S.A., number one!" The old national and ethnic hatreds and ignorance. The old imperial responses to a world where "cells" of terror infect every country, and are spread like a cancer throughout the world's body. The old form of isolationist America dominating the Third World. The old forms of nation-states competing with one another for power and wealth. Now is the time to grasp the truth of our emotional, financial, social, and spiritual interconnectedness.

Our only protection is in our interconnectedness. This has always been the message of the dark emotions when they are experienced most deeply and widely. Grief is not just "my" grief; it is the grief of every motherless child, every witness to horror in the world. Despair is not just "my" despair; it is everyone's despair about life in the twenty-first century. Fear is not just "my" fear; it is everyone's fear—of anthrax, of nuclear war, of truck bombs, of airplane hijackings, of things falling apart, blowing up, sickening, and dying.

If fear is only telling you to save your own skin, there's not much hope for us. But the fact is that in conscious fear, there is a potentially revolutionary power of compassion and connection that can be mobilized en masse. This is the power of fear. Our collective fear, which is intelligent, is telling us now: Find new ways to keep this global village safe. Find new forms of international cooperation that will root out evil in ways that don't create more victims and more evil. Leap out of the confines of national egos. Learn the ways of peace. Find a new ceremony of safety so that not just you and I but all of us can live together without fear.

This will take all of our creative power and ingenuity, as much and more than the intelligence and power we have put into constructing smart bombs and nuclear warheads.

Our despair is asking us to be conscious, to consciously change our meaning story as a human race. Why are we here? What is the purpose of human existence? Are we meant to live in a world like this? Is this dawning of the twenty-first century, with all its foreboding, going to be the beginning of a century of darkness and death? Or the beginning of humanity's awakening to its own purpose?

This is my vision: that just as the twenty-first century has brought us a new kind of terror, a new kind of war, it can also bring us a new kind of international cooperation, a new kind of peace. The seeds are there—in our collective tears and terrors, our collective sorrow for the world. In the collective intervulnerability of humanity's dark emotions, we are pointed to a new world: a world where fear gives way to the joy of living in peace, where grief expands us into interfamilial compassion for the human race, where despair moves us to look squarely into the face of evil in the world and live with open eyes, hearts, and minds, searching together for a new world order.

This is my vision and the vision of millions on the planet today. May God and Goddess grant us the wisdom to heal through our dark emotions as a species and bring the gifts of gratitude, joy, and faith, of compassion and courage, to our children and our children's children.

In the years and decades ahead, may we look back upon this grim moment and remember it as the turning point—not to an era of worldwide conflict that heightened the divisions of religion and nationality, imperialism, racism, and patriarchy that are dividing and destroying us, not as a tragic moment that led to more and more suffering and terror on earth, but, rather, as the moment when we humans finally began to amass the collective courage we need to bring peace to the world.

May we all find peace in these turbulent times.

Miriam Greenspan
*October 11, 2001*
*Boston, Massachusetts*

# Notes

CHAPTER 2. VULNERABILITY

1. Stephen Mitchell (trans.), *The Book of Job* (New York: Harper Perennial, 1992), 7.
2. Ibid., 21.
3. Ibid., 54.
4. Ibid., 88.

CHAPTER 3. HOW DARK EMOTIONS BECOME TOXIC

1. See Daniel Goleman, *Emotional Intelligence* (New York: Bantam Books, 1995), chap. 11, "Mind and Medicine," pp. 168–76, for an overview of the research on toxic emotions.
2. See Paul Foxman, *Dancing with Fear: Overcoming Anxiety in a World of Stress and Uncertainty* (Northvale, N.J.: Jason Aronson, Inc., 1998).
3. Joan Vennochi, "The Clock Is Running Out on Gore," *Boston Globe* (November 18, 2000).
4. For the term "emotional pornography," I am indebted to Roger Gottlieb.

CHAPTER 4. THE ALCHEMY OF THE DARK EMOTIONS

1. Goleman, *Emotional Intelligence*, 4.
2. Candace B. Pert, *Molecules of Emotion: Why You Feel the Way You Feel* (New York: Scribner, 1997), 312.
3. Mihaly Csikszentmihalyi, *Flow: The Psychology of Optimal Experience* (New York: Harper Perennial, 1990).
4. For more information on insight meditation, see *Seeking the Heart of Wisdom* by Joseph Goldstein and Jack Kornfield (Boston: Shambhala Publications, 1987).

CHAPTER 5. FROM GRIEF TO GRATITUDE

1. C. S. Lewis, *A Grief Observed* (New York: Bantam Books, 1961), 61.
2. Ibid., 42.
3. Ibid., 85.
4. American Psychiatric Association, *Diagnostic and Statistical Manual of Mental Disorders*, 4th ed. (Washington, D.C.: American Psychiatric Association, 1994), 684.

## Chapter 6. From Despair to Faith

1. Cross-National Collaborative Group, "The Changing Rate of Major Depression: Cross National Comparisons," *Journal of the American Medical Association* (December 2, 1992).

2. William Styron, *Darkness Visible: A Memoir of Madness* (New York: Vintage Books, 1990), 82.

3. Sandra Salmans, *Depression: Questions You Have, Answers You Need* (Allentown, Pa.: People's Medical Society, 1995), 27.

4. Goleman, *Emotional Intelligence*. For a bird's-eye view of the recent research literature documenting the rise in depression in the United States and worldwide, see Goleman's discussion of the subject, pp. 240–45.

5. Joanna Macy, "Despair Work: Healing the Self through Healing the Planet," in John E. Nelson and Andrea Nelson (eds.), *Sacred Sorrows: Embracing and Transforming Depression* (New York: Jeremy P. Tarcher/Putnam, 1996), 115.

6. Salmans, *Depression*, 26.

7. Peter D. Kramer, *Listening to Prozac* (New York: Viking, 1993), 253.

8. See William S. Appleton, *Prozac and the New Antidepressants* (New York: Plume, 1997), 28–32, for various theories of depression, summarized. See also Joseph Glenmullen, *Prozac Backlash: Overcoming the Dangers of Prozac, Zoloft, Paxil, and Other Antidepressants with Safe, Effective Alternatives* (New York: Simon & Schuster, 2000), a rigorously researched book on the side effects of the new antidepressants and how these are denied and hidden by the pharmaceutical companies.

9. Germaine Greer, *The Change: Women, Aging and the Menopause* (New York: Fawcett Columbine, 1991), 107.

10. Styron, *Darkness Visible*, 5.

11. Ibid., 80.

12. See Salmans, *Depression*, 60–69, for statistics and summary of theories of women's higher incidence of depression.

13. Miriam Greenspan, *A New Approach to Women and Therapy* (Blue Ridge Summit, Pa.: Tab Books, 1993), 182–205 and 300–15. See these sections of the book for a more complete discussion of the relationship between women's depressions and internalized anger.

14. Macy, "Despair Work," in *Sacred Sorrows*, 117.

15. Kramer, *Listening to Prozac*, 272.

16. Rabbi Nachman, *Restore My Soul*, trans. by Avraham Greenbaum (Jerusalem: Breslov Research Institute, 1980), 17.

## Chapter 7. From Fear to Joy

1. See American Psychiatric Association, *Diagnostic and Statistical Manual of Mental Disorders*, 4th ed., 393–444, for the psychiatric criteria for these disorders.

2. Quoted in Jeffrey Kluger, "What Scares You?" *Time*, April 2, 2001, 62.

3. *Boston Globe*, "On Grieving Campus, He Offers Reassurance," February 1, 2001.

4. Adam Trombly, Interview, *Wildfire*, March 1992.

5. These sentence completions are adapted from a workshop on Deep Ecology led by Joanna Macy.

## CHAPTER 8. WE LIVE IN THE WORLD AND THE WORLD LIVES IN US

1. Theodore Roszak, Mary E. Gomes, and Allen D. Kanner (eds.), *Ecopsychology: Restoring the Earth, Healing the Mind* (San Francisco: Sierra Club Books, 1995), 14.

2. James Hillman, "A Psyche the Size of the Earth," in Roszak et al., *Ecopsychology*, xxii.

3. Janet L. Surrey, "The 'Self-in-Relation': A Theory of Women's Development," in Judith Jordan, Alexandra Kaplan, Jean Baker Miller, Irene Stiver, and Janet Surrey (eds.), *Women's Growth in Connection: Writings from the Stone Center* (New York: Guilford Press, 1991), 51.

4. *Boston Globe*, Oct. 15, 2000.

5. Ervin Staub, *The Roots of Evil: Genocide and Individual Responsibility* (New York: Cambridge University Press, 1989), 86–88.

6. *Boston Globe*, "Getting Away with Murder: Charlestown's Code of Silence Means Most Neighborhood Killings Remain Unsolved," October 11, 1992.

7. This was written before many alarming allegations of sexual abuse by numerous Catholic priests came to light in the spring of 2002.

8. Susan Griffin, *Eros and Everyday Life: Essays on Ecology, Gender and Society* (New York: Doubleday, 1995), 44.

## CHAPTER 9. GLOBAL HEALING IN A BROKENHEARTED WORLD

1. Joanna Macy, *Despair and Personal Power in the Nuclear Age* (Philadelphia: New Society Publishers, 1983), 2.

2. A ray of hope in a field dominated and constricted within the narrow confines of the psychiatric model is the advent, in the past several years, of a new ecological model of psychology, called "eco-psychology." For an introduction to this way of thinking, see Theodore Roszak, *The Voice of the Earth* (New York: Simon and Schuster, 1992), and Roszak, Gomes, and Kanner, *Ecopsychology*.

3. Chögyam Trungpa, *Shambhala: The Sacred Path of the Warrior* (Boston: Shambhala Publications, 1985), 45–46.

4. All quotes are from Colin Greer, "Will We Help Them Save the World?" *Parade* magazine, February 28, 1999.

## CHAPTER 10. THIRTY-THREE EMOTIONAL EXERCISES

1. Quoted in Bonnie Dankert, "The Place of the Heart," *Orion Society Notebook*, Autumn/Winter 1995, vol. 1, no. 2, p. 8.

2. See Paul Pearsall, *The Heart's Code* (New York: Broadway Books, 1998), and Doc Childre and Howard Martin, *The Heartmath Solution* (New York: HarperCollins, 1999), for research on the heart's brain.

3. I am indebted to Jan Surrey for the metaphor of an "emotional palette."

4. For more specific instructions in how to practice *tonglen*, see *The Wisdom of No Escape* by Pema Chödrön (Boston: Shambhala Publications, 1991), pages 56–64.

5. This exercise is adapted from a course in Womancraft taught in Boston in 1975 by Ann Valliant. It appears in a different form in Diane Mariechild, *Mother Wit: A Guide to Healing and Psychic Development* (Freedom, Calif.: Crossing Press, 1989).

6. C. G. Jung, *Psychological Reflections: A Jung Anthology* (1953), vol. 10, p. 46. From *The Meaning of Psychology for Modern Man* (1934), in *Bartlett's Familiar Quotations*, p. 754.

7. Gabrielle Roth, *Maps to Ecstasy: Teachings of an Urban Shaman* (San Rafael, Calif.: New World Library, 1989).

# Bibliography

EMOTIONS

Benett-Goleman, Tara. *Emotional Alchemy: How the Mind Can Heal the Heart.* New York: Three Rivers Press, 2001.

Childre, Doc, and Howard Martin. *The Heartmath Solution.* New York: HarperCollins, 1999.

Damasio, Antonio. *The Feeling of What Happens: Body and Emotion in the Making of Consciousness.* New York: Harcourt, 1999.

Goleman, Daniel. *Emotional Intelligence.* New York: Bantam Books, 1995.

Pert, Candace. *Molecules of Emotion: Why You Feel the Way You Feel.* New York: Scribner, 1997.

GRIEF

Henry, DeWitt, ed. *Sorrow's Company: Writers on Loss and Grief.* Boston: Beacon Press, 2001.

Lewis, C. S. *A Grief Observed.* New York: Bantam Books, 1961.

Moffat, Mary Jane, ed. *In the Midst of Winter: Selections from the Literature of Mourning.* New York: Vintage Books, 1982.

DEPRESSION/DESPAIR

Breggin, Peter R. *Talking Back to Prozac: What Doctors Aren't Telling You about Today's Most Controversial Drug.* New York: St. Martin's Press, 1994.

Casey, Nell, ed. *Unholy Ghost: Writers on Depression.* New York: HarperCollins, 2001.

Curtiss, A. B. *Depression Is a Choice: Winning the Battle without Drugs.* New York: Hyperion, 2001.

Glenmullen, Joseph. *Prozac Backlash: Overcoming the Dangers of Prozac, Zoloft, Paxil, and Other Antidepressants with Safe, Effective Alternatives.* New York: Touchstone, 2000.

Huber, Cheri. *The Depression Book: Depression As an Opportunity for Spiritual Growth.* Mountainview, Calif.: Keep It Simple Books, 1991.

Jack, Dana Crowley. *Silencing the Self: Women and Depression.* New York: HarperCollins, 1991.

Kramer, Peter D. *Listening to Prozac.* New York: Viking, 1993.

Macy, Joanna. *Despair and Personal Power in the Nuclear Age.* Philadelphia: New Society Publishers, 1983.

Martin, Philip. *The Zen Path through Depression*. New York: HarperCollins, 1999.

Nelson, John E., and Andrea Nelson, eds. *Sacred Sorrows: Embracing and Transforming Depression*. New York: Jeremy P. Tarcher/Putnam, 1996.

Norden, Michael J. *Beyond Prozac: Brain-Toxic Lifestyles, Natural Antidotes and New Generation Antidepressants*. New York: ReganBooks, 1995.

Salmans, Sandra. *Depression: Questions You Have, Answers You Need*. Allentown, Pa.: People's Medical Society, 1995.

Solomon, Andrew. *The Noonday Demon: An Atlas of Depression*. New York: Scribner, 2001.

Styron, William. *Darkness Visible: A Memoir of Madness*. New York: Vintage Books, 1990.

## LITERARY WORKS

Blake, William. *The Portable Blake*. Arranged by Alfred Kazin. New York: Viking Press, 1946.

Eliot, T. S. *Collected Poems, 1909–1962*. New York: Harcourt, Brace & World, 1934.

Huxley, Aldous. *Brave New World*. New York: Harper Perennial, 1932.

Lowry, Lois. *The Giver*. Boston: Houghton Mifflin, 1993.

Miller, Arthur. *Broken Glass*. New York: Penguin Books, 1994.

Mitchell, Stephen, trans. *The Book of Job*. New York: HarperCollins, 1979.

Roethke, Theodore. *The Collected Verse of Theodore Roethke: Words for the Wind*. Bloomington: Indiana University Press, 1966.

## PHILOSOPHY

Camus, Albert. *The Myth of Sisyphus and Other Essays*. New York: Vintage Books, 1955.

Frankl, Viktor E. *Man's Search for Meaning*. New York: Pocket Books, 1959.

## HEALING

Achterberg, Jeanne. *Imagery in Healing: Shamanism and Modern Medicine*. Boston: Shambhala Publications, 1985.

Cousins, Norman. *Anatomy of an Illness As Perceived by the Patient: Reflections on Healing and Regeneration*. New York: Bantam Doubleday Dell, 1981.

Levy, Naomi. *To Begin Again: The Journey toward Comfort, Strength, and Faith in Difficult Times*. New York: Ballantine Books, 1998.

Noble, Vicki. *Shakti Woman: Feeling Our Fire, Healing Our World*. New York: HarperCollins, 1991.

Orloff, Judith. *Guide to Intuitive Healing*. New York: Three Rivers Press, 2000.

Reis, Patricia. *Through the Goddess: A Woman's Way of Healing*. New York: Continuum, 1991.

Roth, Gabrielle. *Maps to Ecstasy: Teachings of an Urban Shaman*. San Rafael, Calif.: New World Library, 1989.

Young-Eisendrath, Polly. *The Resilient Spirit: Transforming Suffering into Insight and Renewal*. Reading, Mass.: Addison Wesley Publishing Co., 1996.

## MEDITATION

Chödrön, Pema. *The Wisdom of No Escape and the Path of Loving-Kindness*. Boston: Shambhala Publications, 1991.

Goldstein, Joseph. *The Experience of Insight: A Simple and Direct Guide to Buddhist Meditation*. Boulder: Shambhala Publications, 1983.

————, and Jack Kornfield. *Seeking the Heart of Wisdom: The Path of Insight Meditation*. Boston: Shambhala Publications, 1987.

Suzuki, Shunryu. *Zen Mind, Beginner's Mind*. New York: Weatherhill, 1970.

Trungpa, Chögyam. *Meditation in Action*. Boston: Shambhala Publications, 1996.

## PSYCHOLOGY

Csikszentmihalyi, Mihaly. *Flow: The Psychology of Optimal Experience*. New York: Harper Perennial, 1990.

Greenspan, Miriam. *A New Approach to Women and Therapy*. Blue Ridge Summit, Penn.: Tab Books, 1993.

Grof, Stanislav, and Christina Grof. *The Stormy Search for the Self: A Guide to Personal Growth through Transformational Crisis*. Los Angeles: Jeremy P. Tarcher, 1990.

————, eds. *Spiritual Emergency: When Personal Transformation Becomes a Crisis*. Los Angeles: Jeremy P. Tarcher, 1989.

Herman, Judith Lewis. *Trauma and Recovery*. New York: Basic Books, 1992.

Jordan, Judith V., Alexandra G. Kaplan, Jean Baker Miller, Irene P. Stiver, and Janet L. Surrey. *Women's Growth in Connection: Writings from the Stone Center*. New York: Guilford Press, 1991.

Jung, C. G. *The Undiscovered Self*. Boston: Little, Brown and Co., 1957.

Lifton, Robert Jay, and Eric Markusen. *The Genocidal Mentality: Nazi Holocaust and Nuclear Threat*. New York: Basic Books, 1990.

Roszak, Theodore. *The Voice of the Earth*. New York: Simon & Schuster, 1992.

————, Mary E. Gomes, and Allen D. Kanner, eds. *Ecopsychology: Restoring the Earth, Healing the Mind*. San Francisco: Sierra Club Books, 1995.

Staub, Ervin. *The Roots of Evil: The Origins of Genocide and Other Group Violence*. Cambridge: Cambridge University Press, 1989.

Staub, Sylvia, and Paula Green. *Psychology and Social Responsibility: Facing Global Challenges*. New York: New York University Press, 1992.

SPIRITUALITY

Dass, Ram, and Mirabai Bush. *Compassion in Action: Setting Out on the Path of Service*. New York: Bell Tower, 1992.

———, and Paul Gorman. *How Can I Help? Stories and Reflections on Service*. New York: Alfred A. Knopf, 1986.

Des Pres, Terrence. *The Survivor: An Anatomy of Life in the Death Camps*. New York: Pocket Books, 1977.

Eliach, Yaffa. *Hasidic Tales of the Holocaust*. New York: Avon Books, 1982.

Galland, China. *Longing for Darkness: Tara and the Black Madonna*. New York: Viking, 1990.

Gottlieb, Roger. *A Spirituality of Resistance: Finding a Peaceful Heart and Protecting the Earth*. New York: Crossroad Publishing Co., 1999.

Greenbaum, Avraham, trans. and ed. *Garden of the Souls: Rebbe Nachman on Suffering*. Jerusalem: Breslov Research Institute, 1990.

———, trans. *Rabbi Nachman: Restore My Soul!* Jerusalem: Breslov Research Institute, 1980.

Hanh, Thich Nhat. *Teachings on Love*. Berkeley: Parallax Press, 1998.

Henderson, Joseph L., and Maud Oakes. *The Wisdom of the Serpent: The Myths of Death, Rebirth, and Resurrection*. Princeton: Princeton University Press, 1990.

Mariechild, Diane. *Mother Wit: A Feminist Guide to Psychic Development*. Trumansburg, N.Y.: Crossing Press, 1981.

Moody, Raymond A. *Life after Life*. New York: Bantam Books, 1975.

Perera, Sylvia Brinton. *Descent to the Goddess: A Way of Initiation for Women*. Toronto: Inner City Books, 1981.

Tarrant, John. *The Light Inside the Dark: Zen, Soul, and the Spiritual Life*. New York: HarperCollins, 1998.

Trungpa, Chogyam. *Shambhala: The Sacred Path of the Warrior*. Boston: Shambhala Publications, 1985.

Whitaker, Kay Cordell. *The Reluctant Shaman: A Woman's First Encounters with the Unseen Spirits of the Earth*. New York: HarperCollins, 1991.

Winkler, Gershon. *The Soul of the Matter: A Jewish Kabbalistic Perspective on the Human Soul before, during, and after Life*. New York: Judaica Press, 1982.

Woodman, Marion, and Elinor Dickson. *Dancing in the Flames: The Dark Goddess in the Transformation of Consciousness*. Boston: Shambhala Publications, 1996.

ECOLOGY

Colborn, Theo, Dianne Dumanoski, and John Peterson Myers. *Our Stolen Future: Are We Threatening Our Fertility, Intelligence, and Survival?* New York: Plume, 1997.

Kaza, Stephanie, and Kenneth Kraft, eds. *Dharma Rain: Sources of Buddhist Environmentalism*. Boston: Shambhala Publications, 2000.

Macy, Joanna. *World As Lover, World As Self*. Berkeley: Parallax Press, 1991.

## WOMEN AND SOCIETY

Griffin, Susan. *The Eros of Everyday Life: Essays on Ecology, Gender and Society.* New York: Doubleday, 1995.

———. *A Chorus of Stones: The Private Life of War.* New York: Anchor Books, 1992.

# Acknowledgments

For more than a decade, this book has been a devotion, a compulsion, a spiritual practice, a haven, a monkey on my back, and a labor of love. The spark of its conception came to me, not from me; so I thank, first of all, the spirits who chose me as their vessel. It's to you I owe my gratitude for granting me the stamina and patience to see this through, despite the fact that mine is not a writer's life. Especially, I thank you, Aaron, for waking me up so many years ago and keeping me going when things got rough.

In the intervening years, between this book's otherworldly conception and its birth into this world, a lot of life was lived and the book grew. And many wonderful people contributed to its gestation and growth—none of whom are in any way responsible for its shortcomings.

To those whose stories are told here in disguised form: you know who you are, and I thank you from the bottom of my heart for your courage, your openness, your resilience, and all that I've learned from being a companion on your journeys.

Marie Cantlon was the first to hear this book's song. As an ongoing source of encouragement, information, and hands-on assistance in how to write a book proposal and a book, your generous help in getting this book off the ground will always be appreciated.

I want to thank the members of the Global Therapy Group—Janet Surrey, Sarah Conn, Anne Yeomans, and Mary Watkins—for our meetings between 1989 and 1992, which were crucial to getting this book out of my head and onto the page. Your early close readings and feedback on the main ideas gave me the encouragement I needed to go forward. Sarah's work on the self-world connection, Anne's work on healing in dark times, Mary's work on the pathology of individualism, and Jan's work on the self-in-relation have profoundly influenced me. A special thanks to Jan Surrey for our early talks about emotions. I am grateful for your support throughout the years, for our shared commitment to a reshaped world that values human connection and liberation, and for your friendship.

I am grateful also to Sylvia Hammerman, David Hammerman, Claudia Harris, and Ann Drake. Our group focus on spirituality and psychology for four years was a fount of support, for both my work and my life. I am indebted to Ann Drake for instructing me in the wisdom of the shamanic healing arts, and for the generous donation of her beautiful home by the sea in the summer of 1999, which allowed me the rare opportunity to write in uninterrupted peace.

To the women of Greenfire in Tenants Harbor, Maine—Maria Marta Aris-Paul, Judith Carpenter, Connie Chandler-Ward, and Rosanna Kazanjian—my loving thanks for holding me in your collective lap. Your warmth and wisdom, loving-kindness, sense of humor, healing genius, and great food will always be remembered with enormous gratitude. What you did for me you do for many. Bless you.

For two years the members of my Writers Group—Marie Ashe, Kate Nace Day, and Mary O'Brien—encouraged me to dig in, write from the heart, and get to the point. The book is all the better for your wise counsel and suggestions.

I am grateful for the early support from Demaris Wehr, Bev Harrison, and Carter Heyward in attending to the main ideas in embryonic form. I thank also Lisa Lebduska, Director of Communications across the Curriculum at Worcester Polytechnic Institute, for your gracious comments on chapter 1. For reading the book proposal and getting back to me so quickly with smart comments, I thank Kaethe Weingarten. I also thank Christina Rago for your skillful editorial assistance on chapter 6 and our fruitful conversation about despair.

My deepest gratitude to Joanna Macy for your support for this project, for the tears you cried when you saw my drawings of my own journeys through the dark, for writing *Despair and Personal Power in the Nuclear Age,* and for all you do for the sake of the planet.

I am indebted to Kate O'Shea—Goddess of Organizational Skills—for helping me organize my desk, my study, and this book. More than anyone, you know my impairments in these realms. Despite this, you graciously and competently took on the project of helping me put what I knew into form. I thank you also for your spirited support as a friend. Deborah Taylor and Carol Hymowitz read the book proposal and chapter 1 and encouraged me to keep going. I thank you always for your friendship, listening ear, and love. To Bella Rosner, the Queen of Hearts, thanks from my body and soul for your skillful acupuncture and bottomless compassion. I am grateful to Rich Borofsky for your healing wisdom when I needed it most, and for connecting me to my editor at Shambhala, Eden Steinberg.

If a book is like a baby, this long pregnancy was helped along in its final and critical stage by Eden Steinberg. I'm grateful for your keen intelligence, careful attention, and helpful suggestions, for your courage in pushing me to clarify my way of approaching the personal stories, and, most of all, for your passionate support for this work. My thanks to all at Shambhala Publications for your commitment to producing high-quality, beautiful books that appeal to the mind, heart, and spirit, and for being so wholeheartedly behind this one. Also, for your persistence in finding a name for the baby.

My gratitude always to Lewis Randa for harboring my daughter Esther, educating her in the ways of peace, and for your generous donation of a room at the Peace Abbey in Sherborn, Massachusetts, where I found rest and renewal to continue. Your work makes the world a better place.

The work of this book has been on the road in various forms for many years, and there are several venues that deserve to be noted. I thank: the former Interface Institute in Boston for the "Befriending the Dark Emotions" courses I taught in the early 1990s; Anne Simpkinson, publisher of *Common Boundary*, for your solid support and appreciation of my writing and for soliciting and publishing "Befriending the Dark Emotions" in 1998; Anne Yeomans, founder of the Women's Well, for inviting me to do workshops on healing through the dark emotions" for five years in the 1990s. These circles of women were always wonderful places to teach and learn.

Thanks also to the Massachusetts School of Professional Psychology for hosting the course "Toward a New Model of Psychotherapy: Connecting the Personal and the Global," and to Richard Dearing and the Interfaith Pastoral Institute in Winnipeg, for your gracious reception to these ideas. Even further back, I am grateful to Richard Carreiro for inviting me to speak at the University of Manitoba in 1988. The therapists and educators I met in Winnipeg will hold a special place in my heart.

My mother, Aidla Greenspan, read chapter 1 and told me I wrote beautifully. Parental bias aside, you have been the primal support for everything I do. I thank you and my father, Jacob Greenspan, for teaching me through the model of your lives the resiliency of heart and spirit in the aftermath of unbearable sorrows.

I thank my children, Anna and Esther, for putting up with a mom who was too distracted too much of the time, and for asking me, "How's the book going?" year after year after year. Your patience has been much appreciated. May I be worthy of the lessons you teach.

Zucky, you were at my side all through these years, a constant, comforting feline friend. Your consideration in waiting until the day I finished the book before departing for the next world is much appreciated. I miss our interspecies communication.

It's customary for authors to thank someone "without whom, this book would never have been written." Never did those words apply more than to my long-time soul's companion, Roger Gottlieb. Never has so much been asked of one person for so long. Thirteen years is a charm, and you stood by me through all of it. You listened to me, clarified my fuzzy thinking, edited my redundancies, and endlessly boosted me on. This would be enough, but it's the least of it. Because of you, I could write without worrying that our family's special needs would overwhelm us. For hands-on parenting, you have earned the little-known title of Most Devoted Dad of All Time, year after year. When nothing in our lives afforded me the luxury of being a writer, your labor and devotion made it possible.

In the words of E. B. White about Wilbur's friend Charlotte: "It is not often that someone comes along who is a true friend and a good writer." I'm five-ways blessed: you are my truest friend, gifted writer, astute editor, loving husband, and father most rare. Without you, this baby would not have seen the light of day. May your many virtues be amply rewarded.

# About the Author

Anna Gottlieb

Miriam Greenspan is an internationally known psychotherapist, writer, and speaker whose pioneering book, *A New Approach to Women and Therapy,* helped to establish the field of women's psychology. Her work has been featured in *Self, Ms., New Woman, Psychology Today, Common Boundary, Shambhala Sun,* and *Body and Soul* magazines, and her writing has been widely anthologized. She lives in Boston with her husband and two daughters.

Ms. Greenspan welcomes inquiries, comments, or requests for workshops and speaking engagements. Please e-mail her at GreenspanM@aol.com for more information.

*(continued from page i)*

"Written with grace, clarity, and humility, this book beautifully integrates the psychological, spiritual, and political wisdom necessary for personal and social transformation."

—RABBI MICHAEL LERNER, editor, *Tikkun* magazine and author of *Spirit Matters: Global Healing and the Wisdom of the Soul*

"This riveting book is a powerful, urgent appeal for a transformation of our values and the way we conduct our lives. The author is a therapist but she writes not only for other therapists, who will deepen and expand their practice from their reading, but for all of us who struggle daily not to be defeated by the global darkness in which we live."

—SOPHIE FREUD, Professor Emerita, Simmons College School of Social Work

"This is a profound and liberating book. Miriam Greenspan helps us to discover the life-redeeming power of the very emotion we most fear. Thus she opens ways to both our integrity and our freedom."

—JOANNA MACY, author of *Widening Circles*